The Substance of EU Democracy Promotion

Governance and Limited Statehood

Thomas Risse is Director of the Center for Transnational Relations, Foreign and Security Policy at the Otto Suhr Institute of Political Science, Freie Universität Berlin.

This ground-breaking monograph series showcases cutting-edge research on the transformation of governance in countries with weak state institutions. Combining theoretically informed and empirically grounded scholarship, it challenges the conventional governance discourse which is biased towards modern developed nation-states. Instead, the series focuses on governance in Africa, Asia and Latin America including transnational and transregional dimensions.

Located at the intersection of global governance and international relations on the one hand, and comparative politics, area studies, international law, history and development studies on the other, this innovative series helps to challenge fundamental assumptions about governance in the social sciences.

Titles include:

Amichai Magen, Thomas Risse and Michael A. McFaul (*editors*)
PROMOTING DEMOCRACY AND THE RULE OF LAW
American and European Strategies

Susanne Buckley-Zistel and Ruth Stanley (*editors*)
GENDER IN TRANSITIONAL JUSTICE

Markus-Michael Müller
PUBLIC SECURITY IN THE NEGOTIATED STATE
Policing in Latin America and Beyond

Tanja A. Börzel and Christian Thauer (*editors*)
BUSINESS AND GOVERNANCE IN SOUTH AFRICA
Racing to the Top?

Tanja A. Börzel and Ralph Hamann (*editors*)
BUSINESS AND CLIMATE CHANGE GOVERNANCE
South Africa in Comparative Perspective

Malika Bouziane, Cilja Harders and Anja Hoffmann (*editors*)
LOCAL POLITICS AND CONTEMPORARY TRANSFORMATIONS IN THE ARAB WORLD
Governance Beyond the Centre

Anja P. Jakob and Klaus Dieter Wolf (*editors*)
THE TRANSNATIONAL GOVERNANCE OF VIOLENCE AND CRIME
Non-State Actors in Security

Marianne Beisheim and Andrea Liese (*editors*)
TRANSNATIONAL PARTNERSHIPS
Effectively Providing for Sustainable Development?

Daniel Jacob
JUSTICE AND FOREIGN RULE

Anne Wetzel and Jan Orbie (*editors*)
THE SUBSTANCE OF EU DEMOCRACY PROMOTION
Concepts and Cases

The Substance of EU Democracy Promotion
Concepts and Cases

Edited by

Anne Wetzel
Postdoctoral Fellow, University of Mannheim, Germany

Jan Orbie
Associate Professor, Ghent University, Belgium

Editorial matter, selection and conclusion © Anne Wetzel and Jan Orbie 2015
Individual chapters © Respective authors 2015

All rights reserved. No reproduction, copy or transmission of this publication may be made without written permission.

No portion of this publication may be reproduced, copied or transmitted save with written permission or in accordance with the provisions of the Copyright, Designs and Patents Act 1988, or under the terms of any licence permitting limited copying issued by the Copyright Licensing Agency, Saffron House, 6–10 Kirby Street, London EC1N 8TS.

Any person who does any unauthorized act in relation to this publication may be liable to criminal prosecution and civil claims for damages.

The authors have asserted their rights to be identified as the authors of this work in accordance with the Copyright, Designs and Patents Act 1988.

First published 2015 by
PALGRAVE MACMILLAN

Palgrave Macmillan in the UK is an imprint of Macmillan Publishers Limited, registered in England, company number 785998, of Houndmills, Basingstoke, Hampshire RG21 6XS.

Palgrave Macmillan in the US is a division of St Martin's Press LLC, 175 Fifth Avenue, New York, NY 10010.

Palgrave Macmillan is the global academic imprint of the above companies and has companies and representatives throughout the world.

Palgrave® and Macmillan® are registered trademarks in the United States, the United Kingdom, Europe and other countries.

ISBN 978–1–137–46631–0

This book is printed on paper suitable for recycling and made from fully managed and sustained forest sources. Logging, pulping and manufacturing processes are expected to conform to the environmental regulations of the country of origin.

A catalogue record for this book is available from the British Library.

A catalog record for this book is available from the Library of Congress.

Contents

List of Figures and Tables	vii
Acknowledgements	viii
Notes on Contributors	x
List of Abbreviations and Acronyms	xvi

1 The Substance of EU Democracy Promotion: Introduction and Conceptual Framework 1
Anne Wetzel

Part I Alternative Reflections on the EU as a Liberal Democracy Promoter

2 Law Perspective: Praise Undeserved? The EU as a Democracy Promoter: A Sceptical Account 27
Dimitry Kochenov

3 Political Economy Perspective: Fuzzy Liberalism and EU Democracy Promotion: Why Concepts Matter 35
Milja Kurki

4 Critical Social Theory Perspective: Embeddedness as Substance: The EU's Socialized Approach to Democratization 47
Jessica Schmidt

5 Governance Perspective: Democratic Governance Promotion Through Functional Cooperation 58
Anne Wetzel

Part II Country Chapters

6 Addressing the Remnants of a Communist Past Through Accession: Slovakia and the Czech Republic 71
Eline De Ridder

7 Different Trajectories yet the Same Substance: Croatia and Turkey 85
Canan Balkır and Müge Aknur

8 Promoting Democracy in Post-Conflict Societies: Bosnia and Herzegovina and Kosovo   104
   Labinot Greiçevci and Bekim Çollaku

9 Power Relations Meet Domestic Structures: Russia and Ukraine   117
   Susan Stewart

10 Neither Integrated Nor Comprehensive in Substance: Armenia and Georgia   134
   Hrant Kostanyan

11 Democracy Through the Invisible Hand? Egypt and Tunisia   149
   Vicky Reynaert

12 When Security Trumps Democracy: Israel and Palestine   162
   Benedetta Voltolini and Federica Bicchi

13 Favouring Leaders over Laggards: Kazakhstan and Kyrgyzstan   177
   Fabienne Bossuyt and Paul Kubicek

14 Democracy Promotion in Restrictive Environments: Ethiopia and Eritrea   193
   Karen Del Biondo

15 Responding to Political Crises in the South Pacific: The Solomon Islands and Fiji   208
   Maurizio Carbone and Karen Del Biondo

16 Much Ado About Nothing? Brazil and Venezuela   223
   Andrea Ribeiro Hoffmann

17 Comparing Country Cases: Output-Oriented EU Democracy Promotion?   236
   Anne Wetzel and Jan Orbie

Annex: Summary of Substance and BTI Values   255

References   259

Index   296

Figures and Tables

Figures

1.1	The concept of embedded democracy	5
1.2	EU democracy promotion agendas	9

Tables

12.1	CBSS projects by theme in Israel and West Bank/Gaza (2007–2010)	171
13.1	Relative power positions of Kazakhstan and Kyrgyzstan	179
15.1	Indicators of embedded democracy	216
15.2	Selected indicators Solomon Islands and Fiji	217
A.1	Summary of substance of EU democracy promotion based on country case studies	255
A.2	BTI values	257

Acknowledgements

This book presents the results of a research project on the substance of European Union (EU) democracy promotion.[1] It would not have been possible without the contribution of financial support and the commitment of a number of enthusiastic collaborators. In terms of the former, the authors gratefully acknowledge funding by the Swiss National Science Foundation in the form of a Research Fellowship for project co-leader Anne Wetzel, and by the European Commission in the form of a Jean Monnet Information and Research Activity. While the research fellowship was decisive in getting the project started and to the success of its initial phase, the selection of the project for funding through the EU's Lifelong Learning Programme allowed us to invite the contributors of this edited volume to an authors' workshop, held at Ghent University in March 2012, to discuss the individual chapters that now comprise this book. Moreover, the Jean Monnet Activity offered a unique possibility to enter into a dialogue with policy-makers and members of civil society dealing with democracy promotion.[2]

All of the project events were supported by the Centre for EU Studies (CEUS) at Ghent University, Belgium, in cooperation with the Mannheim Centre for European Social Research (MZES) at the University of Mannheim, Germany. The public events related to the topic of this book were generously hosted by the Centre for European Policy Studies (CEPS), Brussels. We owe particular thanks to Michael Emerson, Hrant Kostanyan, Karel Lannoo and Jackie West.

The successful organization of these meetings involved a number of people. Fabienne Bossuyt and Vicky Reynaert were members of the team applying for the Jean Monnet Activity. Together with Eline De Ridder, they formed part of the project's key staff and efficiently and enthusiastically helped in arranging the events, maintaining e-mail lists and keeping the website up to date.

Beyond the key staff, who were also involved in early conceptual discussions, the project benefited tremendously from exchanges with other researchers based at Ghent University, especially Francis Baert, Olivia Rutazibwa, An Schrijvers, Ramin Shafagatov and Syuzanna Vasilyan. Over the course of time, the project received valuable input at a number of conferences, such as that of the European Consortium for Political

Research (ECPR), Porto, 2010; University Association for Contemporary European Studies (UACES), Bruges, 2010; European Union Studies Association (EUSA), Boston, 2011; and at the European Union in International Affairs (EUIA) III Conference, Brussels, 2012. In particular, the comments by Federica Bicchi and Hylke Dijkstra helped to sharpen the project's focus and conceptual basis. Similarly, Frank Schimmelfennig's very helpful comments on the initial findings (published in the *European Foreign Affairs Review*, Vol. 16, No. 5) have been taken up in this book. More general input was gratefully received from Ian Manners and Michelle Pace. Finally, the editors would like to thank the book's anonymous reviewer for suggestions on the manuscript.

During the preparation of the manuscript, Laurence Cooley provided useful proofreading assistance, while the references were edited by Péter Gyülvészi. We wish to thank the MZES for financial support of these editing tasks. While working on the book, both editors enjoyed the privilege of being temporarily hosted as guest researchers at different places. Jan Orbie would like to thank the National Centre for Research on Europe at the University of Canterbury. Anne Wetzel expresses her thanks to the Weatherhead Center for International Affairs at Harvard University. We also gratefully acknowledge the reproduction of two figures in the manuscript from the introductory article in the *European Foreign Affairs Review*, Vol. 16, No. 5.

Our sincere thanks go to the contributors, who each agreed to write a chapter on the substance of EU democracy promotion from their particular scholarly perspective or based on their regional expertise, and who agreed to revise various draft versions in line with the conceptual framework in order to achieve a coherent book. Needless to say, beyond their single chapters, the project has benefited from collective discussions and individual exchange between the editors and contributors.

Finally, we thank the series editor, Thomas Risse, for accepting this title for the 'Governance and Limited Statehood' series and Christina Brian and Ambra Finotello from Palgrave for their assistance during the publication process.

Notes

1. For more information, see the project website under http://www.eu-ipods.eu/.
2. For transcripts of the project's public forum and the expert meeting, see http://www.eu-ipods.ugent.be/publications; for a video summarizing the public event, see https://www.youtube.com/watch?v=3fSLUDO9nJc.

Contributors

Editors

Anne Wetzel is a Postdoctoral Fellow at the Mannheim Centre for European Social Research (MZES), University of Mannheim, Germany. Her research interests include EU democracy promotion and the EU in international organizations. Since 2010, she has been co-leader (with Jan Orbie) of the research project on the substance of EU democracy promotion funded by the Swiss National Science Foundation and the EU's Jean Monnet Programme. She has published in *Journal of European Public Policy* (2009), *Democratization* (2011), *European Foreign Affairs Review* (2011), *Journal of European Integration* (2014), *Cambridge Review of International Affairs* (2015) and in various edited volumes.

Jan Orbie is Associate Professor at the Department of Political Science and Director of the Centre for EU Studies at Ghent University. His research and teaching focus on the 'soft' dimensions of EU external relations. He has published various articles and chapters on these topics. He has also edited books on EU trade and development politics (with Gerrit Faber, 2007 and 2009), on European external policies (2008) and on Europe's global social policies (2008), and special issues of *European Foreign Affairs Review* (2009, 2011), *Res Publica* (2008), *Journal of Contemporary European Research* (2013), *Contemporary Politics* (2014) and *Cambridge Review of International Affairs* (2015).

Contributors

Müge Aknur is Assistant Professor of International Relations at Dokuz Eylül University in İzmir, Turkey. She holds a master's in International Relations from George Washington University and a PhD in political science from McGill University. She is the editor of *Democratic Consolidation in Turkey* (2012). Her research interests include democratization, democratic consolidation, civil–military relations, foreign policy analysis and Middle Eastern politics. She has published articles on Turkish civil–military relations and political liberalization in the Middle East, and book chapters on Turkish foreign policy.

Canan Balkır is Professor of Economics, Jean Monnet Chair in European Economic Integration and coordinator of the Jean Monnet Centre of Excellence at Dokuz Eylül University, İzmir, Turkey. Her research spans European Studies, focusing on economic integration, trade issues, the economics of EU–Turkey relations, EU retirement migration to Turkey and Europeanization. Her recent publications include *Europeanisation of Public Policy in Southern Europe* (co-edited with Tolga Bolukbasi and Ebru Ertugal, 2014); 'Europeanisation and Dynamics of Continuity and Change: Domestic Political Economies in the "Southern Periphery"' in *South European Society and Politics* (2013) and book chapters 'Economics and the Politicisation of Civil Society: The Turkish-Cypriot Case' (with Galip L. Yalman, in T. Diez and N. Tocci (eds.) *Cyprus: A Conflict at the Crossroads*, 2009) and 'Turkey, the New Destination for International Retirement Migration' (with Berna Kirkulak, in H. Fassmann, M. Haller and D. Lane (eds.) *Migration and Mobility in Europe: Trends, Patterns and Control*, 2009).

Federica Bicchi is Associate Professor in the International Relations of Europe in the Department of International Relations at the London School of Economics and Political Science. She holds a PhD in political science from the European University Institute in Florence, Italy, and has spent research periods at Stanford University, New York University, the University of Siena and the Freie Universität Berlin. Her research interests include EU foreign policy towards its Southern neighbourhood, on which she has published, *inter alia*, *European Foreign Policy Making toward the Mediterranean* (2007), as well as the construction of knowledge within the EU foreign policy system. She is co-editor of the special issue of *Mediterranean Politics* on *The Politics of Foreign Aid in the Arab World* (2014).

Fabienne Bossuyt is Assistant Professor in the Department of Political Science at Ghent University in Belgium. In addition to contributing book chapters to a number of edited volumes, her articles have appeared in, *inter alia*, the *European Foreign Affairs Review*, *European Integration Online Papers*, *Comparative European Politics*, *Journal of Contemporary European Studies*, *Cambridge Review of International Affairs* and *Journal of Contingencies and Crisis Management*. She is currently preparing a monograph on the EU's influence in Central Asia.

Maurizio Carbone is Professor of International Relations and Development and Jean Monnet Professor in EU External Policies in the

School of Social and Political Sciences at the University of Glasgow. He has published widely on EU external relations, foreign aid and the politics of international development, as well as Italy's foreign and development policies. Publications include *The European Union and International Development: The Politics of Foreign Aid* (2007), *Policy Coherence and EU Development Policy* (ed., 2009) and *The European Union in Africa: Incoherent Policies, Asymmetrical Partnership, Declining Relevance?* (ed., 2013). His research has also appeared in numerous journals, including *Cambridge Review of International Affairs, Contemporary Politics, European Foreign Affairs Review, Global Governance, International Relations, Journal of European Integration, Journal of International Development, Third World Quarterly* and *West European Politics*.

Bekim Çollaku is the Kosovo Prime Minister's Chief of Staff. Prior to joining the Cabinet of the Prime Minister, he worked as Assistant Lecturer in the Department of Political Sciences at Pristina University, and as a researcher in the Kosovar Institute for Policy Research and Development (KIPRED). He holds a master's in international studies, obtained at Newcastle University, UK, and is currently a PhD candidate in the Centre for EU Studies, Department of Political Science at Ghent University, Belgium.

Karen Del Biondo is a Postdoctoral Fellow in the Kolleg-Forschergruppe 'The Transformative Power of Europe' at the Freie Universität Berlin. She received her PhD from Ghent University in Belgium and was subsequently a Postdoctoral Fellow at the Center on Democracy, Development and the Rule of Law, Stanford University. Her research focuses on the EU's cooperation with Africa, particularly in the areas of democratization, peace and security and development. Her articles have appeared in the *Journal of Common Market Studies, Third World Quarterly, Cambridge Review of International Affairs, European Foreign Affairs Review, Journal of Contemporary European Research* and *Studia Diplomatica*.

Eline De Ridder worked as Associate Professor at the Centre for EU Studies of Ghent University. She has contributed to a number of journals and edited volumes on topics including EU enlargement, democratization, the fight against corruption and the development of civil society. Currently, she is a policy officer at the Flemish Department of Education and Training.

Notes on Contributors xiii

Labinot Greiçevci received an MA in political science from Manchester University, UK, and his PhD in political science from Ghent University, Belgium. He has held research posts as an Honorary Research Fellow at Manchester University, and Visiting Researcher at VU Amsterdam and Oxford University. His teaching and research interests include international state-building, the external affairs of the EU, and EU–Western Balkans relations. He has published extensively in peer-reviewed journals. Currently, he is CEO at the Research Institute of Development and European Affairs (RIDEA), a think-tank based in Pristina, where he also teaches at ESLG College.

Dimitry Kochenov holds the Chair of EU Constitutional Law at the University of Groningen in the Netherlands. His research focuses on EU citizenship, EU human rights and the principles underlying the EU legal order. He has acted as a consultant for the Government of the Netherlands on the EU law aspects of the constitutional reform of the Caribbean possessions and the government of Malta on EU citizenship issues. Among his latest edited volumes are *Europe's Justice Deficit?* (co-edited with Gráinne de Búrca and Andrew Williams, 2014), *EU Citizenship and Federalism* (forthcoming) and *The Enforcement of EU Law* (co-edited with András Jakab, forthcoming).

Hrant Kostanyan is a Special Research Fund Fellow at the Centre for EU Studies, Department of Political Science at Ghent University. He is also an Associate Research Fellow at the Centre for European Policy Studies (CEPS) Foreign Policy Unit, Brussels. His research focuses on EU foreign policy institutions and decision-making and institutions, primarily on the European External Action Service, the European Neighbourhood Policy and the EU's relations with its Eastern neighbours and Russia. Articles have appeared in, *inter alia*, *Journal of Southeast European and Black Sea Studies*, *Journal of Contemporary European Research* and *European Foreign Affairs Review*.

Paul Kubicek is Professor of Political Science and Director of International Studies at Oakland University, Michigan, USA. His articles on Central Asia have appeared in *Europe-Asia Studies*, *Third World Quarterly* and *Journal of Eurasian Studies*. He is currently finishing a book on the role of Islam in Muslim-majority democracies.

Milja Kurki is Professor in the Department of International Politics at Aberystwyth University. She is the author of *Causation in International*

Relations (2008) and *Democratic Futures: Revisioning Democracy Promotion* (2013), and editor of a number of texts on IR theory and democracy promotion. Recent publications include *Democracy Promotion: A Critical Introduction* (with Jeff Bridoux, 2014). Between 2008 and 2012, she was the Principal Investigator of the European Research Council funded project 'Political Economies of Democratisation'.

Vicky Reynaert holds a master's in EU studies and an advanced master's in European Union law. She obtained her PhD in political science from Ghent University, defending a dissertation on the Euro–Mediterranean relationship, in particular on the political economy of EU democracy promotion policy in the region and the identity the EU is creating for itself and others through its policies. She has published several articles and book reviews in academic journals including *Mediterranean Politics* and *European Foreign Affairs Review*.

Andrea Ribeiro Hoffmann is Lecturer at the Otto Suhr Institute and Research Fellow of the Kolleg-Forschergruppe 'The Transformative Power of Europe', both at the Freie Universität Berlin. Among her most recent publications are a chapter on 'Gender Mainstreaming in Mercosur and in Mercosur-EU Trade Relations' in an edited volume on *Gender Equality Norms in Regional Governance* by Anna van der Vleuten, Anouka van Eerdewijk, Conny Roggeband (2014); and a co-authored article on 'Explaining the Enforcement of Democracy by Regional Organizations: Comparing EU, Mercosur and SADC', with Anna van der Vleuten in *Journal of Common Market Studies* (2010).

Jessica Schmidt is a Postdoctoral Fellow at the Centre for Global Cooperation Research, Duisburg, Germany. Her research is broadly located at the intersection between political theory and international relations. She is interested in shifting ontologies of governing and their impact on the understanding of democracy as well as complexity theory and new materialism. She has previously published in *International Relations*, *Resilience* and *European Journal of International Relations*.

Susan Stewart is Deputy Head of the Eastern Europe and Eurasia Research Division at the German Institute for International and Security Affairs (SWP) in Berlin. She specializes in the areas of Russia's relations with its post-Soviet neighbours and the foreign and domestic policy of Ukraine, as well as the EU's Eastern Partnership initiative. She holds a BA in Slavic studies from Harvard University, an MA in International

Relations from the Fletcher School of Law and Diplomacy at Tufts University, and a Dr. rer. soc. from the University of Mannheim. Currently she is pursuing a comparative analysis of civil society development in Russia and Ukraine.

Benedetta Voltolini holds a PhD from the London School of Economics and is currently Lecturer in International Relations in the Department of Political Science at Maastricht University. She has spent research periods at Sciences Po Paris, Freie Universität Berlin and the EU Institute for Security Studies, Paris. Her research interests include lobbying in EU foreign policy, the Arab–Israeli conflict and EU democracy promotion in the Middle East and North Africa (MENA) region. Recent publications include 'EU Democracy Assistance in the Mediterranean: What Relationship with the Arab Uprisings?' in *Democracy and Security* (with Federica Bicchi, 2013) and 'The Role of Non-State Actors in EU Policies Towards the Israeli-Palestinian Conflict', *EUISS Occasional Papers* (2012).

Abbreviations and Acronyms

ACP	African, Caribbean and Pacific countries
ALBA	Bolivarian Alliance for the Peoples of Our America
BiH	Bosnia and Herzegovina
BRIC	Brazil, Russia, India and China
BTI	Bertelsmann Transformation Index
BYuT	Bloc Yulia Tymoshenko
CAN	Andean Community
CBSS	Country-Based Support Scheme
CDES	Brazilian Council for Economic and Social Development
CEE	Central and Eastern Europe
CEECs	Central and Eastern European countries
CFSP	Common Foreign and Security Policy
CIB	Comprehensive Institution Building Programme
CIVETS	Colombia, Indonesia, Vietnam, Egypt, Turkey and South Africa
CSB	Civil Service Bureau
CSO	civil society organization
CSF	Civil Society Fund
CSP	Country Strategy Papers
DCFTA	Deep and Comprehensive Free Trade Area
DCI	Development Cooperation Instrument
DG	Directorate General
DG DEVCO	DG Development and Cooperation
DG Relex	DG for External Relations
DIP	Democratic Institutions Programme
EaP	Eastern Partnership
EAR	European Agency for Reconstruction
EC	European Commission
ECJ	European Court of Justice
ECLO	European Commission Liaison Office
EDF	European Development Fund
EEAS	European External Action Service
EED	European Endowment for Democracy
EESC	European Economic and Social Committee
EIDHR	European Instrument for Democracy and Human Rights
EMP	Euro-Mediterranean Partnership

EMPA	Euro-Mediterranean Parliamentary Assembly
ENP	European Neighbourhood Policy
ENPI	European Neighbourhood and Partnership Instrument
EOM	election observer mission
EP	European Parliament
EPA	Economic Partnership Agreement
EPRDF	Ethiopian People's Revolutionary Democratic Front
ESDP	European Security and Defence Policy
EU	European Union
EULEX	European Union Rule of Law Mission in Kosovo
EUMM	EU Monitoring Mission
EUPM	EU Police Mission
EUSR	EU Special Representative
FH	Freedom House
FLP	Fiji Labour Party
FYROM	Former Yugoslav Republic of Macedonia
GDP	Gross Domestic Product
GSP+	Generalised Scheme of Preferences plus
HAC	Armenian National Congress
HRDO	Human Rights Defender's Office
HR/VP	High Representative of the Union for Foreign Affairs and Security Policy
IEOM	International Election Observation Mission
IFIs	international financial institutions
IFM	Isatabu Freedom Movement
IMF	International Monetary Fund
IPA	Instrument for Pre-Accession Assistance
ILO	International Labour Organization
JAP	Joint Action Plan
JHA	justice and home affairs
MEF	Malaita Eagle Force
MEDA	Mesures d'accompagnement financières et techniques
MEP	Member of the European Parliament
NATO	North Atlantic Treaty Organization
NGO	non-governmental organizations
NIF	Neighbourhood Investment Facility
NIP	National Indicative Programme
NSA-LA	Non-State Actors and Local Authorities in Development Programme
OAS	Organization of American States
ODA	Official Development Assistance

ODIHR	Office for Democracy and Human Rights
OECD	Organisation for Economic Co-Operation and Development
OPPD	Office for Promotion of Parliamentary Democracy
OPT	Occupied Palestinian Territory
OSCE	Organization for Security and Co-Operation in Europe
PA	Palestinian Authority
PACE	Parliamentary Assembly of the Council of Europe
PARLACEN	Central American Parliament
PARLATINO	Latin American Parliament
PARLASUR	Mercosur Parliament
PCA	Partnership and Cooperation Agreement
PDAP	Policy Dialogue and Advice Programme
PFDJ	People's Front for Democracy and Justice
PIF	Pacific Islands Forum
PSCAP	Public Sector Capacity-Building Programme
SAA	Stabilisation and Association Agreement
SAP	Stabilisation and Association Process
SAP	Structural adjustment programme
SAPD	Stabilization and Association Process Dialogue
SCAF	Supreme Council of Armed Forces
SIGMA	Support for Improvement in Governance and Management
TAIEX	Technical Assistance and Information Exchange
TEU	Treaty on the European Union
UfM	Union for the Mediterranean
UN	United Nations
UNASUR	Union of South American Nations
UNDP	United Nations Development Programme
UNMIK	United Nations Interim Administration Mission in Kosovo
UNRWA	United Nations Relief and Works Agency

1
The Substance of EU Democracy Promotion: Introduction and Conceptual Framework

Anne Wetzel

When, in October 2009, the European Parliament adopted its resolution on democracy building in the European Union's (EU) external relations, it urged the EU 'to publicly endorse the UN General Assembly's 2005 definition of democracy as the reference point for its own democratisation work' (European Parliament 2009: Art. 7). This call is remarkable because it exemplifies the thin conceptual basis of EU democracy promotion. At that time, it represented a further step in ongoing attempts to define the meaning of 'democracy' in EU external actions. Eventually, however, the call went unheard. To this day, the EU has not (yet) accepted a single definition of democracy that guides its democracy promotion activities. Scholars have recently come to the conclusion that the conceptual basis of EU democracy promotion can be summarized as 'fuzzy liberalism' (see the chapter by Milja Kurki in this edited volume).

Against this background, the question that guides this edited volume is *what* the EU promotes in the absence of a clear conceptual basis for its democracy promotion policy and how we can explain the content of EU democracy promotion. This is relevant for several reasons. The EU is one of the world's major democracy promoters.[1] As Michael Meyer-Resende, Director of Democracy Reporting International, and Dick Toornstra, Director of the Office for Promotion of Parliamentary Democracy (OPPD) at the European Parliament, state, '[c]larity on what Europe means by "democracy" would be in the interest of transparency and fairness towards foreign partners' (2009). Mapping the substance of EU democracy promotion contributes to such transparency. At the same time, knowing what the EU aims to promote is fundamental when it comes to the assessment of its success as a democracy promoter. Finally, the study of the substance of EU democracy promotion and the factors that shape this substance contributes to our understanding of the EU as an international actor more generally. Given the unique nature of the EU's internal system of governance (Laffan 1998), the question emerges: which values does the EU further outside its territory and which factors contribute to shaping this substance?

The book contributes to a new research agenda on the substance of democracy promotion by systematically mapping the substance of EU democracy promotion and explaining it. It deals with the substantive, democracy-related content that is being promoted by the EU towards third countries through various activities. In doing so, it partly builds on the results of earlier exploratory works on the substance of EU democracy promotion (Wetzel and Orbie 2011a).

The analysis starts from a puzzling finding of the existing literature. While the EU is found to promote liberal democracy in general, it is at the same time often accused of neglecting liberal democracy's core values in its concrete democracy promotion activities. Taking this dual finding as a point of departure, the book employs an adapted model of embedded liberal democracy for mapping the substance of EU democracy promotion. This model is employed in relation to 22 country case studies. In addition, the volume advances hypotheses about the factors that determine this substance. It elaborates on the expectations that the substance may be shaped by (a) the differences in power between the EU and a target country; (b) EU internal institutional factors; (c) differences in the target countries' domestic contexts; and (d) differences in the interorganizational field in the third country. These hypotheses are addressed in all of the country case chapters. Finally, since democracy is a contested concept and the focus on embedded liberal democracy implies a neglect of other forms of democracy (Schimmelfennig 2011), the book includes four contributions to the discussion from the angles of law, critical theory, political economy and governance that put the framework into perspective by offering alternative takes on the substance of democracy promotion. While these elaborations cannot be exhaustive, they do indicate avenues for further research on the topic.

This introductory chapter presents a short review of the literature that guided the choice of the adapted model of embedded democracy. This model is presented in the subsequent section of the chapter. In the third part of the chapter, hypotheses on the substance of democracy promotion are developed and concepts are operationalized. Finally, the chapter provides an outline of the structure of the book and of our case selection.

Anne Wetzel 3

The substance of EU democracy promotion: Some puzzling evidence

Despite the abundant literature on EU democracy promotion (for example Jünemann and Knodt 2007, Magen *et al.* 2009, Youngs 2010a), its substance has received little systematic attention. When scholars address substance, they come to different conclusions about its nature. On a general level, the EU is found to promote liberal democracy (Carothers 1997, Ayers 2008: 3, Risse 2009: 249, Kurki 2010). In a remarkable number of cases, however, the EU seems to neglect the classical elements of liberal democracy (such as civil and political freedoms, checks and balances; see for example Held 2006: 56–95). Youngs and Pishchikova, for instance, characterize EU democracy promotion as tending towards 'a technocratic, rules-export, governance focus' (2013: 25). Similarly, Hout summarizes that the governance-related strategies of EU development policy 'display a technocratic orientation and are instrumental to deepening market-based reform in aid receiving countries' (2010: 3). Holden analyses the EU's democracy promotion policy in the Middle East and comes to the conclusion that the EU promotes hegemonic polyarchy, the major thrust of which consists of 'neo-liberal reform, the opening of markets, and legal and economic integration' (2010: 608). Huber, in turn, sees a clear dominance of state-capacity building measures in the EU's democracy assistance in the Middle East and North Africa (2008: 53). These findings are also supported by Reynaert's study on the EU's policy towards the Southern Mediterranean countries, which concludes that 'the promotion of the civil society, the functioning of the state, and the core elements of democracy are oriented to the promotion of a market-based economy' (2011a: 623). As a result, the EU is found to focus on the promotion of a good governance agenda (Reynaert 2011a: 637). Carothers sees European democracy promotion as following a 'developmental approach', which gives emphasis to socio-economic concerns, state capacity and good governance (2009). Börzel's work, which compares a wide range of target countries, suggests that the question of substance is not one of 'either/or', but of gradation. She finds remarkable variation in the EU's activities, ranging from the promotion of reforms related to input legitimacy and supporting democratic government or governance to reforms related to output legitimacy and thus more to effectiveness (2009).

In order to take these findings into account, we adopt an adapted model of embedded liberal democracy comprising both the core elements of liberal democracy and elements such as state capacity, governance and civil society that have been highlighted by some researchers.

Mapping the substance of EU democracy promotion

Against the background of the above-mentioned dual finding regarding the content of EU democracy promotion activities, we take the democracy models developed by Linz and Stepan (1996a) and Merkel (2004) as a point of departure for the mapping exercise.[2] These works are particularly suitable because they offer a broad conceptualization of liberal democracy.[3] They encompass interlocking core institutions of democracy and supporting external conditions, both of which have been found to be important elements of EU democracy promotion. At the same time, these models allow us to keep core conditions and enhancing external conditions conceptually separate.

Although the two conceptualizations overlap, they also differ, in particular with regard to the question of whether some issues belong to the definitional core or the context of democracy, and the fine-graining of categories. For Linz and Stepan, the five conditions for a democracy are civil society, political society, rule of law, state apparatus and economic society. Democracy, in turn, is dependent on the existence of a state (Linz and Stepan 1996a: ch. 1). Merkel's model of embedded democracy maintains that 'liberal democracy consists of five partial regimes: a democratic electoral regime, political rights of participation, civil rights, horizontal accountability, and the guarantee that the effective power to govern lies in the hands of democratically elected representatives' (Merkel 2004: 37). Furthermore, it accounts for requisites that have an influence on the quality of democracy but 'are not defining components of the democratic regime itself' (Merkel 2004: 44). Figure 1.1 illustrates the concept.

With a view to our aim of mapping the substance of EU democracy promotion, we have decided to mainly follow Merkel's model, but adapt it with a view to aspects of Linz and Stepan's conceptualization of the five areas. This was done for several reasons. First, Merkel's model is more accurate for our purposes here. For instance, it allows us to distinguish more clearly between civil rights and civil society and to disaggregate complex issues such as the rule of law. Also, a major advantage in view of the domestic context hypothesis is that the Bertelsmann Transformation Index (BTI 2012a, 2012b) follows this model and can thus be applied in almost all country chapters. Secondly, we do not follow Linz and Stepan's suggestion of including an institutionalized

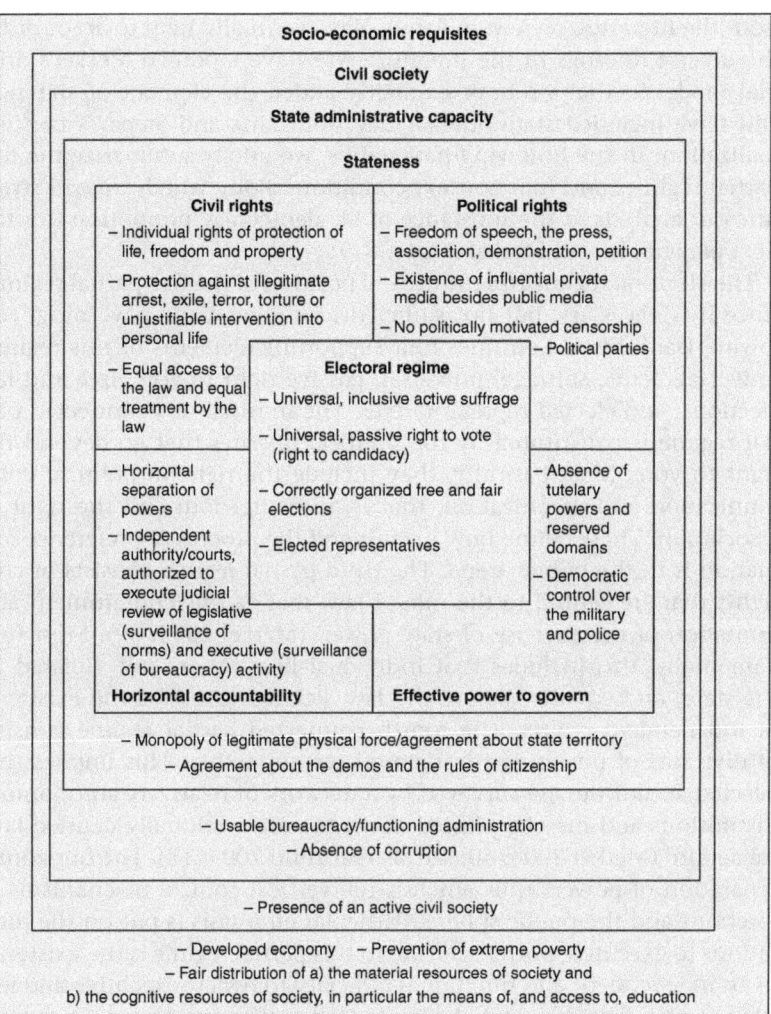

Figure 1.1 The concept of embedded democracy
Source: Adapted, based on Merkel (2004: 37).

market in the definition of democracy but rather see them as distinct issues (cf. Beetham 1997; for a discussion of the relationship between democracy and economy see also Kurki's contribution to this edited volume). Thirdly, Merkel's model helps to clarify the distinction between core aspects of liberal democracy and some related elements that emerge from the literature review and thus may eventually help to account for the diverse findings in the literature. We have modified Merkel's original model in that we have explicitly added the element of stateness and have included state bureaucracy from Linz and Stepan's conceptualization. In the following paragraphs, we briefly summarize the five partial regimes and four context conditions along which we will structure our analysis of the substance of EU democracy promotion (for the next paragraphs, see Merkel 2004: 38–9).

The electoral regime has the central position of the five partial regimes since it is necessary, but not sufficient, for democratic governing. Following Dahl, Merkel outlines four supporting elements of this regime: universal, active suffrage; universal, passive right to vote; free and fair elections; and elected representatives. The most closely connected partial regime is constituted by the political liberties that go beyond the right to vote. Most basically, they include the right to political communication and organization, that is, press freedom and the right to association. These define how meaningful the process of preference formation is in the public arena. The third partial regime consists of civil rights that are central to the rule of law, that is, the 'containment and limitation of the exercise of state power' (Merkel 2004: 39). Most fundamentally, this includes that individual liberties are not violated by the state, and equality before the law. Related to this is the existence of independent courts. The fourth connected partial regime consists of divisions of power and horizontal accountability. This implies that 'elected authorities are surveyed by a network of relatively autonomous institutions and may be pinned down to constitutionally defined lawful action' (Merkel 2004: 40; see also Morlino 2004: 18). The horizontal separation of powers thus amends the vertical control mechanisms of elections and the public sphere. Particular emphasis is put on the limitations to executive power. Central to this partial regime is the existence of an independent and functional judiciary to review executive and legislative acts. The last partial regime is the effective power to govern. This means that it is the elected representatives that actually govern and that actors not subject to democratic accountability should not hold decision-making power. In particular, there should be no tutelary powers or reserved policy domains (Merkel 2004: 41–2; see also Valenzuela 1992: 62–6).

While these five partial regimes are understood to be the defining components of a democracy, there are some more conditions that, while not part of the definition itself, shape the 'environment that encompasses, enables, and stabilizes the democratic regime' (Merkel 2004: 44).

Damage to these conditions might lead to defects in, or the destabilization of, democracy. However, it is important to add that the promotion of the external conditions alone does not necessarily further democratization. On the contrary, a sole focus on the context conditions can even be to the detriment of democratization (for example, Fukuyama 2005: 87–8).

The first of the external supporting conditions is stateness, understood as the ability of the state to pursue the monopoly of legitimate physical force. Where the monopoly of authority and physical force is not institutionalized, it cannot be democratized (Merkel et al. 2003: 58). Following Linz and Stepan, a state is indispensable for democracy: 'No state, no democracy' (1996b: 14). Although this strict connection between state and democracy can be disputed (Beetham 1999: 4–5), it is consistent with the traditional liberal democratic definitions of democracy that focus on 'governmental activity and institutions' at the state level (Held 2006: 77). Stateness is seen to be problematic when the territorial boundaries and the eligibility for citizenship are disputed (Linz and Stepan 1996: ch. 2). It also 'implies that the organs of the state uphold monopolistic control in a basic military, legal, and fiscal sense' and that there are no competing power centres exercising control in these areas (Bäck and Hadenius 2008: 3).

The second external context condition, which, in contrast to Merkel's original framework and our own earlier work, we have separated from stateness, is state administrative capacity. It refers to a capable administration. As Linz and Stepan put it, democracy relies on 'the effective capacity to command, regulate, and extract'. The bureaucracy must be usable by the democratic government (Linz and Stepan 1996: 11). In a broader sense, this condition refers to good governance, in particular to the output-related understanding. It includes in particular the effective government component of good governance promotion, which deals with the 'administrative core of good governance' and implies 'improving governance through strengthening the government and its administration' (Börzel et al. 2008: 10).

The third external context condition is the presence of civil society. This is the 'arena of the polity where self-organizing groups, movements, and individuals, relatively autonomously from the state, attempt to articulate values, create associations and solidarities, and advance their interests' (Linz and Stepan 1996: 7). The importance of this context condition stems from the assumption that a well-developed civil society strengthens democracy by generating and enabling 'checks of power, responsibility, societal inclusion, tolerance, fairness, trust, cooperation, and often also the efficient implementation of accepted political programs' (Merkel 2004: 47). The promotion of civil society is often seen as a part of good governance promotion and can be both input and output-oriented. While the former orientation stresses the empowerment of non-state actors in policy-making 'in order to improve the democratic quality of decision-making processes', the latter refers to the strengthening and/or inclusion of non-state actors in the policy implementation process with the aim of either producing better policies or better implementing policies. The case studies will, as far as possible, indicate which orientation EU civil society promotion follows in each specific instance (Börzel et al. 2008: 10).

The fourth external condition that has an influence on the state of democracy is the socio-economic context. On the one hand, this condition accounts for the link between economic development and the capability to sustain democracy, which has proven to be very stable (Ingelhart and Welzel 2009). On the other hand, it reminds us that a certain level of socio-economic equality is necessary for meaningful political equality: 'Only when citizens are secured and educated by means of a sufficiently developed social and economic status will they be able to form independent opinions as *citoyens*' and participate in the political process (Merkel 2004: 45; see also O'Donnell 2001: 27–9).

On this basis, and with regard to the above-mentioned puzzle, we distinguish five possible types of democracy promotion that differ with regard to the substance that is being promoted:

I: **Externally embedded liberal democracy promotion**: besides the five partial regimes, the EU also significantly supports the advancement of the external conditions.
II: **Liberal democracy promotion**: the EU mainly promotes the five partial regimes of liberal democracy.
III: **Partial liberal democracy promotion**: the EU mainly promotes some partial regimes while it neglects others, for example 'electoralism'.
IV: **External conditions democracy promotion**: the EU mainly supports the advancement of the external conditions.
V: **No liberal democracy promotion**: there are no activities related to the support of any partial regime or context condition (even though the EU may refer to some actions as democracy promotion).

Anne Wetzel 9

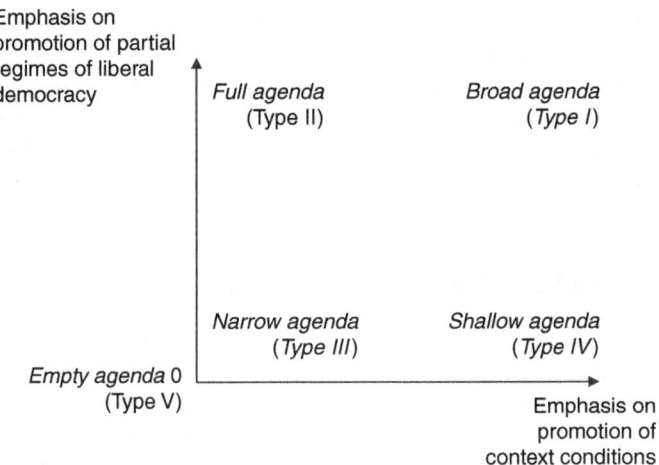

Figure 1.2 EU democracy promotion agendas

We can map the substance of EU democracy promotion in third countries as in Figure 1.2, distinguishing between a 'full', 'broad', 'narrow' and 'shallow' liberal democracy promotion agenda.

In order to map the substance of EU democracy promotion, we take into account not only activities that are explicitly labelled as such, but all activities that are potentially conductive to the development of any of the partial regimes or context conditions. Thus, for instance, while cooperation on social matters is sometimes separated from democracy, for example in the Commission's progress reports in the enlargement framework (see the respective chapters), we treat it as a democracy promotion activity because it contributes to advancing the socio-economic context condition. Yet we are aware that a sole focus on social issues may not lead to democratization. We have elaborated on this tension elsewhere (Wetzel and Orbie 2011b, Wetzel and Orbie 2012). Conversely, activities labelled as democracy promotion are only counted as such when they are designed to develop any of the partial regimes or context conditions (regardless of their actual effectiveness). For instance, the 'Democracy, Good Governance and Stability' Platform established under the EU's Eastern Partnership actually comprises a range of activities that would not be considered as democracy promotion, such as police cooperation on drug trafficking, migration, fight against cybercrime, and coping with natural and man-made disasters (Eastern Partnership 2012).

The terms 'narrow' and 'shallow' are not meant to refer to a 'worse' form of EU democracy promotion. The EU might have good reasons not to pursue a broad democracy promotion strategy in a certain country. In some instances, such as in Brazil or Israel, the state of democracy is already rather advanced. In other cases, such as Eritrea, the third country government's willingness to cooperate on democracy promotion is low.

Explaining the substance of democracy promotion

While the description of the substance of EU democracy promotion is an important achievement in itself, this book also aims to identify which factors have an influence on this substance. Based on previous, more exploratory work on the substance of EU democracy promotion that revealed variation in the substance (Wetzel and Orbie 2011b), we broadly follow the three explanations developed by Lavenex and Schimmelfennig on the EU external governance (2009) and add one additional factor in order to formulate hypotheses on the substance of EU democracy promotion. Importantly, the hypothesized explanatory factors are not completely independent of each other. As will be elaborated below, there are potential interlinkages between them, so they should not necessarily be seen as competing and indeed may even form certain constellations.

1. **Power:** the substance of EU democracy promotion towards a third country will be determined by the EU's capabilities and the constellation of interdependence between the EU and the third country and the EU's security interests.
2. **Institutions:** the substance of EU democracy promotion towards a third country will generally be determined by the EU's internal template. However, the internal template may vary according to the policy-makers that are involved. Thus, the substance will eventually reflect the most influential policy-makers' templates.
3. **Domestic context:** the substance of EU democracy promotion towards a third country will be determined by the domestic context in the third country. On the one hand, the EU may address 'deficient' dimensions and tailor the substance accordingly. On the other hand, the EU may leave the shaping of the substance mainly to the third country.
4. **Interorganizational context:** the substance of EU democracy promotion towards a third country will be determined by the context

of the 'interorganizational field' in which the EU operates in a third country.

Power

The factor 'power' is based on systemic explanations of the substance of EU democracy promotion by looking at the EU's and the third country's power positions. The overall argument is that the stronger the EU's power position is vis-à-vis the third country, the broader can be the agenda of democracy promotion. Eventually, however, the EU will promote what is in its security interests. In a weak power position, the substance of EU democracy promotion will be constricted. However, as we will elaborate below, there are different theoretical opinions about what determines the power position. While neorealism focuses on capabilities and their relative significance, neoliberal institutionalism stresses issue-specific interdependence.

According to neorealism, the first concern of states is their own survival in the anarchical international system. Thus they aim first of all for security. States are conceptualized as instrumentally rational unitary actors, which pursue their goals on the basis of cost-benefit calculations, and in view of the power hypothesis we assume the same for the EU. In striving for security, states aim to extend their autonomy and influence, since both are conductive to it. Influence refers to the will of a state to control its environment and the decisions of other states (Baumann *et al.* 2000). Robert Gilpin, a representative of the so-called 'hegemonic stability theory', writes that

> as the power of a group or state increases, that group or state will be tempted to try to increase its control over its environment. In order to increase its own security, it will try to expand its political, economic, and territorial control; it will try to change the international system in accordance with its particular set of interests.
>
> (Gilpin 1981: 94–5)

Such influence can, in principle, include the promotion of democracy. As Andrew Moravcsik summarizes, the promotion of norms such as human rights is compatible with realism (2000: 221–2). Stephen Krasner maintains that realism offers an explanation for the establishment of human rights regimes based on the 'capabilities and commitment of those states that supported each of these regimes' (1993: 141). While realist arguments on norm promotion are derived from different lines of thought within this theoretical tradition, there is a strong instrumental tone (see also Wolff and Wurm 2011: 82–3). This corresponds with the utilitarian reading of the democratic peace theorem. As Wolff and Wurm summarize, 'the instrumental value of democracy suggested by democratic peace research implies that a democratic state prefers for any given international "partner", other things being equal, a democratic instead of a non- or semi-democratic regime' (2011: 80).

Because of the instrumental character of democracy promotion, that is, the fact that it 'is one instrument among others that is applied to the extent that it contributes to the "real" aims that guide foreign policy' (Wolff and Wurm 2011: 87), we can expect that when influence in the form of democracy promotion is to the detriment of security (modified neorealism, see Baumann *et al.* 2000: 10), the EU will not pursue this goal (Wolff and Wurm 2011: 83; see also Jünemann 2009), even when it is in a powerful position. In fact, studies on international democracy promotion suggest that 'when democracy clashes with more central foreign policy interests, democracy promotion is often compromised' (Schraeder 2003: 33). This trend has also been confirmed for the EU (Olsen 2000, K. E. Smith 2008: 165–7, Schimmelfennig 2012: 16). While inconsistency has been analysed mainly with regard to the instruments employed or not employed by the EU (Knodt and Jünemann 2008, K. E. Smith 2008: 165–7), it can be expected that the same holds true for the substance that the EU promotes. One dilemma is that democratization processes may (temporarily) lead to instability, the empowerment of radical parties and even civil war, which may affect the EU's security (Andrés Viñas 2009, Jünemann 2009, Powel 2009, Börzel and van Hüllen 2014).

The disposition of striving for influence is the same for all states and – by analogy – for the EU. However, the room that states have for action to pursue autonomy and to influence goals depends on their power position. This position, in turn, is influenced by a state's capabilities, keeping in mind the overall distribution of capabilities. Capabilities are often defined in political, economic and military terms. They are seen as fungible and thus translate into the general power of a state, which can be used to pursue goals. As a result, relations with other states are determined by the power (a)symmetries:

> Relations with weaker states are determined by the dependence of the latter, which will be all the greater the weaker those states are. Powerful states can instrumentalize this dependence, for example, by tying the granting of development aid or the provision of diplomatic support to conditions. By instrumentalizing both positive and

negative sanctions, states can increase their influence over weaker states [...].

(Baumann *et al.* 2000: 12)

The neoliberal institutionalist approach corresponds with neorealism in several assumptions. States are seen as unitary, utility-maximizing actors. However, with regard to power, it takes a different view. Neoliberal insitutionalists see states in a struggle for welfare gains rather than power. From this perspective, military capabilities are less relevant than neorealism suggests because the international system is characterized by complex interdependence, which makes military resources less fungible. As a consequence, states can pursue other goals than maximizing power. Also in contrast to neorealism, interdependence is conceptionalized to be issue-specific. Asymmetries in issue-specific dependence can be regarded as a source of power and thus as a bargaining advantage (Keohane and Nye 1989 (1977): ch. 1).

Thus, we arrive at the hypothesis:

If the EU is in a more powerful position vis-à-vis the third non-democratic country, it will promote the substance that is in its security interest. The more the EU expects democracy promotion in a third non-democratic country to lead to a loss of its own (perceived hard and soft) security, the more the EU will promote shallow democracy. In these cases, we may expect a particular emphasis on stateness and/or effective governance, in order to ensure stability. Otherwise, it will promote liberal or externally embedded liberal democracy. Conversely, when the third country is in a similar or even stronger power position, the EU will at best promote shallow democracy.

The EU's power position is operationalized as 'strong' when the EU's capabilities are stronger than those of the target country, 'equal' when capabilities are similar and 'weak' when the EU's capabilities are weaker than those of the target country. Issue-specific interdependence in a sector salient for the EU is in favour of the EU when the target state perceives itself to be more dependent on EU cooperation, 'equal' when the target state and the EU perceive themselves to be equally dependent on cooperation and in favour of the third country when the EU perceives itself to be more dependent on the target sate's cooperation.

The countries included in the book show variance with regard to capabilities and interdependence. The EU is in a strong power position in terms of capabilities and favourable asymmetric interdependence in cases such as Bosnia, the Czech Republic, Georgia and Tunisia, but in a less strong position in others, as is the case with Russia. Also, the EU perceives democratization to entail potential threats to EU security in some cases, such as Palestine, Egypt and Tunisia, whereas it does not in others, such as Slovakia, Turkey, Fiji and the Solomon Islands.

Institutions

The institutionalist explanation emphasizes the role of EU internal institutions in shaping the substance of democracy promotion. Although neo-institutionalism is not a unified approach from which hypotheses can be derived, it draws our attention to both the importance of normative rules and existing templates and the importance of rules structuring the policy process. Roughly speaking, who is in charge of democracy promotion policy and which norms and/or templates guide the action of the respective policy-makers is decisive.

Neo-institutionalism does not provide a single valid definition of institutions. Rather, different elements of institutions are prioritized by different strands within neo-institutionalism. While some scholars stress the regulative pillar, others focus on the normative or cognitive systems. From the latter two, we can derive certain expectations regarding the substance of EU democracy promotion.

Scholars who stress the normative pillar emphasize the 'normative rules that introduce a prescriptive, evaluative, and obligatory dimension into social life' (Scott 2001: 54). For actors in certain positions, behaviour is guided by roles that make some objectives and actions appropriate. With regard to democracy promotion, the 'cultural' or normative approach to the democratic peace is particularly relevant in this regard (Wolff and Wurm 2011: 83–4). This links up with Sedelmeier's account of the impact of EU identity on the enlargement policy (Sedelmeier 2005). It is assumed that policy-makers act within the EU's normative structure. Democracy is part of the EU's normative basis (Manners 2002). The EU has clearly adopted the role of 'democracy promoter' (Sedelmeier 2006a, Jünemann 2009) and thus democracy promotion can be seen as part of the EU's identity as well as the collective identities of policy-makers both within the EU institutions and its member states. However, this role conception is still diffuse (Sedelmeier 2006a: 127). With regard to the substance, for example, there is no single definition of democracy that can be promoted. Nevertheless, there is an 'evaluative standard'. Still, such behavioural prescriptions do not automatically translate into respective policy decisions. Rather, '[t]he effect of the EU's role-construction [...] is uneven across different groups of policy-makers that are involved' (Sedelmeier 2005: 31; see also Scott 2001: 55). As a result, 'the notion of the EU's role as a collective property of EU identity allows for an uneven normative effect of identity across different groups of policy-makers' (Sedelmeier 2005: 31).

Scholars who stress the cultural-cognitive element of institutions attach particular importance to 'the shared conceptions that constitute the nature of social reality and the frames through which meaning is made' (Scott 2001: 57). They point to the power of routines, templates and scripts (Hall and Taylor 1996: 948, Scott 2001: 57–8, 68). This is close to Hall's assertion that 'policymakers customarily work within a framework of ideas and standards that specifies not only the goals of policy and the kind of instruments that can be used to attain them, but also the very nature of the problems they are meant to be addressing' (Hall 1993: 279). Following this approach, it can be assumed that the substance of EU democracy promotion reflects EU internal templates that are externalized. Again, these templates do not have to be the same across different groups of policy-makers. Rather, different 'cultural frameworks' (Scott 2001: 57) may lead to different interpretations of what democracy promotion implies and the degree to which it should be prioritized.

Thus, in order to explain the substance of EU democracy promotion, we have to take into account who is involved in policy-making, which depends on the structure of the EU internal policy process. (Historical) institutionalism has paid particular attention to the distribution of power through institutions. Instead of conceiving individuals as freely contracting, researchers following this approach 'are more likely to assume a world in which institutions give some groups or interests disproportionate access to the decision-making process' (Hall and Taylor 1996: 941). Sedelmeier also points to the importance of the (rule-based) structure of the policy process (2005: 40–2).

Thus we can formulate the following overall hypothesis:

> The substance of EU democracy promotion will differ depending on the sub-system(s) in charge/policy-makers involved in the formulation of EU policies towards a third country.

A sub-system is understood here as a group of policy-makers that is formed along a particular cleavage, which can be sectoral or institutional (Egeberg 2005). We can expect the substance to vary along sectoral sub-systems (such as development policy, trade, security, but also enlargement and European Neighbourhood Policy context) (Egeberg 2005: 106) and institutional sub-systems (predominance of the Commission, Council, or more recently the European External Action Service (EEAS)) (Egeberg 2005: 108–9). They are related insofar that in some sectors, certain organizational sub-systems are more important than others (for example, while the Commission is strong in trade and development policy, security issues are dominated by the Council and the EEAS).

We can expect the substance to vary according to the sectoral sub-systems involved. On the basis of the different templates and paradigms, we can formulate the following more concrete expectations about the substance:

> The higher the degree to which sub-systems with a 'development background' are involved in policy formulation and implementation, the more shallow EU democracy promotion will be, with a particular stress on the component of socio-economic development.

As Thomas Carothers points out, policy-makers from a development background may follow different norms and scripts: 'the initial separation between democracy aid and development aid was not just organizational. It was also conceptual, methodological, and psychological. Democracy promoters conceived of their work as a fundamentally different enterprise from development aid for the simple but powerful reason that its goal was political, not socioeconomic' (Carothers 2010: 13). With regard to the current situation, he finds that while this initial difference has diminished to some degree, 'taking [...] *democracy* seriously as an integral part of the development enterprise remains a bridge too far' and thus hesitations persist (Carothers 2010: 24–5).

> The higher the degree to which sub-systems with an 'enlargement background' are involved in policy formulation and implementation, the broader EU democracy promotion will be.

Enlargement represents a particular case of democracy promotion because the process aims at the eventual EU membership of the candidate country. This is why it can be expected that the EU as a community of values attaches particular importance to democratic elements. As outlined in the so-called Copenhagen criteria established in 1993, this community has made EU membership conditional on the compliance with democratic values.

Apart from sectorally different paradigms, we can expect the substance to vary according to the organizational sub-systems involved:

The higher the degree to which EU member states are involved in policy formulation and implementation, the more the substance will resemble the template favoured by the most dominant member state(s).

Apart from democracy promotion through the EU, member states have national democracy promotion policies in place. These differ with regard to significance and geographical focus. To some degree, they also differ in substance and addressees (Youngs 2006: 20–3, Youngs 2008). We expect that these national policy characteristics are also reflected at the EU level and may eventually shape the substance of EU democracy promotion.

The involvement of EU member states is operationalized as 'weak' when democracy promotion policy towards a third country is mainly Commission-driven and involves member states (through the Council) only to a limited degree. It is 'strong' when democracy promotion policy towards a third country involves one or several member states to a high degree. It is difficult to judge the situation for the recently established EEAS but it seems that the involvement of member states is made diffuse, because they have to share the 'stage' with other actors (Kostanyan 2012).

The cases included in this book are characterized by the pre-eminence of different EU institutions in democracy promotion, such as (former) Directorate-General (DG) Relex in Georgia and Armenia (now shared with the EEAS), DG Development/DEVCO in Ethiopia and Eritrea, and DG Enlargement in the Czech Republic, Bosnia and Turkey. Venezuela, on the other hand, represents a case where a particular EU member state (Spain) plays a major role.

Domestic context

The expectation that domestic factors of the third country influence the substance of EU democracy promotion is based on the assumption that the EU employs a tailor-made approach for every targeted country, that is, it adjusts the substance of democracy promotion to the specific situation within the third country. In extreme cases, it may employ a demand-driven approach and leave the definition of substance mainly to the target country. This expectation follows the more recent attention that the 'structure of resonance' variable, that is, the domestic context, has received in research on the EU's choice of democracy promotion instruments (Knodt and Jünemann 2008: 276–7). In general, tailor-made approaches can be driven by functional necessity or efficiency considerations, or by legitimacy and resonance (Lavenex and Schimmelfennig 2009: 804).

Scholars have indeed shown that although 'the strategies and instruments are pretty much similar across regions and countries, the way in which the EU employs them varies enormously depending on the specific regional or national contexts' (Börzel and Risse 2009: 48; see also van Hüllen and Stahn 2009: 118).

It is not only scholars who are increasingly paying attention to the domestic contexts and preconditions when investigating democracy promotion strategies; the EU also states that it is aware of the varying resonance of democracy promotion in different countries. As a consequence, it aims to develop 'tailor made country strategies' with regard to the promotion of democracy (European Commission and High Representative 2011a: 8; for a similar statement on governance see European Commission 2003a: 17).

We can think of two different scenarios within this explanation. In the first case, the EU takes into account the local circumstances but stays in the 'driving seat' with regard to the substance of democracy promotion. Such a scenario is expressed in the EU's reflection that 'while the overall objectives of the EU's human rights and democracy policy remain valid and unaltered' it sees the advantages of 'an approach that seeks to match objectives in a country with the realities on the ground' (European Commission and High Representative 2011a: 8). In the second case, the EU leaves the main initiative in shaping the substance to the third country. In this case, '[t]he starting point should generally be the countries' own assessments of needs and how these can be addressed' (European Commission and High Representative 2012a: 11).

In the first case, it can be expected that the substance that the EU advocates in third countries in order to promote democracy is tailored to the domestic situation of the country in question and follows identified 'incompatibilities'. In order to assess the quality of the framework's components in the country cases, and the level of conflict, we use the BTI.[4] It covers almost all of the countries that are analysed in this volume, and is available in its present form from 2006 onwards, with the most recent version being for 2014. In contrast to other indices such as the Freedom House index or the World Bank's Worldwide Governance Indicators, it has the advantage that it covers all of the components and is fine-grained enough that it allows us to assess all the components of the framework individually.

The substance of EU democracy promotion will differ depending on 'shortcomings' in the third country.

Post-conflict countries or countries with limited statehood represent a particular case in this regard. Scholars have found that the transition from an autocracy to a partly democratic regime entails a heightened danger of war. War is particularly likely when governmental institutions are especially weak (Mansfield and Snyder 2002: 298). Consequently,

> Where attempts to promote democratic transitions contribute to or occur in the face of weakened central governmental institutions, there is a risk of adverse foreign-policy consequences. Put more positively, policies to foster democratic transitions should be accompanied by efforts to mold strong, centralized institutions that can withstand the intense demands on the state and political elites posed by high-energy mass politics. Before pressuring autocrats to hold fully competitive elections, the international community should first promote the rule of law, the formation of impartial courts and election commissions, the professionalization of independent journalists, and the training of competent bureaucrats.
> (Mansfield and Snyder 2002: 334)

The EU seems to heed this advice. As Börzel shows, in its efforts to promote good governance, the EU reacts to limited statehood by stressing output-oriented objectives, that is, the strengthening of government and its administration, or the implementation capacity of non-state actors. Conversely, when statehood is intact, the EU focuses on input-oriented objectives, that is, the establishment of a functioning public sphere for interest articulation and aggregation, or the bottom-up empowerment of non-state actors in domestic decision-making processes (2009: 4, 38). Thus, in this particular case, we might expect the EU to forego emphasis on the core aspects of democracy in order to allow for peaceful transitions:

> In post-conflict constellations and countries with limited statehood, the EU will mainly pursue shallow democracy promotion, in particular state-building and good governance.

With regard to the second case, in which the EU may leave the shape of the substance of democracy promotion mainly to the third country, we may expect that third countries design the substance of democracy promotion in a way that comes closest to the acceptable level of EU interference in internal affairs, their own ideas of democracy and their domestic institutional structures:

> The substance of EU democracy promotion is demand driven and depends on the degree of political will of the government to undertake democratic reforms and the particular ideas of democracy.

The degree of political will of the government is partly assessed by using the BTI.[5] It is operationalized as 'defensive' when the government is reluctant to initiate any democracy-related initiatives, which is, among other things, indicated by a BTI score between 1 and 5 for Q17.1; as 'open to liberal democracy' when the government is willing to initiate democracy-related initiatives (BTI score between 6 and 10), and as 'open to alternative/country specific models of democracy' when the government is willing to initiate initiatives related to specific models of democracy. It should be noted that even in cases when the EU aims to remain in the driving seat, it may not be able to promote democracy because of the reluctance of the target state's government.

The domestic context of countries included in the book varies significantly. First, there is a difference in the domestic level of democracy, ranging from minor and very specific deficiencies, as in Brazil, Israel and the Czech Republic, to deficiencies in all components, as in Ethiopia and Eritrea. In addition, there are differences in the target countries' openness towards democracy promotion, ranging from rather defensive, as in Eritrea, to rather open, as Ukraine was, albeit temporarily.

Interorganizational context

The EU is not the only international democracy promoter, and not necessarily the most important one in any given target country. It may thus coordinate the substance of democracy promotion with other actors, including its own member states. The literature on interorganizational coordination has defined such coordination in different ways, ranging from merely 'an attribute of any decision that takes its environment into account' to 'a deliberate activity undertaken by an organization or an interorganizational system to concert the decisions and actions of their subunits or constituent organizations', which 'includes coordination at any level of the organization or interorganizational system, from interactions between individuals to the structure of interorganizational networks' (Alexander 1993: 331). Groups of organizations may form 'interorganizational fields', which in turn may be more or less centralized, ranging from loosely linked networks (feudal field) and alliances (mediated field) to corporate empires (guided field) (Alexander 1993: 340).

Donor coordination between the EU and its member states is demanded by Article 210 of the Treaty on the Functioning of the European Union. In addition, Article 21 of the Treaty on European Union establishes that the EU 'shall promote multilateral solutions to common problems'. With regard to the implementation of these provisions, the common format for Country Strategy Papers (CSPs), as outlined in the Common Framework for Drafting CSPs, states that the documents 'must provide as accurate and comprehensive a picture as possible of the programmes of the Member States and other donors, indicating how they complement each other' (European Commission 2006a: 19). It can thus be hypothesized that

> The substance of democracy promotion will differ depending on the EU's interorganizational coordination with other international democracy promoters within the third country. With increasing centralization, the substance of democracy promotion in a country is likely to be shaped by the dominant actor, be it the EU or other actors.

A dominant actor is an actor that has the greatest material and immaterial resources at its disposal.

There is variance with regard to the constellation of external actors engaging in democracy promotion, ranging from the EU as a dominant actor, as in Bosnia and Kosovo, to the EU as a subordinated actor, as in the Solomon Islands and Fiji.

Interlinkages between factors

As already pointed out above, there are potential interlinkages between the single factors, so the hypotheses are not completely independent of each other. For example, if the EU is in a less favourable power position, the substance may to a large extent be shaped by the degree of political will in the third country and its government's agenda. In turn, institutional factors will certainly not come to the fore in such a case. In a similar way, the institutional factor within the EU is related to the domestic context, insofar as some EU institutions may be more open to tailor-made approaches and ownership than others. The same is true for interorganizational cooperation, which may be favoured more by some institutions than others. The EU's position in an organizational field may depend not least on its power position. Thus, the factors are not necessarily 'competing', but we should be open to discovering certain constellations of factors that shape the substance of EU democracy promotion. Further research on the interaction of factors could take a closer look at certain constellations.

Application to country cases

In the 11 country chapters that follow, the framework and hypotheses presented above are applied to 22 case studies. As already discussed above, countries were selected in such a way as to ensure variation in explanatory variables.

The analyses of the substance of EU democracy promotion focus mainly on implementation activities, that is, output in terms of policy analysis (Jann and Wegrich 2003: 79–80). However, they will also take into account the results of the preceding policy formulation process, that is, declarations of intent, statements about intended activities and goals. These are usually laid down in documents such as plans, programmes, declarations and laws (Jann and Wegrich 2003: 79–80). In the case of EU democracy promotion, two different types can be distinguished. The first relates solely to the EU and includes among others Commission Communications, Strategies (such as the EU Strategy on Central Asia) and Council Conclusions or Joint Declarations (such as the European Consensus on Development). The second type includes declarations and statements that are made jointly by the EU and the third country and includes among others the European Neighbourhood Policy (ENP) Action Plans and CSPs. In contrast to these two types, which are at the declaratory level, the subsequent policy implementation refers to the concrete interventions that aim to change the addressees' behaviour. This includes, among other measures, financial support and specific decisions (Jann and Wegrich 2003: 80). With regard to EU democracy promotion, implementation would cover diverse items such as Council Statements, the provision of financial support through various instruments, the imposition of sanctions or awarding a country the Generalised Scheme of Preferences plus (GSP+) status, election observation missions and political dialogue, as well as Twinning and Technical Assistance Information Exchange (TAIEX) projects.

Information on the EU's democracy promotion activities was collected by the authors through document analysis, personal interviews in the EU and in third countries, and via the secondary literature.

Based on these sources, each chapter provides an exhaustive qualitative assessment of the EU's policy. In order to be able to compare the cases and discover more general tendencies in the substance of EU democracy promotion, each author, in addition to the qualitative assessment, assigns values for the EU's implementation activities regarding each component. Values are assigned on a scale ranging from 'no or very minor attention' (−), through 'some' (+) and 'focused' (++), to 'major' (+++) attention. These values were discussed intensely at an authors' workshop held at Ghent University in March 2012, and with the authors individually. While in cases of 'no or minor attention', we see (almost) no EU activity on an issue, 'some attention' means that the EU addresses an issue sporadically or continuously, but with little intensity. 'Focused attention' stands for systematic, repeated or continuous and directed attention that might be backed up with financial resources. 'Major attention' entails an intense direction of (material and/or non-material) resources towards a component.

The time frames covered in each chapter vary slightly due to country characteristics, but all of them except the chapter on Slovakia and the Czech Republic cover the period of about the last ten years.

Notes

1. See, for instance, the figures on 'government and civil society – general' in the Organisation for Economic Cooperation and Development – Development Assistance Committee (OECD-DAC 2014).
2. Please note that these frameworks were not originally developed to describe the substance of democracy promotion. However, we maintain that they offer a valuable starting point for this endeavour.
3. Suitability refers to our specific purpose here. It does not imply an approval of the EU's policy, nor an (implicit) acknowledgement of liberal democracy as a universal and superior democratic model. Furthermore, it should be noted that liberal democracy as a particular and historically specific model of democracy (Parekh 1993) is not the only form of democracy promoted by the EU (see also the chapters 4 and 5 in this edited volume) but rather, as the literature suggests, the dominating one.
4. See http://www.bti-project.de/. For the assessment of the single components, the following items are used: 'electoral regime', Q2.1; 'civil rights', Q3.4; 'political rights', average of Q2.3 and Q2.4; 'horizontal accountability', average of Q3.1 and Q3.2; 'effective power to govern', Q2.2; 'stateness', average of Q1.1 and Q1.2; 'state capacity', average of Q 1.4 and Q15.3; 'civil society', average of Q5.2, and Q16.4; and 'socio-economic development', Q6.1. The level of conflict is assessed using Q13.3.
5. The degree of political will of the leadership to cooperate with international actors is covered by Q17.1.

Part I
Alternative Reflections on the EU as a Liberal Democracy Promoter

Part I

Alternative Reflections on the U.S. and Liberal Democracy "Promotion"

2
Law Perspective: Praise Undeserved? The EU as a Democracy Promoter: A Sceptical Account

Dimitry Kochenov

The need for sober accounts

A significant reshuffling of the European Union's (EU) approaches to national-level democracy in its member states is urgently required.[1] This should be accompanied by a toning down of the EU's claims externally. Fundamentally, it seems that all the uncertainties and challenges related to the promotion and preservation of democracy internally and externally ultimately relate to the vacuum the Union suffers from at its core (Williams 2010): attempting to construct and enforce an approach to justice which is essentially market-based (for a multi-faceted analysis, see Kochenov et al. 2014a), failing to withstand the scrutiny of the project from outside the market paradigm (for a proposal of how to break this trend, see for example Kochenov 2013a) and making wholehearted democracy-related mobilization of the Union legal system impossible (Weiler 2009: 51). Clarity concerning the substance of EU values, in particular democracy and the rule of law, is lacking (Kochenov et al. 2014b), causing many problems in practice. In this context, democracy largely fails to emerge as a guiding principle of EU law, joining an array of highly imprecise malleable values vaguely indicating the *desiderata* informing the construction of the internal market. To be very clear, the EU *acquis* on democracy is simply non-existent.

The huge literature claiming the contrary notwithstanding, the EU's credentials as a democracy promoter seem quite weak both internally and externally. The Union cannot boast clear standards, developed reliable procedures or the institutional capacity to promote democracy in either of the two spheres. Even the pre-accession strategy (Maresceau 2006: 69), which de facto implied a full submission of the candidate countries to the EU's will and was reported as a huge success, is of questionable value in terms of the outcomes actually achieved, not merely reported. This strategy failed to shape lasting effects, as the examples of Hungary or Romania, experiencing severe problems with democracy and the rule of law (for example Bánkuti et al. 2012, Halmai 2012), inter alia, clearly demonstrate.[2] It is suggested, as I have argued elsewhere (Kochenov 2008a), that the failure can largely be explained by one key consideration: the overwhelmingly weak framing of the substance of democracy promotion provided by the Commission.

As a result, the pre-accession democracy promotion and EU enlargements as such have not only had a profound effect on European constitutionalism. They have also exposed the EU to additional dangers related to having countries deeply problematic from the point of view of core values as full members, rather than solving outstanding problems (Kochenov 2008a), making the issue adherence to the *internal* values, as reflected, *inter alia*, in Article 2 of the Treaty on European Union (TEU), and the reinforcement of democracy in the member states particularly acute. Such dangers are particularly acute today, when apart from a dysfunctional pre-accession democracy promotion, the EU cannot boast any viable internal correction mechanisms to clean up the failures of the pre-accession, to say nothing of the democratization of the wider world: the EU's efforts to normalize the democratic situation even in the closest neighbouring states of Belarus and Ukraine – and indeed in Kosovo (European Court of Auditors 2012), which is an entity of its own creation – have been largely futile. Internally, Article 7 TEU fails to provide much-needed solutions (Sadurski 2010: 385) and other approaches are being tried out (see for example Müller 2013, Closa *et al.* 2014, Kochenov 2014a).

At the same time, that the EU promotes democracy is usually taken for granted,[3] triggering a number of obvious questions. Most importantly, how well founded is this way of thinking about the Union? The main goal of this chapter is to suggest that those eager to praise the Union are somewhat too optimistic concerning its democracy promotion capacity. A very different reading of the EU's failures and achievements in this important field is also possible. Scepticism being a necessary starting point of any scholarly inquiry, it is worthwhile taking scepticism seriously in contrast to a myriad congratulatory accounts. The main point made here is that claims that the EU promotes democracy amount to little more than an approval of a self-congratulatory account of the institutions engaged in a public relations exercise: one of the very few areas where they actually seem to be successful.

In fact, the same argument is not only related to democracy as such, but also applies to the ideals of peace (Williams 2010: Chapter 2), the rule of law (Pech 2013), equality (Kochenov 2010) and the like. Most importantly, the question of the external component of the EU's *raison d'être* remains open (de Búrca 2013: 21). The consequences of the prevailing perspective are twofold: claims of the Union's success are so engrained in our thinking about the Union that its image around the world no doubt benefits from an auto-characterization as a renowned democracy promoter. At the same time, probably taking their own propaganda at face value, the institutions have but a minimal impact on the democratic integrity of the member states, since seemingly not enough is being done to ensure that adherence to the democratic ideal enjoys the place it deserves among the Union's actions.[4]

This chapter approaches the weakness of the EU's democracy promotion from four interrelated perspectives – all of them flashing out deeply problematic developments. The four include the following:

1. The relationship between the EU and democracy at the supranational level: the EU is an unlikely place to look for the standards of democracy;
2. The weakness of the EU's performance both internally and externally in fields unrelated to the *acquis* – of which democracy is part – with a particular focus on the ethical essence of its functioning (Williams 2013) and the missing underlying justice aspect of its law;
3. The lack of external and internal democratic standards which would (or would not) be clearly decipherable in the context of the EU;
4. The lack of instruments to defend such missing standards.

Crucially, the analysis points in the direction of a misconceived distinction between the external and the internal contexts of democracy and rule of law promotion by the EU. The two are intimately interconnected and the EU seems to be largely powerless in both.

The conclusion restates a sketch of a realistic account of the current state of affairs with regard to democracy promotion in the EU externally and internally: the EU cannot provide an example, does not have the standards at hand and cannot boast effective instruments to ensure that democracy is taken seriously by its own member states or by its neighbours – to say nothing of the wider world. A pessimistic account is followed by a set of suggestions to remedy this state of affairs, which includes a growing role for the Union's institutions in monitoring the adherence of the member states to the values of the Union, combined with a toning down of the Union's claims on the international scene. Sometimes it is better to remain silent than multiply hypocritical self-congratulatory accounts of engagement with the world: the Union would benefit from a *Realpolitik* revival at the level of its rhetoric, not only de facto.[5]

The EU and democracy: Key problematic aspects in four steps

The feebleness of the EU as a would-be democracy promoter can be illustrated at a number of different levels. First of all, somewhat obviously, democracy has never been the EU's strong point. On the contrary – and no matter whether one takes the whole democratic deficit debate into account or not – what is absolutely clear is that the EU is not a polity which can sincerely claim any more or less conventional democracy model for itself: it is not democratic in the way that a state would be (for example Føllesdal and Hix 2005; but see Moravcsik 2002). Of course, it is fundamental not to confuse oranges and apples, as Joseph Weiler famously warned (1999: 268). Yet, when we speak about the promotion of democracy, we are not concerned with democratizing other quasi-federal EU-like international organizations and structures (on the use of federal approaches in characterizing the EU and its legal system, see for example Lenaerts and Gutman 2006, Schütze 2009), but with the spread of democracy among states: something the EU cannot provide any viable model for.

Secondly, democracy is of course not everything and should be considered in context. It is a tool for achieving desired results, rather than a result in itself (Van Parijs 2012) – even though the two sometimes go together. Indeed, a democracy of vile persons will be vile (Weiler 2003: 18) – and this is not what anyone could possibly wish to establish and promote, which is why the rule of law, equality and the protection of human rights, alongside a defendable and appealing idea of justice to inform all the above, are indispensable. It is no secret that the EU does not possess any of these. Only the idea of human rights protection, however much it may possibly be undermined by the entry into force of the Charter of Fundamental Rights (Pescatore 2003, Knook 2005), can be treated as a reality in the EU (Van den Brink 2012): all the other fundamentals and, particularly, equality, justice and the rule of law are not really there (Kochenov 2013b). Gráinne de Búrca is absolutely right: in the context of the Union, equality is just a rhetorical device to justify predetermined outcomes (1997: 14); moreover, the moral stance of the Court of Justice of the European Union (ECJ) is not clear either (Kochenov and Plender 2012: 393–5) and the reading of justice – as masterfully exemplified by Andrew Williams in a most credible account (Williams 2009) – amounts to nothing more than sticking to some market-oriented idea proclaimed by the drafters of the EU treaties (Williams 2009). In other words, the EU, given its nature, is a very poor candidate to be a standard setter, not only in the field of democracy as such, but also in all the related fields, which are necessarily connected with democracy, whether we like it or not.

Thirdly, and this point is in direct connection with the previous two, EU law on democracy is non-existent. Consequently, there is no *acquis* to fall back on and no democracy standards to promote either internally or externally (Kochenov 2004; for the general context of EU values promotion see Cremona 2011, Herlin-Karnell 2013). Democracy is outside of the EU's realm, as are justice and related notions, the arguments for embracing them notwithstanding (Poiares Maduro 2012, Kochenov *et al.* 2014b). The values of Article 2 of the TEU are thus quite a strange animal, when approached from the general context of the *acquis* (for example Kochenov 2014b). Crucially, standards cannot really come from the member states either, since the member states embrace a large number of radically different models. Democracy in Poland is very different from that in the Netherlands and in the UK. In this context, to speak about the EU promoting democracy in the world is akin to asking my beloved orange cat, however smart, to give truck-driving lessons. The results are presented as and are thus confined to enormous expenses (Ogerschnig 2012), without any expectation or chances to preserve any change in the majority of contexts (European Court of Auditors 2012). The EU spends, equating this activity with democracy promotion and approaching the latter through its own spending. Moreover, crucially, the EU's democracy promotion rhetoric ignores the democracy drive in democratizing countries themselves – a crucial point made by Wojciech Sadurski (2013): whether the EU should be credited for what is actually happening on the ground is frequently most unclear, to say the least. The logical connection between the EU's engagement and the success of democratization, although assumed by the Commission to be clear, is missing (Kochenov 2008a).

Although the law is not there, the Treaties contain a number of political promises, reflected in the values on which the EU is built, which are assumed to be shared with its member states (Article 2 of the TEU), and also in Article 7 of the TEU, which is designed to bring the member states deviating from those values back to compliance (for an analysis, see Sadurski 2010). Given the wording of this provision, however, it is crystal clear that the values are viewed primarily through the prism of the political – not as legal obligations, which explains the exclusion of the ECJ from the procedure introduced by this provision. In other words, member state-level democracy is not within the sphere of the EU's competences, no matter what actually goes on in the member states concerned, unless a political exception governed by Article 7 of the TEU is made. Crucially, since the provision does not provide any usable standards of democracy assessment as such, to view democracy as an enforceable legal requirement in the context of EU law would be an overstatement.

Fourthly, the deployment of the values, which Article 7 of the TEU is designed to protect in the different and difficult context that is the EU's external relations, demonstrates with clarity that they are deprived of any clearly decipherable content. This is so, since adherence to them is a usual starting point for third countries that already enjoy a contractual relationship with the EU to participate in the European Neighbourhood Policy (Kochenov 2009) or its geographically attuned offspring, the Eastern Partnership (Kochenov 2011). To claim that Ukraine, Azerbaijan and the Palestinian Authority share the same values with the EU would be an affront, if taken seriously (Kochenov 2009). However, values, as such, are not really taken seriously in the EU – not even internally – which is probably the reason why Article 7 of the TEU has never actually been used.

Conclusion

A careful overview of the *acquis* and the way in which EU law functions internally demonstrates that democracy is not a real principle of law, but an exclusively political 'value' underlying the Union and its member states, able to boast virtually no binding legal content. Unenforceable and vague, it adds little to the way the EU, famous for its democratic deficit, actually functions.

There is no doubt about the fact that this is a big problem, which is strongly felt in the Union, especially in the context of EU member states deviating from the democratic path. Illustrations of this are numerous, ranging from Jörg Haider's Austria to the recent developments in Hungary and Romania (Bánkúti *et al.* 2012, Halmai 2012). Ironically, the EU's response did not become any more consolidated or convincing following the introduction of Article 7 in the treaties, which was supposed to build on the Austrian example and was clearly inspired by the prospect of the big-bang enlargement (Sadurski 2010). Nothing close to the legal mechanisms to protect and promote democracy has in fact been incorporated into the *acquis*. This value chiefly remains outside the scope of EU competence,[6] which directly affects the EU's ability to promote it, triggering legal-theoretical debate concerning the possible use of EU citizenship provisions (von Bogdandy *et al.* 2012), or systemic infringement actions (Scheppele 2013), or a newly created Copenhagen Commission (Müller 2013) – *inter alia* – to fill in this important gap in turbulent times.

Most importantly, we should fully realize the importance of the fact that the recent problems of democratic governance actually arose in the Central and Eastern European countries:[7] those which were subjected to the highest possible degree of scrutiny in the field of democracy and the rule of law promotion (for analyses see for example Inglis 2000: 1178, Maresceau 2001, Hillion 2002, Beurdeley 2003: 43), that is exactly the same scrutiny, which gave the Commission its self-congratulatory rhetoric and had already been branded by scholars too numerous to be mentioned as a success, even before these countries actually joined the Union. This certainly says a lot about the worth of the Union's reported success in the field – at least as far as the organization of the promotion of democracy in the context of the legal-political regulation of enlargements goes (for analysis of the legal side of the preparation of enlargements, see for example Ott and Inglis 2002, Kochenov 2008a: especially chapters 1 and 2).

Notes

1. A draft of this paper was presented in Princeton in April 2014. I am grateful to Jan-Werner Müller for the kind invitation.
2. The European Commission has traditionally made a direct connection between the concepts of democracy and the rule of law (see Kochenov 2008a).
3. Enlargement is rightly viewed as a potent foreign policy and democratization tool (see Pridham 2005, Vachudová 2005, Zielonka 2006).
4. The fact has been recognized even by Commission Vice-President Viviane Reding (see Reding 2013).
5. Democracy is not on the agenda at all, in building better relations with the worst dictatorships in the world, be it Saudi Arabia or Turkmenistan (see, for example, Boas 2012).
6. To which recent case law equally testifies; for example Case C-286/12 *Commission v. Hungary* [2012] not yet reported.

7. Besides Romania and Hungary, one could also cite Latvia, Estonia and Slovenia, where large chunks of the population were simply deprived of political rights upon the proclamation of independence – developments that the EU failed to counter effectively during the preparation of these countries' accession to the EU (for overviews, see for example Kochenov 2008b, Poleshchuk 2009 and the literature cited therein).

3
Political Economy Perspective: Fuzzy Liberalism and EU Democracy Promotion: Why Concepts Matter

Milja Kurki

This book studies the substance of European Union (EU) democracy promotion, a very pertinent study indeed today. While EU democracy promotion is much talked about – including its contribution to the EU's 'normative power' role in world politics – its content has received comparatively little scholarly attention. This is problematic because the EU's broad range of activities in support of democracy cannot be assumed to be 'consistent and coherent', even as the EU itself constantly calls for the manifestation of such qualities.

Avoiding the close study of 'substance' is also problematic because, in failing to pay close attention to what is actually being supported by the EU in its democracy assistance, the distinct conceptual premises of the EU's democracy promotion can easily go unanalysed or unappreciated. Drawing on a wider four-year study of conceptual foundations of democracy promotion,[1] it is suggested here that the EU's wide-ranging democracy promotion activities can be seen to take place within a uniquely vague, or 'fuzzy', conceptual framework vis-à-vis many other actors, such as the US, the international financial institutions (IFIs) or political foundations and non-governmental organizations (NGOs).

Arguably, what is unique about the EU is that, from the relatively late beginnings of its democracy promotion efforts in the mid-1990s, the meaning of the idea of 'democracy' itself has been left undefined within the EU's central decision-making bodies – notably, in the work of the European Commission and the Council. While most scholars accept that in the early years of EU democracy promotion there was a great deal of confusion as to what kind of democracy the EU was to promote via accession and its external relations (see for example Pridham 2005, Kochenov 2007, K.E. Smith 2008), it is often overlooked that even today, as the EU's instruments and policy statements on democracy promotion have matured and proliferated and now provide a great deal of technical detail as to what it expects from democratic states, it is still not clear what the EU 'stands for'. It seems that the EU works with a very broad, but at the same time vague definition of 'democracy' in its democracy promotion efforts. While many documents indicate the kinds of values and practices of democratic governance the EU promotes – liberty, equality, solidarity – no specific conceptually systematic 'model' of democracy emerges from EU democracy promotion, nor, it follows, is there a clear 'ideological' vision within the EU as to what democracy means (Kurki 2013).[2] In fact, the outlines of multiple potential models of democracy seem to arise from EU activities across different Directorate-Generals (DGs) and little evidence exists that systematic thought is dedicated to deliberating over what exactly the EU's value-preferences should be, and how these should translate to its activities.

The conceptual vagueness of EU democracy promotion is of course understandable, for the EU has to function within a political and bureaucratic context which seems to deny the possibility of a singular, clear and definitive idea of democracy. In a politically pluralist Union, characterized by a diverse set of historical experiences of the idea and structures of democracy, no singular coherent democratic tradition can easily emerge as the guiding light of EU democracy promotion. While in the US-led democracy promotion agenda, 'liberal democracy' has, certainly since the end of the Cold War, formed the core reference point of what democracy promoters understand by democracy (reflecting the deep embeddedness of liberal democratic thinking in the US (T. Smith 2004, 2011, Kurki 2013), the EU context for democracy promotion is arguably more complex. This is because in the practice of democratic governance in Europe, 'liberal democratic' ideals have always competed with 'social democratic', 'reform liberal', 'participatory democratic' and even 'global democratic' ideals. Even as relative agreement has been reached in the US on liberal democracy (if not on the exact model of liberal democracy), in Europe it has not been self-evident that democracy means 'liberal democracy'. Indeed, as Sheri Berman (2006) contends, the experience of democratic governance in Europe has been rather more 'social democratic' in nature. This model of democracy has entailed the expansion of democratic decision-making to the sphere of the economy and thus challenges the separation of economic and political spheres essential to the liberal model (or at least the more 'liberal' variants of 'liberal democratic practice').

Given the conceptual indeterminacy of the concept of democracy in Europe, it is no surprise that EU democracy promotion rhetoric is also fuzzy (Kurki 2012, 2013). It also follows that it is no surprise that where EU democracy promotion practices and instruments 'hit the ground', somewhat different ideals as well as realities may emerge from EU activities, as the chapters in this study so provocatively demonstrate. Because conceptual issues precondition the multifarious practices of EU democracy promotion, this chapter seeks to shed light on these pre-existing conceptual contours which condition the many different facets and faces of EU democracy promotion on the ground. I wish here, then, to contribute to the study of the substance of EU democracy promotion through a conceptual angle. I do not examine the substance of EU democracy promotion as delivered on the ground. I wish to instead do two things that contextualize the excellent empirical studies that are advanced here.

First, I wish to examine the overall conceptual, and thus also ideological, 'confines' within which EU democracy promotion practices work (for conceptual frameworks define and reflect our value systems and thus ideological orientations). I seek to explain the reasons for, and highlight the significance of, the EU's unique 'fuzzy liberalism' in democracy promotion. I point to not only the potential for openness but also the curious forms of 'depoliticization' this fuzziness leads to.

Second, I reflect briefly on the problems and prospects of such democracy promotion in the current world order. The EU leads the way in the promotion of a form of 'depoliticized' democracy and in so doing is, it could be argued, rather successful in a world order which is also changing and in which 'liberal principles' are no longer self-evident (Koivisto and Dunne 2010, Dunne and Flockhart 2013, Kurki 2013). While contradictions abound in the promotion of a fuzzy and depoliticized vision of democracy, it also facilitates, or at least does not contradict, the Union's interest-seeking in today's changing world order. Conceptual frameworks of democracy promotion arise out of somewhere; they are in complex ways predicated on and responsive to the structural positions and interests, as well as the identities, of democracy promotion actors. It is important to appreciate this in order to have a better sense of both the substance and the conceptual contours of EU democracy promotion in world politics.

Liberal democracy and models of democracy – A conceptual-ideological angle

This book sets up as its guiding aim the study of the substance of EU democracy promotion in reference to the idea of liberal democracy. Based on the existing literature, the editors follow a mainly liberal model of democracy and ask the questions: what kind of liberal democracy promotion emerges from the substantive practices of EU democracy promotion; and is it a one-size-fits-all approach, or are there different extents and modes of liberal democracy promotion that the EU engages in?

The analytical framework set up here serves the purposes of the study well and the focus on 'liberal democracy' is understandable, for the discourse of liberal democracy does indeed serve as one core reference point of EU policy frameworks on democracy. Yet, to simply look for liberal democratic democracy promotion when examining the EU may leave our understandings of democracy and EU democracy promotion incomplete. In my view, it is important to critically reflect on the pluralistic conceptual and thus ideological sets of meanings that the idea of 'liberal democracy' can take on (as is also suggested by the editors), and also to recognize that ideals beyond liberal democracy may structure and inform EU democracy promotion conceptually (see also the other alternative reflections in this book). To do so, we need to appreciate some basic dynamics of the contested idea 'democracy'.

Democracy as a contested concept

Democracy is a famously contested concept and takes on various different political meanings for different political actors. A key debate within democratic theory revolves around whether liberal democracy, or other social democratic, participatory democratic, deliberative or radical models of democracy should serve as the reference point for how we understand democracy's meaning (see for example Held 2006). Even liberal democracy, democratic theorists point out, is a contested notion: it has no singular meaning but, in fact, is a 'cluster concept' which can be understood in more and less liberal and more and less democratic ways (Freeden 1996).

The question that concerns us here is: what is the role of such conceptual, and ultimately ideological, contestation over democracy's meaning in the EU's discourse on democracy promotion, if any? Is it the case that not only 'substantial' but also 'conceptual' incongruence (or even contestation) characterizes EU understandings of democracy? If so, this surely has an effect on shaping the practice of EU democracy promotion. While the theoretical setup of this book does not centrally focus on the exploration of conceptual or ideological contestation or debate about democracy's meaning in democracy promotion practice (assuming, as it does, a mainly liberal democratic reference point as defined by Merkel), the 'Political Economies of Democratisation' project based at Aberystwyth University between 2008 and 2012 has studied these conceptual bases in detail. We have studied the discursive practices of EU democracy promotion in reference to a wide-ranging set of possible democratic ideologies (social democracy, participatory democracy and global democracy as well as different variations of liberal democracy), thus attempting to gain a sense of the way in which normative debate or contestation over the exact aims and *finalités* of EU democracy promotion is framed in EU discourses. Such discourses concern us here because they provide the context within which substantive aspects of EU democracy promotion in specific contexts are developed: conceptual context is not insignificant to the determination of the substance of democracy promotion (while also not being the only determinant of the substance of democracy promotion). The institutionalist hypothesis presented in the introductory chapter resonates with this and is worth exploring in further research.

What is also significant to note is that the Aberystwyth project has studied conceptions of democracy in EU discourse on democracy promotion within a theoretical framework that acknowledges the politico-economic content of different models of democracy, including liberal democracy. This approach draws attention to the fact that while, within the liberal democratic tradition of thought, thinkers perceive the economic sphere as independent of the political, or at best as a 'condition' of successful democratization, we need to in fact trace the complex and significant interactions of economic and political thought and how it relates to the idea of democracy. We point out, for example, that among participatory or social democratic strands of thought, democracy has an inherently economic meaning: democracy should extend to structuring not only of the political but also of the economic, for no real democracy can emerge in a context of undemocratic or non-democratic economic decision-making. The agenda of democratization, then, for these thinkers should not be limited to the political sphere, nor its study. Even variants of liberal democratic thinking, it is argued, are politico-economic in nature, for embedded within liberal democratic thought are specific understandings of the relationship between economics and politics (with classical liberals separating the workings of the market and democracy, neoliberals seeing economic freedom as essential for liberal democracy and reform liberals seeking to control economic liberties in defence of working democratic equality of opportunity).

But what is the relevance of this study for our understanding of EU democracy promotion? With regard to the EU, the focus of the Aberystwyth study has been on trying to understand the conceptual drivers and contours of EU democracy promotion. Focus has been placed specifically on key Council and Commission-generated policy guidance and documentation on democracy promotion.

Conceptual foundations of EU democracy promotion

The research has found that one of the key characteristics of EU democracy promotion is that it is uniquely under-determined in its conceptual and thus also ideological orientations. First, there is a distinct lack of clear definitions of democracy in the EU discourse, as the EU 'outsources' definitions of democracy and hence normative justifications for its support to external actors, such as the UN or the Organisation for Economic Co-operation and Development (OECD), or, as Carbone (2011) illustrates, to other state actors.

There is also a lack of specificity as to interpretation of the context within which democracy's meaning is to be understood. Many concepts – equality, justice, rights, elections – are thrown around in the discourse, but their specific meanings in relation to each other and hence the specific hierarchies of values the EU stands for remain unspecified. As Michael Freeden (1996) reminds us, it is all-important to appreciate how value systems exactly 'de-contest' and link concepts to each other – this is what gives ideological meaning to concepts and narratives. Mere 'litanies' of values in and of themselves mean little; it is hierarchies of concepts in narratives which give meaning to values. Thus, concepts such as 'equality' or 'democracy' can be understood in very different ways by, say, libertarians or socialists, although both will make reference to the same concepts: what matters is how equality and democracy are related to other values (for example rights, property and constitutions or socio-economic development, autonomy and majoritarianism).

A close analysis shows that there is a lack of clear hierarchies of values in EU discourses. Unlike in the US, where democracy is fairly solidly – although not uniformly (since various traditions of liberal democratic thinking can be seen to characterize the US scene) – tied to the concepts of liberty, economic freedom, electoral procedures and entrepreneurial liberal civil society (thus 'liberal' hierarchies of values providing a clear-cut 'liberal' interpretation of democracy), the same does not arise in the EU. Here, alternative reference points – social justice, labour rights and even participatory democracy – are made reference to as part of traditional liberal discourse. It is this lack of specificity and broadness of the seemingly liberal democratic discourse which gives rise to what I have elsewhere called 'fuzzy liberal' democracy promotion (Kurki 2012, 2013).

Now, fuzzy liberalism, it could be argued, is not merely an accidental or coincidental characteristic of EU democracy promotion: it is an essential part of its discursive framing of democracy and democracy promotion and, in fact, could be described as the EU's 'politico-economic model of democracy' in its democracy work. What it entails is a fuzzy rhetorical set of moves, which sees democracy as a relatively openly defined, broadly liberal but potentially more pluralistic (for example potentially 'social democratic') concept. While at its core it focuses on liberal democratic notions, liberties, rights and elections, the EU discourse also makes reference to the social and economic contexts of democratization and integrates – sometimes very heavily – the idea of development within democratization.

Crucially, for us, the ideological orientation of the model of democracy is undecided: it is not a highly liberal Hayekian liberal democratic model that is advanced (as it arguably was during the Bush years in the US [2001–2009]), nor is it a social democratic one (as advocated by some political foundations, such as the Friedrich Ebert Stiftung or the Olof Palme Centre), nor a Hobsonian 'reform liberal' model (as advocated by 'moderate' 'centrist' liberals in the US and Europe). Nor are participatory ideals incorporated to such an extent as to result in consistent or meaningful participatory democracy promotion – alongside or as the core conceptual focus of EU democracy promotion. This leaves things distinctly open for interpretation in terms of what kind of democratic (and economic) ideology emanates from EU democracy promotion.

Such fuzziness is, of course, a very practical quality in EU democracy promotion. While in some contexts democracy comes to mean socio-economic development, in another it can take on electoral forms, and in another can be reduced to the economic restructuring of states. It is important to note the possibility of a broad range of 'substances' that arises from this broad conceptual basis. Indeed, this book shows with great lucidity these different outcomes that can ensue from EU democracy promotion, partly as a result of its enabling conceptual fuzziness.[3]

My aim here is not so much to contribute to these studies (although I have also analysed how conceptual fuzziness turns concrete in specific contexts; see Kurki 2011a, 2011b, 2011c, 2013), but to emphasize the conceptual origins and impact of this under-determination of objectives.

What is crucial to note is that this under-determination arises in crucial respects from the lack of interest in developing specific normative orientations given the political and economic contestedness of the idea of democracy in the EU context. As in so many other policy areas, contesting and debating democracy's meaning is considered hazardous. The European Parliament-affiliated Office for Promotion of Parliamentary Democracy summarizes some of the reasons for this: the debates on which kind of democracy is best are ultimately without an answer and potentially fractious. The Office's report suggests that instead of seeking 'the EU model', a model of democracy most reflective of European experience, European democracy promotion should proceed on the basis of the most broad-based and universal definitions available, that is, the most widely accepted UN definitions. This is seen as advantageous diplomatically in allowing criticisms of Eurocentrism and particularism to be avoided, and at the same time can ensure that the EU's support for multilateral global politics can be reaffirmed (OPPD 2009: 5). Arguably, avoiding this debate also sidesteps the potential fractitiousness of the politics of democracy on the European scene, where indeed the 'European Union consists of 27 Member States, each with their own form of democracy, shaped by history, culture and circumstance' (OPPD 2009: 5).

This is not all. Arguably, the EU's curious positioning in the world system – that is, its dual role as a great 'liberalizer' of global trade and defender of 'social democracy' inside Europe – necessitates that it shows sympathy both to liberal and to more social democratic ends. Indeed, as McCann (2010) points out, the success of EU's internal 'solidaristic' social democracy depends on the success of 'liberal' economic and political governance abroad. The result is arguably a curious need to fudge debate on what the EU stands for, inside and out. Conceptual foundations are always tied – even if indirectly – to real social and political interests and the structural positions of actors.

Fuzzy becomes concrete

An important point to note about the EU's conceptually fuzzy agenda is that, while seemingly pluralistic, and while enabling many and contradictory agendas in some instances, it also enables and maintains a strange 'depoliticizing' dynamic in EU action.

Whereas the US has been caught up in supporting specific groups of democrats in target countries, in the EU such accusations can be more easily fudged. While the US commitment to liberal democracy means it wears its ideological colours more openly on its sleeve (even as not all American democracy promoters necessarily understand exactly the same thing by 'liberal democracy'), this is not the case with the EU's fuzzy liberalism, which is very difficult to 'pin down' to any specific ideological orientation. As a result, as if to compensate for the lack of clear political and ideological direction and responsibility-taking by political authorities, the implementation and governance of EU democracy promotion funding tends to become very technocratic in nature (Kurki 2011b, 2013).

The EU uses various managerial and technical instruments to disperse funding. However, under an illusion of 'neutrality', the hidden political biases and content of these instruments are not reflected on; democracy promotion is perceived as a rather technical exercise. It is standards of modern 'good governance' in the European Neighbourhood Policy (ENP) or the demands of funding instruments in civil society support that decide who is assisted and how (Kurki 2011c). While this depoliticization has its benefits, it also has its downsides.

This is because within depoliticization lurk often implicit neoliberal ideals. In EU civil society funding through the European Instrument for Democracy and Human Rights, for example, hidden neoliberal preferences structure aid and cooperation with civil society groups (Kurki 2011c). Thus, even when overt neoliberal economic agendas are not present (as they are in the ENP or in trade policy), in the sphere of civil society support there is an interest in encouragement of entrepreneurial and 'non-anti-European' civil society. This preference is not overt, intended, strategic or political but rather arises from hidden tendencies in management demands, language and structures of financing within the EU structure (Kurki 2011c). This leads to a 'fuzzy (neo) liberalism' gaining rather a hard technocratic and depoliticized edge in its implementation on the ground. Even 'social' service delivery work seems, in the EU, to work through neoliberal management processes, which inevitably influences the authenticity of any 'social democratic' tendencies in such support (Kurki 2013). Thus, for example, NGOs come to act almost as private actors in delivery of now ('privatized') competitively awarded contracts relating to social services.

This is not to say that every democracy assistance official – in DG Development and Cooperation (DEVCO), for example – abides by or actively encourages a technocratic neoliberal economic model. Democratization aims and funding can also cut against these directions in EU democracy promotion. Indeed, because of the fuzziness of the discourse one could argue that the EU is an actor whose democracy promotion is potentially the only one to be constituted by ideologically 'clashing sets of models' and visions (Kurki 2011b). Despite seemingly being in line with other actors in some respects, it is strikingly different from many of the other actors in democracy promotion. The IFIs and the US hold much more specific and liberal understandings of democracy and democracy promotion. They are somewhat less inclined to make nods to social democracy, although some small nods in 'reform liberal' ideas have emerged in these contexts in recent years.

The fuzziness of EU discourse, then, may be read in a positive rather than merely negative light. It certainly holds great promise for a different, more pluralistic type of democracy promotion. Yet, on the basis of the analysis we have conducted, we are also forced to note that this promise, as practised, fails to result in concrete value pluralism today. The promise of EU pluralism at present translates to a reality of fuzziness with neoliberal tendencies implicitly coming through in practices of democracy promotion.

EU democracy promotion in a changing liberal world order

What does this analysis tell us of the EU as an actor? The debates with regard to this tend to revolve around the issue of whether or not the EU is a normative actor, and of what specific kind. Manners (2006) has argued that there is a unique social model core to EU activity and that this defines its role in the world order. Others (Youngs 2010b) argue that the EU is no longer any kind of committed normative actor. In this book, various sets of reasons are given for the orientations of the substance of EU democracy promotion – from bureaucratic politics to local contexts of democratization. My reading of these debates is different. I argue that the EU's ideological predilections reflect its unique internal composition but also its unique ability to reflect changes in the world order.

The US – the originator of the idea of democracy promotion – has always been an ideologically committed international actor. Its commitment to liberal internationalism has been relatively unwavering and this is reflected in its democracy promotion: while the US promoted reform liberalism and social democracy in the immediate post-Second World War period, since the mid-1980s the US has firmly focused on the promotion of 'liberal democracy', with preference since the Bush years being given to a rather more extremely liberal vision of liberal democracy. This model is now shifting, albeit incompletely, to a different set of more 'reform liberal' ideals (Kurki 2013).

The EU, on the other hand, has always been a more functional technocratic entity, the normative ideals of which have always followed as a secondary consideration to pragmatic interest-oriented cooperation.

What is interesting to note is that in some regards it is the big-L – explicitly ideological – liberal interventions of the US which are most problematic today – in a decreasingly big-L liberal world order. With this in mind, it is no surprise that the EU has arguably been in a much better position to reflect the shifts in the world order in recent years towards a far less openly ideological and 'big-L liberal' (Koivisto and Dunne 2010, see also Chandler 2009) world order.

With the rise of the BRICs (Brazil, Russia, India and China) and the CIVETS (Colombia, Indonesia, Vietnam, Egypt, Turkey and South Africa) and with the decline of Western power in relative terms, liberal hegemonic ideas too have come under some questioning and are decreasingly pushed on the global scene. The Bush debacles demonstrated for many the consequences of hubristic beliefs in world affairs, and the financial crisis has for many put the nail in the coffin of unquestioned Western supremacy in political or economic matters.

With this in mind, the EU's unique fuzzy liberalism, contextualized within a rather depoliticized discourse, works arguably rather well – if not for all democratic actors 'on the ground' – for the EU's own interest and value projection. It is arguably less open to overt ideological contestation by target states and populations and in its pragmatic and technocratic edge seems to be about cooperative modernization rather than ideological lecturing, something attractive to democratizing populations today. The upshot, or undercurrent, of the policies is not always so very different from those of other actors – a (neo)liberal, and as such politico-economically 'liberal capitalist', democracy is often encouraged in the target states – but the way of approaching democracy promotion and how it is packaged differs. In the post-ideological age that many argue we are moving towards, this form of 'implicitly liberal' democracy promotion may just be the best way to go (Chandler 2009, Koivisto and Dunne 2010, Kurki 2013).

Conclusion

Democracy promotion is a contradictory exercise: it involves promoting a normative model of an idea which is essentially contested. EU democracy promotion is even more curious: it involves promotion of an undefined model of a contested idea, often through technocratic means of delivery. While the substance of EU democracy promotion, then, is curious, so are its conceptual foundations. Lack of clarity and specificity is palpable, yet the EU can be remarkably successful (measured by its own terms) in conditioning states into acceptance of its fuzzy normative ideals. This tells us interesting things about the curious nature of the EU as a normative power – it seems a politically or ideologically 'hollow' type of international actor (Chandler 2009) – but also about shifts and changes in the liberal world order, where big normative ideals work less and less well and managerial 'small-l liberal' ideals do much of the work of structuring both ideas and power relations.

Notes

1. The research leading to these results has been funded by the European Community's Seventh Framework Programme (FP7/2007-2013) ERC grant agreement 202 596. The 'Political Economies of Democratisation' project was based at Aberystwyth University between 2008 and 2012. Its full findings in relation to the EU have been presented in numerous publications such as Kurki (2011a, 2011b, 2011c, 2012 and 2013). All views are those of the author.
2. By ideological, here I refer to the political meaning-context within which democracy is understood. As a contested political concept, democracy is not just neutral, but conceptual debates on it are tied in intricate ways to ideological debates. Thus, a right-wing liberal will define democracy's core values (liberty, equality), and thus the concept's ideological content and meaning, differently from a social democrat (socio-economic equality, solidarity, justice). Conceptual and ideological meanings, then, are tied together in how democracy is thought about.
3. However, my own analytical approach does not assume the centrality of liberal democracy or seek to define levels of meaning/depth to it. Rather, I am interested in analysing the differences in the ideological orientations in how the economic and political are integrated. The Merkelian line of analysis here, then, does not work in my own framework: even a model where the economy is separated from democracy constitutes a specific (liberal) politico-economic model of democracy, and thus a specific variation of the liberal democratic and democratic theory tradition.

4
Critical Social Theory Perspective: Embeddedness as Substance: The EU's Socialized Approach to Democratization

Jessica Schmidt

Introduction

Over the past 20 years, governance has evolved into the main trope in international relations, the question of 'world order' and the problem of how to capture state–society relations. 'While there is no internationally agreed definition of governance', the 2003 European Commission Communication on Governance and Development explains, 'the concept has gained in importance' (European Commission 2003a: 3). Consequently, the question of the substance of democracy and approaches to democratization and democracy promotion has found itself right at the centre of this 'governance turn'. This governance turn – and the suspicion that 'somehow' it is affecting democracy and its promotion – has thus instigated this volume (see the introductory chapter). While the rise of governance in framing and addressing international problems (Dillon and Reid 2000, Duffield 2001, Larner and Walters 2004, Neumann and Sending 2010, Roberts 2010), generally, and regarding the EU specifically (Kohler-Koch and Rittberger 2006, Youngs 2009, Chandler 2010, Lavenex and Schimmelfennig 2011, Wetzel 2011) has gone far from unnoticed in academic discussions, this turn to governance, in fact, begs us to pause for a moment. It is, at this point, worth looking at the broader epistemological shifts that have occurred and ask how EU discourses on democratization have come to operate within them. The objective of this contribution is thus limited: it seeks to denaturalize what, seemingly without much reflection, has come to be understood as the essence of democracy: democratic governance.

The concern here, therefore, is less whether it is liberal democracy that can be pertinently claimed to underpin the EU's approach to democratization, but rather to ask what has come to be the current imaginary of democracy: what has come to be the referent object of democracy since the end of the Cold War? Where is it located and what is its objective? What kind of problem is democracy in its current complexion thought to be addressing?

In order to tackle these questions, this chapter refers to the trajectory of different ontologies of governing from sovereign power of the law via disciplinary power of the homogenizing norm to population governance of optimizing local realities as traced by Foucault. However, the aim here is not to take Foucault's elaborations on techniques of governing as an ahistorical and universal framework for analysis. Rather, the chapter looks at the permutations within the European discourses on democratization and argues that to an extent Foucault's work is helpful in giving an impulse for highlighting, contextualizing and problematizing these tweaks and shifts at play in contemporary understandings of democracy.

Having said this, I will argue that democracy as approached by the EU no longer primarily seeks to address the question of how authority is exercised and who is in power, but rather is concerned with optimizing local life through participatory practices, capacity building and inclusion. It is not so much political institutions that are to be democratized, but the coping and management capacities of individuals, communities and societies. With the focus on democratic practices and processes, democracy and democratization are increasingly perceived in sociological terms. The crucial question for EU approaches, thus, has somewhat moved away from whether democracy is better fostered via 'top down' or 'bottom up' measures. Instead, both society and the state are increasingly understood in terms of their mutual embeddedness, comprising complex social relations. And it is these relationships that need to be managed and optimized by members of any given society themselves. In the governance turn of democracy, capacity building and inclusion, therefore, come to play a pivotal role. In other words, the rise of governance is also a rise of the social (on the latter, see Owens 2012). The substance of EU democracy promotion, therefore, can be said to rest with embeddedness itself. That is, democracy, in being 'socialized', has no specific or separate 'regime' within which it takes place and through which it can be implemented, but rather is understood and promoted as something that is lived and actualized in everyday interactions. What this chapter therefore challenges is the idea that the substance of EU democracy promotion can be adequately captured through an analytical framework that is based on (adapted) 'models' of democracy.

The chapter will proceed as follows. After briefly outlining the dominant perception of democracy into which the EU's democracy agenda was born after the end of the Cold War, it will contextualize the challenges this approach faced through recourse to Foucault's investigations on shifting rationalities of governing. It will then draw out how the shifting role of norms demonstrated by Foucault can help us understand the reconceptualization of democracy within European discourses as addressing social relationships in their local environment.

With regard to the EU's democracy agenda, the chapter will mainly focus on the Communications of 2003, 2006 and 2009 (European Commission 2003a, 2006b, 2009a), which all deal with the issue of democratic governance, and additionally, on two EuropeAid handbooks from 2005 and 2008 on the same theme.[1] This situates the democracy discourse as dealt with in this contribution within a broader development agenda.[2]

Representative government and democracy engineering: Exporting the formal framework

The EU's democracy agenda emerged alongside its own transformation from an economic into a political entity and the general seismic changes in the international environment that accompanied the collapse of the Soviet Union (European Commission 1995, Youngs 2001a: 4). While the end of the Cold War marked an important caesura in international relations, it also meant the culmination of a universalist understanding of democracy (most famously captured by Fukuyama 1992), which coined the initial European approach to democratization.[3]

In the 1990s, the initial understanding of democracy and the international democracy promotion agenda were still markedly influenced by the notion of minimal or procedural democracy associated with the work of Joseph Schumpeter, Robert Dahl (Smith 2000, Light 2001) and Adam Przeworski (Pouligny 2000), who decisively moved away from 'normative' democratic theory to a more 'realistic' and 'descriptive' modelling. Consequently, the academic debates and respective knowledge production that served as the basis for its policy operationalization centred on questions regarding adequate institutional and constitutional frameworks. Hence, up until the mid-1990s the idea prevailed that democracy – conceived to consist of formal-institutional principles and processes, such as political rights, separation of public authority and elections – could be designed, crafted and eventually exported (Di Palma 1990, Pridham *et al.* 1997 [1994], see also Olsen 2000: 148–9, Agné 2014: 50). The site of democracy as well as the target of democratization, in other words, was the institutional arrangements and procedures that framed the public exercise of authority.

Making similar observations, Marina Ottaway described this optimistic and enthusiastic approach that characterized the early post-Cold War period as the 'Leninist option' (1997, 2003). Ottaway likens Western democratization efforts to Lenin's idea of top-down engineering 'socialist man' in the absence of preconditions that would lead to his natural evolution. Early post-Cold War democracy promotion was driven by the idea that 'democratic man' could be fostered by taking a similar shortcut. The Western approach thus was to employ '[e]xternal pressure, support, and expertise' which, it was understood, could 'make elections happen, strengthen parties, and create institutions'. The underpinning assumption was that the question of the feasibility and appropriateness of democracy promotion rested with the general political logics and functionalities of formal-institutional design; the particularities of local context played a secondary role since they formed the object of transformation. This assumption, crucially, was expressive of 'the belief that deliberate plans can change the society in the desired directions' (Ottaway 1997: 10). This belief is emblematic of the liberal-modern paradigm that, however, was already in decline. Early democracy promotion and democratization efforts were grounded in the idea of linear historical trajectories and the possibilities of transforming local contexts according to an externally provided and forward-looking ideal. Their conceptual starting point consisted of the vision of a prefabricated future for those lagging behind.

Foucault, the embarrassment of governing and the sociological turn

The Leninist option of producing democratic subjects and societies 'from scratch' through top-down institution building quickly failed because, as Ottaway (1997: 12–14, 2003: 320–1) argues, it was overambitious and overburdened. Not only did it fail, but in response to its own failure a shift in the understanding and locale of power and effective governance occurred, which displaced the site of democracy from political structures to social processes.

In order to conceptualize this shift, I briefly resort to Foucault's studies on the changing approach to punishment (a form of intervention or government) as well as the rise of a form of governance through the organic norm rather than the artificial law (1991, 2009). In engaging with the emergence of different modalities and rationalities of governing in the West, Foucault roughly distilled three ontologies of governing: the rule over territory (sovereign-interventionist law), disciplinary capacity building of individuals in a multiplicity (disciplinary power as the standardizing norm) and the governance of populations (regulatory power of the organic norm) – which are ordered along a spectrum of increased thrift and decreased immediacy in the mode of its exercise. While sovereign power *rules over* and directly intervenes upon the inhabitants of a territory, the latter two modes *govern through* norms that work more indirectly through and on the social fabric. In addition to the distinction between ruling over and governing through, the latter two norm-based forms of governing differ from each other with regard to the nature and origin of the norm. Whereas capacity building occurs through an externally imposed norm that serves as the standard according to which individuals need to be transformed (Foucault 2009: 56–7), the governance of populations occurs through already-existing norms whose effective and positive elements need to be optimized and facilitated (Foucault 2009: 19–23). A precondition for this latter form is a political ontology of inextricably embedded subjects.

From sovereign power to population governance, governing itself becomes ever less openly interventionist and ever more lenient, gentle and therapeutic (Foucault 1991). The 'line of flight' that characterizes the spectrum of governing, however, is not only characterized by greater leniency; rather there is an increasing embarrassment with regard to the open exercise of power, an 'increasing difficulty in judging, as if one were ashamed to pass sentence' (Foucault 1991: 304). Whereas sovereign rule is exercised as open punishment and through the interventionist event, disciplinary mechanisms operate through externally prescribed norms. As they seek to enable the subject to live up to a norm or standard and prevent its violation, these mechanisms necessarily entail constant supervision and attention to detail (Foucault 2009: 44–5). As Foucault has pointed out, while both disciplinary government and sovereignty existed simultaneously, with the growing embarrassment to authoritatively judge and intervene, the latter has gradually been colonized by the former; the law, in other words, is being turned into a process of normalizing and homogenizing (individual and collective) subjects. Unsurprisingly, what this provoked is a veritable 'inflation of the juridico-legal code' (Foucault 2009: 7) and the proliferation of institutions and instances concerned with capacity building and supervision. We could call this shift a shift from government based on formal principles and institutions to governance based on social effectiveness. This approach leads not only to a growing awareness of social fabric and processes, but also to the overstructuration of social life. By the same token, it also requires the participation of an increasing number of people involved in the process of transforming subjects and building their capacity to make them 'capable of living within the law and of providing for [their] own needs' (Foucault 1991: 18). With this extension of governing concerns and their displacement into the social, new knowledge was required that paid attention to the social fabric and social processes within which capacity building was to occur. With this requirement, however social context turned into an irreducible reality that could no longer be ignored. This marks the beginning of what Foucault observed as the 'emergence of the naturalness of the species within the political artifice of a power relation' (Foucault 2009: 21-2) – and, for simplicity's sake, also can be said to provoke the shift from a governing rationality of standardizing to one concerned with optimizing.

Relationships, networks of social life and milieus begin to fill the empty space of the externally provided norm that underpinned the transformative-homogenizing mechanisms of disciplinary power. No longer is it possible to think of the space and object of governing as a *tabula rasa* in which the disciplinary norm as a prescriptive future can operate. Society and the social context of actors emerge as a reality of governing: populations always already exist and possess an indigenous dynamic to which ways of governing need to adapt. Whereas disciplinary power is based on an ontology of an 'empty, artificial space', which it constructs through the normative ideal, the optimizing norm of population governance 'works on a given' (Foucault 2009: 19). Its rationality is considerably more modest: '[i]t is simply a matter maximising the positive elements' (Foucault 2009: 19). While less perfectionist and ambitious, 'society', at the same time, is becoming essentialized and naturalized; it is the reality to which governing must adapt and react in order to be both effective and non-judgemental. Whereas before the independent variable was the norm and society the dependent one, now it is society which constitutes the independent variable – the angle from which governing needs to be approached – and the norm that is dependent. Crucially, we see a shift in the ontology of governing from a paradigm of transformation according to a prefabricated future to a paradigm of optimizing what 'is' but what follows its inner, contingent rules, processes and dynamics.

These trajectories and modifications in the objective (from standardizing on the basis of prescriptive norms to optimizing based on context-dependent norms), site (from externally imposed to internally given) and rationale (from working on an artificially constructed space to working through the given) of governing provide us with a helpful toolkit to understand the sociological reinterpretation of institutions and subsequently the substance of democracy in European approaches to democratization in the aftermath of the Leninist option. Based on her experience as a democracy promotion practitioner, Béatrice Pouligny captured a crucial development with significant implications for the 'substance of the democratic project itself' (2000: 18). The failure of democracy promotion thus far rested with the promoters' 'classical and formal' understanding of 'institutions'. This, she argues, ignored the diverse and complex reality of institutions as a 'body of socially sanctioned means' as it appears from a sociological and anthropological perspective (Pouligny 2000: 18). For democracy promotion to be effective, the 'nature of this diversity must be seized' (Pouligny 2000: 18). This means that 'outsiders must take up the call of sociology and anthropology to insist upon an awareness of the routines and complexities of the processes shaping institutions, in the (fluid) conjoining of the social and the political spheres' (ibid.: 19). This demand has indeed been picked up. There is a distinct move away from formal-institutionalist approaches or frameworks. In the EU approach, not only can we see a new truth being vested into the 'in between' of institutions and society but also a growing prevalence accorded to the local situation 'as it is', expressed in an emphasis on ownership, capacity and inclusion.

Context, management and participation: Democratizing local life

After having declared in 1998 that 'elections alone will not necessarily make a country a democracy' (European Commission 1998a: 5), a significant number of policy documents and practitioner handbooks published by the European Commission over the past ten years address the issue of democracy and democratization in terms of a concern with governance (2003a, 2006b, 2009a, EuropeAid 2005, 2008). Governance 'refers to *rules, processes, and behaviour* by which interests are articulated, resources managed, and power exercised in society' (European Commission 2003a: 3, emphasis added). Obviously, these rules, processes and behaviour refer to a sphere that is not and cannot be captured and regulated by a politico-legal framework as such. Rather they denote social characteristics, that is, norms that shape and guide relationships as well as how people act. Crucially, these implicit rules and behaviour within the 'Leninist approach' were perceived to be the result of setting up political institutions and did not require separate attention. As such, the 'concept of good governance,' the EU declared in 1998, 'remains implicit in a political and institutional environment respecting human rights, democratic principles and the rule of law' (European Commission 1998a: 8). Now, however, norms and behaviour have moved into the limelight of what is to be understood as the site of democracy: 'Overall the approach of EU Member States to governance is shifting from an initial focus limited to economic efficiency towards a greater concern for issue of democracy, justice and participation' (European Commission 2003a: 18). With this shift in focus from democratizing the institutional edifice to democratizing the relationships it is comprised of, the underpinning norms and subjective behaviour, the European democracy agenda takes a journey that is close to Foucault's observations: (a) democracy proliferates and (b) the governance context first becomes a reality and then a given.

More than exporting institutions and promoting elections, democratic governance in EU discourses is closely linked to local ownership, capacity building and enabling participation and inclusion (European Commission 2006b). Being increasingly concerned with subjective behaviour and the management of relationships rather than institutional arrangements for the democratic control over the exercise of authority, there is, in a sense, no form or 'limit' to democracy: it has no specific locus, event, principle or realm – such as government, decision-making or elections – but is a constant process encompassing all spheres of society. All sectors both provide a potential platform for optimizing behaviour and self-management but also, in the absence of a reliable institutional framework, require democratized subjects and their participation. 'Democratic governance processes cannot be reduced to one specific component' (European Commission 2009a: 4). Hence, '[d]emocratic governance is to be approached holistically, taking into account all its dimensions (political, economic, social, cultural, environmental, and so on) [...]. Accordingly, the concept has to be integrated into each and every sectoral programme' (European Commission 2006b: 6). Institutions, for sure, do not simply disappear – the same way sovereign power does not simply disappear – but they undergo a significant reconceptualization. Most pointedly, this is captured by EuropeAid's handbook on capacity development. '[I]nstitutions', the handbook elaborates, 'denotes resilient social structures formed by norms and regulations which provide solidity and meaning to social life' (EuropeAid 2005: 11).[4]

As a consequence of this relational focus and the deinstitutionalization of governing, a reality is being created that is predestined to become intractable: there is always already a context; people are always already embedded in social relationships and interact based on inherent norms, processes and rules. Governance is a fact. Moreover, its dynamics follow inner, contingent rules and thus elude positive outside knowability. As such, rather than a democratic model providing the normative starting point into which societies must be transformed, it is the local environment around which democracy must be moulded with the aim of optimizing what is given. As a EuropeAid handbook for practitioners explains, '[D]emocratic governance is a domestic issue as recognized by the EC [European Commission], and consequently governance support cannot be based on blueprints or one-size-fits-all solutions or show immediate results, but requires a realistic and incremental approach based on the current governance reality' (EuropeAid 2008: 6, see also European Commission 2003a: 17). In such a situation, one needs to 'act strategically'. Acting strategically means 'refrain[ing] from adopting normative approaches or exercising hands-on control' (EuropeAid 2008: 6) but rather strengthening capacity and inclusion. '[C]apacity can be defined as the ability to perform tasks and produce outputs, to define and solve problems and make informed choices' (EuropeAid 2005: 5).[5]

If we put the different strands of behaviour, social resilience, capacity and inclusion together, the following picture with regard to the EU's understanding of democracy and approach to democratization evolves. The reference object of democracy is not primarily the political system which would have transformative power over society. Rather, what is to be democratized are management capacities – the ability to perform tasks and define problems based on the local realities and immediate parameters. Inclusion is thus essential if self-management is the objective. The full democratization of management capacities, in turn, aims at social resilience – being able to cope and make the best of things that cannot be changed. The approach adopted is not to transform political systems and societies according to a prescriptive template but to therapeutically optimize local contexts so as to enable individual and collective subjects to secure their well-being, manage their socioeconomic relationships and resume in case of disruptions. While this is certainly a significant shift away from the civilizing mission reverberating in the Leninist approach, it does not exactly result in a move towards emancipation or seeking to bring about political agency. Rather, implicitly, the message of democracy as governance seems to be that not much can be actively done about the world but to cope and adapt.

Conclusion

This chapter has sought to provide a conceptual narrative – and certainly other stories could have been told – on the 'governance turn' and its impact on the substance of democracy by referring to the trajectory of different ontologies of governing traced by Foucault. In asking about the referent object of democracy, its position and role in the European imaginary, significant permutations have surfaced that challenge analytical frameworks and assumptions that seek to excavate this substance through 'models' of democracy. Concretely, the chapter found that rather than a revival of a liberal *mission civilisatrice*, where societies had to be made fit to 'live up to' democratic standards, it is democracy itself that is being moulded around local ways of living and well-being. This may not be the imperialism of power projection and superior knowledge; but it may well be a more subtle imperialism of low expectations, necessity and adaptation. In a way, the substance of 'democratic life' has been aptly – albeit perhaps inadvertently – summarized by the World Movement of Democracy (2010): '[D]emocracy is like oxygen. When it is there, you can breathe and you don't even notice that you are breathing.'

Notes

1. The empirical material used in the following sections has been selected to the extent that it points to a changing rationale in EU democracy promotion. In other words, this chapter's aim is to illuminate and conceptualize an intriguing tendency that resonates with the logics of governing drawn out by Foucault but does not claim that the EU world is indeed congruent with a 'Foucauldian world'.
2. It is increasingly (but unsurprisingly, as this contribution seeks to demonstrate) difficult to speak of democracy promotion occurring *within* the context of development; rather, to the extent that development has become understood to be human-centred (see Sen 1999) at the same time as democracy has come to be conceived 'not only [as] a political system but also [as] a social form of processes and interrelationships' (Large and Sisk 2006: 7), these areas increasingly collapse into each other (see also Carothers 2010).
3. The EU's democratization agenda initially focused particularly on providing electoral assistance (European Commission 1995: 20) and on influencing political elites (Youngs 2001a: 191–2, Raik 2004). Moreover, the EU, in one of its earliest documents on democratization, subscribed to the 'setting-up of

Jessica Schmidt 57

new democratic institutions' in third countries (European Council 1991). Following an institution-centric model of democracy, the EU had little difficulty aligning itself with the 'international community' of democracy engineers and proclaimed to take a ' "hands-on" approach...to actively supporting the transition to democracy' (European Commission 1995: 20). Even when the 'governance agenda' began to emerge in the context of development, democratic governance at first was still perceived mainly in formal-institutional terms (see European Commission 2001a: 16).

4. This de-institutionalized, socialized understanding of the locale and meaning of democratic governance is also mirrored in the EU's more recent 'rights-based' approach (Council of the European Union 2013: 56). While centring on the link between human rights and democracy, the understanding of human rights and the agencies targeted for bringing about 'positive change' (Council of the European Union 2013: 34) have little to do with a juridico-political understanding of rights. Rather, the focus is on civil society organizations that are encouraged to 'empower' people to 'know and claim their rights' (Council of the European Union 2013: 8). In this context, it is women particularly that are sought to be empowered to participate politically, socially and economically. Empowerment here is the opposite of entitlement. Civil society organizations by definition are not in a position to implement these rights through public government; they can only enable individuals to manage their own situation better (and raise awareness about the existence of vulnerable others).

If human rights are universal – and, by extension, democracy is a universal right, too – and all humans are endowed with these rights qua being human, in a political-legal understanding this would mean that international actors that have declared themselves able to judge upon these issues (such as the EU) would have the obligation to actively remove all forces responsible for their violation.

5. The handbook highlights that its definition is similar to the one proposed by the OECD (Organisation for Economic Co-operation and Development), which reads: 'capacity is the ability of people, organisations and society as whole to manage their affairs successfully' (quoted in EuropeAid 2005: 5).

5
Governance Perspective: Democratic Governance Promotion Through Functional Cooperation

Anne Wetzel

Democracy promotion has so far mainly been studied with a (sometimes implicit) model of liberal democracy in mind (for example Schimmelfennig et al. 2006, Magen et al. 2009). The same is true for the democratization literature (O'Donnell and Schmitter 1989: 4–14, Schmitter and Karl 1991). Taking its point of departure in the existing literature (see the introductory chapter), this edited volume follows this conventional perspective by employing a framework of 'embedded liberal democracy' – and in doing so potentially reinforces an existing bias. While 'embedded liberal democracy' exceeds by far minimalist definitions of democracy, it can still be said to (partly) miss the substance of some specific activities that different perspectives on democracy promotion would put at their centre. This chapter deals with 'democratic governance' as one of these under-addressed substances.[1] More particularly, it will focus on 'democratic governance' as the substance that the European Union (EU) promotes in third countries through functional cooperation in transgovernmental networks. It proceeds as follows. The first section will briefly introduce democratic governance promotion as a complementary EU democracy promotion strategy. The next section will present a short overview of the literature on democracy promotion through transgovernmental relations. The third part turns to the question of which substance is being promoted by a transgovernmental approach. More particularly, it will refer to a definition of democratic governance as conceptualized in a recent research project on EU democracy promotion through functional cooperation.[2] The chapter concludes with a brief discussion of the implications for research on EU democracy promotion.

Anne Wetzel 59

Democratic governance promotion as a complementary EU strategy

In the early 2000s, an EU approach to democracy promotion emerged that was different from, yet complementary to, prevailing models. Scholars increasingly recognized 'the incorporation of democracy-related components into good governance initiatives' (Youngs 2001b: 363). One of the reasons was the limited feasibility of existing EU democracy promotion strategies, especially in the absence of a membership perspective for the target countries. As Richard Youngs summarizes, '[i]n all areas, from China to Morocco, from Eastern Europe to Central America, access has been easier through governance projects', which were 'increasingly used as a "foot in the door" to work capable of impacting on broader democratic dynamics' (2001b: 363). The European Commission explicitly acknowledged the democratizing potential of such an approach in 2001 (2001a: 6):

> To promote human rights and democratisation objectives in external relations, the EU draws on a wide-range of instruments [...] Some are more innovative, and potentially underused, namely Community instruments in policy areas such [as] the environment, trade, the information society and immigration which have the scope to include human rights and democratisation objectives. These tools should be used in a coherent manner, to achieve synergy and consistency and to ensure maximum effective use of resources to promote sustainable development and respect for human rights and democratisation world-wide.

The Commission's approach was subsequently supported by the Council of the European Union (2001a: III, IV).

More than a decade later, the European Commission, together with the High Representative, confirmed this approach, especially with a view to the European Neighbourhood Policy (European Commission and High Representative 2012b: 18):

> The EU's values of respect of human rights, democracy and the rule of law underpin the EU and define cooperation among its Member States; they are also reflected in the EU's laws, norms and standards. Taking over EU norms and standards through sector cooperation [...] will promote such values. Sector reform and cooperation thus contributes to better political and economic governance, political

and administrative transparency and accountability, socio-economic development, conflict prevention and resolution, state building, and civil society involvement. In many sectors, notably transport and energy, the Commission is developing a special focus on the ENP region and intends to develop this approach more widely.

This democracy promotion approach is different from the more traditional ones of 'top-down' leverage and 'bottom-up' linkage on several accounts (for details, see Lavenex and Schimmelfennig 2011). It is distinct in its focus on reforms in policy sectors, the use of the transgovernmental channel and, most importantly in the view of this edited book, the promotion of a particular kind of substance: democratic governance.

Democracy promotion through transgovernmental networks

Cross-border cooperation of officials below the level of governments has been dealt with under the label of 'transgovernmental relations'. In their oft-cited work, Keohane and Nye first of all distinguish the term 'transgovernmental' from the term 'transnational'. Whereas 'transnational' is restricted to non-governmental actors, the term 'transgovernmental' is used to refer to sub-units of governments, namely, 'when they act relatively autonomously from higher authority in international politics' (Keohane and Nye 1974: 41). Keohane and Nye define transgovernmental relations as 'sets of direct interactions among sub-units of different governments that are not controlled or closely guided by the policies of the cabinets or chief executives of those governments' (Keohane and Nye 1974: 43). It is the lower-level bureaucracies which are covered by this definition. The top level of leadership is explicitly excluded (Keohane and Nye 1974: 43–4). Building on this work in a second wave of research on trangsovernmental relations, Anne-Marie Slaughter's research starts from the assumption that the state, instead of disappearing, is disaggregating into its separate, functionally distinct parts – courts, regulatory agencies, executives and legislatures (Slaughter 1997: 184, 2000: 200, 2004: 5). These parts create networks[3] with their counterparts across borders, which leads to particular forms of cooperation. Networks are defined as 'a pattern of regular and purposive relations among like government units working across the borders that divide countries from one another and that demarcate the "domestic" from the "international" sphere' (Slaughter 2004: 14). This mode of governance, in which states interact with each other not

Anne Wetzel 61

only through their foreign offices but also through sub-state channels, is seen as a reaction to a new generation of international problems.

Research on transgovernmental networks has shown that they have an impact on the domestic adoption of internationally promoted policies and their subsequent enforcement in the case of insider-trading regulation (Bach and Newman 2010). Furthermore, it has been shown that they play a role in policy learning and transfer in the fields of welfare, labour market and social policy (Legrand 2012). Before the European Commission referred to transgovernmental democracy promotion, Slaughter had already presented reasons why transgovernmental networks may be considered to be conductive to democracy promotion too. First of all, disaggregating the state makes it possible to assess the (democratic) quality of single sub-state institutions or agencies, regardless of the overall level of democracy or autocracy of that state. Through cooperation in transgovernmental networks, the problem of labelling the whole political system as democratic or non-democratic when the real picture may be much more diverse can be avoided (Slaughter 1997: 186, 2000: 202). This again may make it possible 'to disaggregate the many complex elements of democratic legitimacy in ways that permit more nuanced and contextual strategies for democratization' (Slaughter 2000: 202). So, instead of using wholesale democracy promotion strategies, tailored approaches for particular sectors of a country could be pursued. Slaughter sees this as a particularly valuable approach because 'it sidesteps strategies that require identifying a core "liberal democratic order" that must be "enlarged", an approach that often seems above all to reinforce perceptions of an exclusive democratic for which many would read "Western" – club' (2000: 227). As will be shown below, this kind of disaggregation has a fundamental impact on the substance that is being promoted.

Secondly, Slaughter points to the fact that transgovernmental networks offer 'less public and potentially more effective channels for the transmission of norms of democratic accountability, governmental integrity, and the rule of law' (2000: 202). So, whereas intergovernmental meetings are accompanied by massive media coverage, these meetings proceed mostly unobserved and, in general, seem to remain largely unaffected by the turbulences of (high-politics) disputes (Pollack 2005: 906). This characteristic is especially conductive to the socialization mechanism described below.

Thirdly, by focusing primarily on (alleged) functional questions, the networks can circumvent or mediate cultural clashes that often appear when democratic governance is directly defined and promoted

(Slaughter 2000: 202). Furthermore, they might allow for the depoliticization of issues.

Connected to the third argument is the fourth: that promoting democratization processes through transgovernmental networks may make them less vulnerable to nationalist and cultural opposition (Slaughter 2000: 203). The fifth and sixth arguments maintain that democracy promotion strategies of both socialization and leverage are likely to work. To start with the latter, the argument is that in transgovernmental networks, actors can use concrete and differentiated issue-specific leverage. Technical assistance to build regulatory capacity or other expertise in a particular issue area can be made conditional on meeting predefined criteria (Slaughter 2000: 228). Incentives can be offered and pressure can be applied to particular institutions while others are bolstered (Slaughter 2004: 203). Socialization and learning (Slaughter 2000: 229), on the other hand, are fostered by the manageable size of the networks dealing with particular issues, regular interaction that promotes the building of trust, development of personal relationships, a sense of common enterprise and also opportunities for informal sanctions or rewards (Slaughter 2004:198–200). That changes of attitude and the development of a sense of collegiality can result from regularized coordination is also stated by Keohane and Nye. In the longer run, this can lead to changing policies or affect policy implementation (1974: 45).

Finally, Slaughter presents arguments that focus on potential power shifts in the domestic arena in favour of pro-democratic actors through 'capacity building' (Slaughter 2000: 228–9) and information exchange (Slaughter 2000: 228). Moreover, Keohane and Nye point to the fact that processes of 'transgovernmental coalition building' can occur through transgovernmental networks (1974: 46–7). Related to this is another argument by Slaughter that members of a transgovernmental network can justify a reform agenda in domestic debate by stressing the peer pressure in this network and the need to comply with rules that other similar agencies have already adopted (2000: 229).

Democratic governance as substance of democracy promotion

While democracy promotion through leverage and linkage aims to promote democratic institutions at the state level and democratic culture at the level of society (and often, indirectly, at the state level) respectively (Lavenex and Schimmelfennig 2011), what is the substance of democracy advanced through functional cooperation? When Slaughter writes about the democratization potential of transgovernmental networks, she primarily has in mind 'spreading democratic accountability, governmental integrity, and the rule of law' (1997: 186). She sees the capability of transgovernmental networks not so much in 'returning power to the people' but rather in 'preventing the abuse or usurpation of that power through the rule of law and honest and effective government' (2000: 229). It is noticeable that she does not mention any concrete institutions at the state level. Since transgovernmental cooperation is primarily aimed at addressing policy problems at the sectoral level, the democratic substance that is being promoted through this channel is related to this level, too. In order to distinguish it from democracy at the state level, current research on this topic has conceptualized the substance promoted by the EU through this approach as 'democratic governance', consisting of the principles of transparency, accountability and participation (Freyburg et al. 2007, Freyburg et al. 2015).

Most fundamentally, this conceptualization does not share the state-centric focus of conventional definitions of democracy. Rather, it builds on a range of attempts to conceptualize democracy beyond the state. Given the limited space available here, we can briefly mention only some of these. Regarding notions of democracy 'below' the state level, Philippe Schmitter (1992) and Schmitter and Imco Brouwer (1999) present a disaggregated understanding of democracy that stands out from the mostly state-centric transformation studies. With regard to democracy promotion in particular, Schmitter and Brouwer suggest analysing democracy promotion measures at the partial regime[4] or meso level (1999: 38). Another conceptualization of democracy 'below' the state level is Paul Hirst's theory of associative democracy (for example 1993), which belongs to the family of participative democratic theories (for an overview see Schmidt 2008: 236–53). It is relevant for the conceptualization of democracy at a sectoral level because it addresses the democratization of the intermediate level between state and society (Schmidt 2008: 237). A similar point is made by Dahl, who sees the improvement of 'democratic institutions within countries' as necessary for the adaptation to the present transformation of democracy. Dahl acknowledges that '[w]hat form these might take is hard to say', but they are likely to include institutions for enhanced participation below the level of the state (1994: 33). Attempts to conceptualize democracy 'below' the state level are complemented by approaches to democracy 'above' the state. Here, in particular, scholars of European governance have questioned state-centric notions of democracy as appropriate descriptions and benchmarks for the EU polity and offered alternative understandings (see for example Majone 1998, Héritier 1999, Bartolini 2005, Cheneval and Schimmelfennig 2013).

A second fundamental characteristic of the notion of democratic governance is its focus on underlying principles rather than concrete institutions embodying them. As such, it follows Beetham's concept, according to which democracy can refer to every situation in which collectively binding decisions, or decisions for a collective, are taken (Beetham 1999: 4–5). This is why it is 'the principles that are central to the question of definition; institutions are secondary and derivative, and may take different forms in different contexts' (Beetham 1999: 4).

Governance is here defined with reference to 'how the rules of the political game are managed' (Hyden *et al.* 2004: 2) at the sectoral level. More particularly, it is asked whether the rules that 'provide the context in which policy and administration are carried out' (Hyden *et al.* 2004: 2) meet certain democratic standards. 'Democratic', in turn, is defined following the literature on democratic theory that suggests a focus on the key principles of democratic politics such as 'access', 'transparency' and 'accountability' (Dalton *et al.* 2003a, Dalton *et al.* 2003b). This is also in line with the literature that refers to 'democratic governance' in order to characterize the management of public affairs according to those principles (Brinkerhoff 2000: 602).

Transparency is conceived broadly, following Christopher Hood's definition of it as the 'conduct of business in a fashion that makes decisions, rules and other information visible from outside' (2010: 989). As this definition suggests, transparency can be related to issues and procedures. The former covers access to issue-specific information, while the latter refers to the availability of information about sectoral decision- and policy-making.

Accountability is understood as the answerability of public officials that consists in enforced requirement to justify policy action under the threat of sanctions (Schedler 1999: 14). Importantly, this understanding also includes administrative accountability that 'reviews the expediency and procedural correctness of bureaucratic acts' and professional accountability, which '"watches" over ethical standards of professionalism' (Grant and Keohane 2005: 29) and forms an important part of the accountability of public officials (Schedler 1999: 28, Endnote 23). Accountability can take a horizontal or vertical form (Diamond *et al.* 1999: 3, Schedler 1999: 25), that is, it can be exercised between independent state agencies or between civil society and the state, respectively.

Finally, participation refers to non-electoral forms of taking part in politics (for example Verba 1967: 55, Sørensen and Torfing 2005: 201, 195), such as the involvement of non-state actors in administrative decision-making and policy implementation, and can range from selective participation of non-state actors with no voting rights to open and full admittance to rule-making.

Since transparency, accountability and participation are general principles of democratic governance, in practice they can take very different forms, for example in the existence of freedom of information or sunshine laws, ombudsman-type institutions, various forms of citizen participation and public consultation before issuing new regulations, the citizenry's access to (functioning) courts and possibilities of judicial review, inclusive processes of agenda formation, financial audits and sectoral representation (for examples from OECD [Organisation for Economic Co-operation and Development] countries, see Cain *et al.* 2003).

Implications for the study of EU democracy promotion

This chapter has presented 'democratic governance' as a substance of EU democracy promotion that is only partially covered by the adapted framework of embedded liberal democracy. The framework potentially covers some aspects of the principles of transparency, accountability and participation under its components. For instance, the principle of participation may be addressed by support for civil society, transparency may be addressed by support for independent media as part of political rights, and judicial review, as well as the fight against corruption, may eventually strengthen the principle of accountability. Still, some gaps remain, as the framework does not offer room for instances such as obligations to hold public hearings and consultations, obligations for authorities to publish annual reports or statistical data, and monitoring of political processes and results by citizens at the sectoral level (see also Schimmelfennig 2011). To be sure, democratic governance and liberal democracy are not incompatible (although some friction may be anticipated, for instance with regard to the relationship between direct participation and representation). Also, EU democratic governance promotion does not replace the promotion of the partial regimes of liberal democracy.[5] Rather, it takes place alongside it, as references to the promotion of closer interaction between non-governmental organizations (NGOs) in local communities or the envisaged integration of civil society into policy processes in Susan Stewart's chapter show, for instance (for the same finding with regard to Kosovo, see also Fagan 2015). While this shows that studies on democracy promotion should in general place (more) emphasis on this so far largely ignored substance, the most pressing question here is certainly what the exclusion of democratic governance from the framework of analysis means for the results of this edited volume. With regard to one of the main findings, namely that the EU, based on its particular 'nature', tends to promote output-democracy as a default option, the inclusion of democratic governance in the analysis would add to rather than contradict it. As Frank Schimmelfennig has already pointed out, the promotion of democratic governance is closely connected to the notion of the EU as a 'regulatory state' (2011: 731). Since the concluding chapter makes exactly the same point for the adapted model of embedded liberal democracy, inclusion of the analysis of democratic governance is likely to strengthen the argument about the significance of the EU's internal characteristics for the substance of its external democracy promotion. Furthermore, given that the EU's cooperation with third countries in policy sectors is, to a large degree, driven by the desire to manage interdependence, and it is sectoral officials that are in charge rather than 'democracy promoters', it can be expected that the cooperation favours output- rather than input-related democratic governance. Again, this would be congruent with the overall findings of this volume. Eventually, however, this can only be established by further research.

Notes

1. Other alternative, even if complementary, substances can include deliberative democracy (for instance, Dryzek 2009).
2. This project was jointly conducted by Tina Freyburg, Sandra Lavenex, Frank Schimmelfennig, Tatiana Skripka and Anne Wetzel at the National Center for Competence in Research 'Challenges to Democracy in the 21st Century' (NCCR Democracy), funded by the Swiss National Science Foundation (SNSF). Parts of the chapter rely on joint research with the above-mentioned project members. The author wishes to thank the SNSF and the NCCR Democracy for their support.
3. Slaughter is not consistent in the usage of terms to describe these networks. She calls them 'transgovernmental networks' (1997: 195, 196), 'government networks' (1997: 197, 2000: 204, 2004: 13), 'transnational government networks' (2000: 200) or, in the case of judicial networks, 'transnational judicial networks' (2000: 2004). Furthermore, unlike Keohane and Nye (1974), she does not clearly distinguish the state level or governmental level from the sub-state or sub-governmental level when she refers to these networks (2000: 204). In order not to confuse transnational and transgovernmental networks and to avoid connotations of intergovernmentalism, I will use the term

'transgovernmental networks' for interactions among sub-units of different governments.
4. Note that Schmitter and Brouwer's definition of partial regimes is different from the one employed in this edited volume.
5. This also speaks to the view that democratic governance at the level of state administration cannot be considered an equivalent or substitute for the democratization of a polity.

Part II
Country Chapters

Part II
Country Chapter

6
Addressing the Remnants of a Communist Past Through Accession: Slovakia and the Czech Republic

Eline De Ridder

Introduction

Enlargement is often considered to be the European Union's (EU) most successful foreign policy tool (Zielonka 2006, De Ridder *et al.* 2008). The integration of candidate countries into the EU grants the Union unique leverage over the domestic developments of third countries. This leverage is not limited to transposing EU legislation to future member states, but provides the EU with a wide array of possibilities of impacting upon the development of democracy in the candidates for membership. At the same time, however, limits to the Union's scope of influence can be identified.

This chapter examines what kind of democracy the EU promoted during the Eastern enlargement. While a wide range of scholars (for example Pridham 2005, Schimmelfennig *et al.* 2005, Vachudova 2005) have analysed the ways in which the EU supported democracy in the Central and Eastern European candidate countries, the substance of EU pre-accession democracy promotion has only seldom been the subject of systematic examination (with the notable exception of Kochenov 2004, 2008a). This chapter contributes to bridging this research gap by classifying the EU's democracy promotion in the Central and Eastern European countries (CEECs) along the partial regimes and external conditions of democracy promotion that were outlined in the introductory chapter. In addition to determining what kind of democracy the EU has supported in the CEECs, various factors shaping the content of EU democracy promotion in the Eastern enlargement are identified.

In what follows, the focus lies on the principle of conditionality, which played a central role in the promotion of reform in Central and Eastern Europe (CEE) (Dimitrova and Pridham 2004, Schimmelfennig and Sedelmeier 2005: 210, Schimmelfennig *et al.* 2005, Sedelmeier 2006b: 28). Two kinds of pre-accession conditionality have been identified: democratic conditionality and *acquis* conditionality (Schimmelfennig and Sedelmeier 2004, 2005). While the latter concerns the transposition of the specific rules of the Union's *acquis communautaire*, the former involves compliance with the Union's criteria on democracy, the rule of law and human rights. The chapter at hand relies on primary sources, interview and secondary literature. Part of the analysis is based on the author's PhD thesis.

EU democracy promotion during the Eastern enlargement

While in the run-up to the Eastern enlargement the EU could rely on several mechanisms, the key instrument for promoting democracy in the CEECs was the mechanism of conditionality. From the very beginning of the transformation process in CEE, the EU made the development of institutional links and the provision of financial and technical aid conditional upon compliance with its basic democratic principles (Schimmelfennig and Sedelmeier 2004: 669, 2005: 211–12).

The basis of the accession conditionality applied by the EU during the Eastern enlargement was formed by the Copenhagen criteria. Established in 1993 at the Copenhagen European Council, they not only reflect the economic concerns of the Union (a functioning market economy) and the duty to take on the obligations of membership (the *acquis communautaire*), but also the political goals the EU wanted to achieve in CEE, that is, stability of institutions guaranteeing democracy, the rule of law, human rights, and respect for and protection of minorities (see also De Ridder *et al.* 2008: 244–5). In 1995, the Madrid European Council added administrative and institutional capacities as another criterion. Two things are remarkable about these criteria: first, they show that in the Eastern enlargement the EU came to see itself as a legitimate actor to deal with issues that did not fall within the scope of the *acquis communautaire*, and second, that the EU did not provide further definitions of these all-encompassing criteria (cf. the chapter by Dimitry Kochenov in this volume).

The application of pre-accession conditionality in the Eastern enlargement roughly splits into three periods (Dimitrova 2005: 75). During the first (1989–1993), the focus was on democratic stability in general.

Political conditions to this end (that is, respect for democratic principles and human rights) were integrated in the Trade and Cooperation Agreements and the Association Agreements which the European Communities concluded with the different CEECs. While democratic and human rights criteria remained a crucial component during the second period (1993–1997), the EU paid increasingly greater attention to the internal market *acquis*, as well as the promotion of democratic change in CEE by criticizing national policy choices and institutional developments.

The third period of EU conditionality started in 1997 and lasted until the conclusion of the enlargement process. In this period, accession conditionality became more complex due to the application of new tools of conditionality by the Union. An elaborate system of legal-political tools, which have been referred to as 'Copenhagen-related documents' (Kochenov 2004: 6–10, 2008a: 67–79), was created to ensure the day-to-day monitoring of the candidate countries' compliance with the Copenhagen criteria and to compensate for the broad and overencompassing character of the latter. Copenhagen-related documents include the general reports issued by the Commission, which offered an annual analysis of the progress of the whole bulk of the candidate countries towards accession; annual individual country reports of the Commission, that is, the Opinion and Regular Reports; and the Accession Partnerships in the form of Council Decisions, which outlined the main priorities to be met by each candidate country individually. These documents were highly connected, as the Accession Partnerships were largely drawing on the reports. In the Copenhagen-related documents, the EU specified its democratic membership criteria. This broader scope of the EU's democracy promotion explains the scope of the chapter on the third period of EU conditionality in the Eastern enlargement.

Inserted into the framework of conditionality, the provision of financial aid also became an important incentive for CEECs' transformation. The bulk of financial help was distributed through the Phare programme (1989–2006), which aimed to stimulate political and economic reform in CEE. The provision of financial aid was conditional upon compliance with the Copenhagen criteria as interpreted in the Copenhagen-related documents. In order for countries to be eligible for Phare support, the following criteria had to be met: commitment to the rule of law, respect for human rights, the establishment of multi-party systems, the holding of free elections and the implementation of economic liberalization (K. E. Smith 2004: 70–1). The requirements here are also very general, with the exception of the criterion on free elections, which clearly addresses the electoral regime.

In 1992, a separate Phare *democracy* programme was set up with the sole aim of promoting the development of pluralist democracy and the rule of law in the CEECs. While the programme mainly supported the external condition of civil society, it is crucial to bear in mind that the sum of money involved was relatively small, amounting to just 1 per cent of total Phare and Tacis funding (ISA Consult 1997, Pridham 2005, Sasse 2005: 5).

Democracy promotion in the Czech and Slovak pre-accession process

In what follows, the EU's pre-accession democracy promotion activities towards the Czech Republic and Slovakia are examined with the aim of identifying their substance (the values are summarized in Table A.1 in the Annex[1]). Although Prague and Bratislava were united in one country until 1993, their democratic development varied widely after the split of Czechoslovakia. While the Czech Republic became a democratic frontrunner, Slovakia was clearly struggling to establish the basic principles of democracy. Bratislava, however, made a remarkable U-turn after Prime Minister Vladimír Mečiar was ousted from power in October 1998 and replaced by a reform-oriented government headed by Mikuláš Dzurinda. Democratic reforms were implemented at a very high pace and Slovakia succeeded in catching up with the remaining applicant countries.

The diverging development of democracy was clearly reflected in the EU's treatment of the two countries. The Czech Republic and Slovakia were initially classed by the Commission as belonging to the opposing extremities of the spectrum of compliance with the pre-accession standards (Scherpereel 2009). In the mid-1990s, the EU had issued (the only ever) two démarches on Slovakia, which denounced the authoritarian behaviour of the Mečiar government.[2] While the first démarche remained general and vague, expressing the hope that Slovakia would consistently follow the way of democratic reforms (Duleba 1997: 215), the second was harsher in its wording. It voiced misgivings about the contemporary political and institutional tension in the country, denounced the concentration of power in the hands of the government, called for the restoration of opposition representation in government bodies and expressed concern about the deepening conflict between the prime minister and the president (Duleba 1997: 216, Slivkova 1999: 8,

Vachudová 2005: 156). These demands and concerns primarily reflect the EU's growing worries about horizontal accountability in Slovakia.

Furthermore, while the Czech Republic was among the first countries to be granted candidate status in 1997, Slovakia was the only country from which this status was withheld because of its failure to meet the Copenhagen political criteria. Only after Prime Minister Mečiar was replaced by a liberal government in 1998 and necessary reforms were carried out was Slovakia officially recognized as a candidate country in December 1999.

A textual analysis of the Commission Reports and Accession Partnerships allows us to examine how the EU detailed the general democratic conditions for membership in the accession process of the Czech Republic and Slovakia.[3] This in turn enables us to delimit the substance of democracy promoted by the EU in the accession process of the Czech Republic and Slovakia.

The structure of the Commission Reports dealing with the two countries is identical. In the first chapter, the European Commission assesses the democratic development of a candidate country. This chapter is subdivided into two larger parts, addressing democracy and the rule of law on the one hand, and human rights and the protection of minorities on the other. In general, the first subchapter consists of an assessment of the structure and functioning of the parliament, executive and judiciary, and an evaluation of the anti-corruption measures implemented by the candidate country. When assessing legislative power, the European Commission also briefly reports on the question of free and fair elections. Under the banner of democracy and the rule of law, the Commission has thus focused on elections, horizontal accountability and the external condition of state administrative capacity. When reporting on the separation of power in the candidate countries, the Commission also touches upon civilian oversight over the secret services, the military and the police, addressing the democratic regime of effective power to govern. These references, however, constitute but a very small part of the Commission's democratic assessment.

The subchapter on human rights and the protection of minorities primarily promotes the democratic regimes of political and civil rights. The assessment is subdivided into three parts: civil and political rights; economic, social and cultural rights; and minority rights and the protection of minorities. In the first part, the European Commission assesses a wide range of civil and political rights in the candidate countries, such as the freedom of association and assembly, the freedom of expression, access to the courts, electoral rights, protection against arbitrary arrest, ownership rights, respect for privacy and the occurrence of inhumane or degrading treatment. The subchapter on economic, social and cultural rights reports on the freedom to engage in trade union activity, the right to strike, the right to a minimum means of subsistence and social security and the fight against racism. The final part on minority rights reports on the political representation of minorities and their right to maintain their own identity, to be educated in their own language and to use their own language in contact with administrative authorities.

In the third chapter of the Commission reports, which assess compliance by the candidate country with the Union's *acquis communautaire*, various elements are addressed that have contributed to the strengthening of democracy in the CEECs. References to economic and social cohesion are found in the chapters on industrial policy, on social policy and employment and on regional policy. In the last-mentioned chapter, the Commission assesses the preparation of the Czech Republic and Slovakia for future participation in the cohesion and structural funds. The chapter on justice and home affairs (JHA) contributes to the promotion of horizontal accountability and state administrative capacity when addressing issues such as the functioning of the judiciary and the fight against corruption, fraud and money laundering.

In its assessment of the democratic situation in the candidate countries, the European Commission frequently draws on reports of international organizations including the Council of Europe, the Organization for Security and Co-operation in Europe (OSCE) and the United Nations (UN), and at times relies on international instruments to assess progress. This is particularly evident in the case of the fight against corruption and the protection of human and minority rights, where the European Commission reports on the ratification of international conventions drawn up by the Council of Europe, the UN or the Organisation for Economic Co-operation and Development (OECD). The EU's use of international instruments has been explained by the lack of own standards and models (Sasse 2005, De Ridder 2009).

The Regular Reports form the basis for the Accession Partnerships. These documents are adopted by the Council on the proposal of the Commission and set up individual short- and medium-term priorities to be met by individual countries on their way towards accession. Reflecting the division between *acquis*-related and non-*acquis*-related conditionality discussed above, the Union's main concern lies with an effective transposition and future implementation of Community legislation: four fifths of the objectives identified in the agreements are linked to the third Copenhagen criterion of adopting the *acquis communautaire*.

The *acquis*-related objectives by default address the adequate implementation of Community rules. Various priorities established in the field of JHA, though, touch upon the partial regimes or external context conditions, such as the functioning and independence of the judiciary, the strengthening of public financial control functions and the effective fight against corruption. While the first two priorities promote the democratic regime of horizontal accountability, the objective of fighting corruption relates to the external condition of state administrative capacity. The latter condition has also been strengthened by the Council's administrative criteria, which amount in the case of the Czech Republic to 6 per cent of the priorities and in the case of Slovakia to 7 per cent.

In the Accession Partnerships, a number of objectives can be discerned which address the economic and social cohesion of the candidate countries. Sixteen per cent of the Czech objectives and 15 per cent of the Slovak ones thus promote the external condition of the socio-economic context.

Only a minority of the objectives, however, have been identified by the European Commission as democratic criteria: 5 per cent for the Czech Republic and 9 per cent for Slovakia. The bulk of the democratic criteria address issues of minority protection and the integration of the Roma population. Further reference is made to strengthening media independence and laws which guarantee press freedom. While issues of minority protection may address both civil and political rights, the latter two objectives promote the democratic regime of political liberties. The 2002 Partnerships for both countries also establish as political objectives the fight against corruption and the independence of the judiciary, issues which are by default treated in the agreements as *acquis*-related priorities.

For Slovakia, an additional democratic priority was outlined in 1998 on the functioning of non-governmental organizations, which relates to the external condition of civil society. The first Slovak Accession Partnership also promotes the electoral regime when it urges Bratislava to provide free and fair presidential, national and local elections. The latter two conditions, which cannot be found in the agreements drawn up for the Czech Republic, are country-specific and reflect the domestic situation within Slovakia, which was at the time of publication of the first Accession Partnership (March 1998) still governed by Prime Minister Mečiar.

Our analysis of the Czech and Slovak Accession Partnerships shows that the EU has promoted various regimes and external conditions of democracy in these agreements. For both candidate countries, the partnerships have supported the democratic regimes of political liberties, civil rights and horizontal accountability, as well as the external conditions of state administrative capacity and the socio-economic context. In the case of Slovakia, which was struggling much more than its neighbour to establish the basic principles of democracy, the first Accession Partnership in addition promoted the electoral regime and the context condition of civil society.

To conclude our textual analysis of the reports and partnerships, we point to the fact that until 1998 some smaller country-specific differences can be discerned. These relate to the different democratic path chosen by both candidate countries in the aftermath of the split of Czechoslovakia. However, from 1999 onwards – after the Mečiar regime in Bratislava was replaced by a pro-democratic government – the EU has promoted similar regimes and external conditions of democracy in the Czech Republic and Slovakia.

Next to democratic conditionality, financial support was an important incentive applied by the EU to promote domestic reform in CEE. In order to identify the substance of democracy promoted by the EU via the provision of financial aid, we carried out an analysis of all Phare projects set up under the Czech and Slovak National Programmes.[4]

Some of the Phare projects have been developed with the sole aim of promoting compliance with the political criteria for membership. The money allocated to these projects amounts to 5 per cent of the total Phare budget for the Czech Republic, and 8 per cent for Slovakia. In both countries, the majority of these funds (94 per cent in the case of the Czech Republic and 79 per cent for Slovakia) were dedicated to a strengthening of civil society and the promotion of minority tolerance and the integration of the Roma community. In addition, democratic projects were set up in Slovakia with the aim of strengthening the judiciary, fighting corruption and modernising the state administration. These three domains were covered by Commission funding for Prague too, where they were marked as *acquis*-related projects (see below).

A substantive share of the Phare financial aid projects (37 per cent for the Czech Republic, 55 per cent for Slovakia) supported an effective transfer of the *acquis communautaire* and compliance with the EU's economic membership criteria. While the main objective of the *acquis*-related projects was to guarantee an effective transfer of Community law, some of them have actively contributed to the consolidation of democracy. This is particularly evident for JHA projects, which provide money to support the fight against corruption and economic crime, and to strengthen the independence and operation of the judiciary. These projects have allowed the EU to support horizontal accountability and state administrative capacity in the Czech Republic and Slovakia.

A large part of the Phare funds has also been dedicated to supporting economic and social cohesion in the applicant countries. Thirty per cent of the money allocated to Prague and 23 per cent of the funds for Bratislava have been used to support this aim. The bulk of this financial help (88 per cent for the Czech Republic, 83 per cent for Slovakia) supported the candidate countries' preparation for future participation in the cohesion and structural funds.

To conclude, the EU has also promoted the context condition of administrative capacity by setting up Phare projects to support administrative reform in both countries. These projects account for 5 per cent of the total funding for the Czech Republic and 10 per cent of the funding allocated to Slovakia.

Our analysis of the Czech and Slovak Phare projects allows us to conclude that the pre-accession financial aid allocated by the European Commission to both Prague and Bratislava primarily supported horizontal accountability, state administrative capacity and the socio-economic context of democracy promotion. Large amounts of money were allocated to support economic and social cohesion, and to a lesser extent administrative reform in both candidate countries. Various projects – democratic or *acquis*-related – also contributed to a strengthening of the judiciary and the fight against corruption. While democracy promotion projects were set up that primarily supported minority protection and civil society development, these constituted but 4–7 per cent of the total amount of Phare aid allocated to the Czech Republic and Slovakia.

Explaining the substance of EU democracy promotion during the Eastern enlargement

Our analysis of the Czech and Slovak accession process has revealed that the EU primarily promoted the democratic regime of horizontal accountability and the external conditions of state administrative capacity, civil society and socio-economic development. In the accession process of the CEECs, the substance of EU democracy promotion tended towards a broad agenda, which was characterized by its vague nature. In what follows, the factors shaping the content of EU democracy promotion in the Eastern enlargement are identified.

Power

During the Eastern enlargement, the power relationship between the EU and the candidate countries was highly asymmetrical. The desire of the countries of CEE to join the EU was higher than the EU's wish to expand its number of member states (De Ridder *et al.* 2008: 240), which explains the Union's superior bargaining power. As a result, the EU could make the granting of rewards conditional upon compliance with its rules. It also provided the EU with the power to shape its neighbouring countries according to its own image, not least by exporting the *acquis communautaire*.

In the Eastern enlargement, the promotion of democracy did not clash with the EU's security interests. Since it is to the Union's own benefit to be surrounded by stable consolidated democracies, one would expect the EU to promote liberal or externally embedded liberal democracy. As has been demonstrated above, the EU engaged in partial liberal democracy promotion and the promotion of three out of four external conditions, resulting in a narrow and shallow form of democracy promotion. Rather than relying on power-based explanations, this content can be explained by the specific starting conditions of the CEECs at the beginning of the EU's Eastern enlargement process (see below).

Institutions

Regardless of the fact that the EU's Eastern enlargement was characterized by a complex actor constellation, the European Commission managed to establish itself as the main protagonist of the EU's accession conditionality (Pridham 2007: 353). The Commission's Directorate General for Enlargement was involved intensely in the Eastern enlargement process as the single most important actor in the application of the EU's accession conditionality (Maniokas 2004: 28, Pridham 2007: 353). In addition, the Commission was in charge of monitoring and reporting on compliance with the EU's membership criteria by the various candidate countries (Grabbe 1999: 22, Hughes *et al.* 2004: 527).

The Commission engaged in monitoring the EU's accession conditionality by publishing its progress reports. One of the downsides of this annual reporting exercise was the general and vague nature of the documents. This was particularly striking in the EU's assessment of democratic developments in the candidate countries, where the Commission frequently called for 'major efforts' to improve the situation, without specifying the means to reach this objective (Grabbe 2006: 24). This vagueness has to be linked to the fact that the EU never reached any conceptual clarity on what constitutes a consolidated democracy. Instead, the EU conditions on democracy have been pragmatically handled and developed incrementally without involving any comprehensive review or understanding of liberal democracy (Pridham 2006: 381). The EU has been very slow in developing a definition of its political criteria, because it did not possess institutional templates for any of these conditions. The EU set the political criteria for the candidates, but these criteria largely remain outside EU-level responsibilities (Grabbe 2001, Olsen 2002, Bulmer and Radaelli 2005).

Domestic context

Soon after the fall of communism, the CEECs were involved in a parallel process of Europeanization and democratization. The fact that democratic institutions, rules and procedures were still in the process of consolidation enhanced the scope for the EU to promote democracy within the region. While European integration has benefited the process of democratization in CEE, it is important to note that by the time the EU actively stepped in to determine the scope and direction of domestic reform, most countries of CEE had already completed the initial phase of democratic transition and had chosen the path of liberal democracy (Schmitter 2001: 40, Whitehead 2001: 4–5). In this process, the EU and its member states were used as role models (see also De Ridder *et al.* 2008: 244). This implies that certain basic criteria of democracy were already in place and required no further incentives or support from the EU. This partly explains why the EU paid minor attention to, for example, the promotion of free and fair elections in the case of the Czech Republic, or the effective power to govern and the external condition of stateness in both countries examined.

Our analysis of the conditionality instruments and financial aid revealed that the EU has promoted similar regimes and external conditions of democracy in the Czech Republic and Slovakia. Smaller country-specific differences can only be discerned in the first documents, published in 1997 and 1998. As mentioned above, these are to be linked to the domestic developments inside Slovakia, which was ruled by an undemocratic government until the autumn of 1998. Regardless of the vagueness and general nature of the content of its demands, the EU has addressed the same regimes and context conditions of democracy in its relations with the CEE candidate countries, as shown from the values assigned in Table A.1. The fact that the EU has promoted identical aspects of democracy in the Czech Republic and Slovakia can be explained by the fact that both countries were facing similar larger problems (for example the independence of the judiciary, the fight against corruption and the development of civil society), which they shared with other post-communist countries in the region.[5] The CEECs displayed specific socio-economic characteristics, resulting from more than 40 years of communist rule, which determined the process of Europeanization that took place in the region (Grabbe 2003: 305, Maniokas 2004: 17, Sedelmeier 2006b: 19). These post-communist characteristics, together with the problems and weaknesses linked to the transformation processes in CEE (Dimitrova 2002: 175), have influenced the design of conditionality and democracy promotion in the Eastern enlargement.

Interorganizational context

After the fall of communism, the EU was by no means the only actor involved in the CEECs. In no other region of the world has the impact of international factors on the transition process been so extensive as in CEE (Rupnik 2000: 57). After 1989, the region quickly became the playground of a myriad of international organizations, stepping in with the aim of promoting economic and democratic reform.

It has been generally accepted that the leverage of the European Community, and later the EU, has widely exceeded the changes brought about by other international organizations such as the International Monetary Fund (IMF), the North Atlantic Treaty Organization (NATO), the Council of Europe and the OSCE (Petrovic and Solingen 2005: 282, 284). Although the EU has been the dominant actor in the promotion of consolidated democracy in CEE, it did at times rely on reports of international actors and international instruments to assess the situation of democracy inside a candidate country. This is particularly evident in the case of the fight against corruption and the protection of human and minority rights, where the European Commission in its reports makes note of the (lack of) ratification of international conventions drawn up by the Council of Europe, the UN or the OECD. The EU's use of international instruments has been explained by the lack of own standards and models (Sasse 2005, De Ridder 2009).

Conclusion

In the Eastern enlargement, the EU supported the process of democratization in the CEECs by applying democratic conditionality and providing financial and technical support to democratic reform in the region. An analysis of the Copenhagen-related documents and the Phare projects elaborated in the accession process of the Czech Republic and Slovakia reveals that the EU primarily supported the democratic regime of civil rights and horizontal accountability and the external conditions of state administrative capacity, civil society and socio-economic development. The substance of the EU's democracy promotion in the Eastern enlargement may thus be situated between narrow and shallow democracy promotion, and was characterized by its vague and general nature.

Various factors are consistent with the EU's substance of democracy promotion in CEE. During the Eastern enlargement, the EU held a stronger bargaining position than the candidate countries, which explains why, in theory, not one single democratic issue could escape the monitoring exercise of the European Commission. The fact that the EU, regardless of its dominant position internationally and its superior position vis-à-vis the target countries, did not engage in (externally embedded) liberal democracy promotion can be explained by the domestic situation inside the region. Most countries in the Eastern enlargement had established the basic criteria of liberal democracy by the time the EU appeared on the scene. The EU did not, therefore, engage in a full or broad liberal democracy promotion agenda.

In the Eastern enlargement, the European Commission developed itself as the main protagonist of the Union's accession conditionality. Due to the lack of a general understanding inside the EU of what constitutes a consolidated democracy, the Commission did not apply a clear institutional template to promote democracy in the Eastern enlargement. But regardless of the vagueness and general nature of its demands, the EU addressed the same regimes and context conditions of democracy in its relations with the CEE candidate countries. Similar problems and challenges, linked to the process of transition and to a communist heritage, explain the fact that the EU promoted identical aspects of democracy in the Czech Republic and Slovakia.

Notes

1. The Copenhagen-related documents examined in the chapter were issued between 1998 and 2004. As mentioned above, the transition facility (running until 2006) has been included in our analysis of the Phare financial aid for the CEE candidate countries.
2. A first démarche was issued on 24 November 1994, a second on 25 October 1995.
3. A textual analysis has been carried out of the Opinion Reports (1997) and subsequent Regular Reports (1998–2002) and of the short- and medium-term

priorities and objectives contained in the Accession Partnerships. The reports can be accessed under http://ec.europa.eu/enlargement/archives/key_ documents/glossary_2005_en.htm, date accessed 20 May 2014.
4. Since details on the financial aid provided by the Commission to the Czech Republic and Slovakia under the Phare and Tacis democracy programme are no longer available, this programme could not be included in our analysis. In 1998 Phare was reoriented from a demand driven to a supply driven instrument. Since the programme supported the CEECs' preparations for membership only after 1998, the period before has not been included in the analysis. This decision has been reinforced by the fact that no adequate information on the Phare projects developed in the Czech Republic and Slovakia before 1998 could be provided by the European Commission. Between 2004 and 2006, the projects were part of the Phare transition facility, which has been included in the research. Phare funds have been distributed through several programmes, depending on the beneficiary countries involved. The bulk of the financial aid was distributed through the national programmes, which were developed for each candidate country separately. These programmes form the basis of the analysis carried out in this chapter.
5. Information obtained on 14 January 2009 in an interview with a Commission official working in DG Enlargement.

7
Different Trajectories yet the Same Substance: Croatia and Turkey

Canan Balkır and Müge Aknur

Croatia and Turkey began European Union (EU) accession negotiations on the same date, 3 October 2005. The opening of negotiations with Croatia was a classic case of trade-off bargaining between member states. Austria laid down Croatia's start of negotiations as a condition for the opening of negotiations with Turkey. Turkey has long been in the queue for accession, since it first signed the Agreement of Association, known as the Ankara Agreement, on 12 September 1963, which sought to integrate the country into a customs union with the European Economic Community (EEC) while acknowledging the ultimate goal of membership (EEC-Turkey 1963). Croatia was the second country to sign a Stabilisation and Association Agreement (SAA) with the EU in 2001. Following Croatia's application for EU membership in February 2003, the European Council of December 2004 decided that accession negotiations would be opened. After an initial period of crisis in the negotiations, Croatia's accession finally took place in July 2013.

Based on its initial application in 1959, Turkey became an associate member after the signing of the Ankara Agreement in 1963. Following the 1987 application for full membership, which the EU postponed, citing Turkey's political and economic situation, and the Kurdish issue as well as the Cyprus conflict, Turkey had no option but to conclude the customs union with the EU in line with the Additional Protocol, which took effect on 1 January 1996. Through the EU–Turkey Customs Union, Turkey has become part of the European internal market and has been required to adopt large parts of the *acquis*, regardless of its membership process (Balkır 2010: 1). Turkey was finally accepted as a candidate country at the Helsinki Summit of December 1999, on an equal footing with other potential candidates, after which it initiated democratization reforms, including two major constitutional packages in 2001 and 2004, and nine legislative packages between February 2002 and July 2004. Compared to those of other candidate countries, Turkey's application process has been the lengthiest. There is still no accession date envisaged. The main areas of concern for the EU have been population, size, geographical location, economics, military potential, and cultural and religious identity, and since Turkey started formal negotiations, conditionality has dominated the process. The absorption capacity of the Union has also been cited as an obstacle to Turkish membership.

As defined at the European Council in Copenhagen in 1993, the first step for a country to meet the key criteria for accession is to have stable institutions guaranteeing democracy, the rule of law, human rights, and respect for and protection of minorities. This chapter aims to map the substance of EU democracy promotion in Croatia and Turkey and identify the factors that account for the differences in the EU's approach to these countries. Although, in both cases, EU democracy promotion started earlier than the granting of candidate status, as this is itself a reward for certain prior democratic reforms, the period under analysis is 1999–2012 for Turkey and 2004–2012 for Croatia, based on their years of candidacy.

EU democracy promotion in Croatia and Turkey

Croatia and Turkey are two countries that are significantly different, yet both have experienced the same candidate framework, including democratic conditionality. Compared to a small post-war state such as Croatia, Turkey is a big country both geographically and demographically. Both countries are parliamentary republics, with the Turkish Republic established on 29 October 1923, and the Republic of Croatia founded on 8 October 1991. However, while both countries are secular republics, the historical legacy of Western civilization has made it easier for the EU to offer membership to Croatia, as Turkey's historical, cultural and religious legacy as the predominantly Muslim successor of the Ottoman Empire makes it harder for the Union to offer membership (*Schimmelfennig* and Scholtz 2010). In other words, EU member states have remained sceptical about Turkey's Europeanness. Croatia, on the other hand, has always been considered European, and its accession has been considered as serving the EU's strategic interests in regional security and conflict prevention (European Commission 2007a: 11).

The EU's programme of democracy promotion in both Turkey and Croatia, as expressed in Progress Reports, Commission Communications,

Strategy Papers, Opinion Papers and financial allocations, has focused primarily on political and civil rights, as well as horizontal accountability. In Turkey, the EU has also paid major attention to which institutions have effective power to govern (see also summary Table A.1 in Annex).

The EU's role in promoting democracy in Croatia

Throughout the 1990s, the authoritarian rule of President Franjo Tudjman and his party, as well as issues inherited from the collapse of Yugoslavia, hindered Croatia's application for EU membership. It was only after the elections of 2000 that the Croatian approach to the EU changed, when membership began to be perceived as a way to confirm the democratic credentials of the newly established state. The revision of the constitution in November 2000 moved Croatia from a semi-presidential system to a fully parliamentary system.

The first partial regime, the electoral regime, was rated 10 during 2006 and 2010 and 9 in 2012 by the Bertelsmann Transformation Index (BTI 2012a), since there are no constraints on free and fair elections in Croatia. The 2012 Monitoring Report (European Commission 2012a) mentions some shortcomings with regard to the 'maintenance of the voters' list'. The 2011 Progress Report demands the 'strengthening of the State Electoral Commission' (European Commission 2011a). Thus, the EU paid some attention to elections until Croatia's eventual accession, mainly to the need for 'universal, inclusive active suffrage' and 'correctly organized free and fair elections'. The main problems in this area concerned the status of minorities who were residents of Yugoslavia, primarily the Serbian minority who had been victims of Croatia's wartime nationalism. The EU emphasized that Croatia should allow 'citizens of the Union residing in Croatia, who are not Croatian nationals, to vote and to stand as a candidate in municipal elections and in elections to the European Parliament' (European Commission 2004a: 59). Concerning this issue, in 2007 and 2008 the EU continued to insist on legislative improvements to ensure the adequate verification and updating of residence data (European Commission 2007b: 7, 2008a: 6).

Concerning civil rights as the second partial regime, the BTI index rated these 9 in 2006 and 2008 and 8 in 2010 and 2012, noting that civil rights were guaranteed by the constitution and respected by all state institutions (BTI 2012b: 21). The EU paid major attention to civil rights in Croatia, mainly concentrating on minority rights and the return of refugees (European Commission 2008a,b: 32, 2009b: 35, 2010a: 30–1, 2011b: 32). This was reflected in the Opinion on Croatia's Application for Membership of the EU, which concluded that Croatia needed to make additional efforts in the fields of minority rights and return of refugees, and that Croatia needed to maintain 'full cooperation' with the International Criminal Tribunal for the former Yugoslavia (ICTY) (European Commission 2004a: 120–21). Refugee return has been one of the priority sectors for Community Assistance for Reconstruction, Development, and Stabilisation (CARDS) to Croatia.

Croatia's relations with the ICTY caused the suspension of the ratification of its SAA, and accession negotiations were postponed just the day before they were due to start (16 March 2005) as a result of the ICTY's critical assessment of Croatian efforts to capture the fugitive general, Ante Gotovina, as being neither timely nor sufficient. Negotiations restarted following the arrest of General Gotovina in December 2005.

Freedom of thought, conscience and religion are guaranteed by the Croatian constitution. No particular problems in the exercise of freedom of religion were mentioned in the Progress Reports, with the exception of the ruling of the European Court of Human Rights (ECHR) on violations concerning religious education in public schools and nurseries and state recognition of religious marriages (European Commission 2011a: 10).

In contrast, concerning equal treatment under the law and anti-discrimination, the position of minorities has been an urgent and major priority for the EU (European Commission 2005a: 21), as Serb and Roma minorities have continued to face economic and social discrimination (European Commission 2008b: 32, 2009b: 35, 2010a: 30, 2011b: 32). The 2011 Progress Report also reflects the EU's continued attention to the poor living conditions and challenges remaining with respect to the Roma (European Commission 2011a: 51–2). Discrimination and unequal treatment before the courts received repeated criticism from the Commission (European Commission 2005b: 19, 2007b: 14, 2009c: 14, 2011a: 12).

Regarding the prohibition of torture and inhuman or degrading treatment or punishment, civil rights are generally respected in practice. The EU's concern about single violations is not made explicit but rather can only be inferred indirectly from references to the ECHR ruling against Croatia in the Šečić case (European Commission 2007b: 51), as well as some discrimination complaints (European Commission 2011a: 11, 51) and numerous complaints about police treatment of citizens, including excessive use of force (European Commission 2009c: 11, 2010b: 10, 2011a: 9) to the ombudsman.

The right to privacy (including respect for private and family life, home and communications) is guaranteed by Croatia's constitution. Property rights are generally assured but there are delays in property repossession. Problems with the restitution of property that was confiscated during the Yugoslav regime were highlighted as concerns in several Progress Reports.

Concerning the third partial regime, political rights, while BTI rated association and assembly rights as a 10 between 2006 and 2012, freedom of speech showed a decrease from 10 in 2006 to 8 in 2008 and 7 in 2010 and 2012. That is, freedom of expression in Croatia changed from being unrestricted to partially limited (BTI 2012b: 19). The EU paid focused attention to political rights, noting certain problems remaining from the previous authoritarian regime, such as 'freedom of speech', 'freedom of press' and 'existence of influential private media besides public media' (European Commission 2008b: 31, 2009b: 35, 2009c: 12, 2010a: 30, 2011a: 50). Although almost all the Progress Reports concluded that 'freedom of expression, including freedom and pluralism of the media, is provided by law and is generally respected', beginning in 2006, in parallel with the decrease shown in the BTI, the reports repeatedly noted that undue political pressure was applied to editors and journalists, while there were also threats against and intimidation of journalists working on cases of corruption and organized crime.

Concerning horizontal accountability, the fourth partial regime, the BTI rated separation of powers in Croatia as 9 in all reports between 2006 and 2012, indicating that there is a clear separation of powers with mutual checks and balances (2012b: 20). Concerning independent judiciary, the BTI rating showed an increase from 7 in 2006, 2008 and 2010 to 8 in 2012. The EU paid major attention to horizontal accountability, the key focus being on the independence and impartiality, and efficiency, of the judiciary (European Commission 2006c: 33, 36, 2007a: 31, 2008b: 31, 2009b: 18, 2010a: 15), concluding that 'a culture of political accountability is lacking' (European Commission 2009b: 34). Judicial reform was a priority of the 2008 Accession Partnership (Council of the European Union 2008a), and numerous measures were implemented, including EU-funded projects to rationalize the court network, and to strengthen the efficiency, independence, accountability, impartiality and professionalism of the judiciary.[1] Significant challenges remained, so that even in the 2011 Accession Treaty (Council of the European Union 2011: Art. 36/Annex VII) the Commission was still closely monitoring Croatia's progress in the area of the judiciary.

Regarding effective power to govern, the fifth partial regime, the BTI rated Croatia as 10 in 2006 and 2008 and 9 in 2010 and 2012, which indicates that democratically elected representatives have the effective power to govern and do not permit any other individual or group to maintain de facto power. In line with BTI rating, the EU paid minor attention to the effective power to govern.

Concerning the first external condition, stateness, Croatia's BTI ratings of 9.5 for 2006, 2008 and 2012 and 9 for 2010 show that there is no competition with the state's monopoly on the use of force throughout the entire territory, and that there is a general agreement on citizenship, with no major groups being excluded from citizenship. The EU paid focused attention to stateness, focusing on the unsolved issues about state territory and the demos and rules of citizenship. The EU demanded concrete steps towards reaching permanent solutions on all border issues with Slovenia, Serbia, Montenegro, and Bosnia and Herzegovina (European Commission 2006d: 18, 2007b: 16, Council of the European Union 2008a). In addition, impunity and the issue of double citizenship in the region continued to concern the EU (European Commission 2010b: 10).

Regarding the second external condition, state administrative capacity, all BTI on basic administrative structures from 2006 to 2012 rated 10, indicating that these structures were providing all expected public services (BTI 2012b: 17). The reform of state administration was one of the key priorities of the 2008 Accession Partnership. The EU paid focused attention to public administration reform, useable bureaucracy, functioning administration and strengthening administrative capacity, especially at a local level (European Commission 2010a: 29, 34, 2011b: 31). Many projects were financed in this area through the Instrument for Pre-Accession Assistance (IPA) and Technical Assistance Information Exchange (TAIEX) programmes.[2]

Croatia's anti-corruption policy earned a BTI rating of 7 between 2006 and 2012, indicating that some of the government's integrity mechanisms had limited effectiveness (BTI 2012b: 40). In line with this rating, the implementation of the anti-corruption strategy and the legal framework to combat corruption were a main concern of the EU. The fight against corruption and organized crime was another priority of the 2008 Accession Partnership and was mentioned in all Progress Reports until 2011, and in the Accession Treaty of 2011 (Council of the European Union 2011: Art. 36/Annex VII).

Regarding the third external context condition, civil society, the BTI rated Croatian interest groups at 8, showing that they reflected social interests quite well. Nonetheless, the EU still mentioned the situation of civil society and continuing problems such as weak analytical and financial capacities in its 2005 and the following Progress Reports (European Commission 2005b: 19, 2011a: 10). The EU's focused attention on the presence of civil society can also be seen from its strategy papers and the financial support given to civil society to help conduct and sustain *acquis*-based reforms and development under the IPA and the Civil Society Facility (European Commission 2011a: 4).[3]

The last external condition, socio-economic development, was rated 8 by the BTI, throughout the period 2006 to 2012, indicating that poverty and inequality are limited and barely structurally ingrained. Still, the EU paid focused attention to socio-economic development in Croatia.

Concerning the prevention of extreme poverty in Croatia, poverty/social inclusion is mentioned in some Progress Reports (European Commission 2006d) and in the strategy papers, the difficult living conditions of Croatia's Roma minority are referred to. In each Strategy Paper, the Commission concluded that Croatia is a functioning market economy and that it should be able to cope with competitive market pressure within the Union in the medium term, provided that it continues to implement its reform programme to remove remaining weaknesses. The IPA has been the main programme through which the EU enhanced regional development (35.4 per cent of total IPA funding) and rural development (17.2 per cent of the total) during 2007–2013.

The EU was mainly concerned with addressing the problem of unemployment and with facilitating the process of privatization, while external indebtedness was regarded as the key vulnerability of the economy. The labour market has been an area of criticism in the Progress Reports. According to the EU, high unemployment, particularly of youth and minorities, remained a pressing economic problem, along with the large size of the economically inactive population. Meanwhile, private sector development has been rather slow (European Commission 2007b: 21), requiring EU support for market reforms, promoting an investment climate, developing business-related infrastructure and reducing the role of the state in the economy by privatizing large state-owned companies and public utilities.

The EU also paid attention to the requisites for ensuring the social inclusion of national minorities in the country's economic and social life, including public bodies, through education and employment. Almost 9 per cent of IPA funds have been granted in the area of human resources development.[4]

To sum up, on the basis of the five possible types of democracy promotion that are identified with regard to the substance that is being promoted, the EU's involvement with Croatia can be classified as externally embedded liberal democracy promotion since the EU, besides the five partial regimes, also significantly supported the advancement of external conditions by paying its focused attention. Concerning partial regimes, while the EU paid major attention to civil rights and horizontal accountability, it paid focused attention to political rights. In addition, it paid some attention to the electoral regime and minor attention to the effective power to govern. The EU paid focused attention to all external conditions. Accordingly, we can map the substance of EU promotion in Croatia as following a 'broad agenda'.

The EU's role in promoting democracy in Turkey

Following the decision to open accession negotiations with Turkey, the EU continued to monitor the progress of political reforms closely mainly by paying major and focused attention, respectively, to the majority of the partial regimes and external conditions.

Concerning the electoral regime, the EU paid some attention to the issue of electoral democracy in Turkey, where free and fair elections are held regularly and conducted properly as can be seen by its BTI rating of 8. The EU's Progress Reports mainly concentrated on the issue of inclusive active suffrage because of the 10 per cent electoral threshold for parliamentary representation as well as the underrepresentation of women and minorities in parliament (European Commission 1999: 9, 2004b: 46, 2007c: 7–8, 2010c: 8, 2011c: 9).

Regarding civil rights, in line with a BTI score that increased from 6 in 2006 and 2008 to 7 (which means that civil rights are guaranteed, but are partially or temporarily violated or not protected in some parts of the country), in 2010 and 2012 the EU paid major attention to the issue through Progress Reports, Commission Communications and the Turkey 2007 Accession Partnership by mainly focusing on human rights violations that are mainly related to the conflict with the Kurdistan Workers' Party (PKK) and the prevention of torture and ill-treatment (European Commission 1998b: 14–15, 1999: 10–11, 2000: 15, 2001b: 22, 2002: 23, 29, 2010a: 62, 2012b: 18, Council of the European Union 2008b: 7).

European Instrument for Democracy and Human Rights (EIDHR) projects gave macro-grants ranging from €200,000 to €700,000 in order to promote human rights in unions and schools, to enhance access to justice, improve civil rights in southeastern Turkey, promote the prevention of torture and assist the establishment of rehabilitation centres for torture survivors (Delegation of the European Commission to Turkey 2008, European Commission 2010d).[5]

In stating their concerns with regard to minority rights[6] in Turkey, the EU Progress Reports, Commission Communications and the Turkey 2007 Accession Partnership paid major attention to this issue by concentrating on cultural diversity, promotion of respect for and protection of minorities in accordance with ECHR decisions, legal protection of minorities, minority education, languages, broadcasting, participation in public life, reducing attacks on minority religions by extremists and enhancing tolerance (European Commission 2003b, 2004b, 2005c, 2006e, 2007c, 2008c, 2010a, 2011b, 2012b). The EU criticized Turkey for not signing the Council of Europe Framework Convention for the Protection of National Minorities or the European Charter for Regional or Minority Languages (European Commission 2009d: 27–8, 2010c: 31, 2011c: 38). The EIDHR gave grants that ranged from €47,000 to €400,000 to projects that aimed at combating discrimination and promoting minority rights, and that concerned social problems faced by minorities and the use of minority languages (Delegation of the European Commission to Turkey 2008).[7]

Concerning political rights, the third partial regime, the BTI values indicate that these rights were partially limited between 2006 and 2012, but generally there were no outright prohibitions on independent political or civic groups or press. The EU paid major attention to this issue, mainly focusing on the area of the freedom of speech, thought, press, association and assembly. Specifically, every single Regular/Progress Report written between 1998 and 2012 and every Commission Communication criticized various articles of the anti-terror law and penal law for charging and sentencing elected politicians, journalists, writers, trade unionists or non-governmental organization workers for statements, public speeches, published articles or books that allegedly endangered the unity of the state, its territorial integrity, secularism or respect for the formal institutions of the state. Turkey's 2007 Accession Partnership highlighted the need for full respect of freedom of expression and the implementation of reforms concerning the freedom of association and peaceful assembly in accordance with the ECHR (Council of the European Union 2008b: 8). The EIDHR gave grants to projects to raise Turkish citizens' awareness about restrictions on freedom of thought and expression, particularly concerning the media (European Commission 2008d).

Regarding the fourth partial regime, horizontal accountability, Turkey's BTI values suggest that there were partial or temporary restrictions of checks and balances, which, however, improved up until 2012. Nevertheless, occasional political influence on the judiciary or corruption in courts still existed. In its Progress Reports, Community Conclusions, IPA[8] and Turkey 2007 Accession Partnership, the EU paid major attention to the issue by concentrating on problems concerning the independence, impartiality and efficiency of the Turkish judiciary, particularly the High Council of Judges and Prosecutors (HSYK) in the handling of the Şemdinli bombing[9] and Ergenekon cases[10] and its harmony with ECHR decisions (European Commission 2006e: 7–8, 22, 2007c: 10, 58, 2008c: 6, 10, 2009d: 6, 11, 2010c: 7, 2011b: 72–3, 2012b: 17, Council of the European Union 2008b: 6–7).

The fifth partial regime concerning the effective power to govern had a BTI score of 7 in 2006 and 2008, with an improvement in 2010 and 2012 to 8 and 9 respectively, which indicates that enforcement of special interests by power groups over elected representatives is no longer possible. The EU paid focused attention to this issue by constantly criticizing the power that the Turkish military exerted in politics through both institutional and non-institutional mechanisms and the dominant role it played in the National Security Council. This was reflected in every single Regular and Progress Report between 1998 and 2012. The Communication Conclusions of 2011–2012 (European Commission 2011b: 72), the 2012 Progress Report (European Commission 2012c: 13) and the Turkey 2008 Accession Partnership (Council of the European Union 2008b: 6) all emphasized the need to consolidate civilian oversight of the security forces, particularly regarding the introduction of parliamentary oversight of the defence budget, opening of the decisions of the Supreme Military Council to civilian judicial review, and the prevention of the General Staff's exertion of direct or indirect pressure on political issues.

Concerning the first external supporting condition, stateness, a BTI rating of 7.5 indicated the Turkish state faced challenges to its monopoly over the use of force and state identity. The EU paid focused attention to this issue. While the EU noted the intensification in PKK terrorist attacks and listed it as a terrorist organization (European Commission 2010c: 18–19, 63, 2011b: 75, 2012b: 18), its main focus was on civil rights (rather than on stateness and Turkey's territorial integrity), repeatedly indicating that the Turkish government's fight against terrorism should be conducted with due respect for human rights and rule of law (European Commission 1998b: 10, 14–15, 1999: 6, 10–11, 2010c: 17, 35, 2012c: 12).

Considering the agreement about the demos and the rules of citizenship, the EIDHR Turkey Programme gave grants to projects on issues of identity and citizenship to combat discrimination on the grounds of racial, ethnic, religious and linguistic identities (Delegation of the European Commission to Turkey 2008).[11] The Turkey 2008 Accession Partnership also paid attention to the 'peaceful settlement of border disputes' by advising the continuation of efforts to resolve any outstanding border disputes and commit to good neighbourly relations (Council of the European Union 2008b: 10).

Concerning state administrative capacity as the second external context condition, basic administration according to the BTI increased from 8 in 2006 and 2008 to 9 in 2010 and 2012, which means that – by and large – a functioning administration is in place. Anti-corruption policy scored 5 throughout 2006, 2008 and 2010, before increasing to 6 in 2012, which indicates the government's will to combat corruption but the still limited effectiveness of integrity mechanisms. Concerning functioning state administration, the EU paid focused attention to the issue in every Progress Report between 2005 and 2012 and in the 2009–2011 Commission Communications under the title of 'public administration'. It pointed out the need to improve transparency and accountability, establish an ombudsman, strengthen external auditing and public financial management and controls, and modernize the civil service (European Commission 2009b: 67, 2010a: 61, 2011b: 72).

Moreover, with regard to the efficiency of the judiciary, through Progress Reports the EU paid focused attention by pointing out the amendments to the laws on the Court of Cassation and the Council of State that aimed to deal with the backlog of cases and packages aiming at speeding up judicial procedures further (European Commission 2012c: 71, 2011c: 14–15).

The EU also focused on state administrative capacity through the IPA by allocating €2.256 and 4.9 billion to Turkey to enhance institutional capacity and the quality of legislation for the periods of 2007–2010 and 2007–2013, respectively. Among the components of this assistance, 'Transition Assistance and Institution Building', which was allocated €1.7 million for 2007–2013, included *acquis* alignment, public administration reform, and justice and home affairs reforms (Republic of Turkey, Ministry of EU Affairs 2011).

The EU also paid focused attention to corruption, particularly highlighting the need to increase transparency of political financing, to end the broad scope of immunities and to establish impartiality in processing anti-corruption cases. It suggested the Turkish government adopt a national anti-corruption strategy (European Commission 2008c: 11–12,

2009d: 12–13, 2010a: 62, 2010c: 14–16, 2011b: 72, 2011c: 19, 2012a: 17–18, Council of the European Union 2008b: 7). In addition, the EU contributed €1.35 million through projects such as 'Reform of Public Administration, Fostering Ethics in the Turkish Public Administration'.[12]

Regarding the third external context condition, civil society, the Turkish interest groups score according to the BTI increased from 7 in 2006 and 2008 to 8 in 2010 and 2012, showing that the representation of social interests is getting broader. The EU's focused attention on Turkish civil society organizations mainly concentrated on legislative and bureaucratic obstacles, enhancement of their administrative and communication skills, and encouragement of civil society dialogue between Turkey and the EU (European Commission 2005c: 109, 2006e: 15, 2009d: 6, 2010c: 6, 2011c: 5, 27–8, 2012a: 6). The 2008 Accession Partnership concentrated on the further strengthening of the domestic development of civil society and its involvement in the shaping of public policies. It also pointed out the need to facilitate and encourage open communication and cooperation between all sectors of Turkish civil society and its European partners (Council of the European Union 2008b). Under both the national programme and the Civil Society Facility, greater EU financial support was provided to civil society, in particular to strengthen the capacity of civil society organizations and encourage a civil society dialogue between Turkey and the EU (Ketola 2010: 86, European Commission 2011c: 5).[13] The EU funding for Turkish civil society organizations was allocated mainly for the purpose of supporting democratization.

Socio-economic development, as the fourth external condition, was rated as 5 in 2006, 2010 and 2012 (with the exception of a 6 in 2008), indicating that poverty and inequality are pronounced and partially structurally ingrained. The EU paid major attention to economic development in Turkey. For example, the project 'Strengthening Institutional Capacity of Centre for Labour and Social Security Training and Research' concentrated on developing the labour market through a better skilled labour force, and improving working conditions, social security services and occupational health and safety. The project also focused on training and research to realize its targets in line with the EU's social policy and employment *acquis* (European Commission 2011d). The 2008 Accession Partnership, under the title of 'labour rights and trade unions', also focused on the alignment of union rights to EU standards and the relevant International Labour Organization conventions (Council of the European Union 2008b: 9).

As regards social development, the EU paid major attention to education in every Progress Report between 2005 and 2012[14] and in the Accession Partnership. The focus was on improving the general level of education and professional training efforts by paying special attention to youth and women (European Commission 2010c, 2011c, 2012c, Council of the European Union 2008b). The 'Human Resources Development' component of the IPA aimed to increase the level of investment in human resources through raising the level of education for girls and people of all ages (Republic of Turkey, Ministry of EU Affairs 2011).

The 2010, 2011 and 2012 Progress Reports (European Commission 2010c: 70, 2011c: 80, 2012c: 66) focused on the lack of progress in the field of social inclusion. The 'Human Resources Development' component of the IPA also focused on enhancing employment capacity in the poorer regions. The 2012 Progress Report (2012c: 65) also focused on regional disparities, particularly concerning the low employment and participation rates in the southeastern region. The same component also looked at inclusion, aiming to increase the access of disadvantaged people to the labour market and improve their social protection. The EU allocated €474.1 million to this component for the period of 2007–2013 (Republic of Turkey, Ministry of EU Affairs 2011).

To sum up, the EU's democracy promotion in Turkey can be classified as externally embedded liberal democracy promotion since the EU, besides the five partial regimes, also significantly supported the advancement of external conditions (see Table A.1 in Annex). Concerning the partial regimes, the EU paid major attention to democracy promotion in Turkey with regard to civil rights, political rights and horizontal accountability; it also paid focused attention on the effective power to govern, while paying some attention to the electoral regime. Concerning external conditions, the EU paid major attention to socio-economic development and focused attention on stateness, state administrative capacity and civil society. Accordingly, we can map the substance of EU democracy promotion in Turkey as a 'broad agenda'.

Explaining the substance of democracy promotion in Croatia and Turkey

The EU has promoted more or less the same substance in Croatia and Turkey, but with a marked difference regarding effective power to govern and a difference in intensity concerning political rights and socio-economic development. In the case of Turkey, the EU confronted the country with an exceptionally broad approach to democratization, on which it has placed a lot of emphasis with conditionality rather than incentives (Balkır and Soyaltın 2010: 43). Overall, we conclude that the substance is similar because it is very much driven by the strong EU power position and the common institutional framework, and is aimed at similar domestic contexts, with a slightly better performance from Croatia. While the EU cooperates with other international actors in both countries, these do not significantly shape the substance of its democracy promotion.

The power/interdependence explanation

The EU is more politically and economically powerful than both Croatia and Turkey. Therefore, both Turkey's and Croatia's relationship with the EU started out as an asymmetric interdependence in favour of the EU. While this asymmetric relationship continued until accession in the case of Croatia, in the case of Turkey, without a clear prospect of reward the EU lost credibility and even legitimacy in certain aspects (Kramer 2009: 4). This was mainly the result of the EU's forcing of controversial conditions on Turkey that had not been imposed on any other EU candidate and the harsh reactions Turkey received to its membership from dominant EU members such as France and Germany.

The institutionalist explanation

Although both Turkey and Croatia were under the same enlargement Directorate-General and framework, EU democracy promotion in Croatia, with a credible membership perspective and societal identification with Europe, has followed a much more linear process than in Turkey. Along with the European perspective given by the Balkan Stability Pact, key member countries, such as Germany and Austria, have supported Croatia's accession from the beginning.

In the case of Turkey, the involvement of EU key member states was much more vocal and negative. In the case of Turkey, through Regular/Progress Reports, Communications, the Accession Partnership Document and the financial allocations given under the IPA and EIDHR, the EU has paid significant attention to the delivery of democracy promotion messages. The EU has paid particularly major attention to civil and political rights, horizontal accountability and socio-economic development in Turkey. In the initial stages of candidacy, the EU's criticisms have been constructive rather than destructive, and Turkey's enthusiastic efforts to carry out these reforms in the early 2000s were well received by the European Commission.

However, the institutions, particularly the Commission, started losing influence as Turkey lost enthusiasm for the process, initially when Cyprus was given full EU membership. Following Turkey's refusal to implement the Additional Protocol to Cyprus, the EU decided to freeze the opening of eight *acquis* chapters, and imposed the condition that no chapter could even be provisionally closed until Turkey met its obligations. This opened the way to other blockages by member states. Under the Sarkozy government, France blocked five chapters on the grounds that their opening would hinder French plans to restrict Turkey to qualifying for a position short of full EU membership. Six more chapters were also unilaterally blocked by Cyprus in December 2009.[15] In addition, proposals such as 'privileged partnership', and giving 'less than full membership' showed that some prominent EU members, such as France and Germany, were not committed to Turkey's membership at all (EUobserver 2009). Moreover, both France and Austria declared that they would put Turkey's membership to a public vote through referendums.

The domestic explanation

Because the substance of EU democracy promotion varies depending on the weaknesses of the candidate country, the EU's slightly broader agenda towards Turkey than towards Croatia can be, to a large extent, explained by differences in the two countries' domestic contexts. Croatia's democratic problems were generally due to its being a post-conflict country, required to reconstruct its national identity and abandon the legacy of Tudjman. Its existing democratic shortcomings were not severe during the period under analysis, as can be seen in Croatia's high BTI scores on the partial regimes. Consequently, the EU mainly focused on the rule of law, judicial independence and the impartiality of the courts, and minority rights. Croatia also had to improve its record in the fight against corruption and organized crime. The governing political elites legitimized themselves by initiating these required reforms and the Croatian case became an example of domestic political empowerment through the EU membership perspective (Vachudova 2005).

In the Turkish case, the substance of EU democracy promotion largely corresponds to the domestic shortcomings. Thus, the EU pays comparatively little attention to elections, which are generally not seen as problematic. On the other hand, it focuses strongly on the socio-economic context, which remains weak. Also, Turkey is one of the few instances in which the EU promotes the effective power to govern.

This is an explicit reaction to the strong role of the Turkish military in domestic politics. It is interesting to note that although the substance of democracy promotion in Turkey has remained constant over time, the reaction to it by the governing Justice and Development Party (AKP) has changed. Although the EU remains in the driving seat when defining the substance of democracy promotion, the AKP government looked at it as an à la carte menu from which it could choose whatever it preferred. Such policy was also encouraged when conditionality rather than the incentives dominated the negotiation process and the EU began to lose both legitimacy and credibility in the eyes of the Turkish public.

From a comparison of the substance of EU democracy promotion with the BTI values for Croatia and Turkey, it emerges that the EU seems to be 'over attentive' to democracy in the two countries. In some instances, it pays more attention than the BTI judgments would suggest, such as with regard to civil rights or state capacity in Croatia or horizontal accountability in Turkey. This may to some degree be ascribed to the enlargement context that is characterized by the existence of templates and routine monitoring mechanisms.

Interorganizational context

Regarding the interorganizational context, the EU is able to coordinate the substance of democracy with other actors, including its own member states and/or international organizations. The EU's democracy promotion in Croatia seems to have received cooperation from member states such as Germany and Austria, the ECHR, the UN and the Organization for Security and Co-operation in Europe (OSCE). Germany also provided financial and logistical support to Croatia, especially via 'twinning projects'. The EU referred to ECHR decisions in Croatia concerning violations regarding religious education and the state recognition of religious marriages, discrimination and excessive use of force by the police (European Commission 2011a: 9–11). In addition, the EU also made Croatia's full cooperation with the UN ICTY in The Hague a condition for opening accession negotiations at the European Council of December 2004. Consequently, Croatia's lack of cooperation with the ICTY caused the freezing of negotiations from March to October 2005. Moreover, the OSCE conducted election observation missions in Croatia in 2007 and 2011 (OSCE 2014a).

In the case of Turkey, the coordination of the substance of democracy with other actors is mainly evident in the EU's reference through Progress Reports and Accession Partnerships to the need for full respect for minority rights and the freedom of expression and freedom of association and peaceful assembly in accordance with the ECHR (European Commission 2003b, 2004b, 2005c, 2006e, 2007c, 2008b, Council of the European Union 2008b: 8). Similar to Croatia, the OSCE also carried out election observation missions in Turkey in 2002, 2007 and 2011 (OSCE 2014b). Furthermore, the fourth external condition, the socio-economic context, is developed via two external anchors, namely, the EU's economic conditionality and the 2002 International Monetary Fund (IMF) stand-by agreement.

To conclude: the EU's use of broad democracy promotion in Croatia can be best explained by institutionalist and domestic approaches. In the case of Turkey's troublesome membership process, the EU's use of broad democracy promotion can be explained by institutionalist and power-based approaches in the early stages of the process, and by the domestic approach in the later stages.

Notes

1. The following EU-financed projects are examples: 'Support for the rationalization of the court network' (IPA/2011/022-954/1); 'Strengthening the efficiency of the judiciary in the Republic of Croatia' (IPA /2010/022-460); 'Professional development of judicial advisors and future judges and state attorneys through the establishment of a self-sustainable training system' (IPA/2009/21661).
2. Examples of projects financed under IPA are 'Restoration and equipping of the premises for PNUSKOK Osijek and Rijeka' (IPA/2011/ 022-954/3), 'Implementation of the General Administrative Procedures Act' (IPA 2008/020-329), 'Flexible Facility for Reinforcement of Administrative Capacity' (IPA/2010/022-460) and 'Strengthening the PAAFRD capacities for meeting the challenges arising from the CAP and the CFP reforms and the post-2013 period' (IPA/2011/022-954/9). Regarding the fight against corruption, there have also been a range of TAIEX events such as a seminar on anti-corruption policies and preventive measures, October 2007 (JHA25511), a workshop on anti-corruption and conflicts of interest, October 2011 (JHA46457), and a seminar on how to fight corruption, May 2007 (JHA24370).
3. 'Enhancing the capacities of the civil society sector for the monitoring of implementation of the EU *acquis*' (IPA 2008/020-329); 'Enhancing the sustainability and the development of civil society organizations (CSOs) as proactive social actors in the implementation of the EU *acquis*' (IPA/2009/21661); 'Assisting civil society organizations in developing, implementing and monitoring public and *acquis*-related policies' (IPA /2010/022-460); and 'Active civil society for ensuring durability of policy reforms in post-accession Croatia' (IPA /2011/022-954/2).
4. IPA Component IV – Human resources development was used for enhancing access to employment and sustainable inclusion in the labour market, reinforcing social inclusion of people at a disadvantage, enhancing

human capital and employability, and technical assistance with the Human Resources Development Operational Programme (Republic of Croatia 2007).
5. Some of these projects are 'All human rights for all: Programme for the promotion of awareness and respect for human rights among DİSK (Confederation of Turkish Revolutionary Labour Unions) members'; 'Promoting human rights in primary and secondary school textbooks'; 'Enhancing access to justice in southeastern Turkey'; 'Justice for all'; and 'Project concerning the treatment and rehabilitation centres for torture survivors' and 'Rehabilitation of torture victims', which includes Argentina, Brazil, Madagascar, Morocco and Thailand besides Turkey (see Delegation of the European Commission to Turkey 2008).
6. According to the 1923 Treaty of Lausanne, minorities in Turkey consist exclusively of non-Muslim religious communities, that is, Jews, Armenians and Greeks. Without prejudice to the treaty, the Turkish authorities consider Turkish citizens as individuals with equal rights before the law, rather than as individuals belonging to the majority or to a minority (European Commission 2007c: 21).
7. Among these projects included 'Promoting the rights of minorities: Promoting Roma rights in Turkey'; 'Combating discrimination and promoting minority rights in Turkey'; and 'A modern method to voice the social problems of minorities living in İstanbul'.
8. In order to ensure the proper functioning, effectiveness and efficiency of the judiciary in line with the EU standards, the IPA initiated a project titled 'Towards an effective and professional justice academy' (European Commission 2010e). The IPA Decentralised National Programmes of September 2009 initiated two projects titled 'Enhancing the role of the supreme judicial authorities in respect of European standards' (CRIS Number: TR080101), and 'Strengthening the court management system' (Phase II of TR 06.01.04, CRIS Number: TR080102).
9. In the Şemdinli incident, two non-commissioned officers were indicted and a land forces commander was accused of bombing a bookstore in the predominantly Kurdish town of Şemdinli in November 2005 in which one person was killed and others were injured. The interference of the General Staff to protect the non-commissioned officers caused the High Council to dismiss the Şemdinli prosecutor from office in April 2006. The disproportionate character of this decision raised doubts about the independence of this council from other state institutions.
10. The Ergenekon trials refer to the trials of a large number of people including the military officers, journalists and academicians who are accused of forming a terrorist organization and attempting to overthrow the government and undermine its operations by use of violent means.
11. These projects include 'All together from the past to the future' and 'Citizenship and nationalism: Are we aware?' Another EIDHR report included 'Disrupting the shield of silence: Bringing forth narratives of displacement towards a reconciliatory national dialogue' (see European Commission 2008d).
12. 'Fostering ethics in the Turkish public administration, Turkey' (European Commission n.d.a), 'Reform of public administration'.

13. 'Promotion of the civil society dialogue between Turkey and the European Union', which ran from 2006 to December 2009, was committed to awarding grants amounting to €19.3 million. In total, 119 projects were awarded grants, and in each case a Turkish organization partnered with an organization from an EU member state or another candidate country (Ketola 2010: 86).
14. The Regular Reports of 1998–1999, under the title of 'Education, training and youth', and the Progress Reports between 2000 and 2004, under the title of 'Education and training', all paid attention to education.
15. The Enlargement Strategy Paper published on 12 October 2011, by the EU Commission includes the proposal of creating a 'positive agenda' in Turkish-EU relations. The positive agenda process foresees informal talks and the exchange of views between the EU Commission and Turkey on the blocked chapters as well.

8
Promoting Democracy in Post-Conflict Societies: Bosnia and Herzegovina and Kosovo

Labinot Greiçevci and Bekim Çollaku

Introduction

For more than a decade, the European Union (EU) has been involved in the Western Balkans. It has played various roles in the region. In some countries, such as Bosnia and Herzegovina (hereinafter, Bosnia or BiH) and Kosovo, it has acted as a kind of 'international protector', without excluding the use of its conditionality mechanism. In other cases, including Albania, Croatia, the former Yugoslav Republic of Macedonia (FYROM), Montenegro and Serbia, the EU has merely used the 'carrot and stick' of conditionality to stabilize and put these states on their EU integration pathways. Moreover, the EU also played the role of 'facilitator' in the peaceful disintegration of the union between Serbia and Montenegro, and of 'conflict preventer' and 'interlocutor' in the case of FYROM during the conflict there in 2001. The EU and other international actors have invested a lot of energy and money in the region. A certain degree of progress has been achieved, at least in terms of establishing negative peace (the absence of war; see Donais 2005: 32) in the region, but this stability remains fragile, while its future is to some degree contested. The major positive developments appear to be Croatia's accession to the EU and the deal between Kosovo and Serbia on principles for the normalization of relations, both of which were achieved in 2013.

Kosovo and Bosnia remain, to some extent, international protectorates. The EU does not seem to have a clear strategy for their future or for the rest of the region, apart from the discourse that 'the future or perspective of the region rests with the EU'. This chapter discusses the EU's democracy promotion in the post-war period in each of the two cases. In the case of Bosnia, this process is analysed from 1995 onwards, whereas in the case of Kosovo we examine the period from 1999 onwards, with a focus on the last decade. The chapter finds that, in both cases, the EU has promoted a broad substance, with varying intensity regarding the single components and a general tendency towards the shallow end (see summarized in Table A.1).

The substance of EU democracy promotion in Bosnia: Partial regimes

Following a devastating war in Bosnia that started in 1992, the Dayton Peace Agreement was successfully negotiated in November 1995 (Yannis 2002). The agreement represents 'the institutionalization of ethnicity' in Bosnia (Slye 1996: 459). Bosnia is divided into two distinctive entities: the Federation of Bosnia and Herzegovina and the Republika Srpska. The Bosnian Serbs were effectively granted 49 per cent of Bosnian territory 'even though according to western leaders the Bosnian Serbs had perpetrated a war of aggression and ethnic cleansing [...] and crimes against humanity' (Economides 2003: 119). Dayton involved various international actors, including the EU, the UN, the Organization for Security and Co-operation in Europe (OSCE) and the US in the process of peace-building and consequently in promoting democracy in Bosnia. The most significant donors in the area of democracy promotion are the European Commission, Sweden, the US, the Netherlands and Norway (Sebastian 2010: 3). This reflects the complex landscape of the involvement of various international actors in promoting democracy in Bosnia (*cf.* hypothesis 4).

In Bosnia, several cycles of elections have been held in order to establish state, entity and municipal governments. These elections have been free and fair, but they have not resulted in much change in political life in Bosnia, because the winners have been wartime nationalists. The EU has been active with regard to this partial regime through providing financial means, addressing the issue of elections in its progress reports, through applying conditionality and through its involvement via the Office of the High Representative, who formerly also acted as the EU Special Representative to Bosnia. With regard to the first point, in 2005 the EU allocated €31.3 million to good governance and institution building, which is also linked to elections (European Commission 2005d). On the ground, however, the OSCE was the key actor in organizing and promoting democratic elections and the electoral system.

Since 1996, the OSCE has been responsible for organizing and monitoring elections. Nonetheless, election-related issues were also tackled in the European Commission's progress reports on Bosnia, which is one of the conditionality mechanisms of the EU. As a result of Bosnia's noncompliance with international election standards, the Council of the EU has refrained from taking a positive decision on the entering into force of Bosnia's Stabilisation and Association Agreement (SAA). In order to address this issue, in 2013 the EU launched a facilitation process to assist the country's political representatives in reaching a compromise agreement to bring the constitution and the election law into compliance with European standards and principles (European Commission 2013a: 7).

Civil rights (for example prevention of torture, protection of freedom and property, equal access to the law) have been mentioned in all EU progress reports on Bosnia since 2005 (European Commission 2005d: 20, 2006f: 13–14, 2007d: 15–16, 2008e: 16–17, 2009e: 15–16, 2010f: 16–17, 2011e: 15–16, 2012d: 16, 2013a: 16). In addition, the EU has occasionally funded civil rights projects through the European Instrument for Democracy and Human Rights (EIDHR) and the Instrument for Pre-Accession Assistance (IPA). Among the former, in 2009, Bosnia participated in an EIDHR project on torture prevention and among the latter, in 2007, Bosnia received support for its Human Rights Ombudsman.

Political rights, such as the right to free speech and the freedom of the press, are addressed in EU progress reports (European Commission 2005d: 20–1, 2006f: 14, 2007d: 16–17, 2008e: 17–18, 2009e: 17, 2010f: 17–18, 2011e: 16–17, 2012d: 16–17, 2013a: 17) and are mentioned in the form of conditionality, but were substantively promoted by other international actors, mainly the OSCE and the UN. Still, the EU has supported the promotion of political rights through financial means. Between 2007 and 2010, support to the media was one of the priorities of the IPA component I, 'Transition Assistance and Institution Building' (European Commission 2007e, 2008f).

With regard to the effective power to govern, the UN and OSCE were more involved. The EU paid some attention to this component in its progress reports, in particular with a view to civilian oversight over the military (European Commission 2006f: 11, 2007d: 12, 2010f: 12) and the police (2012d: 55).

Regarding horizontal accountability, the progress reports regularly point to the weak state-level government structures, in particular the Parliamentary Assembly and the government (European Commission

2009e: 9–11, 2010f: 9–11, 2012d: 9–11) and the weaknesses of the judicial system, including the issue of judicial independence (European Commission 2005d: 16–17, 2006f: 11–12, 2007d: 12–13, 2008e: 13, 2009e: 12–14, 2010f: 12–14, 2011e: 11–13, 2012d: 12–14, 2013a: 12–14). The EU has supported this component through financial allocations and a range of projects. The reform of the judicial system has been a priority of IPA component I since 2007 (European Commission 2007e, 2008f, 2011f: 10), and has received funding ever since (Europa 2014a). In 2011, the EU–BiH Structured Dialogue on Justice began (Europa 2014b). In addition to the justice sector, the EU has allocated €4.7 million to enhance the capacity of parliaments, with a particular focus on accession (Project CRIS Decision Number 2012/23589).

The EU's promotion of external conditions in Bosnia

The issue of stateness has regularly featured in the progress reports, which point to border issues (European Commission 2005d: 25, 2006f: 20, 2007d: 22, 2008e: 23, 2009e: 23–4, 2010f: 23–4, 2011e: 22–3, 2012d: 22–3, 2013a: 21–2), the question of citizenship (European Commission 2005d: 24, 2006f: 17) and the status of the Republika Srpska (European Commission 2007d: 7, 2008e: 7). The input of the EU in promoting stateness in Bosnia mainly consists of the presence of different EU police and military missions (mostly from 2005 onwards) that assisted in developing the ability of the Bosnian state to pursue the monopoly of legitimate physical force. Within the framework of the Common Foreign and Security Policy (CFSP) and the European Security and Defence Policy (ESDP), the EU has contributed through three different mechanisms: the EU Special Representative (EUSR), the military deployment EUFOR-ALTHEA and the EU Police Mission (EUPM, until 2012). In practice, this means that 'the EU runs the police force, taking over from the United Nations at the end of 2002, and the military, taking over from NATO (North Atlantic Treaty Organization) at the end of 2004, and manages Bosnia's negotiations with the World Bank' (Chandler 2010: 81). First, the EUSR can impose and supervise everything in 'high politics', which is how EU input is channelled in Bosnia, as a weak state. Chandler (2010: 81) notes that the EUSR mandate includes the power to impose legislation directly and to dismiss various elected government and public officials. Similarly, he has had to try to accommodate the interests of the different ethnic communities in Bosnia.

In terms of financial assistance, the following is illustrative: approximately €28.8 million of European funds were provided in

2005 to support the EUPM, the OHR and the EUSR (€20 million, €8.5 million and €0.27 million, respectively) (European Commission 2005d). Although by 2005 the EU had become the most important actor with regard to state-building, it pursued this issue in a 'disjointed and haphazard manner' (Bieber 2011: 1785).

The EU used to channel its input on the issue of the monopoly of legitimate physical force through its military mission, EUFOR-ALTHEA. The number of troops deployed under EUFOR-ALTHEA in 2006 was around 6,000 (European Commission 2006f), and this subsequently decreased to around 1,900 troops (European Commission 2010f). In addition to contributing to a safe and secure environment in Bosnia, EUFOR has contributed to reforming the military mechanisms of the Bosnian state. By 2014, the troop numbers had reduced to 600 (European Commission 2013a).

The EU has tried to promote capable state administration and good governance in Bosnia, mainly through the Stabilisation and Association Process, which was launched in 2000.[1] It has assessed the state of public administration in every progress report since 2005 (European Commission 2005d: 14–16, 2006f: 9–10, 2007d: 10–12, 2008e: 11–12, 2009e: 11–12, 2010f: 11–12, 2011e: 10–11, 2012d: 11–12, 2013a: 11). The same is true for corruption and anti-corruption policy (European Commission 2005d: 18–19, 2006f: 12, 2007d: 14–15, 2008e: 14–15, 2009e: 14–15, 2010f: 14–15, 2011e: 14, 2012d: 14–15, 2013a: 14–15). The EU's focus on this component is motivated not least by the fact that a functioning administration is necessary for the implementation of the SAA (see European Commission 2003c: 10), which was signed in 2008 but has not yet entered into force. The development of the legislative framework and administrative capacity to allow for proper implementation of the SAA was set in 2005 as an EU condition for concluding negotiations on the Agreement. The 2007 progress report repeated that 'public administration reform will also be required before the SAA is signed' (5). Similarly, the EU assisted through the EUPM, whose mandate focused chiefly on helping Bosnian authorities in their fight against organized crime and corruption (European Commission 2010f). With regard to financial support, public administration reform and institution building have been priorities of IPA component I since 2007 (European Commission 2007e: 14, 2008f: 16–17, 2011f: 15–17). The same applies to the fight against corruption (European Commission 2007e: 14, 2008f: 17, 2011f: 10). Between 2001 and 2008, under the Community Assistance for Reconstruction, Development, and Stabilisation (CARDS) and IPA programmes, the EU spent almost €50 million on public administration reform (European Commission 2011f: 25).

The third external condition of 'embedded democracy' is civil society. From 2005 onwards, the EU has continuously tracked the development of civil society in its progress reports (European Commission 2005d: 22, 2006f: 15, 2007d: 16–17, 2008e: 17–18, 2009e: 17, 2010f: 17, 2011e: 17, 2012d: 17, 2013a: 11). In the case of Bosnia, the aim of the international community (including the EU) has been to promote and consequently build some kind of 'social groups' and non-governmental institutions/organizations (NGOs). With regard to funding, however, civil society was largely overlooked, while the majority of funding was allocated to refugee return (Sebastian 2010). Thus, as an example, Bosnia received €20 million annually between 2001 and 2003 for refugee return, whereas civil society and the media received less than €3 million in 2001 and only €1 million in 2003 (ibid.). This illustrates the fact that EU funding for civil society was not a priority compared to other sectors until 2006, but is in accord with the policy orientations of the other international actors. However, there was a change in EU policy in this respect from 2006 onwards. Hence, between 2007 and 2010, civil society was mentioned as a priority under the IPA programme component I (European Commission 2007e: 14, 2008f: 17). Under the IPA programme, the EU allocated €3 million in 2007 as assistance to civil society for different projects focusing on strengthening local democracy and increasing the capacity of civil society, followed by €3.5 million in 2008 and €3 million in 2009 (European Commission 2007d, 2008e, 2009e). In 2010, EU support to civil society in Bosnia was primarily oriented towards anti-corruption measures, environmental protection, local democracy and networks of civil society organizations (European Commission 2010f). Since 2008, Bosnia has benefited from the IPA Civil Society Facility. Between 2011 and 2013, it received €8.5 million under this scheme (European Commission, 2012e: 8). In addition, civil society has been promoted by the EIDHR (see Europa 2014c). In general, the EU's approach is characterized by an instrumental understanding of civil society, that is, it is seen as a means to achieve other objectives (such as transforming society in general, monitoring or watchdogging the government).

The last external condition of 'embedded democracy' is the socioeconomic context. In the aftermath of the war in Bosnia, the international community started the process of post-war economic reconstruction. Although the EU is not the only actor in this area, it has been a key actor. It has regularly paid attention to labour rights, employment, education and social protection in its progress reports (European Commission 2005d: 22–3, 2006f: 15–17, 2007d: 17–18, 2008e: 18–19, 40–3, 2009e: 18–19, 41–4, 2011e: 17–19, 40–4, 2012d: 17–19, 38–42,

2013a: 18, 37-9). EU financial assistance to Bosnia in the first ten years after the end of the war in 1995 totalled more than €2 billion (European Commission 2005d), channelled through various programmes such as Phare, OBNOVA and CARDS (ibid.). In 2006, EU pre-accession financial assistance allocated to Bosnia reached €51 million (European Commission 2006f), which included funds for social development. The socio-economic context has been a priority under IPA component I since 2007 (European Commission 2007e: 116–17, 2008f: 18, 2011f: 20–1). In 2009, the EU allocated more funds under IPA to Bosnia compared to previous years and the figure reached a total of €89.1 million (European Commission 2009e). The rationale behind the increasing of funds for Bosnia was linked to the idea of alleviating the impact of the financial and economic crisis in the country (ibid.). Overall, the EU allocated almost €47 million in IPA funds to social development between 2007 and 2010 and €40 million between 2011 and 2013 (European Commission 2011f: 12). Apart from the EU, other international actors were involved in promoting socio-economic development in Bosnia (the IMF, the World Bank and so on).

In brief, it could be said that in the case of Bosnia, the EU agenda of democracy promotion was chiefly broad, with a tendency towards the shallow end. While the context conditions receive evenly high attention, the partial regimes are addressed to a varying degree, with the major focus on elections (law) and horizontal accountability.

The EU's promotion of democracy in Kosovo: Partial regimes

In spite of the EU's presence within the United Nations Interim Administration Mission (UNMIK) since 1999, the EU has continued to gradually build its field presence in Kosovo. The first EU agency that was established in post-war Kosovo after the EU pillar of the UNMIK administration was the European Agency for Reconstruction (EAR). This was followed by the establishment in the mid-2000s of the European Union Monitoring Mission (EUMM). Subsequently, in April 2004, the first Personal Representative of the EU High Representative for the CFSP in Kosovo was appointed. The EU presence in Kosovo was further enlarged in September 2004, when the European Commission opened a new Liaison Office (ECLO) in Kosovo. Similarly, in mid-2006, a new office – the EU Planning Team – was established in Pristina to prepare the circumstances for the new EU mission in the field of the rule of law (that is, the current EULEX mission) in Kosovo.

Moreover, the majority of EU member states have their own liaison offices and embassies in Pristina and when those who held the EU's rotating presidency had their offices in Pristina, they consequently played a role in representing the Union in Kosovo. The next sections will discuss the substance of democracy promotion of the above-mentioned EU agencies and will review those that were more active in this terrain.

As in the case of Bosnia, the key role of promoting free elections rested with the OSCE, which has attempted to establish democracy at the local level (Tansey 2009). Between 2000 and 2007, the OSCE in Kosovo organized five elections and established national electoral institutions (OSCE 2011). Nonetheless, the EU also paid focused attention to this component. For one, it funded the 2001 parliamentary elections in Kosovo, to the tune of €2.5 million (EAR 2002). Even more importantly, elections have formed part of the EU's conditionality since 1997 (European Commission 2012f: 2). The 2008 European Partnership mentions elections as a priority (Council of the European Union 2008c: 62). Shortcomings have been addressed in progress reports (for example European Commission 2011g: 6). The EU has sent two election observer missions (EOMs) in 2013 and 2014 (Europa 2014d) and Members of the European Parliament also visited Kosovo in the context of elections in 2009, 2010 and 2011 (European Commission 2010g: 5, 2011g: 5). With regard to the 2014 EOM, the Head of the EU Office in Kosovo/EUSR and the Heads of Mission of the EU Member States present in Kosovo make clear that the 'findings will be the guidance [...] for Kosovo's EU future!' (Head of EU Office in Kosovo et al. 2014).

Civil rights have received some attention. They have been mentioned in all EU progress reports on Kosovo since 2005 and in the European Partnership (Council of the European Union 2008c). A particular focus has been placed on property rights and minority rights (Council of the European Union 2008c), in particular the situation of the Serb minority in Kosovo. The latter is reflected in IPA funding, where human and minority rights were mentioned as priorities between 2007 and 2011 (European Commission 2007f: 14, 2008g: 14, 2009f: 13).

Both the EU presidency and the Personal Representative of the EU High Representative of the CFSP have been involved in promoting the political rights to participation in Kosovo. The goal of these offices was to collect more information about ongoing political processes in Kosovo and to assist these processes (for example inter-ethnic issues). Similarly, the EU has mentioned political rights in its regular progress reports (for example European Commission 2005e: 17–19, 2011g: 15–16) and in the European Partnership (Council of the European Union 2008c). Overall, the EU has paid some attention to political rights, which, according to the Bertelsmann Transformation Index (BTI 2012a), are not overly problematic.

Horizontal accountability, by contrast, has attracted major attention. On the one hand, there is a focus on insufficiencies in the judicial system. This can be traced in the progress reports since 2005. The establishment of EULEX in 2008, the largest civilian mission ever launched under the CFSP so far, confirms the importance attached to this issue by the EU. The strengthening of the judicial system has also been a consistent priority of IPA funding (European Commission 2007f: 14, 2008g: 14, 2009f: 13, 2011f: 11). On the other hand, the EU has focused on the effective functioning of the government and the parliament. Again, there have been frequent mentions in the progress reports, including of parliamentary oversight of the executive branch (European Commission 2005e: 10–11, 2010g: 7–8, 2013b: 6–9). However, it has received less IPA funding. Similarly, the Structured Dialogue on the Rule of Law was launched in 2011 and this is an ongoing process (European Commission 2011i).

As in the case of Bosnia, the EU has paid some attention to the effective power to govern in Kosovo. This issue has been tackled within the European Commission's progress reports on Kosovo (in particular from 2010 onwards), with a particular emphasis on the civilian oversight of security forces (European Commission 2010g: 9, 2011g: 10, 2013b: 10).

The EU's promotion of external conditions in Kosovo

The EU has played a role in the process of promoting the external supporting context of stateness in Kosovo, for example, through the work of the EU Planning Team for the EULEX mission, which started in 2006. Similarly, the EAR and ECLO programme on integrated border management – another EU project related to the Kosovo Police Service – was intended to strengthen the institutional capacities of the Kosovo police and to further develop the work of the border/boundary management agencies in Kosovo (EAR 2008). The final intention was to make these Kosovo agencies and institutions work in line with the Guidelines for Integrated Border Management in the Western Balkans and with the EU standards (ibid.). Likewise, the work of the EULEX mission in Kosovo, since 2008, is also part of the EU's contribution towards promoting stateness in Kosovo. The EU's progress reports have mentioned the problem of Serb parallel administrative structures (European Commission 2005e: 12–13, 2013b: 6). However, in relation to state-building, it should also be noted that five EU member states do not recognize Kosovo. Although the EU has sought to present a 'unified position' and became a 'key state-builder' in Kosovo, the same overall assessment as above in the case of Bosnia applies (Bieber 2011: 1785, 1789-790).

State administrative capacity has received major attention. Both public administration and the issue of corruption have received much attention in progress reports since 2005 and as priorities in the European Partnership (Council of the European Union 2008c: 62-3). An array of related projects have been carried out by the EU. For instance, the EAR supported the establishment of the Institute for Public Administration to train civil servants and provided the Statistical Offices of Kosovo with technical assistance (EAR 2004). There have been IPA projects on the 'Support to Public Administration Reform' since 2010, and under different names in earlier years (Europa 2014e).

According to rough calculations, IPA funding for public administration reform between 2007 and 2010 was €106.22 million and €20.35 million for the years 2011-2013 (European Commission 2011h: 13). Much emphasis with regard to public administration is on its effective working (*cf.* output governance). When analysing the state administrative capacity, the EU frequently assesses how the former deals with European integration issues. Regarding this dimension, in recent years the EULEX role has been of crucial importance, in particular in fighting corruption and organized crime (see European Commission 2010g, 2011g, 2013b).

Attention to civil society was minor in 2005-2006 but has increased since 2007. It has been mentioned continuously in the progress reports, although not necessarily under a separate heading. The EU has also continually emphasized the need for the Assembly of Kosovo (parliament) to increase civil society involvement. In addition, it has provided substantial financial support to civil society organizations. Of more than 300 civil society projects that the EU supported in Kosovo (1999-2006), 60 were dedicated to Serbian and Roma minorities (EAR 2007), which links up with the above-mentioned attempts to promote minority rights as part of 'civil rights'. Similarly, the ECLO contributed through EIDHR, which was implemented in Kosovo for the first time in 2007. In essence, the purpose of EIDHR was to strengthen the role of civil society in promoting human rights and democratic reform (ECLO 2008). This consistent support has continued in subsequent years. Civil society was mentioned as a priority in IPA multi-annual planning documents between 2007 and 2011, among others through mainstreaming this issue in other programmes (European Commission 2007f: 14, 2008g: 14,

2009f: 13). Under the Civil Society Facility 2011–2013, Kosovo received €3.3 million (European Commission 2012e: 9). Thus, between 2010 and 2012, the EU provided assistance for a wider range of issues and activities than any other donor in the civil society sector (Fagan 2014). In addition to funding, the EU has also engaged in a concrete dialogue with civil society. In the framework of the Stabilisation and Association Process Dialogue (SAPD), the 2013 cycle of SAPD meetings was completed by a plenary meeting and a civil society plenary meeting in July (European Commission 2013b). These kinds of meeting with civil society have been regular in recent years.

Regarding socio-economic context, economic and social rights have received continuous attention in progress reports (for example European Commission 2005e: 19–21, 2010g: 16–18), as have issues of employment, social security and education (for example European Commission 2005e: 20, 30, 2010g: 36–9, 2013b: 34–6). Employment, social policies, education and research were listed as priorities in the 2008 European Partnership (Council of the European Union 2008c: 64–5). Between 2007 and 2011, socio-economic issues were mentioned as priorities of IPA funding (European Commission 2007f: 17, 2008g: 16, 2009f: 15–16). Concretely, IPA projects included programmes on education and employment (2008, 2009, 2012 and 2013), social welfare (2011) and education (2007, 2010; see Europa 2014e).

As in the case of Bosnia, the EU agenda of democracy promotion in Kosovo was chiefly broad, with a tendency towards the shallow end of the spectrum, that was even a bit more pronounced than in Bosnia. While the context conditions have received evenly high attention, the partial regimes are addressed to a varying degree, with major focus on horizontal accountability, followed by elections.

Explanations

In terms of capabilities and interdependence, the EU is clearly more powerful than the two Western Balkan states discussed in this chapter. The enlargement framework presents a situation of asymmetric interdependence in favour of the EU. This relates in particular to issues such as visa facilitation. Still, the EU's power should not be overestimated. For one, enlargement fatigue and perceived double standards have negative consequences for the credibility of eventual EU membership as the reward for reforms. In addition, not all national elites in Bosnia and Kosovo welcome the EU's efforts, which Pickering summarizes as follows: 'how can the EU compel democratic institutional reform at the national level when powerful political elites in Bosnia & Hercegovina, particularly among Bosnian Serbs, and Kosovo Serbs continue to focus on shoring up power among their ethnically based constituency while they stall or undermine reforms demanded by the EU?' (Pickering 2011: 1942). Overall, however, the substance promoted is compatible with the expectations of the power hypothesis.

Another factor, that has shaped the substance against the background of the EU's powerful position, is the particular domestic context, to which the EU has adjusted the substance of democracy promotion in both Bosnia and Kosovo. In other words, it has had to take into account the fact that these cases are post-conflict states, which are ethnically divided and have limited statehood (for example Džihić and Wieser 2011: 1806). Both countries have a BTI value of '5' with regard to conflict intensity (BTI 2012a), which points to divisions among the society and elites. In this sense, the EU has had to try and accommodate the interests of various ethnic communities within a post-conflict context. This is one factor that has stimulated the EU to promote components such as horizontal accountability, state capacity and socio-economic context more than the partial regimes of civil and political rights. In other words, the EU has had to prioritize its agenda and, based on the circumstances on the ground, it has had to first invest money and energy reconstructing these countries and building up effective state institutions, and only then shift its attention to the components of partial regimes. At the same time, according to the BTI values for Bosnia between 2006 and 2012 (see BTI 2012a), the external conditions were more problematic than the partial regimes. Thus, the EU prioritized the more 'deficient' components. Similarly, in Kosovo the EU prioritized more those components that are characterized by low scores (BTI 2012a). Somewhat surprising is the fact that the EU did not put most of its attention on stateness, although this is seen as the overarching problem in both Kosovo and Bosnia and the EU is, in fact, a key actor in this regard. The institutionalist explanation helps to shed light on this seeming contradiction. While many elements of the substance of EU democracy promotion resemble the templates of the Eastern enlargement (see the chapter by De Ridder in this volume), the EU lacks templates and experience with regard to state-building and thus finds it difficult to formulate clear expectations. Secondly, and also related to institutions, there is no unity between EU agencies and member states, as becomes particularly clear in the case of the (non)recognition of Kosovo (Bieber 2011: 1793).

With regard to the interorganizational context, there is some tendency to share the workload in these two states, such as with the OSCE in the case of elections, and although the conditions that the EU finds for democracy promotion have been shaped by other external actors, such as the Dayton Agreement, the substance of EU democracy promotion does not follow an externally determined agenda. On the contrary, in Kosovo, the EU increasingly sets the reform agenda more than any other actor (see also Fagan 2015).

Note

1. The Stabilisation and Association Process (SAP) was confirmed as the policy framework for advancing the EU perspective of the Western Balkans states at the European Council summit in June 2003. It is also known as 'Thessaloniki Agenda', since it was adopted in Thessaloniki.

9
Power Relations Meet Domestic Structures: Russia and Ukraine

Susan Stewart

In the years immediately after the collapse of the Soviet Union, the European Union (EU) had two priorities regarding the countries to its east. The first was to establish a working relationship with the Russian Federation as the official successor to the USSR. The second was to respond to the increasingly insistent aspirations being formulated by the previous satellite states of the USSR in Central and Eastern Europe to 'return to the fold', which implied EU accession. The second priority resulted in ten states from the former socialist bloc joining the EU in 2004/2007. As for the first, the EU signed a Partnership and Cooperation Agreement (PCA) with Russia in 1994. The outbreak of the first war in Chechnya in 1995 delayed the entry into force of the agreement, but did not shake the assumption on which it was based: that Russia and the EU shared a fundamental commitment to democracy and the rule of law, and that Russia was on a clear path towards implementing these values. This assumption set a course for EU democracy promotion efforts in Russia that continues to have important implications to this day.

As for the other former Soviet republics (except the three Baltic countries, which became EU member states), the EU did not turn its attention fully towards them until shortly before the 2004 Eastern enlargement. Realizing that with the enlargement its borders would change significantly, creating new EU neighbours, the EU devised a 'European Neighbourhood Policy' (ENP) to address the altered situation.[1] While other elements of the EU's agenda in its eastern neighbourhood (energy concerns, social and economic issues) took priority over components dealing with democracy and the rule of law, these latter areas have nonetheless consistently been present in the EU approach to the countries to the east, which are now dealt with within the 'Eastern Partnership' framework. The 'Arab Spring', which occurred just as the EU was reviewing its Neighbourhood Policy, motivated the European Commission to propose a stronger emphasis on democratization and to incorporate greater incentives for partner countries successfully engaging in it (the so-called 'more for more' approach). This approach was reinforced in May 2012 with the publication of the Joint Communication entitled 'Delivering on a new European Neighbourhood Policy'. Unexpected actions by Russia and some Eastern Partnership (EaP) countries (Ukraine in particular) in the run-up to and following the Vilnius summit in November 2013 have further called into question the premises and instruments of the EaP, as well as the basis for the EU's relationship with Russia.

The role of democracy in the documents

The key documents relating to the ENP, as well as those dealing with EU–Russia relations, invoke the importance of democracy in two ways: as a value to which both sides of the relationship are committed, and as a goal to work towards in the partner countries. Part of the relationship is considered to consist of EU assistance with democratization in the eastern neighbourhood. However, there are clear differences between the approach to the ENP partner countries on the one hand, and Russia on the other.

The primary documents through which the policy towards the eastern neighbourhood can be traced are the 'Wider Europe – Neighbourhood' Communication of March 2003 (European Commission 2003d), the Strategy Paper on the European Neighbourhood Policy (published as a Commission Communication in May 2004), and the Communication on the Eastern Partnership of December 2008 (European Commission 2008h). In the 'Wider Europe' text, many of the aspects of liberal democracy as elaborated in the embedded democracy framework outlined in the introductory chapter are linked: 'Democracy, pluralism, respect for human rights, civil liberties, the rule of law and core labour standards are all essential prerequisites for political stability, as well as for peaceful and sustained economic development' (European Commission 2003d: 7). In the ENP Strategy Paper, such general considerations give way to more specific references to the importance of strengthening democracy in particular countries (especially Belarus) or through certain instruments (such as the European Instrument for Democracy and Human Rights, or EIDHR). Finally, in the Eastern Partnership Communication, the role of democracy appears to be reinforced. First of all, as part of this 'more ambitious partnership', 'additional, tangible support for their [the partner countries'] democratic and market-oriented reforms' is foreseen, and one of four policy platforms is dedicated to 'democracy, good governance and stability' (European Commission 2008h: 2–3). Perhaps most importantly, a certain element of conditionality connected to democratic development was introduced:

> A sufficient level of progress in terms of democracy, the rule of law and human rights, and in particular evidence that the electoral legislative framework and practice are in compliance with international standards, and full cooperation with the Council of Europe, OSCE/ODIHR and UN human rights bodies will be a precondition for starting negotiations [on an Association Agreement] and for deepening relations thereafter.
> (European Commission 2008h: 4)

Thus there appears to be a tendency towards specifying and intensifying the role democratic development should play in the EU's relations with its neighbours, as well as continuity in linking democracy with other goals (stability, good governance, rule of law, and so on).

In the early documents dealing with Russia, the EU clearly worked on the assumption that the Russian elite was in the process of consolidating democracy in the country. This is true for both the PCA of 1994 and the Common Strategy on Russia of 1999. This assumption has never been explicitly rejected by either side and is still in place, since the PCA remains valid during negotiations on a new agreement unless abrogated by one of the parties. During the time frame under review here, the relevant documents have been the roadmaps for the Four Common Spaces and, more recently, documents concerning the Partnership for Modernization (Europa 2010, 2014f, 2014g). In the roadmaps, questions of democracy are mentioned only in the sense that democracy is seen as a value common to both Russia and the EU. EU assistance for Russian democratization processes is not mentioned. The only issues which arise in the sense of the embedded democracy framework utilized in this edited volume are fighting corruption and strengthening the independence of the judiciary. The situation with the Partnership for Modernization is similar. In this case there are no major documents outlining the objectives and instruments of the programme. However, the 'Work plan for activities within the EU-Russia Partnership for Modernisation' indicates that a subfield of cooperation on 'Strengthening the fight against corruption, ensuring the effective functioning of the judiciary, fighting money laundering' has been included.

120 *Cases: Russia and Ukraine*

Nonetheless, the two points directly addressing corruption and judicial reform are at this stage 'preliminary EU proposals' rather than 'agreed projects/activities'. Judging from the work plan, there does not appear to be any agreed-upon activity dealing directly with any of the aspects of liberal democracy as defined in the introductory chapter. Thus while the EU does not officially appear to have given up on the idea of Russia as a consolidating democracy, its rhetoric indicates that the democracy promotion agenda has been reduced to a few elements.

This brief review of the documents reveals a significant difference in the substance and intensity of EU democracy promotion regarding the eastern ENP partner countries on the one hand and Russia on the other. In the ENP and the Eastern Partnership, democracy plays a major role, both as a prerequisite for the EU goals of stability and economic development in the neighbourhood and as a goal of reforms in the partner countries to be supported by the EU. The fact that Belarus was initially excluded from the ENP (and was only included in the multilateral aspect of the EaP) due to its inadequate record on democracy and human rights also sends a signal about the importance attributed to democracy in the ENP context.[2] In the case of Russia, the documents indicate minimal emphasis on issues of democracy. The EU has tended to treat Russia as a country pursuing democracy as an objective, or at least to assume that democracy represents a value shared by the EU and Russia equally. Beyond this assumption, questions of democratic development have played a very small role in the documents. As will be shown below, on the level of praxis this has translated into a much more superficial approach to democracy promotion than in the case of the ENP partner countries, exemplified here through the experience of Ukraine.

EU democracy promotion in Ukraine: Domestic structures are key

Two characteristics become clear when the substance of EU democracy promotion in Ukraine is analysed (see summary in Table A.1 in Annex). First, there is a very broad approach which attempts to cover a wide range of aspects. This holistic effort means that the EU has been trying to address most of the partial regimes of democracy through its rhetoric and activities, as well as the four external conditions. Second, the emphases placed on certain areas have changed, in particular after the election of Viktor Yanukovych to the presidency in February 2010.

Within the field of electoral democracy, the EU has primarily been active in supporting the organization of free and fair elections. In particular, in December 2004, during the Orange Revolution, the EU was instrumental in helping to work out a compromise between the camps of the Orange forces under Viktor Yushchenko and the 'party of power' under then President Leonid Kuchma. This compromise allowed for the organization of a third round of presidential elections which, in contrast to the first two rounds, was declared largely free and fair, and which made possible the election of Yushchenko to the Ukrainian presidency. Since then, less visible but equally important contributions to free and fair elections, such as sending delegations of election observers, have solidified the EU's presence in this realm, even if it has remained weaker than that of other actors. Regular treatment of election-related issues in the ENP Progress Reports on Ukraine confirms the systematic concern present in the EU regarding the free and fair nature of Ukrainian elections. In 2012 the EU focus on elections was especially intense, since the October parliamentary elections were perceived as a litmus test of the Ukrainian political leadership's willingness to implement key democratic standards and thereby improve Ukraine's chances of signing and ratifying an Association Agreement with the EU (Ashton and Füle 2012a). There was only a very small EU presence at the Ukrainian local elections in 2010. However, any presence at all is rather unusual when elections are held at the local level. Thus this participation reflects a heightened concern in the EU about the status of free and fair elections in Ukraine, which was again visible with regard to the early presidential elections held in May 2014.

With regard to political liberties and political rights of participation, the EU has also been quite active. The focus has been primarily on the media. In addition to providing training for journalists, the EU has supported Ukrainian media more generally to ensure pluralism and the presence of a variety of opinions, on political topics in particular (Europa 2011). On the level of the European Parliament, cooperation has been institutionalized between the Bloc Yulia Tymoshenko (BYuT) and the European People's Party on the one hand, and between the Party of Regions and the Progressive Alliance of Socialists and Democrats on the other, although the latter's agreement with the Party of Regions was allowed to expire in 2012.

Both free and fair elections and a free and pluralist media were increasingly endangered under the presidency of Viktor Yanukovych (Haran 2011, Sushko and Prystayko 2011). In the media realm, specific incidents involving harassment of journalists or television and radio stations were repeatedly raised by the EU side in dialogue with Ukraine. In addition, concern was voiced about freedom of association and demonstration, since certain types of political protest were limited or prevented by the Ukrainian security services after Yanukovych came to power. Thus at least on the rhetorical level, the EU heightened and extended the areas of its concern after the change in president and government took place in 2010. The clearest examples of this are (1) the EU's emphasis on the trial of Yulia Tymoshenko and (2) its refusal to initial the Association Agreement as originally intended at the EU–Ukraine summit in December 2011.[3] This indicates that the EU is tailoring its efforts to domestic developments in Ukraine, even going so far as to initially cut assistance earmarked for the Ukrainian government due to its failure to ensure transparency in the public procurement process.

Civil rights have been only a limited focus of the EU with regard to Ukraine, in part because they were not seen as a significant problem under the Orange governments. There has been increased interest involving individual cases since 2010, sparked largely by the campaign pursued by Yanukovych and the Azarov government against previous government officials, including but by no means limited to former Prime Minister Yulia Tymoshenko (Levy 2011). Here again, this new focus is evidence of the EU modifying the substance of its democracy promotion according to domestic developments within Ukraine, and is in line with the findings of the Bertelsmann Transformation Index (BTI 2012a), which indicates a sharp drop in the rating for civil rights from 2010 to 2012. The EU has issued repeated warnings against using the judicial system selectively for political purposes (Kyiv Post 2011). Another issue which has arisen within this category is the treatment of asylum seekers and refugees within Ukraine (Bez Kordoniv 2010, Human Rights Watch 2010a). This is of particular concern to the EU within the context of the 'action plan' on visa liberalization presented to Ukraine by the EU at the EU–Ukraine summit in November 2010 (Kyiv Post 2010).

In the area of horizontal accountability the main concern of the EU has been the independence of the Ukrainian judiciary, which has been steadily decreasing since 2008 according to the BTI. One example of this concern in practice is a twinning project with the Ukrainian Academy of Judges (Europa 2009). Also, the EU has been disturbed by the fact that the changes to the Ukrainian constitution agreed upon in 2004 introduced a certain amount of overlap and uncertainty with regard to the division of powers between the President and the Prime Minister. Experts from the EU on the Venice Commission of the Council of Europe have consistently taken part in advising Ukraine on constitutional issues, and clear signals came from the EU following

Yanukovych's election about the need for constitutional clarity and the willingness of the EU to contribute to this process. In particular after the decision of the Ukrainian Constitutional Court in October 2010 to revert to the 1996 Constitution, with its stronger role for the president and clearer definition of competences within the executive branch, the EU has argued for a transparent and systematic process of constitutional revision, rather than a manipulation of the courts in the short-term interests of those in power (Council of the European Union 2010). Emphasis on constitutional reform has continued after Yanukovych's departure, in particular with regard to decentralization of power between the central and regional levels.

Effective power to govern, in the sense it is addressed in this edited volume, has not been a focus of EU interest in Ukraine, nor has it been a particularly problematic area.

The EU has been clearly involved in activities related to three of the four external conditions affecting the development of democracy. In the area of 'state administrative capacity', the EU has been particularly concerned with the emergence of a functioning administration and with efforts to fight corruption. The issue of a functioning administration is crucial for the EU's cooperation with Ukraine, because agencies need to work well and be able to coordinate with one another for the successful implementation of accords reached with the EU. For this reason, in 2010 the EU devised the Comprehensive Institution Building Programme (CIB) as part of the Eastern Partnership, which (in the Ukrainian case) intends to focus on strengthening those institutions responsible for implementing the Association Agreement negotiated with Ukraine. However, even before the Eastern Partnership was launched, the EU was attempting to foster the development of a functioning administration, for example through formats providing training and advice. These efforts continued in 2011, with €70 million allocated for 'Reform of the Administrative Legal Framework and Civil Service in Ukraine' (European Commission 2011j: 18). With regard to corruption, the EU has strongly advocated a package of anti-corruption laws which was repeatedly postponed by the Ukrainian authorities, but has finally been passed. In addition, the EU has jointly carried out projects with the Council of Europe focused on fighting corruption in Ukraine (Council of Europe 2009).

The EU has also become increasingly involved in supporting civil society development in Ukraine. In particular, the EU offers grants to non-governmental organizations involved in certain areas considered especially relevant by the EU, although these areas can change over time. Some of these grants are made available through EIDHR, which, like the EU in general, attempts both to strengthen the capacity of Ukrainian civil society and to utilize civil society organizations to promote approximation to EU standards. For example, the EU has funded the Ukrainian branch of Counterpart International to promote aspects of civil society development and has fostered closer interaction between non-governmental organizations (NGOs) in local communities with their local administrations for the fulfilment of social needs in the towns and villages involved. The EU also organizes events to explain its programmes to interested Ukrainian civil society activists and tries to assist them in the complex process of applying for funding (Stewart 2009). In 2011 the EU established a 'Neighbourhood Civil Society Facility', which in the Ukrainian case is intended 'to promote the effectiveness of policy dialogue in Ukraine' as well as to assist Ukrainian civil society organizations in cooperating with international NGOs and civil society organizations in the EU member states (Delegation of the European Union to Ukraine 2012). Through the Civil Society Forum of the Eastern Partnership, the EU has sent a signal that it believes civil society input into government-initiated processes to be valuable. Such a signal has also been given to Ukraine explicitly through the Association Agenda of 2010, which was designed to prepare the way for implementation of the Association Agreement further down the road. The Agenda speaks of 'integrating civil society into policy processes in Ukraine' as an objective (EU/Ukraine 2009). The important role played by civil society in the 'Maidan' movement has reinforced its importance as an actor in the Ukrainian context for the EU.

Finally, the EU has made an effort to be involved in the improvement of socio-economic parameters in Ukraine. Prior to the financial and economic crisis, the EU attempted to address socio-economic issues through its Action Plan with Ukraine, which contained a section entitled 'Social situation, unemployment, poverty reduction' and related projects. The Association Agenda continued this approach to a certain extent through the inclusion of a section on 'Social co-operation', which deals in particular with social protection mechanisms and anti-discrimination measures related to the labour market. Through the negotiations on an Association Agreement with Ukraine, which is to include a deep and comprehensive free trade area, the EU is attempting to contribute to the emergence of a more developed economy in Ukraine (and, of course, one which is more compatible with EU norms and standards). Elements of the above are clearly present in the Support Package for Ukraine agreed by the European Commission in March 2014.

Susan Stewart 125

This section has shown that the EU has covered a very wide swath in terms of democracy promotion regarding Ukraine. It should be noted that, compared to other areas (the energy sector; trade concerns), comparatively few resources have been invested in EU democracy promotion in Ukraine. However, when addressing questions of substance, it is clear that the EU has pursued a holistic approach, dealing with a wide variety of issues relating to democracy on the level of both rhetoric and action. Furthermore, the approach is not static, but rather changes in the presidency and government in 2010 brought about a heightened concern with democratic development in Ukraine, which has led to a more critical rhetoric and has had consequences for the EU's actions towards Ukraine as well. This speaks for the EU's ability to tailor its efforts to the changing situation in the country. This ability has been further tested since the emergence of the Maidan movement in November 2013 and the ensuing developments, especially the overthrow of President Yanukovych and the de facto loss of Ukrainian territory to Russia in early 2014.

Exploring why the EU has altered its approach towards democracy promotion in Ukraine in recent years can help shed light on the relevance of the various hypotheses outlined in the introductory chapter to this volume. First of all, during the Yushchenko presidency, the EU did not see significant grounds to distrust Ukraine's overall commitment to democracy and the rule of law. The election of Yushchenko in the context of the Orange Revolution, when demands for free elections and less corruption were in the forefront, created an initially positive environment for EU democracy promotion in Ukraine. Yushchenko's desire to intensify relations with Western entities such as the EU and NATO (North Atlantic Treaty Organization) increased the level of trust and led to a situation in which projects oriented towards democracy promotion could be carried out without major obstacles within Ukraine. Although Ukraine's development under Yushchenko was seen by the EU as problematic, this was attributed to infighting within the Ukrainian political establishment rather than to calculated attempts to thwart EU intentions regarding the country.

EU attitudes have changed under the Yanukovych presidency. Initially the EU was clearly willing to work closely with Yanukovych, considering that he was legitimately elected and hoping that, as he claimed, consolidation of political forces would be utilized to push through reforms in a variety of areas while preserving existing achievements in democracy and the rule of law. However, as time passed, EU concern with the absence of reforms combined with democratic regression grew, particularly in the light of EU intentions to finalize the text of an Association Agreement with Ukraine. Although the Ukrainian negotiating team regained the necessary impetus to complete the negotiations by autumn 2011, reports on the deteriorating situation concerning the courts and the rule of law in general, combined with mounting evidence of selective justice designed to persecute the political opposition, motivated the EU to focus on the Tymoshenko trial. It became a 'litmus test' of Ukraine's commitment to upholding the rule of law, and a positive outcome (that is, freedom and permission to participate in politics for Tymoshenko) came to be linked by the EU with the option of signing the Association Agreement. Tymoshenko's eventual conviction and sentence of seven years in prison infuriated many EU officials and member state politicians, who had believed that Yanukovych understood the EU demands and intended to comply. Thus EU–Ukraine relations temporarily came to a standstill.

These developments point to a strong case for the third set of hypotheses regarding domestic context. As time passed, it became increasingly clear to those EU officials dealing with Ukraine that the Ukrainian political context had changed significantly with the shift from Yushchenko to Yanukovych. While both rhetorically professed a commitment to democracy and the rule of law, under Yanukovych this was strongly counteracted on the level of actions. His desire to cement his power and create material benefits for his loyal supporters led to serious democratic backsliding and sabotaged any potential for movement towards a rule-of-law-based state. While some member states may have welcomed the opportunity to reduce cooperation with Ukraine, on the whole the worsening domestic context drove the EU to postpone a hoped-for success (the Association Agreement) out of frustration and concern with losing credibility by offering substantial opportunities for economic integration to a neighbour drifting towards authoritarianism.

It is likely that elements of a power-based explanation (hypothesis 1) have also entered into the EU's calculations regarding Ukraine. Ukraine's relative weakness vis-à-vis the EU may have stimulated the EU to pursue democracy promotion more vigorously than would otherwise have been the case. The EU's primary interest concerning Ukraine is in its role as an energy transit country. With other pipelines (Nord Stream, possibly South Stream or a Trans-Adriatic Pipeline in future) coming into play and with the gas market in flux due to a variety of factors (shale gas, changing attitudes to nuclear power, greater availability of liquefied natural gas, or LNG), the EU may feel even less constrained in upcoming years to limit its democracy promotion efforts in Ukraine. However, it is safe to say that up to now the domestic structures hypothesis explains EU democracy promotion activities in Ukraine to a greater extent than the power-based hypothesis.

Less important have been questions of institutional context within the EU and the issue of the interorganizational field in the Ukrainian case. On the whole, DG Enlargement has tended to set the tone for the EU approach to Ukraine, although DG Relex and later the European External Action Service (EEAS) have also been involved. While DG DEVCO and DG Trade have played certain roles, these have been minor compared to that of DG Enlargement. On the member state level, Poland has played an extremely active role in serving as Ukraine's advocate within the EU. With regard to the interorganizational field, two factors are important. First, the US became much more active more rapidly than the EU with regard to democracy promotion in Ukraine. This has had an impact both on which topics have become typical for the Ukrainian NGO discourse and on which actors are available to work with the EU. Second, as elsewhere, the fact that the OSCE (through the Office for Democracy and Human Rights, ODIHR) has been quite involved in election monitoring in Ukraine has meant that the EU has played a lesser role in this field than it might otherwise have. Nonetheless, these developments explain the substance of EU democracy promotion efforts in Ukraine less (or less directly) than do power relations and especially domestic structures.

EU democracy promotion in Russia: Power relations and domestic structures interact

The Russian case differs from the Ukrainian one in two ways. First, the substance of democracy promotion with regard to Russia is considerably more superficial in the sense of being pursued with less intensity and depth, although it is spread over a large variety of areas. Second, power-based explanations play a larger role in accounting for the substance of democracy promotion in the Russian case.

Democracy promotion pertaining to the electoral regime has involved some election observation with the participation of EU member states, for example through the OSCE, but problems have arisen, provoking 'regret' on the part of the EU (European Union 2008a). In the run-up to the Duma elections of 2 December 2007, the Russian government imposed such tight restrictions on the would-be election observers that the ODIHR, which was responsible for sending the observers, declined to fulfil its role (OSCE 2007). The right to candidacy in Russian elections is also problematic, since opposition candidates (or parties) are often disqualified from participating on technicalities. The EU has not been overly active in this sphere, but the European Parliament has repeatedly issued resolutions criticizing the election process in both parliamentary and presidential elections in Russia. Following both the Duma elections in December 2011 and the presidential elections in March 2012, numerous critical statements were issued by EU officials, expressing their unease regarding biased media coverage, harassment of independent election monitors, detention of opposition activists and limitations on competition (EurActiv 2011, Ashton 2012a).

With regard to political liberties and political rights of participation, there are major problems in Russia with freedom of the media and of assembly, as reflected by the low score of 4 for the last three BTI measurements. However, the EU has not been particularly active on this score, with the exception of the European Parliament. The Parliament as a whole, and even more often individual members, have been vigorous in condemning Russian legislation and practice in these fields (Hautala 2010). Members of the European Parliament (MEPs) have called attention to violations of freedom of assembly more than once and have also participated in demonstrations (European Forum 2010). In addition, the EU regularly voices concern with the low level of media freedom in Russia in official forums. However, there are few if any concrete projects to deal with this problem on the ground.

With regard to civil rights, human rights consultations between Russia and the EU have been institutionalized, despite their relative lack of effectiveness. More prominent, however, are individual cases on which the EU has taken certain action. One of these involved the lawyer for the firm Heritage Capital, Sergei Magnitsky, who died in a Russian prison after having been repeatedly denied medical treatment for an urgent and serious condition. The European Parliament has proposed introducing sanctions on those officials whose collusion in Magnitsky's death can be proven. Another, even more visible case is that of Mikhail Khodorkovsky, a Russian businessman and owner of the energy firm Yukos, who has served about eight years in Russian prisons for tax evasion. MEPs went to Moscow to observe part of the trial, which suffered from various procedural flaws. Furthermore, High Representative Catherine Ashton stated after the verdict that the EU was concerned and disappointed with 'irregularities in the proceedings' and that the EU expected Russia to live up to its commitments in the realm of human rights and the rule of law (Khodorkovsky Center 2010).[4] In the summer of 2012, the trial and conviction of three members of the punk group

'Pussy Riot' for their controversial performance in a Russian Orthodox cathedral provoked a critical and concerned statement by Ashton (2012b). Thus a small number of individual cases have been raised by the EU with the Russian authorities, although treatment of such issues on a more systematic level is missing.

As in Ukraine, the question of the independence of the judiciary is raised by the EU in its dealings with Russia. Here again, the Khodorkovsky case is an example. More generally, the separation of powers in Russia is substituted by the de facto subordination of the legislative and judicial branches to the executive branch. This is rarely addressed by the EU outside of expressions of concern over individual cases. However, the EU has expressed the intention to include questions of rule of law within the Partnership for Modernization. The tentative programme of projects agreed upon at the EU–Russia summit in December 2010 revealed that a section including rule-of-law issues had been included. However, it was lumped together with 'strengthening the legal environment, improving investment and the social climate', and the agreed-upon activities dealt almost exclusively with aspects of these foci unrelated to democracy promotion.

A further similarity to the Ukrainian case is that the EU does not devote much if any attention to questions involving the 'effective power to govern' in Russia, and in fact, this area (along with 'stateness') is rated higher by the BTI than the other categories in the Russian case.

On the whole, the EU line towards Russia in the above realms has become more critical since the return of Vladimir Putin to the Russian presidency in May 2012, although this has made itself felt primarily on the rhetorical level.

With regard to the external conditions, the EU addresses them significantly less in the Russian case than in the Ukrainian one. To some extent, issues of a functioning administration and of corruption are subsumed under the EU intention to promote the rule of law in its relationship with Russia. Here it attempted to connect to former Russian President Dmitri Medvedev's discourse on modernization. The Partnership for Modernization demonstrates an effort to intensify cooperation with Russia by addressing part of Medvedev's rhetorical agenda without completely giving up on the EU's own agenda vis-à-vis Russia, which includes a (weak) democracy promotion component. However, the Progress Report on the Four Common Spaces for the year 2009 makes clear that very few specific cooperation measures have been undertaken in the field of good governance in general, and the subfields of functioning administration and battling corruption in particular (European

Commission 2010h). An initial EU–Russia seminar on anti-corruption issues did take place in December 2011 in Moscow (Permanent Mission of the Russian Federation to the European Union 2011).

The EU clearly considers the presence of an active civil society to be an important external condition for democratic development in Russia, and according to the BTI it is one of the least developed areas. The EU concern is borne out by the attempted emphasis on civil society in the Partnership for Modernization as well as by the decision to establish an EU–Russia Civil Society Forum. In addition, a small number of EIDHR projects conducted in Russia are designed to strengthen civil society organizations and increase their participation in political processes. The EU criticism of the 2012 revisions to (and implementation of) the law governing NGO activity in Russia, including the introduction of the term 'foreign agent' for NGOs engaging in 'political activity' and receiving foreign funding, has been in line with the importance the EU attributes to civil society development.

Economic issues are one of the core areas of EU–Russia relations. This is reflected in the fact that the lion's share of the progress reports on the Four Common Spaces is consistently devoted to the economic space. However, the focus on redistributive issues within the EU–Russia relationship has been minimal.

Both in the documents and in practice, the substance of EU democracy promotion in Russia is much more superficial than it has been in Ukraine, although the breadth of aspects the EU would ideally prefer to cover is similar. What can explain the superficiality of substance in the Russian case? Again a combination of the first set of hypotheses on power relations and the third one on domestic context appears to provide the best chance for understanding EU efforts. However, the power-based explanation plays a greater role here than in the Ukrainian case. Since Russia is an important source of oil and natural gas for the EU, it is widely perceived to have a certain amount of leverage on the EU through the asymmetrical power relations in the energy field. The sense of having to rely on Russia for something as essential as energy, even if the perception of dependency may be overstated, makes many member states keen to cultivate a good relationship with the Russian Federation and therefore reluctant to pursue topics unpleasant to the Russian leadership, of which democracy promotion is certainly one. Since Russia is an immediate neighbour of the EU, other concerns, such as security-related aspects, also play a role, but energy is viewed as the primary source of dependence. Following Russia's annexation of Crimea and intervention in Eastern Ukraine, however, the EU has begun to seriously reflect on accelerating measures to reduce its dependence on Russia in the energy sphere, and security issues have come to the foreground.

The power-related explanation interacts with the one involving domestic context. Despite the perceived dependence on Russia in the energy sphere, EU officials are willing to address questions of democracy and the rule of law with their Russian counterparts, if not in a particularly forceful or systematic manner. However, since the Russian government has a defensive agenda in the sense of the set of hypotheses on the domestic context, meaning that it is 'reluctant to initiate any democracy-related initiatives', the EU efforts are ineffective, and the EU concern with power relations outlined above often prevents the EU from trying to override this reluctance. Thus it is the mutually reinforcing nature of the two factors that explains the superficial substance of EU democracy promotion in the Russian case.

It should, however, be added that the history of EU–Russia relations provides an additional piece of the explanation. In the early 1990s, the EU worked on the assumption that Russia would democratize. The EU was extremely slow to discard this assumption and has yet to come up with a strategy corresponding to Russian realities. This explains in part the piecemeal and unsystematic nature of EU democracy promotion vis-à-vis Russia. Despite the complex and multifaceted nature of the EU–Russia relationship, prior to the establishment of the EEAS it was primarily guided by DG Relex. While the impact of the shift to EEAS on relations with Russia is still unclear, Russia's accession to the World Trade Organization in August 2012 has created a larger role for DG Trade. The EU antitrust case against Gazprom, which was launched in September 2012, implies an at least temporarily active part for DG Competition in the relationship. Thus recent developments would tend to indicate a diversification of the EU institutional environment dealing with Russia, although the consequences of this for democracy promotion efforts are far from evident at this point. However, following Russia's hostile actions towards Ukraine and initial EU sanctions against Russia, it appears possible that there will instead be a contraction of the number of EU actors involved with Russia, since formats such as the negotiations on a new basic agreement and on visa facilitation/liberalization have been put on hold indefinitely. The interorganizational field shows similarities to the one in Ukraine. In the Russian case, the US was also involved earlier and more actively in democracy promotion endeavours, although the expulsion of the US Agency for International Development (USAID) by the Russian authorities in September 2012 could open up new options for the EU to cooperate with Russian civil society organizations. The OSCE has also pursued election observation efforts in Russia, although as mentioned above ODIHR has had difficulties working under the constraints imposed by the Russian side, which has rendered EU actions in this field somewhat more important than in the Ukrainian case. Still, the roles played by the EU institutional environment and the interorganizational field have been much less significant than those of domestic structures and power relations in explaining the substance of EU democracy promotion in the Russian Federation.

Conclusions

A comparison of the outcomes for Ukraine and Russia can be enlightening in several ways. On the level of substance, it is clear that both on paper and in practice there are significant differences in the EU's treatment of the two countries. While a broad democracy promotion template is seen as desirable in both cases, due to various constraints the EU has pursued a much more superficial approach in the Russian case, while genuine breadth has been achieved with regard to Ukraine. However, the superficial nature of the endeavours has been characterized more by less intense engagement in many of the areas analysed, rather than in a focus on significantly fewer areas. Of further interest is that in the Ukrainian case the EU has altered its approach over time, responding to differences between the Yushchenko and the Yanukovych presidencies, and now to the overthrow of Yanukovych and the emergence of an ostensibly more reform-oriented president and government. A more critical attitude to Ukrainian progress in the realms of democracy and rule of law has developed, and linkage between such progress and the EU–Ukraine relationship has become much stronger. This is beginning to happen on the level of EU rhetoric towards Russia under Vladimir Putin as well, but in a slower and more cautious manner. EU indignation at Russian actions with regard to Ukraine may accelerate this process.

The explanations for the EU approach in the respective cases are similar but not identical. Both rely on the hypotheses regarding power relations on the one hand and domestic structures on the other, which may point to a typical explanatory pattern applicable to the post-Soviet region. However, while in the Ukrainian case the domestic context hypotheses take precedence, with power relations playing a smaller role, in the Russian case the two sets of hypotheses are equally important. In fact, it is the combination of the two and their interaction that explain the EU approach to democracy promotion in Russia.

Notes

1. The ENP encompasses not only the EU's eastern neighbourhood, but also the countries to its south, in North Africa and the Middle East.
2. It should be added, however, that the continued inclusion of Azerbaijan in the ENP and EaP, despite its clearly authoritarian government, weakens this signal somewhat and points to contradictions in the EU approach.
3. The Agreement was initialled but the signing was postponed by the EU during the Yanukovych regime due to EU concerns about anti-democratic developments in Ukraine.
4. Khodorkovsky was released in December 2013 and has been living abroad since then. However, whether the criticism from the EU played any role in his release is unclear.

10
Neither Integrated Nor Comprehensive in Substance: Armenia and Georgia

Hrant Kostanyan

Introduction

Shortly after the collapse of the Soviet Union, the European Union (EU) moved to establish contractual relationships with the newly independent states. In 1999 Partnership and Cooperation Agreements (PCA) with Armenia and Georgia were enacted. In view of the 2004 eastward enlargement, the European Neighbourhood Policy (ENP) was established and the South Caucasus countries joined in 2004. Since the initial agreements, the EU's cooperation with Armenia and Georgia has gradually extended. Besides participating in the ENP, they have also been included in the EU's Black Sea Synergy (European Commission 2007g) and the Eastern Partnership (European Commission 2008h). The ENP mid-term review in 2011 was the latest effort to redraw EU policies towards its neighbours. The negotiations of the new-generation Association Agreements were concluded with Armenia and Georgia. However, Armenia refused to sign the agreement with the EU and opted for membership of the Customs Union with Russia, Belarus and Kazakhstan instead. The Association Agreements deepen partner countries' European integration and widen their political relationship with the EU. The Deep and Comprehensive Free Trade Area (DCFTA) that is considered an integral part of the Association Agreement focuses on the economic aspect of the relationship. In addition, the EU concluded visa facilitation/readmission agreements negotiations with Armenia and Georgia and continues visa liberalisation dialogue with Georgia.

Through application of the embedded liberal democracy model, this chapter contributes to the literature (Freire and Simão 2007: 27, Börzel *et al.* 2008, Muskhelishvili and Jorjoliani 2009, Boonstra 2010) by examining and explaining the substance of the EU's democracy promotion in Armenia and Georgia. Whereas the substance of the EU's democracy promotion in Armenia and Georgia is wide-ranging at the level of rhetoric, it is not comprehensive in implementation. Although the EU focuses on most of the partial regimes and context conditions (cf. Table A.1), these components are not integrated and there is an inconsistency in the EU's focus across policy areas. Methodologically, the analysis draws on triangulation of collected data: examination of legal documents, press articles and secondary literature is complemented by interviews with seven relevant EU officials from the European External Action Service (EEAS), the European Commission and member states' permanent representations to the EU, conducted during 2012–2013.

The declaratory level

The EU's official documents related to the neighbourhood have consistently taken a broad approach to the substance of democracy promotion. The seminal 'Wider Europe-Neighbourhood' Communication outlines the EU's objectives of achieving democracy, the rule of law, respect for human rights, stability, security and prosperity in the neighbourhood (European Commission 2003d). The EU's holistic approach has been detailed in various ENP-related documents, such as country reports, strategy papers, National Indicative Programmes (NIPs), the European Neighbourhood and Partnership Instrument (ENPI) regulation, bilateral action plans and annual progress reports.

The EU's official texts reject a 'one-size-fits-all' approach by stressing differentiation between the partner countries as the basis of the neighbourhood policy. Partner countries are called upon to show commitment to political, economic and institutional reforms and the EU's support is conditional on progress towards achieving the targets set (European Commission 2003d: 16). Effective implementation of reforms by a given neighbourhood country, therefore, is viewed as an essential element in its relations with the EU (European Commission 2004c: 13). Moreover, the ENPI regulation provides the basis for the suspension of EU assistance in cases where a partner country does not keep its end of the bargain and does not adhere to principles such as 'liberty, democracy, respect for human rights and fundamental freedoms and the rule of law' (Council of the European Union and European Parliament 2006: Art. 1(3)). The EU's assistance in these cases could be redirected from the government to non-state actors (Council of the European Union and European Parliament 2006: Art. 28). Thus far, such strict measures have been put in place only in relation to Belarus among the EU's Eastern neighbours.

Democracy promotion, human rights and good governance are also part of the EU's Black Sea Synergy that brings together the EU, Armenia, Azerbaijan, Georgia, Moldova, Ukraine, Russia and Turkey (European Commission 2007g: 3-4). Beyond the partial regimes, the Synergy covers 13 priorities that include context conditions such as economic reforms, development and conflict resolution, as well as environment and energy (European Commission 2007g: 3-4).

The bilateral and multilateral tracks of the Eastern Partnership are also far-reaching. The former offers the partner countries the possibility of upgrading their political (through Association Agreement) and economic (through DCFTA) relations with the EU, as well as achieving visa liberalization, facilitating energy cooperation and enhancing the ability of the state to implement reforms through a Comprehensive Institution-Building (CIB) programme. The latter focuses in particular on democracy and good governance, a market economy and sustainable development (European Commission 2008h: 4).

Eight years after the EU's initial neighbourhood Communication, the mid-term review of the ENP, 'A new response to a changing Neighbourhood', promises 'a much higher level of differentiation' (European Commission and High Representative 2011b: 5). Inspired by the events unfolding in the Arab world, the document not only stresses a greater need for differentiation between the partner countries but also identifies attainment of 'deep and sustainable democracy' in the neighbouring countries as the EU's eventual goal.

The authors of the ENP review define deep democracy as the sum of

> free and fair elections; freedom of association, expression and assembly and a free press and media; the rule of law administered by an independent judiciary and right to a fair trial; fighting against corruption; security and law enforcement sector reform (including the police) and the establishment of democratic control over armed and security forces.
> (European Commission and High Representative 2011b: 3)

which are also the main benchmarks for assessing progress and adjusting the extent of the EU's assistance in line with 'more for more' (European Commission and High Representative 2011b: 4) principle of positive conditionality. The proposed reforms are presented as beneficial not only in terms of strengthening democracy but also for creating 'the conditions for sustainable and inclusive economic growth, stimulating trade and investment' (European Commission and High Representative 2011b: 7) and strengthening support for civil society. The EU's described broad approach to democracy promotion is in line with the model proposed in the introductory chapter of this volume.

The ENP bilateral action plans that are jointly adopted by the EU and partner countries go as far as including specific priority areas and deliverables. They address, *inter alia*, the reform of democratic structures related to the partial regimes and context conditions, including but not limited to the judiciary, the fight against corruption, strengthening human rights and the rule of law, aiding economic reforms, facilitating growth and improving the investment climate. However, the differentiation promised by a number of the EU documents produced in the framework of the ENP is not visible in the joint action plans agreed with Armenia and Georgia. The jointly identified priority areas, general objectives and actions are similar for both South Caucasian states, although more differentiation is expected since these two countries are different on a number of issue areas (cf. Table A.2 in Annex). In practice, however, the substance of promoted democracy is slightly more differentiated than what the vague action plans suggest (cf. Table A.1).

Policy implementation

The EU's policies towards Armenia and Georgia tackle a whole host of sectors and issue areas that, to varying degrees, include most of the partial regimes and the external conditions as outlined in the embedded liberal democracy model. In terms of partial regimes, the EU addresses the electoral process, respect for political and civil rights, and horizontal accountability, but does not deal with effective power to govern. This may seem surprising at first sight, yet it is not puzzling because there are no problems with this component in either of the two countries. The sharp decline in effective power to govern in Armenia that the Bertelsmann Transformation Index (BTI 2012a) shows is questionable. To substantiate its argument, the BTI mainly cites infighting within the government (BTI 2012c: 7–8). However, the author of this chapter disagrees with the BTI, since despite the existence of conflicts within the governing elite, there are no tutelary powers or reserved domains in Armenia. Moreover, during the past decade, the Armenian government has been successful in controlling both the military and the police.

With regard to the electoral regime, the EU systematically addresses elections in both Armenia and Georgia in its progress reports. The BTI shows (see Table A.2) that Armenia has systematically experienced problems in pursuing electoral democracy. As an unwritten rule, demonstrations follow elections. The immediate aftermath of the presidential election in 2008 saw the height of these protests. Hundreds of protesters were arrested and injured and ten people lost their lives. After the tragic events of 1 March, the EU expressed deep concern about the post-election violence that led to loss of life and urged Armenian authorities to release those detained unlawfully, conduct an independent investigation into the events and start a dialogue with the opposition with the aim of attaining 'peace and stability in the country' (European Union 2008b). A week later, the EU issued a second statement with similar demands (European Union 2008c) and suspended the ENPI Governance Facility (Zulueta-Fülscher 2008: 5).

As a reaction to the Arab Spring and to the unparalleled competition in the Armenian internal political environment, the EU has put its money where its mouth is and supported the parliamentary (2012) and presidential (2013) elections by spending €1.7 million on electoral monitoring. This support had both short- and long-term goals, such as strengthening the Human Rights Defender's Office (HRDO) and enhancing the administrative capacities of election commissioners and the police (Europa 2012a). A statement of the High Representative of the Union for Foreign Affairs and Security Policy (HR/VP) and the Neighbourhood Commissioner welcomed the progress made in the 2012 parliamentary elections and the presence of six political parties in the National Assembly, while asserting that a number of shortcomings need to be addressed before the presidential election (Ashton and Füle 2012b). The latter was also welcomed by the EU; however, concerns have been raised in relation to 'reported instances of partiality by public servants, claims of misuse of administrative resources, unclear interpretation of campaign financing provisions and cases of pressure on voters' (Ashton and Füle 2013a).

In the area of elections, the EU has taken a slightly less proactive role in Georgia than in Armenia following the Rose Revolution of 2003, which brought Mikheil Saakashvili into power with 96 per cent of the votes cast in 2004's election. Saakashvili's popularity began to show cracks in November 2007, when anti-governmental protests had grown in size, manifesting the first serious opposition to the authorities. As an answer to the protesters' demands to hold parliamentary elections, President Saakashvili imposed emergency rule, cracked down on the demonstrations and called for presidential elections, which he won with 53.47 per cent of the vote. The EU issued a declaration calling the 2008 elections 'an important test' for Georgian democracy and stability (Council of the European Union 2008d). The EU reacted to the following parliamentary elections with similar rhetoric, welcoming the progress made since the previous elections and urging the addressing of shortcomings (Council of the European Union 2008e: 9). The October 2012 parliamentary and the October 2013 presidential elections were hailed by both the HR/VP Ashton and Commissioner Füle (2012c and 2013b).

In terms of political rights, the EU takes an interest in promoting rights such as the freedom of the press, the right of association and to demonstration both in Armenia and Georgia. The state of the observance of these rights and the mechanisms of their improvement are subject to the discussions, *inter alia*, in the bilateral exchanges, negotiations of Association Agreements, the annual EU–Armenia and EU–Georgia Cooperation Councils, as well as EU–Armenia and EU–Georgia human rights dialogues. Some of these agreements, for example the Association Agreements, go as far as to include conditionality clauses.

To a varying degree, freedom of the traditional press (television) has been a problematic area in Armenia and Georgia. More modern forms of press such as online newspapers and portals are relatively free. The EU has raised the issue in its annual progress reports. Moreover, the EU officials have consistently expressed their concerns with both Armenian and Georgian counterparts during the annual human rights dialogues.[1] The EU, however, has paid slightly more attention to press freedom in Georgia than in Armenia through funding, *inter alia*, a large project on 'Strengthening the Media's Role as a Watchdog Institution in Georgia' as part of its reconstruction relief and rehabilitation framework.

The EU has raised similar concerns about the freedom of association and demonstration in both of the South Caucasus countries. When the Armenian authorities allowed the major opposition movement, the Armenian National Congress (HAK), to hold a demonstration in Liberty Square on 28 April 2011, the EU released a statement welcoming the move and expressing hope that future requests by the opposition would be handled in a similar manner (European Union 2011a).

Freedom of assembly has also been a challenge in Georgia, the former government of which often used excessive force to crack down on anti-government demonstrations. During the first post-Rose Revolution crackdown on protests by the law enforcement authorities in 2007, the EU expressed 'deep concern' and urged all sides to search for solutions through a constructive dialogue (Council of the European Union 2007a). Despite a number of critical EU reactions in the past, the Georgian authorities suppressed opposition demonstrations in May 2009 and May 2011. In the case of the former, the EU issued a joint statement with the US, containing no criticism of the government's actions (US/EU 2009). The EU's statement in the case of the latter, which cost the lives of four people, was also not critical (European Union 2011b).

Party politics is weak in both Armenia and Georgia. However, the interaction of Armenian and Georgian parties with the European Parliament is gradually increasing, with a number of Armenian and Georgian political parties becoming members of the European political groups. Finally, through the EuroNest Parliamentary Assembly, the EU brings together 60 Members of the European Parliament (MEPs) and ten parliamentarians from each Eastern Partnership country (except Belarus). The EuroNest facilitates socialization of Armenian and Georgian parliamentarians with their EU counterparts (Kostanyan and Vandecasteele 2013).

The EU also promotes political and civil rights in both Armenia and Georgia through the European Instrument for Democracy and Human Rights (EIDHR). However, the EU has focused more on Georgia than on Armenia when addressing civil rights. The EU has expressed concerns about respect for civil rights and has been a major supporter and donor of the HRDO in Armenia as well as in Georgia. In Armenia, the EU has encouraged reforms aimed at improving the judicial system, promoting the rule of law and the protection of human rights (Europa 2012b). For instance, the EU issued a statement welcoming the release of three HAK activists and called on Armenian authorities to free the rest (European Union 2011a). After the remaining imprisoned HAK members were released under the amnesty proposal by President Sargsyan, the HR/VP Ashton issued a statement welcoming the president's initiative (2011a). The EU also assisted the chamber of advocates, organized training of judges, facilitated the access of vulnerable groups to justice and aided in the creation of the administration of juvenile justice. The EU has aided approximation of Armenia's criminal justice with international norms.

Since the Rose Revolution, protection of civil rights in Georgia has been increasingly problematic. Georgian prisons are in bad condition and overcrowded. The acquittals rate is low (2 per cent in 2011). Arrests of opposition figures and those supporting them have intensified, especially in the aftermath of the large demonstrations of 2007, 2009, 2011 and 2012. In September 2012, the EU officials released two statements condemning the abuse and ill-treatment of prisoners (Delegation of the

European Union to Georgia 2012, European Union 2012a). Moreover, under the former government, the EU pointed out that the rights of workers and core labour standards did not correspond to those of the International Labour Organization (ILO). With regard to civil rights, the EU has put a lot more focus on Georgia than on Armenia in ENP progress reports.

In terms of separation of power and horizontal accountability, the EU has paid particular attention to the judiciary in both Armenia and Georgia, although overall attention has not been very pronounced. The EU's support for the development of the Armenian and Georgian justice sectors was provided through budget support and accompanying technical assistance, which are conditional on specific reforms that the partner countries commit to implementing. A jointly agreed Strategic Action Plan for Judicial Reform 2009–2011 was put in place. The EU has also paid particular attention to the commercial courts in Armenia.[2]

Similar to Armenia, in Georgia the horizontal separation of power across government branches has been fundamentally distorted and accountability mechanisms are dysfunctional. Until the 2012 elections, the parliament was heavily dominated by the ruling party – the United National Movement – and the division between the legislature and the state remained unclear. The parliament did not properly scrutinize the executive, leaving it unchecked and unaccountable. The Georgian judiciary is not only dependent on the executive but also discredited and suffers from a number of structural problems such as those relating to the appointment, reassignment and professionalism of judges. The EU's focus has mainly been on criminal justice in Georgia.[3]

With regard to the external conditions that shape the democracy environment, the EU has made a contribution to stateness, administrative capacity, civil society and socio-economic development in both Armenia and Georgia. On the issue of stateness, the EU has been more involved in Georgia than in Armenia. With regard to the latter, the EU is not an official party to the Organization for Security and Cooperation in Europe (OSCE) Minsk Group consisting of France, Russia and the US, which has been mediating for resolution to the Nagorno-Karabakh conflict. However, the EU supports the work of the Minsk Group. The Nagorno-Karabakh conflict is also raised, *inter alia*, by EU officials in high-level contacts as well as by the European Parliament's resolutions.

The EU is substantially more involved in the Abkhazian and South Ossetian conflicts. It participates in the Geneva process that also includes Russia, Georgia, the US, the United Nations, the OSCE, and the authorities of Abkhazia and South Ossetia. Moreover, since

2008, it has dispatched a civilian EU Monitoring Mission (EUMM) in Georgia. Finally, the EU's Special Representative for the South Caucasus, appointed in 2011, is also specifically called upon to address 'the crisis in Georgia'.

While being more involved in Armenia than in Georgia, in both states the EU has supported the enhancement of administrative capacity including bureaucracy and institutions, especially those that are charged with implementation of EU–Armenia and EU–Georgia agreements. Both South Caucasus countries benefit from the CIB, the Technical Assistance Information Exchange (TAIEX), the Twinning and the Support for Improvement in Governance and Management (SIGMA) programmes.

A high-level EU Special Advisory Group to the Republic of Armenia has been set up to cooperate with the Office of the Armenian President, the staff of the National Security Council, the National Assembly, the government, ministries and agencies. The group aims to transfer EU know-how to Armenian authorities, supporting them, for example, in negotiating the Association Agreement and in the DCFTA negotiations. The EU aids Armenian authorities in the education of the new generation of diplomats through supporting the Diplomatic School at the Ministry of the Foreign Affairs. The EU has also assisted Armenia in the implementation of e-government. Corruption in Armenia, however, remains problematic and the Commission's 2012 progress report states that 'effective implementation' of anti-corruption measures is lacking (European Commission and High Representative 2012c: 5).

As opposed to Armenia, in the immediate aftermath of the Rose Revolution, Georgia undertook important political and economic reforms aimed at combating petty corruption and improving public services. Transparency International's Corruption Perceptions Index 2011 gave the country a 4.1 score on a scale from 10 (very clean) to 0 (highly corrupt), which was a better result than some EU member states (Transparency International Georgia 2011). The EU, however, expressed concerns that 'the Civil Service Bureau (CSB) mainly concentrates on fighting petty corruption in the public service and not on its overall reform' (European Commission and High Representative 2011c: 4). The EU also identified concerns with regard to the absence of regulations on salaries or the training of civil servants in Georgia, as well as with regard to the Civil Service Code (European Commission and High Representative 2011c: 4). Moreover, the EU continues its support for strengthening, *inter alia*, of e-government and the public finance management report.

The EU has provided similar assistance to both Armenian and Georgian civil society, within and beyond the ENP and the Eastern Partnership. The Neighbourhood Civil Society Facility established in

2011, of which Armenia and Georgia are beneficiaries, shows the EU's increasing commitment to the support of non-state actors and civil society at large. For the period of 2011–2013, the Facility focused on three components. Firstly, it aimed to strengthen the capacity of partner countries' civil society through exchanges and training, both in order to promote reforms on the national level and contribute to the improvement of public accountability. The EU views civil society as a partner in process of the ENP's implementation (cf. chapters 7 and 9 on Turkey/Croatia and Ukraine/Russia, respectively). Secondly, it aimed to reinforce the role of the non-governmental organizations (NGOs) 'through support to regional and country projects, by supplementing the funding available through thematic programmes and instruments'. Finally, the Facility aimed to promote a greater role for civil society in bilateral projects between the EU and the partner country (European Commission 2011k).

The Civil Society Forum created in the framework of the Eastern Partnership brings together non-state actors from eastern neighbourhood countries and the EU. It is organized in four working groups following the thematic platforms of the Eastern Partnership, viz. democracy, human rights, good governance and stability; economic integration and convergence with EU policies; environment, climate change and energy security; and contacts between people. Within the framework of the Forum, every partner country has developed a national platform, which brings together NGOs that have an interest in working towards their countries' European integration.

The EIDHR has been an important instrument through which the EU has allocated funding, *inter alia*, to civil society actors. The instrument has five priorities, the second of which is specifically about the strengthening the civil society. The EIDHR focuses on subjects such as gender issues, healthcare, disability-related projects, criminal justice, equal employment opportunities and strengthening labour and trade unions. However, the funding for the so-called Country Based Support Scheme on a yearly basis has remained fairly limited for Georgia and especially for Armenia. The EU also holds a yearly Civil Society Seminar with Armenia and Georgia, focusing on a wide range of issues. Through supporting civil society actors, the EU tries to conduct advocacy in the areas which 'conventionally' have been reserved for the governments. Active civic participation is seen by the EU as an important aspect in increasing the accountability of the otherwise overly powerful executive branches of the Armenian and Georgian governments.

The EU has also contributed to the socio-economic development of Armenia and even more so to that of Georgia. The ENPI NIP 2011–2013 for Armenia identifies socio-economic reform and sustainable development among its priorities. The EU assists Armenia in regional and rural development, supports the improvement of infrastructure in the areas of transport, energy, environment and electronic communications, and human capital development such as education, science and social services. The ENPI NIP 2011–2013 for Georgia identifies regional development, sustainable economic and social development, and poverty reduction among its priorities. The EU has focused on social reforms and protection, regional and sustainable development, including environmental protection, education, skills development and mobility. As opposed to Armenia, the NIP 2007–2010 for Georgia also listed support for economic development as a priority, with the focus on promoting trade and improving the investment climate.

The EU provides macro-financial assistance to Armenia and Georgia. Both South Caucasus countries currently enjoy preferential access to the EU market via the so-called Generalised Scheme of Preferences plus (GSP+). The EU also supports Armenia and Georgia in attracting investments through the Neighbourhood Investment Facility (NIF), which aims to draw supplementary funding, mainly for infrastructure and supporting small- and medium-sized businesses.

In sum, as Table A.1 (Annex) indicates, in Armenia the EU focuses on elections and state administrative capacity, followed by civil society and socio-economic development, more than on political and civil rights, horizontal accountability and stateness. In Georgia, the EU has primarily focused on socio-economic development and, to a lesser extent, on civil rights, elections, stateness, state administrative capacity and civil society. Political rights and horizontal accountability in Georgia have been addressed to a lesser extent. The effective power to govern has been not given attention in either country.

Explaining the substance of promoted democracy

In order to explain the substance of EU democracy promotion in Armenia and Georgia, this section analyses four factors outlined in the introductory chapter of this volume, namely, power, institutions, domestic structure and interorganizational context.

Power

According to the power-based hypothesis, the substance of EU democracy promotion towards Armenia and Georgia is conditioned by the power distribution between the EU and the targeted countries. In line with a neorealist argument, the EU has stronger economic and military capabilities than Armenia and Georgia; therefore, it is in a better position to advance a broad democracy agenda in both countries, promoting its security interests. Moreover, applying the neoliberal institutionalist approach reveals that Armenia and Georgia are more dependent on the EU across policy sectors than the other way round. Both countries benefit from EU financial aid. The EU is the largest trading partner for both South Caucasus states, which are in a similar position vis-à-vis the EU in terms of power constellation and interdependence.

Although power-based hypotheses are relevant to Armenia and Georgia, this assessment has to be nuanced. In Armenia, the EU faces a powerful Russian presence, whereas in Georgia, the Russian influence (except for Abkhazia and South Ossetia) has considerably weakened after the Rose Revolution and especially following the 2008 war. However, the 'Russian factor' has been very much present in the form of energy, trade and stability/security concerns within the implementation of the EU's democracy promotion in Georgia. Moreover, after the latest parliamentary elections in 2012, the new government has made efforts to normalize relations with Russia.

Institutions

The institutionalist hypothesis states that the substance of democracy promoted by the EU can differ based on the involvement of particular actors, including EU member states, EU supranational or intergovernmental institutions, with their specific preferences and interests (for example security, trade or development). In Armenia and Georgia, the substance of the EU's democracy promotion was dominated by the Directorate General for External Relations (DG Relex) and has been taken over by the EEAS after the enactment of the Lisbon Treaty in 2009. In the post-Lisbon period, the Commissioner responsible for Enlargement and Neighbourhood policy leads the efforts of the Commission, while relying on the EEAS for assistance. The Commission's DG Development and Cooperation (DEVCO) is in charge of implementing projects and DG Trade negotiates the DCFTA with Armenia and Georgia.

Two elements clarify the choice of DG Relex and the EEAS as the leading EU institutions. Firstly, the EU's relationship with Armenia and Georgia is primarily political and aid as well as trade are regarded as rather supplementary to political considerations.[4] Armenia and Georgia are beneficiaries of EU aid, for which the Commission and the EEAS share responsibility. Both partners are 'insignificant' for the EU in terms of trade.⁵ Secondly, there is more than one member state that has an interest in the region. Member states such as Poland, Romania, France and Germany arguably have different templates of democracy promotion. This points to the absence of one dominant template from the member states' side. In sum, Armenia and Georgia are tackled by the same actors from the EU side and the political issues are given a priority.

Domestic structure

The domestic structure explanation assumes that the EU takes into account the domestic constraints and opportunities of a given country where the EU promotes democracy. On the one hand, the EU might 'tailor' its policies taking into consideration the domestic context. The data in Table A.2 (Annex) that is extracted from the BTI represents the 'shortcomings' in Armenia and Georgia, respectively. The BTI 2012, however, does not take account of the parliamentary and presidential elections in Armenia and Georgia.

Georgia has higher scores on the BTI than Armenia in electoral regime, political rights, horizontal accountability and effective power. By contrast, Armenia scores better on stateness. For civil rights, civil society and socio-economic development, the scores are similar. Comparison of the BTI with the findings illustrated in the Table A.1 reveals that the EU focuses on a number of domestic shortcomings (for example electoral regime, socio-economic development), and to a lesser extent on others (for example political rights, horizontal accountability), in implementation of its democracy promotion in Armenia and Georgia. Georgia does well in terms of elections but the EU still pays focused attention to this issue, while horizontal accountability and political rights, which are assessed as worse, receive less EU attention. In Armenia, where horizontal accountability and political rights receive a very poor assessment, the EU still pays only limited attention. In other components, 'deficiencies' and 'attention' seem to fit better: for example elections in Armenia; socio-economic development, stateness and state administrative capacity in Georgia.

Both Armenia and Georgia pursue a European integration agenda. However, since the Rose Revolution, Georgia has been more open towards EU democracy promotion than Armenia, both in terms of domestic enthusiasm and acceptance. The 'inconsistencies' in the substance of the democracy that is promoted are due to the difference in the degree of political will of the respective governments since the substance is tailored by the EU based on the consensus between the EU on the one hand, and Armenia and Georgia on the other hand.

Interorganizational context

The interorganizational context also has relevance in both the Armenian and the Georgian cases, especially with regard to the electoral regime. In practice, the EU is not in charge of election observation in the region and has an arrangement with the OSCE, whose Office for Democratic Institutions and Human Rights (ODIHR) takes the lead in electoral observations in the OSCE member states. However, besides the ODIHR, the International Election Observation Mission (IEOM) includes the OSCE Parliamentary Assembly, the Parliamentary Assembly of the Council of Europe (PACE) and the European Parliament. EU leaders systematically base their statements on the findings of the ODIHR reports. Moreover, UN agencies and the Organisation for Economic Co-operation and Development (OECD) cooperate with the EU through implementation of the TAIEX, Twinning and SIGMA programmes designed to strengthen, among other things, administrative capacity. The EU also issued a joint statement with the US in relation to the Georgian government's crackdown on demonstrations in 2009.

Conclusion

This chapter has analysed the substance of EU democracy promotion in Armenia and Georgia. In rhetoric, the EU has consistently taken a wide-ranging approach and consistently covered a whole host of areas in its efforts to promote democracy in the two countries. EU documents also promise a differentiation between targeted countries. In reality, although the EU has addressed almost all partial regimes and external conditions in both Armenia and Georgia – albeit to a different degree – it has not been consistent. The EU's democracy promotion in Armenia and Georgia tends towards a shallow agenda and its content can be conceptualized as a combination of partial liberal and external conditions democracy promotion.

This study has also attempted to explain the substance of EU-promoted democracy in Armenia and Georgia through evaluating power-based, institutionalist, domestic structure and interorganizational context hypotheses. The EU has a dominant position vis-à-vis Armenia and Georgia in terms of power distribution. Both targeted countries are also dependent on the EU more than vice versa. On the one hand, these two variables enable the EU to advance a broad democracy agenda in both countries. On the other hand, the EU is not the only player in town and has to factor in a Russian presence.

While testing the institutionalist hypothesis, this analysis found that the Commission's ex-DG DG Relex previously took a lead in promoting democracy in Armenia and Georgia. After the enactment of the Lisbon Treaty, the EEAS replaced DG Relex as the dominant EU institution providing an important 'background template'. The Commission's DG DEVCO and DG Trade, as well as the Commissioner responsible for the ENP, also play an important role. From the side of the member states, there are multiple approaches, and therefore a dominant template is absent. In sum, the institutions are not a decisive factor in shaping the substance of democracy promotion towards Georgia and Armenia, because otherwise the substance should have been more or less identical between the two cases.

The domestic structures hypothesis also holds explanatory power with regard to the substance of EU-promoted democracy in Armenia and Georgia, with the domestic acceptance of EU-promoted democracy being an important condition. The EU has put great focus on election monitoring in Armenia and on socio-economic development in Georgia, which are problematic areas. However, the EU has focused less on political rights and horizontal accountability, which are equally problematic in both countries. Therefore, the substance of the EU's democracy promotion entirely reflects neither the objective deficiencies as identified by the BTI nor the subjectively perceived deficiencies as outlined in EU assessments.

Finally, the interorganizational context hypothesis also has some relevance to the substance of the EU's democracy promotion in Armenia and Georgia. However, it is mostly limited to election observation, where the OSCE's ODIHR leads the effort, with the EU covering the costs and participating in observations through some representatives of the European Parliament. Besides cooperating with the OSCE on election observation, the EU also cooperates with the UN agencies and the OECD in the implementation of the TAIEX, Twinning and SIGMA programmes.

Notes

1. Interview, European Union, 16 January 2013.
2. Interview, European External Action Service, 16 January 2013.
3. Interview, European External Action Service, 18 January 2013.
4. Interview, European Union, 26 January 2012.
5. Interview, European Union, 26 January 2012.

11
Democracy Through the Invisible Hand? Egypt and Tunisia

Vicky Reynaert

Introduction

The establishment of democracy is one of the objectives of the European Union (EU) within the framework of the Euro-Mediterranean Partnership (EMP; established 1995), the Union for the Mediterranean (UfM; established in 2008) and the European Neighbourhood Policy (ENP; established in 2003), the policies designed by the EU to guide its relations with its southern Mediterranean neighbours. In the 1990s, however, the EU hardly focused on the promotion of democracy and human rights, despite the high hopes created by the EMP. This changed in 2002, when the United Nations Development Programme (UNDP) published its first Arab Human Development Report (UNDP 2002). This report, which showed that the Arab region fell considerably below the world average on issues such as democracy and human rights, triggered the European Commission to give a new impetus to the promotion of democratic values in the Mediterranean region. This led to greater (although still limited) attention being paid to democracy and human rights in the EU's policy towards the region. However, this renewed attention to the political situation in the Mediterranean countries did not lead to significant changes in the domestic context of those countries. Following the demonstrations and revolutions of the spring of 2011, the EU reflected on how it could contribute more to the evolution towards democracy in the region. These reflections eventually led to an adaptation of the ENP and to new initiatives regarding democratic governance (European Commission and High Representative 2011b, European Commission 2013c).

150 *Cases: Egypt and Tunisia*

Although the role of the EU as a democracy promoter has been a subject of scholarly interest, there has been less attention to the substance of democracy that the EU furthers in the Mediterranean. Michelle Pace (2009: 45–9) indicates that the EU promotes a 'European-style liberal democracy' in the region, based on the EU's own model and on its democratization strategy for Central and Eastern European countries, but she does not go deeper into what exactly this entails. This chapter therefore examines which of the four context conditions and five partial regimes of an embedded liberal democracy (set out in the introductory chapter of this volume) the EU has been promoting in Egypt and Tunisia, before and after the Arab Spring (2003–2012). The substance of EU democracy promotion in both countries will be studied (see summary in Table A.1, Annex) through an analysis of both the discourse in declaratory documents such as Action Plans and Country Strategy Papers (CSPs) and the implementation of its policy through Common Foreign and Security Policy (CFSP) statements, the financial assistance as laid down in the National Indicative Programmes (NIPs) and budget lines such as the European Instrument for Democracy and Human Rights (EIDHR) (Ashton 2010a, 2011b, 2011c, 2013, Ashton and Füle 2011, Council of the European Union 2004, 2005a, 2005b, 2006, European Commission 2001c, 2001d, 2001e, 2003d, 2004d, 2004e, 2006g, 2006h, 2010i, 2010j, 2013c, 2013d, n.d.b, European Commission and High Representative 2011b, 2011d, European Union 2012b, 2012c). Egypt and Tunisia are chosen as cases because they differ with respect to two of the factors which might explain the substance of democracy promotion, that is, the power of the EU towards the third country and the domestic context. Overall, the EU has more power over Tunisia than over Egypt for economic reasons. In addition, the domestic context also differs. Before the Arab Spring, Egypt was, for example, more tolerant towards civil society organizations (CSOs) than Tunisia. Both countries were also confronted with a regime change after the Arab Spring, so it is possible to study the EU's discourse and look for similarities and differences. The chapter will examine whether the difference in these factors is consistent with the difference in the substance the EU is promoting in each country. It can be expected that the EU will pursue a broader agenda of democracy promotion in Tunisia because it has more power, and the interests of the EU towards the country will also have to be taken into account. Alternatively, it can be expected that the EU will pursue a broader agenda of democracy promotion in Egypt because the political will of the government is stronger than in Tunisia.

Vicky Reynaert 151

The substance of EU democracy promotion in Egypt and Tunisia

The promotion of the external context conditions

Although the EU pursues several objectives in its relations with the Mediterranean countries, its main goal, even following the Arab Spring, is the integration of those countries in its internal market (European Commission 2003d). Therefore, according to the EU's goals, the southern neighbours need to be transformed into market-based economies through economic liberalization. Analysis of the 'Mesures d'Accompagnement Financières et Techniques' (MEDA) programme (1995–2006) and the European Neighbourhood and Partnership Instrument (ENPI; 2007–2013), the EU's main budget lines for the Mediterranean region, shows that the highest share of the financial assistance between 2002 and 2013 was devoted to economic liberalization: 40.6 per cent of the budget in the case of Egypt and 62.1 per cent in the case of Tunisia (projects promoting free trade, privatization and the reform of the private sector; European Commission 2001c, 2001d, 2006g, 2006h, 2010i, 2010j). In addition, research has found that the EU has used MEDA (2002–2006) and the ENPI (2007–2010) as mechanisms to reward countries that have implemented economic reforms such as the development of market-based competition or the recognition of private property and companies, and which combine this with good economic performance. Therefore, Tunisia received a high amount of aid per capita per year in comparison with, for example, Egypt, despite its low democratic performance. Tunisia has a high score on the Bertelsmann Transformation Indices 'development of market-based competition' and 'good economic performance' in both periods, in comparison with Egypt. In addition, the fight against corruption was identified as a sufficient condition for receiving financial assistance (this was the case with Tunisia between 2002 and 2006). Other elements such as the ability of the country's citizens to participate in elections, the freedom of expression, association or the quality of the rule of law, did not play a decisive role (Reynaert 2011b). The geographical budget of the EU was mainly used as an instrument to promote economic liberalization, and thus to support the development of the market. According to the EU, this would lead to socio-economic development, stability and security (European Commission 2003d: 4). Between 2002 and 2013, the EU also provided financial assistance for education, although this assistance was mainly linked to labour market requirements, especially in Tunisia, but also in Egypt. In Egypt, there was, in general, more attention paid towards socio-economic balancing than in Tunisia (with, for example, financial assistance also for public health; European Commission 2001c, 2001d, 2006g, 2006h). Overall, it can be concluded that the EU assigned focused attention to the socio-economic context in Egypt, and some attention to the socio-economic context in Tunisia.

The focus on economic liberalization also has consequences for the EU's support for the state's administrative capacity. Closer examination of the financial assistance shows that the EU supported the reform of the state in both Tunisia and Egypt if it was reformed to support the functioning of the free market and to stimulate trade. The EU supported the reform of the state in Tunisia in order to optimize the market economy, to reduce the administrative barriers for the private sector and to make it possible to implement the National Action Plan Tunisia has concluded with the EU (where the main objective is the integration of the country in the EU's internal market; European Commission 2001d: 21, 2006h: 28). This is also the case in Egypt. Its CSP 2007–2013 mentions that 'modernization and development of public services, including improvement of good governance and measures to combat corruption and encourage transparency of public finance are major priorities for Egypt' (European Commission 2006g: 21). It is important to note that this kind of aid for the state's administrative capacity is often referred to as aid for 'good governance'. Although the EU defines 'good governance' rather broadly in its policy documents, including support for the democratization process, respect for human rights and fundamental freedoms and respect for the rule of law (European Commission n.d.b), it applies a rather narrow definition when it comes to the programming of aid in the Mediterranean region. The focus here is mainly on the efficiency of public administration and the absence of fraud and corruption. In contrast to this focused attention on the state administrative capacity in both Egypt and Tunisia, there was no attention paid to stateness.

Overall, the main objective of the EU's policy towards the Mediterranean region has not changed following the Arab Spring: the goal is still to integrate the Mediterranean neighbours into the EU internal market. Consequently, the promotion of the reform of state administrative capacity also still receives focused attention. In the discourse, the main task of the state is still presented as facilitating access to the EU internal market. Therefore, the state needs to be reformed. Reform of the state is also needed to address security: 'A key element in this [mobility between the EU and the neighbours] is the strengthening of capacity building in the Mediterranean countries on borders/migration/asylum and more effective law enforcement cooperation to improve security throughout the Mediterranean' (European Commission and High Representative 2011b: 6–8). In this regard, there is no real change in comparison with the discourse before the Arab Spring. Nevertheless, in addition to this, the European Commission and the High Representative now argue that these reforms of the state will lead not only to economic development and security, but also to more democracy. In their communication, they state:

> To support democratic transformation, Comprehensive Institution-Building Programmes similar to those implemented with its Eastern neighbours will be set up: they will provide substantial expertise and financial support to build the capacity of key administrative bodies (customs, enforcement agencies, justice) and will be targeted in priority towards those institutions most needed to sustain democratisation.
> (European Commission & High Representative 2011b: 16–17)

However, research has shown that this reform of the state will not necessarily lead to more democracy (Reynaert 2011a: 630).

In contrast to the support for the development of a market economy and state administrative capacity, the EU's support for CSOs played a less important role. A closer examination of the CSPs and NIPs reveals that the EU supported the development of a civil society in both Egypt and Tunisia under MEDA and the ENPI, although far more money went to Egypt than to Tunisia. In Egypt, the EU promoted 'the more effective involvement of civil society in social development' (2002–2006; European Commission 2001c) and the involvement of civil society in the democratic, political, economic and social process. Special attention was paid to the strengthening of the role of CSOs involved in the protection of the environment (2007–2010; European Commission 2006g: 29). In Tunisia, the EU supported a project in order to 'reinforce the civil society' (2002–2006; European Commission 2001d: 38). Tanja Börzel, who examined MEDA, concluded that the support for civil society in the Mediterranean region is first of all a matter of increasing effectiveness (of the public administration) rather than of democratic participation, stating that 'the MEDA assistance programme is largely oriented towards increasing output legitimacy' (2009: 25). Besides the MEDA programme, the EU also used another budget line to support CSOs in the Mediterranean region, that is, the EIDHR. However, research has shown that the EU had serious difficulties supporting CSOs in the Mediterranean countries (and especially in Tunisia) and that it therefore mainly promoted CSOs in the least authoritarian regimes (Israel, the West Bank and Gaza, and Morocco; Karktuli and Bützler 1999: 3). The research of Federica Bicchi (2009) indicates that the EU anticipated the problems that promotion of civil society in the Mediterranean region would bring, and therefore reduced the scope of the financial assistance. This was, for example, the case in Tunisia, where the EU Delegation issued no call for microproject proposals between 2005 and 2007 (Bicchi 2009: 69, 75–6). Consequently, no projects were funded. By contrast, in Egypt, the EU Delegation stuck to the priorities as defined in the EIDHR programming documents in Brussels, and it opened the call for all civil companies in order to circumvent the Egyptian legislation, which requires registration of CSOs (Bicchi 2009: 67). This led to more projects being funded by the EU in Egypt.

In the EU's proposal for a 'new' neighbourhood policy published in May 2011, the creation of a 'partnership of societies' is seen as an important element in the creation of 'deep democracy'. In the new strategy of the EU towards civil society, it is stated that civil society plays 'a pivotal role in advancing women's rights, greater social justice and respect for minorities as well as environmental protection and resource efficiency', and that the EU will help civil society to develop 'their advocacy capacity, their ability to monitor reform and their role in implementing and evaluating EU programmes' (European Commission and High Representative 2011a: 4). In 2011, the EU established a Neighbourhood Civil Society Facility to achieve this objective. The reference to the role of CSOs in monitoring reform and implementing EU programmes indicates that the EU mainly seems to focus on output-oriented tasks. In the previous document on the establishment of a partnership, the European Commission and the High Representative (2011b) indicated that they also wanted to strengthen the social dialogue through a 'social dialogue forum'. Although it seems the EU now also wants to promote the input-oriented tasks of civil society, this should be put into perspective. The main objective of the organization of this social dialogue is to sustain the reform efforts the EU is promoting in the Mediterranean region (which can be seen as part of the implementing task). In other words, civil society has to contribute to the legitimation of the market reforms the EU is promoting.

The promotion of the partial regimes

The EU's support for the electoral regime in both Egypt and Tunisia in the past was very limited, in fact almost non-existent. The EU issued CFSP statements regarding elections in Egypt and Tunisia, but it was always very careful in its criticism of the regimes of Mubarak and Ben Ali. In the case of Tunisia, it issued a declaration in 2004 congratulating Ben Ali 'with his new term as President', and 'encouraging the authorities of Tunisia to continue to improve the framework for elections and to take the necessary steps to ensure that the next elections fully meet international standards. The EU stands ready to offer, in the spirit of Partnership, its assistance in this respect' (Council of the European Union 2004). In 2009, when parliamentary and presidential elections were held again, the EU issued no declaration. In the case of Egypt, the EU made similar declarations as in the case of Tunisia: congratulating Mubarak, expressing its concerns about irregularities, encouraging the government to make further improvements and offering help, electoral assistance or an EU observation mission (Council of the European Union 2005a, Ashton 2010a). However, it is only possible to find one project that actually supported the development of an electoral regime, in the CSP of Egypt for the period 2007–2013. One of the main components of the project was 'to support the government in reforming the electoral system by increasing public participation in political life, revising the voters' list and reviewing the legislative and administrative frameworks' (European Commission 2006h: 28). In addition to MEDA and the ENPI, the EU also had a separate budget line to support elections in third countries. The EU can also send an election observation mission. One of the main criteria is that the governments have to ask for the assistance of the EU with the organization of their elections. Since most of the Mediterranean countries were authoritarian regimes, the EU did not receive many requests for support. Exceptions were Lebanon and the Occupied Palestinian Territories. Since the Arab Spring of 2011, the EU has focused on elections more. It issued several statements about the elections in Tunisia (Ashton 2011b, Ashton and Füle 2011) and Egypt (European Union 2012b, 2012c). Following the Arab Spring, the EU also launched a 'Partnership for Democracy and Shared Prosperity'. In order to benefit from this partnership, the Mediterranean countries are required to hold monitored, free and fair elections (European Commission and High Representative 2011b). This shows a new focus of the EU on the electoral regime, which according to the EU will be used as a rewards-based conditionality mechanism. In the case of Tunisia, immediately after the revolution the EU offered support for the establishment of an appropriate legal framework, which was accepted by the Tunisian National Commission for Constitutional Reform and Elections. In addition, it sent an EU election observation mission, which monitored the elections. In the case of Egypt, the EU provided €2 million to support the organization of elections and it offered to send an EU election observation mission. However, the Supreme Council of Armed Forces (SCAF) declined the offer, as it initially did not want any international observers to monitor the elections. Later on, the European External Action Service (EEAS) eventually sent two electoral experts to assess the conduct of the presidential elections in May–June 2012 (who found that the elections had been fair; European Commission 2013c). In conclusion, we can state that since the Arab Spring, there is more attention paid to elections in the discourse of the EU, but that this does not necessarily imply active support for elections on the ground, as the Egyptian case has shown.

When we look at the support for political and civil rights in Egypt and Tunisia, it is clear that the EU's attention has been rather limited. In Tunisia, we only found one CFSP statement, about the obstruction of the activities of the 'Ligue Tunisienne pour la Défense des Droits de l'Homme', which promotes and protects human rights in the country (Council of the European Union 2005b). Between 2002 and 2013, the EU supported only one project, that is, the development of independent media (European Commission 2001c). In Egypt, there was more attention paid to these objectives, especially after the country established the National Council for Human Rights in 2003. In a reaction to this, the EU gave more assistance for human rights (both political and civil rights: freedom of association, expression, opinion, and the rights of women and children) between 2005 and 2013 (European Commission 2001d, 2004e, 2006h, 2010j). In 2006, it issued a CFSP statement in which it expressed its concern about the measures that the Egyptian authorities had taken against civil society activists (Council of the European Union 2006). The EU also supported political and civil rights through the EIDHR. As mentioned earlier, no microprojects were funded between 2002 and 2007 in Tunisia. In Egypt, there were some projects, but this support principally went to organizations working on the rights of women and children, rather than to organizations working on more controversial civil and political rights, such as those relating to torture (Bicchi 2009: 71–2). This was the case for all Mediterranean countries. The main reason for this bias is that in the context of the EIDHR, there were far more applications from CSOs for projects on children's and women's rights as there was a higher chance that these would be accepted by the authoritarian regimes. However, the EU also did not stimulate support for civil and political rights or political parties through the definition of thematic priorities through its EIDHR policy.

Following the Arab Spring, the EU stated that it wanted to focus more on the strengthening of human rights, and especially on gender equality, discrimination, freedom of religion and the protection of the rights of refugees and beneficiaries of international protection, and therefore that it would strengthen the human rights dialogue with partner governments. Media freedom and free access to information are key objectives according to the discourse of the EU. These are and will remain supported through the EIDHR (European Commission and High Representative 2011b, 2011d). In relation to Egypt, the High Representative issued statements on civil rights, especially on women's rights (Ashton 2011c, 2013). In addition, the EU developed a new instrument, which is central to the new EU strategy to create a 'partnership of societies', the European Endowment for Democracy (EED). The EED will support political parties, non-registered non-governmental organizations (NGOs) or trade unions and other social partners, that is, important political rights (European Commission 2011a, 2013d). Overall, it can be concluded that in the discourse of the EU, there is more attention paid to political rights than before the Arab Spring. However, it remains to be seen how the EED functions in reality. It has already proved to be very difficult to gather the necessary funding to make this new instrument operational.

With regard to horizontal accountability, it can be concluded that the EU mainly gave financial assistance to the executive bodies in both Egypt and Tunisia, which have to implement the policies of the government. In addition, there has also been support for the judiciary. The EU provided €30 million for the modernization of the judicial system in Tunisia between 2002 and 2006, and €20 million for the modernization of the administration of justice and the strengthening of the capacity of law enforcement bodies in Egypt between 2007 and 2013. However, the main objective of this kind of support, which is often referred to as support for good governance, is not necessarily to create a system of checks and balances. In the case of Tunisia in the period 2002–2006, the main goal was to support businesses (European Commission 2001d: 19), while in the case of Egypt in the period 2007–2013, the main objective was to enhance security (combating organized crime, money laundering and terrorism, and the management of migration flows; European Commission 2006h: 30). By contrast, minor attention is paid to the legislative bodies in both countries. There is a political dialogue with the members of parliament of Tunisia and Egypt through the Euro-Mediterranean Parliamentary Assembly (EMPA; since 2003) and the joint parliamentary committees between the European Parliament and the parliaments of both countries. Both initiatives were strengthened after the Arab Spring (European Commission 2011b). In conclusion, it can be argued that the EU has not paid attention to horizontal accountability. Moreover, the EU had also not paid attention to the effective power to govern for elected representatives, despite the fact that, especially in Egypt, the army had important decision-making power without being under democratic control.

Based on this analysis (see also summary in Table A.1), it can be concluded that the EU in the Mediterranean region in general, and in Egypt and Tunisia in particular, mainly focuses on the development of a market-based economy. The EU has also focused on state administrative capacity in Egypt and Tunisia. By contrast, the EU did and still does not address stateness. The EU has paid some attention to the development of civil society in Egypt, but almost none in Tunisia. Furthermore, we have found that the support for the electoral regimes in both Mediterranean countries was almost non-existent, although we can state that the EU paid some attention to elections in Egypt. The support for political and civil rights has also been limited, and here, the EU has paid more attention to these rights in Egypt than in Tunisia. The EU has strongly supported the executive bodies and the judiciary, but there has been far less attention paid to legislative bodies. There has been no attention paid to horizontal accountability. In addition, there has been also no attention on the effective power to govern for elected representatives. Overall, it can be concluded that the EU mainly focuses on the context conditions of democracy promotion, and that it thus has a shallow liberal democracy promotion agenda, defined as 'good governance'.

Explaining the substance of EU democracy promotion in Egypt and Tunisia

Institutionalist explanation

The main objective of the EMP, UfM and the ENP is the integration of neighbouring countries in the EU's internal market. The main policy paradigm for making this integration possible is economic liberalization. The European Commission was/is the main architect of the economic component of the EMP and of the ENP and ensures that the strategy of economic liberalization is applied in the neighbouring countries. It drafts the proposals for the development of the ENP, the country reports, the ENP Action Plans, the progress reports, the CSPs and the NIPs and it takes the lead in the determination of the amount of funding a country receives. The member states have far less influence. Since the entering into force of the Lisbon Treaty, the European Commission has to cooperate with the EEAS, but it is still the main institution responsible for the development of the ENP and the programming of financial assistance. In this regard, there is no differentiation between Egypt and Tunisia – they are part of the same sub-system (the ENP).

Domestic explanation

However, this does not mean that the EU promotes the exact same policy in each Mediterranean country. Differentiation and joint ownership are important policy principles within the ENP. In the CSPs, the EU analyses and discusses the policy agenda of the Mediterranean country and their economic, political and social situation. Based on this analysis (but also on the EU's strategic interest; see below), the EU drafts its NIPs. This means that the EU funds different projects in different countries, based on the policy agenda of the Mediterranean government and on what is possible in the country. This explains the differences in democracy promotion between Egypt and Tunisia, such as, for example, the support for political and civil rights. Between 2003 and 2013, the EU focused more on human rights in Egypt than in Tunisia because the Egyptian government had indicated that it wanted to support human rights through the creation of a National Council for Human Rights. A second example is the support for civil society. The research of Bicchi (2009) indicates that the EU Delegations in both countries anticipated the possibility of promoting CSOs in the calls for proposals for microprojects they issued, but whereas no projects were funded in Tunisia, in Egypt several projects received financial assistance. This suggests that the agendas of the Mediterranean countries are taken into account when the European Commission drafts the CSPs and NIPs, and when the EU Delegations issue calls for proposals. The substance of EU democracy promotion is thus also demand-driven, in the sense that it depends on the degree of 'political will' of the government to address certain elements of an embedded liberal democracy. However this still happens within the overall paradigm of the EU, that is, economic liberalization. In addition, it can be argued that the EU does not really address the shortcomings in third countries since there is, for example, no attention paid to the partial regime 'effective power to govern', although this regime is rather problematic in both Egypt and Tunisia.

Power-based explanation

Another important difference in the policy of the EU towards Egypt and Tunisia is that the EU pushes Tunisia more towards the development of a market-based economy by providing more financial assistance, which is used as a rewards-based mechanism. Tunisia implements economic reforms the EU requests because it is economically dependent on the EU. In this regard, the EU has more power over Tunisia than over Egypt. It pushes the development of a market-based economy because this is in its economic interests, but also because it believes that it will lead to more stability and security. However, despite the economic power of the EU over Tunisia, it has been rather reluctant to promote other elements of an embedded liberal democracy, for example the support for civil society. By contrast, it has proved to be more difficult for the EU to promote economic reforms in Egypt, although it has succeeded in promoting some partial regimes of an embedded liberal democracy. In addition, it can be argued that the security interests of the EU have less of an impact on the substance it is promoting in Egypt. Although Egypt plays an important role in the regional stability in the Mediterranean region, and although it is important in terms of the transport of oil towards the EU, this did not prevent the EU from promoting partial regimes of an embedded liberal democracy.

Interorganizational context

From 1989 until 2007, the EU mainly followed the economic paradigm of the World Bank in the Mediterranean region, which was based on economic liberalization. One of the main conditions for receiving financial assistance from the EU under the MEDA programme was to have a structural adjustment programme (SAP) developed or approved by the World Bank. There was thus coordination with the World Bank. This changed in 2003, when the EU developed the ENP. The main goal then became the integration of the Mediterranean countries into the EU internal market. This objective was integrated into the EU's financial assistance in 2007. Since then, the EU has promoted a European economic model. It still promotes the economic liberalization paradigm, as it did between 1989 and 2007, but this paradigm is now linked to the EU internal market instead of to the policy of the World Bank. For the political aspect of its cooperation with the Mediterranean region, and especially human rights, the EU always referred to the international norms and standards of the United Nations. This changed after the Arab Spring, when the EU started to refer to its own history. Since then, it has tried to promote a European political model (Reynaert 2012).

Conclusion

This chapter has found that the main policy paradigm of the EU in the Mediterranean region, and thus in Egypt and Tunisia, is economic liberalization, which in the Union's view should lead to economic development, security, stability and – as added more recently – democracy. Overall, the EU has in both countries focused more on the promotion of the context conditions for democracy, in particular the socio-economic context and state administrative capacity, rather than on the partial regimes, which leads to the conclusion that the EU has a shallow liberal democracy promotion agenda in Egypt and Tunisia, defined as 'good governance'. Within the context of the EU's policy paradigm promoted in the region, there are differences in the substance of democracy the EU is promoting in Egypt and Tunisia. The EU focuses on different aspects in the two countries: in Egypt there is more attention paid to the electoral regime, to political and civil rights, to the promotion of civil society and also to socio-economic balancing than in Tunisia. By contrast, in Tunisia, there is more focus on the development of the market and state administrative capacity than in Egypt. These differences can be explained mainly by the domestic context of the two countries. The degree of political will of the government plays an important role in determining the substance the EU is promoting in both Egypt and Tunisia. In addition, the economic power of the EU over Tunisia and its economic interests also has an influence on the substance of the democracy the EU is promoting in the country. In conclusion, it can be said that in the Mediterranean region, the EU has promoted a European economic model since 2003 and a European political model since 2011.

12
When Security Trumps Democracy: Israel and Palestine

Benedetta Voltolini and Federica Bicchi

As part of the Mediterranean and the Middle East region, Israel and Palestine[1] are among the countries targeted by European Union (EU) policies aimed at democracy promotion. As democracy and human rights are universal values, it is to be expected that every actor in the world should uphold the standards they set, including inside the EU. The local context of Israel and Palestine, however, is particularly ridden with contradictions and plagued by one of the most intractable conflicts in the world, thus raising a set of considerations that, when taken together, present actors promoting democracy with stark choices. As a consequence, the EU has routinely addressed external conditions for democracy more than democracy itself, embracing a shallow liberal democracy promotion agenda due to the local situation of conflict and the related security concerns.

The most prominent feature of this region is latent or ongoing conflict, with the notable but partial exception of the Oslo years (1993–2000). Small- or large-scale violence regularly breaks out in the region. The Gaza Strip has been the main focal point for violence since Israel's withdrawal from Gaza in 2005, but the border with Lebanon has also witnessed recurrent conflicts and small-scale violence, while the West Bank remains under de facto occupation and constant tension. Israel retains a position of dominance that the Palestinians are in no way able to counter, but do continue to challenge. It is thus no surprise that the main concern of the EU vis-à-vis these two countries is the achievement of security, for all the parties involved but also and especially for its own sake, given the history of spillover effects that the conflict has had on European soil and on European citizens. While there are economic considerations at stake, especially in the case of Israel, and these can

162

and often do trump the search for conflict resolution, security trumps democracy in the eyes of European policy-makers.

Moreover, Israel is a modern democracy and one that measures favourably on a number of parameters – apart from the crucial issue of minorities' protection. According to Freedom House's index measuring political rights and civil liberties, Israel is considered a free country, the only one with this score in the Middle East (Freedom House 2013). Despite this positive assessment, the link made between the Jewish and democratic nature of Israel raises serious doubts concerning the situation of minorities, who are excluded from this definition of statehood. Indeed, the Jewish nature of Israel tends to be prioritized over its democratic features. The Arab minority does not enjoy the same rights as the Jewish Israeli citizens and it is portrayed as a security and demographic threat (Tocci and Voltolini 2011).[2] Therefore, the gist of external democracy promotion actions towards Israel tends to be directed towards this aspect.

For its part, despite its success at the United Nations General Assembly in November 2012, where it was recognized as a 'non-member observer state', Palestine lacks the main attributes of a state and remains under foreign occupation. There is little doubt that any activity aimed at promoting democracy is hampered by the lack of stateness, defined as 'the ability of the state to pursue the monopoly of legitimate physical force' (see the introductory chapter). As Linz and Stepan (1996a: 14) put it, '[n]o state, no democracy'. It is true that the vast majority of countries in the Middle East lack established and internationally recognized borders, as at least part of the border tends to be contested. But this has not stopped countries such as Morocco, for instance, from developing the attributes of stateness. In the case of Palestine, instead, there are multiple centres of power and major fractures in its territorial dimension, most notably in the split between the West Bank and the Gaza Strip. Hamas has been de facto ruling in the Gaza Strip since 2007 and the EU has followed the US in boycotting and then blacklisting Hamas since it won the elections in 2006. In the West Bank, the administrative capacities of the Palestinian Authority (PA) have been beefed up under the leadership of Salam Fayyad, but the debate is very much open about the PA's capacity to 'command, regulate, and extract' (Linz and Stepan 1996a: 11) under occupation. The occupation also deeply affects the socio-economic context in Palestine, limiting the potential for economic growth and the potential for participation in social, economic and political processes.

The conflict, therefore, affects the main external supporting conditions of democracy, as well as the chances of democratic developments in the two countries. It acts as a catalyst for the attention of international actors aiming to support democratic developments in the region. As a rule, the EU, like other external (and internal) players, has tended to address democracy as a second-order consideration, with security and occasionally economic interests taking priority instead. The EU is not devoid of power over the two countries. On the contrary, it potentially wields a large set of economic instruments to prod and cajole them. But the politics of the local conflict has long since engulfed the regional and international dynamics too, limiting the leeway both external and internal actors have.

After describing the EU's approach to Israel and Palestine, this chapter addresses two key issues related to democracy promotion, namely, minority rights in Israel and the EU's reaction to the Hamas victory at the 2006 elections. The chapter then zooms in on a set of projects by definition targeting democracy and human rights, funded under the European Instrument for Democracy and Human Rights (EIDHR). It then deals with competing explanations that attempt to account for the EU's shallow democracy promotion agenda towards Israel and Palestine, before concluding with a few general remarks.

EU democracy promotion in Israel and Palestine

EU democracy promotion policies towards Israel and Palestine rely on a wide range of instruments, including both direct and indirect tools. Moreover, the EU's approach relies on positive conditionality, while negative measures are rarely implemented due to the EU's idea that cooperation and inclusion are more conducive to progress than exclusion (Pace 2010). Against this backdrop, the instruments and policies employed by the EU in the case of Israel and Palestine are declaratory diplomacy, financial assistance and cooperation. EU declarations in support of democratic values and condemning those actions that it does not approve of are frequent, and generally made by the High Representative Catherine Ashton. At the same time, the relationships between the EU and Israel/Palestine are framed by the Barcelona Process/Euro-Mediterranean Partnership (EMP) and the European Neighbourhood Policy (ENP). The ENP represents the legal and policy framework within which EU relations with and policies towards the Mediterranean countries develop. In addition to these geographical and institutional frameworks, the EU can also use some thematic instruments, such as the EIDHR (see Section 3) or the Civil Society Facility, to promote democracy in Israel and Palestine.

The Association Agreements, signed by the EU and each partner of the Barcelona Process, define the contractual and legally binding context in which relationships and policies take place. Democracy is one of the key aspects of these agreements, as Article 2 of the Association Agreements requires the parties to respect democratic principles and human rights. This clause is an essential component, so that its violation can lead to the suspension of the Association Agreement. Yet, this leverage has never been used by the EU, which still prefers a policy of positive conditionality and engagement with the parties, even when human rights are violated. Complementary to the Barcelona Process, the ENP promotes specific objectives and programmes, agreed between the EU and each of its partners. These Action Plans are aimed at fostering reforms in each country and at increasing cooperation with the EU. Mentions of democracy are also made in the ENP Action Plans, which normally devote an entire section to discussing not only the promotion of democratic values but also some policies or key issues that the third country needs to tackle. The EMP and the ENP entail programmes for state-capacity building, such as the modernization of police, administration, the judicial sector and, in some cases, elections (Huber 2008).

While these broad policy frameworks target the state, the EU can also use some thematic instruments. In particular, the EIDHR is aimed at promoting democracy and human rights in the world. It complements the EMP and the ENP by favouring a bottom-up approach which targets and supports civil society actors. Without requiring any consent from the state, the EIDHR funds projects promoted by civil society actors that deal with human rights and democracy, in the belief that the latter can work as controllers of the state and as loci for interest articulation. This idea is also reflected in a more recent thematic instrument called the Neighbourhood Civil Society Facility, which was created for the period 2011–2013 as a consequence of the changes in the neighbourhood and a review process of the ENP. The instrument is aimed at supporting and strengthening civil society, which is seen as the vehicle for further democratization and a necessary condition for democratic reforms to take place. However, the budget of €22 million is very modest, with Israel and the Palestinians receiving €500,000 and €400,000 respectively in 2011, both €500,000 in 2012, and €500,000 and €900,000 in 2013.[3]

Within these institutional and policy frameworks, EU policies target different aspects in Israel and Palestine. In the case of Israel, the main objective of the ENP is to 'gradually integrate the country into European policies and programmes'. Although there is a reference to the 'shared values, including issues such as the promotion and the protection of human rights and fundamental freedoms' and the role of dialogue between the EU and Israel to solve the Arab–Israeli conflict, special attention has been paid to the development and strengthening of economic relations (EU/Israel 2005). This has led to the intensification of cooperation in several policy areas and the signing of numerous agreements, such as an Agreement on Agriculture and Fishery in 2009, and the Agreement on Conformity Assessment and Acceptance of Industrial Products in 2012.

Under the European Neighbourhood Policy Instrument (ENPI), Israel was allocated €14 million for the period 2007–2013 (European Commission 2007h: 2), which is an extremely small amount when compared to the funds received by other countries in the region. For example, between 2007 and 2010 Egypt was allocated €558 million (European Commission 2006g: 3) and Tunisia €300 million (European Commission 2006h: 0, see also Reynaert's chapter). As Huber (2008) stresses, financial support to Israel is mainly meant to improve administration or other state-related functions. The money is mainly spent on activities under the Twinning and Technical Assistance and Information Exchange (TAIEX) instruments. While Twinnings are long-term projects in which EU member states experts work with their Israeli counterparts in order to implement and harmonize EU regulations, TAIEX projects are short-term and meant to help Israel to approximate, apply and enforce EU legislation, as provided for in the ENP Action Plan. For instance, recent Twinning projects have covered equal employment opportunities and telecommunications, while TAIEX activities were focused on transport, data protection and equal opportunities.

Despite rhetorical attempts at linking the bilateral relationship with Israel to its broader policy towards the conflict, concrete steps in this direction have not been taken. As Nathalie Tocci (2007, 2010) points out, the EU has not employed its potential to exert influence on Israel, refraining from implementing any form of negative conditionality. Instead of the 'stick' contained in Article 2 of the Association Agreement, the EU has preferred to engage in positive conditionality and dialogue with Israel. Therefore, condemnations of Israeli policies, such as settlement construction or bills aimed at curbing non-governmental organizations' (NGO) freedom of expression, have been the issue of declarations by the High Representative Catherine Ashton, or on the agenda of EU–Israeli bilateral meetings in Committees and Working Groups established under the Association Agreement. Yet, these instruments have been proven rather ineffective in addressing Israel's democratic credentials with regard to its policies in the Occupied Territories as well as internally towards the Arab Israeli minority.[4]

Similarly, concerns for democracy promotion in Palestine have been limited (Pogodda 2012). The focus has traditionally been on security issues and state-building, with the notable exception of the period 2002–2006 when the Western countries aimed at curtailing Arafat's power by multiplying the sources of authority and decision-making in the PA. Indeed, building state administrative capacity has not always been accompanied by similar measures in terms of stateness. Moreover, little attention has been given to the partial regimes addressing civil liberties, political rights, the separation of powers and elections (see the introductory chapter).

This became evident after the electoral victory of Hamas in 2006. The short parenthesis in 2002–2006, during which the EU's policies aimed to create the position of prime minister, to reform the security sector and modify the procedures for channelling foreign aid, was abandoned in favour of the so-called 'West Bank First' policy. The Gaza Strip, under the control of Hamas, has been ignored since then, only being addressed in terms of humanitarian assistance and aid. The EU's democracy promotion efforts have been directed at the West Bank, supporting the three-year Palestinian Reform and Development Plan launched by the PA in 2008. On the basis of the priorities indicated by the PA in the plan, the EU invested in the four main programme areas, namely, governance, social development, economic and private sector development, and public infrastructure development. At the same time, EU efforts have also been made in the reform of the security sector in the West Bank through the Common Security and Defence Policy (CSDP) mission EUPOL COPPS, whose goal has been to contribute to the establishment of police forces and to advise them on issues of criminal justice or related to rule of law.

Although democracy promotion policies in both countries have been meant to contribute to the establishment of both partial regimes and external conditions, they have been inextricably linked with the Israeli–Palestinian conflict and security concerns. The promotion of external conditions and of partial regimes has been considered in the light of security narratives, that is, a set of assumption that policy-makers use to reduce uncertainty (Pogodda 2012). This leads to evident contradictions in the substance promoted and in failed attempts to put flesh on the bones of EU democracy promotion policies. The 'West Bank First' approach clearly exemplifies this. The support of the EU has contributed to creating the basic conditions of control over the West Bank, which are sufficient to guarantee Israeli security and strengthen the position of the PA as partner in the peace process (or what remains of it). Democracy has always been interpreted through the lenses of the conflict. The EU has therefore turned a blind eye to the non-democratic features of the Abbas government and of Israel due to conflict-related concerns.

Democracy promotion 'à la carte'

The EU's democracy promotion agenda has mainly been framed through the conflict-related lens so that security concerns have trumped more democracy-oriented efforts. This has also led the EU to focus more on the external conditions of stateness, state administrative capacity, civil society, and social and economic requisites, instead of promoting the partial regimes. This is particularly evident in the cases of minority rights in Israel and Hamas's election in Palestine.

The Arab minority in Israel

The case of the Arab minority is an interesting aspect that shows how the EU promotes democracy selectively when it comes to Israel. Since the adoption of the ENP Action Plan, the Commission has judged as unsatisfactory and discriminatory the situation of Arab Israeli citizens as far as land allocation, planning, housing, access to justice, services and education are concerned, and has therefore asked Israel to redress these discriminatory policies (European Commission 2006i, 2008i, 2009g, 2010k). Not only has negative conditionality (via Article 2 of the Association Agreement) never been used to tackle this problem, but EU declaratory policies have also been largely silent on this aspect. The EU has generally avoided dealing with Israel's internal affairs and has preferred to concentrate its declaratory efforts on conflict-related problems and the violations of human rights in the Occupied Territories (Tocci and Voltolini 2011, Euro-Mediterranean Human Rights Network 2011). The issue of the Arab minority is discussed in the EU–Israel informal working group on human rights, but the EU has limited power to monitor Israel's performance in this regard, especially given the informal nature of the setting of discussions. Indirectly, the EU tends to promote minority rights via the EIDHR. By supporting civil society projects that deal with the political and civil rights of disadvantaged sectors of the population such as Arab Israeli citizens, the EU aims to empower local actors and use them to promote some of the partial regimes of its embedded liberal democracy (see Section 3).

Yet, EU policy towards the Arab minority remains quite weak (Tocci and Voltolini 2011). The EU is aware of the situation of the Arab minority, but it has not used its policy tools to address this aspect, for two main reasons. On the one hand, the EU adopts a conflict-related perspective when it comes to Israel. Security concerns dominate and trump EU policies of democracy promotion, as minority issues are disentangled from the conflict, although they are a direct consequence of the 1948 war. In this case, the EU prefers not to antagonize Israel on this topic, in the hope that it will cooperate in the resolution of the conflict, thus missing a key opportunity to develop a proactive policy of democracy promotion. A second reason for avoiding the issue of minority rights is linked to the vague legal status that minority rights have in international and EU law (see Kochenov's chapter for a different approach). Not only are minority rights poorly specified, but there is also no consensus on what they entail, which in turn allows for inconsistent practices among EU member states (Hughes and Sasse 2003, De Witte 2011). Therefore, dealing with minority rights in Israel is seen as opening a 'Pandora's box', with all the uncertainties and security risks that would follow.

The 2006 elections and Hamas's victory

Another key issue where we identify a predominance of conflict-related concerns over democracy promotion efforts is in the domain of elections. Although the EU states that 'elections are an essential basis for sustainable development and a functioning democracy' and it is committed to supporting 'the right to participate in genuine elections' through 'electoral assistance projects and EU election observation missions' (Europa 2013a), the 2006 elections in Palestine provide a different picture. At the invitation of the PA, the EU carried out electoral observation missions on the occasions of the general elections in 1996, of the 2005 presidential elections and of the 2006 parliamentary elections. During the last of these, Hamas obtained the majority of votes in the parliament and was therefore in charge of forming the new government. Although the EU's electoral mission declared the elections fair, transparent and free, the EU did not recognize the Hamas-led government, bowing to the American and Israeli pressure. The Quartet declared that 'all members of a future Palestinian government must be committed to non-violence, recognition of Israel, and acceptance of previous agreement and obligations, including the Roadmap'. It also added the possibility of using negative conditionality in the form of withdrawal of aid, if these principles were not respected by the government (Middle

East Quartet 2006, Tocci 2011). Due to this stance and on the basis of the inclusion of Hamas on the EU's terrorist list in 2003, the EU froze its financial assistance to the PA and suspended its CSDP mission EUPOL COPPS until Hamas agreed on the Quartet's conditions, which Hamas was not prepared to do. A policy of non-engagement (at least formally) followed, thus leading the PA to the brink of collapse. Humanitarian assistance via the United Nations Relief and Works Agency (UNRWA) and the Temporary International Mechanism continued to deliver aid, but it bypassed Hamas and was delivered directly to the population. While the intention of Fatah and Hamas to form a National Unity Government in 2007 seemed to open the possibility of engaging again with Palestine, the takeover of the Gaza Strip by Hamas in 2007 led the Quartet to the adoption of the 'West Bank First' approach, namely, a policy of engagement with the Fatah-led government in the West Bank and a progressive isolation of the Hamas-governed Gaza Strip.

This example shows how the declared substance of EU democracy promotion can change in the implementation phase. While supporting the elections in the Occupied Territories and confirming their regular development, the EU was not willing to accept the results in the light of perceived security concerns and mounting pressure from the US and Israel to boycott Hamas (Gunning 2010). Again, the conflict between Israel and Palestine shapes and determines the content and effectiveness of all other EU policies, which are subordinated to local dynamics.

Zooming-in: The EIDHR

The EU has also developed a thematic instrument aimed at the promotion of democracy and human rights, the EIDHR, which provides direct support for civil society, without requiring the formal authorization of the third country's government to be implemented. By adopting a bottom-up approach, the EU addresses one of the context conditions (civil society) of embedded liberal democracy. While support for civil society is a potentially fruitful way to promote democracy, criticisms have been raised as to the effectiveness of the EIDHR in really pushing for implanting democratic features in third countries, especially in the Mediterranean and the Middle East regions. Human rights projects have often been preferred to activities aimed at challenging authoritarian governments in power (Youngs 2003). For example, in 2002–2006, the EU supported human rights projects in uncontroversial issues such as women's and children's rights, and it avoided funding initiatives on torture (Bicchi 2009, 2010). As Ottaway (2005: 116) argues, '[a]n

Benedetta Voltolini and Federica Bicchi 171

improvement in the rights of women does not threaten the power of the incumbent authoritarian government in the same way as free elections or a free press would'.

More specifically, one of the objectives of the EIDHR, the Country-Based Support Scheme (CBSS), is of particular interest, as it is entirely run by the EU Delegations, which are in charge of issuing the calls, selecting the projects and controlling their implementation. They can therefore tailor the calls for proposals according to the needs and the shortcomings of the country concerned. Moreover, they are largely directed at local actors, thus limiting competition from larger, Western NGOs. Both Israel and Palestine have benefited from the CBSS, with an allocation of funding ranging between €900,000 and €1,200,000 per budget year.[5]

As Table 12.1 shows, around 20 projects were funded in the 2007–2010 period in each country.[6] In Palestine the majority of projects were under the themes 'governance' and 'promotion and protection of human rights and fundamental freedoms', while in Israel the bulk of projects were in the fields of 'human rights dialogues', 'strengthening civil society' and 'fight against racism, xenophobia and discrimination'.[7] The majority of these projects relate to the partial regimes of embedded liberal democracy by dealing with, for example, freedom of association, independence of the media, criminal accountability of the army and so on.

While strengthening civil society remains the primary goal of the EIDHR, its empowerment is seen as functional to promote other aspects of the model of 'embedded liberal democracy', in particular civil and

Table 12.1 CBSS projects by theme in Israel and West Bank/Gaza (2007–2010)

Theme/country	Israel	WB/Gaza
Children	0	3
Death penalty	0	0
Governance	0	4
Human rights dialogues	6	3
Promotion and protection of HR and fundamental freedoms	2	5
Rule of law and justice (penal system included)	2	0
Services	0	0
Strengthening civil society	7	2
Fight against racism, xenophobia and discrimination	6	0
Women	0	1
Total	23	18

political rights, and horizontal accountability. The EIDHR has been used by the EU to promote the rights of the Arab minority and of disadvantaged people (for example Bedouins) living in Israel. Most of these projects tackle discrimination in terms of civil rights, such as the right to property and housing, social rights such as equal treatment in the workplace, education and equal access to resources, as well as political rights. In this way, the rights of the Arab minority are taken into consideration by relying on the work of civil society organizations.[8] For example, the EU funded a project entitled 'Advocating a Just Solution for the Issue of the Unrecognised Villages in the Negev', which aimed at promoting recognition of the villages in the Negev while safeguarding the rights of their residents. As far as Israeli policies in the Occupied Territories are concerned, CBSS projects address both civil and political rights (for example demolitions of houses, access to justice), and issues of the accountability of Israel and its military personnel. For example, Yesh Din Volunteers for Human Rights received a grant for the project entitled 'Israeli Security Forces Criminal Accountability under International Humanitarian Law', which tries to change Israeli policies in the Occupied Palestinian Territories (OPTs) with respect to the criminal accountability of the army.

In Palestine, EIDHR projects focus on administrative capacity, effective governance and horizontal accountability. For example, one project dealt with the establishment of a constitutional court as stipulated by the Palestinian Basic Law and the Constitutional Court Law, thus aiming to promote constitutional and legal reforms as part of the efforts of institution- and state-building. Other projects focus on civil and political rights, such as the project implemented by the NGO Holy Land Trust, which aimed to support the production of TV and radio programming in order to give voice to the Palestinian people and increase freedom of expression and opinion.

While there is a clear intent to go beyond a superficial promotion of shallow democracy, the EIDHR remains a very limited instrument, which can only scratch the surface of the democratic situation in both Israel and Palestine. Although civil society actors are crucial in establishing the conditions for a democratic functioning state, they can only foster democracy to a certain extent. While it clearly helps to promote the context conditions of democracy, the partial regimes are only partially addressed. In a nutshell, the EU recognizes that there are problems, but it mainly deals with them via instruments that have a limited impact, instead of using stronger tools that would be available through the EMP/ENP.

Explaining the substance of democracy promotion

In the light of the policies and instruments that the EU uses in the context of Israel-Palestine, it can be argued that the Union pursues a shallow agenda in both Israel and Palestine. Table A.1 (in the Annex) provides a summary of the elements of the model of embedded liberal democracy to which the EU has devoted attention in the two countries. It has to be noted that giving attention to one aspect does not necessarily lead to full-fledged support, as the cases of Hamas and of the Arab minority show. Therefore, one 'plus' indicates that the EU gives some attention to the issue, but this does not represent its main concern or component of its democracy promotion agenda: it is a sign of limited support. As explained in the previous sections, the support for partial regimes is mainly pursued indirectly by funding projects promoted by civil society actors through the EIDHR. The main goal remains the empowerment of civil society, which is considered a key pillar for the development and enhancement of democratic features. In the West Bank, the EU is also actively involved in supporting state-building activities (both in terms of stateness and state administrative capacity) and socio-economic development by providing a substantial contribution to the reform plans drafted by the PA. Therefore, the EU's agenda remains 'shallow', as external conditions are preferred over partial regimes.

The reasons behind this shallow agenda of democracy promotion are clearly the result of a myriad of different and interrelated factors. Yet, an underling motive shaping EU democracy promotion towards Israel and Palestine is the Israeli–Palestinian conflict and related security concerns, which is in line with the hypothesis on power formulated in the introductory chapter. Indeed, the EU looks at the two countries through a security lens, which inextricably links Israel and Palestine. Therefore, any measure or policy targeting these countries is always framed within the broader picture of the conflict, which in turn trumps any possibility of the full development and employment of EU instruments of democracy promotion. Moreover, the EU's security concern is also influenced by the Israeli and US narratives and positions. In theory, the EU is in a stronger position towards Israel, given the benefits that the latter gains thanks to its relationship with the EU. Yet, this leverage has hardly been used by the EU, whose stance has been dictated by the transatlantic dimension, the historical pasts of its member states and a general EU preference to use positive conditionality and socialization instead of the stick (Tocci 2007, Musu 2010). In contrast, Palestine is heavily dependent on EU financial support and, more generally, it is forced to comply with the external conditions imposed by the Quartet and all other donors. At the same time, however, democracy promotion has been pursued as long as it does not interfere with security goals and with Israeli interests. This power game, and the predominant role of the US, became clear in the case of Hamas's victory in 2006, which led the EU to drop democracy promotion (Pogodda 2012).

Evidently, power relations intersect with the multiplicity of external actors and interests in the region, which inevitably limit the EU's range of action. A complicated set of factors interact to make the context more or less favourable to the dynamics identified in the introductory chapter. Most importantly, given the relevance of security in the region, the role of the US is paramount. Although the EU and the US are part of the Quartet and should coordinate their policies towards the parties of the conflict to reach peace, the US retains the leverage to steer the EU's political stance and policies (De Soto 2007, Tocci 2011). Finally, institutional dynamics within the EU need to be taken into account. Although the External Action Service should be in the driving seat, given that it provides the guidelines and monitors the implementation of all EU policies under the EMP and ENP,[9] and defines the framework for the EIDHR, member states play a role in the political stance towards both countries not only at the declaratory level, but also as far as the room for manoeuvre of EU institutions is concerned. While the EU can push on certain aspects and support certain projects instead of others, the direction of EU policies of democracy promotion is a political decision. Democracy promotion is therefore supported as long as it is in line with the interests of EU member states and the security concerns that shape the lens through which democracy promotion towards Israel and Palestine is considered.

Conclusions

Democracy promotion in Israel and Palestine, despite being among the goals of the EU, is not its primary concern. Instead, the Israeli–Palestinian conflict and the related security concerns take precedence over all other aspects and shape the international efforts aimed at democracy promotion. Although the EU has tried to implement a variety of policies with a view to creating democratic conditions in Palestine and addressing some lacking democratic features in Israel (for example in respect of the Arab minority), it has always sidelined these goals, if security-related matters emerged. In the hope of 'resuscitating' the dead peace process between Israel and the Palestinians, the EU has disregarded the result of the 2006 Palestinian elections, has accepted Abbas as president and leading figure of the PA (even though his mandate has expired) and has invested in Palestinian state-building in the belief that this will increase the chances of peace. Similarly, the situation of the Arab minority has been tackled mainly through the back door, by financially supporting civil society actors promoting projects to reduce discrimination and foster equality. Yet, it has avoided linking the problem to the conflict, of which Arab Israelis are part and parcel, and has avoided any actions that would hamper Israeli willingness in the peace process.

It therefore follows that the local situation characterized by the ongoing conflict between Israel and Palestine has shaped and determined all other policies of external actors, including democracy promotion. The EU has not escaped from this paradigm and has therefore invested in context conditions, especially in the case of the Palestinians. In this way, EU democracy promotion policies mainly contribute to maintaining the Israeli occupation in the West Bank and the façade of a peace process. The conflict has caught everything in its net and has prevented external actors from implementing democracy effectively due to the fear of disrupting the equilibrium that has been created and the security dynamics. Democracy therefore matters only when it is functional and linked to the conflict and any steps aimed at its solution.

Notes

1. 'Palestine' refers here to the West Bank and Gaza Strip.
2. Various NGOs, for example Mossawa, Adalah and Association for Civil Rights in Israel (ACRI), publish reports on the situation of minority rights in Israel, highlighting various acts of discrimination against the Arab minority.
3. Note that the figures for 2013 are forecasts made by the Commission (see European Commission and High Representative 2013).
4. In July 2013, the EU introduced guidelines on funds, prices and grants applicable to Israeli entities and their activities in the territories. On the basis of these guidelines, Israeli entities present or with activities in the Occupied Territories are not eligible to any funds, grants or prizes from EU institutions under the 2014–2020 EU budget and related programmes.
5. The amounts are slightly larger than the other Mediterranean countries, which receive between €600 and 900 million per year.
6. In terms of projects, the average for the other Mediterranean countries is around 14.
7. It has to be noted that since 2009 European NGOs can also be funded under the CBSS, provided that they support local organizations and promote the development of local conditions. In Israel/Palestine, the majority of EIDHR funds are given to local NGOs.

8. For a more detailed account of the discrimination that the Arab minority faces, see the Euro-Mediterranean Human Rights Network report (EMHRN 2011) and the reports and documents of, among others, the Mossawa Center and Adalah.
9. Before the entry into force of the Lisbon Treaty, the role of the European External Action Service (EEAS) was played by Commission Directorate General External Relations (Relex). With the creation of the EEAS, DG Relex does not exist any longer. The money is still administered by the Commission, which, however, acts in line with the guidelines and provisions indicated by the EEAS.

13
Favouring Leaders over Laggards: Kazakhstan and Kyrgyzstan

Fabienne Bossuyt and Paul Kubicek

Introduction

This chapter maps the substance of EU democracy promotion in Kazakhstan and Kyrgyzstan and identifies the factors that shape this substance. In applying the framework and hypotheses presented in the opening chapter of this volume, the empirical analysis focuses on the period 2007–2013.[1] We consider both the EU's discourse and its actual policy implementation. The chapter consists of two parts. The first part sketches the democratic substance promoted by the EU. It finds that the EU does more to promote 'broad' liberal democracy in Kyrgyzstan than in Kazakhstan. In the second part, possible factors are examined that shape the content of the EU's democracy promotion in order to understand the variance between the two target countries. We conclude with a summary of the main findings based upon review of EU documents, interviews and assessments of the extent of democratic reform in both countries.

Substance of EU democracy promotion

Overarching regional policy framework

In mapping the democratic substance promoted by the EU in Kazakhstan and Kyrgyzstan, one should first look at the overarching framework that guides the EU's relations with the five post-Soviet Central Asian countries. This is established in the EU Strategy for a new partnership with Central Asia, that is, the political strategy launched in 2007, and the European Commission's regional assistance strategy for Central Asia, which sets out the goals and guidelines for assistance in 2007–2013.

In the EU Strategy, 'the development of transparent, democratic political structures', together with the rule of law, human rights and good governance, is presented as one of the six priority areas for cooperation with the region (Council of the European Union 2007b). In outlining more specifics, the strategy focuses on the protection of human rights and creation of an independent judiciary, aimed at 'making a sustainable contribution to the establishment of structures based on the rule of law and international human rights standards' (Council of the European Union 2007b: 12–14). Central to these purposes are the human rights dialogues held annually with each of the five countries and the EU Rule of Law Initiative, implemented by the member states in cooperation with the Commission. While attention is paid to the 'partial regimes' of civil rights and horizontal accountability, little emphasis is placed on the promotion of a democratic electoral regime and political rights of participation (Council of the European Union 2007b: 14). Similarly, the regional assistance strategy highlights the promotion of democratization, human rights and good governance, but it is clear, at least judging from funding, that the last item, together with socio-economic development, is more the focus than democratic transition in a narrower sense (European Commission 2007i: 27). For example, in 2007–2013, poverty reduction programmes constituted 40–45 per cent of the budget and good governance programmes – together with economic reform programmes – were allocated 20–25 per cent of the funds (European Commission 2007i: 3). Many of the latter target state administrative capacity and management, both at the national and local level. Certain core aspects of democracy, such as political rights of participation, are promoted through the European Instrument for Democracy and Human Rights (EIDHR), which falls under a separate budget line (see more below). It should be pointed out that the funding allocated to Central Asia under the EIDHR is relatively limited compared to the funding for democratization activities provided under the Development Cooperation Instrument (DCI), the main budget line.

Varying substance of EU democracy promotion

While the EU has common goals across Central Asia, its democracy promotion activities differ among all five countries in the region (cf. Bossuyt and Kubicek 2011) as well as between Kyrgyzstan and Kazakhstan. In both countries, the EU has devoted much attention to the context conditions for democracy. In Kyrgyzstan, the second poorest state in the region, the focus of the EU's activities has been poverty reduction, particularly through the Food Security Programme,

Table 13.1 Relative power positions of Kazakhstan and Kyrgyzstan

Country	Population (in millions)	GDP/capita (current int'l $)	Oil rents (per cent GDP)	Per cent income from ODA
Kazakhstan	16.3	12,115	22.4	0.17
Kyrgyzstan	5.4	2,229	0.7	8.55

Source: World Bank (2010).

which has provided technical assistance and social sector-oriented budget support. As noted earlier, socio-economic development is the largest item in the EU's assistance budget. Its Assistance Strategy Paper explicitly links poverty reduction to democratization, clearly suggesting the importance that the EU attaches in Central Asia to the promotion of the socio-economic requisites for democratization. In this way, the EU wants to enable the poorer states of Central Asia to complete their political and economic transition, and thus to consolidate broader values of democracy, including the rule of law and respect for human rights (European Commission 2007i: 7). As Kazakhstan is economically more advanced and scores better in terms of socio-economic development (cf. Table 13.1), poverty reduction programmes are far less pronounced in the EU's assistance to Kazakhstan.

Both countries have seen significant EU efforts to bolster state administrative capacity, including training for civil service officials and support for local governments. Capacity-building initiatives are especially pronounced in Kazakhstan, where support for public sector reform and modernization in Kazakhstan has attracted significant EU funding over the last decade (European Union 2010: 42). Promotion of good governance, and in particular state administrative capacity, currently dominates the EU's bilateral assistance to the country: in 2011–2013, the latter consisted of support for regional development and local governance (€8 million), judicial reform (€10 million), and enhancement of public service capabilities for social and economic reforms (€12 million) (European Commission 2010l: 16). An important scheme in this regard is the Policy Dialogue and Advice Programme (PDAP), which is designed to establish a close policy dialogue by means of exchanging expertise, best practice and know-how.

The EU also has various initiatives to promote civil society in both Kazakhstan and Kyrgyzstan. Many of these are run through the EIDHR. For example, the EIDHR sponsors annual civil society seminars, which

180 *Cases: Kazakhstan and Kyrgyzstan*

promote discussion between European and Central Asian state and non-state actors and are designed to complement human rights dialogues held at foreign ministerial level. In addition, the EU supports the Non-State Actors and Local Authorities in Development (NSA-LA) programme, which is aimed at strengthening both civil society and municipal governments.

EU democracy promotion efforts also touch more directly on the partial regimes of democracy. With respect to horizontal accountability, EU activities in Kazakhstan have included support for notary reform, institutional development of the court system, support to the Judicial Academy, and strengthening the office of the Ombudsman (European Commission 2007j: 1–2). The fact that the main goal of these projects is to improve the independence of the judiciary suggests that this particular aspect of 'horizontal accountability' takes up an important role in the democratic substance of EU policy. However, one should note that this goal is also linked to the EU's concern with improving Kazakhstan's investment climate (see also Reynaert in this volume), making it more attractive for foreign (not least European) investors – a reflection of the country's strategic value.

Legal and judicial reform is also a focal priority of the EU's assistance to Kyrgyzstan, where its objective is to ensure progress in the capacity and independence of the judiciary, thereby guaranteeing impartiality and effectiveness of prosecution. As in Kazakhstan, the goal is to improve transparency and accountability of the state (European Commission 2010m). Interestingly, however, in Kyrgyzstan the EU's promotion of horizontal accountability goes markedly further, notably by also targeting the Parliament (Europa 2014i).

The EU has also done more in Kyrgyzstan with respect to the electoral regime. This is, as will be elaborated upon below, in part a function of the fact that Kyrgyzstan has had a more competitive political system. Since the overthrow of the Bakiev government in 2010, the EU has increased its support for electoral and political reforms in Kyrgyzstan, including assistance to the design and implementation of legislative and constitutional reform and technical and financial support for elections in 2010 and 2011.

Other core aspects of democracy, such as political rights of participation and civil rights, are promoted primarily through the EIDHR. In Kyrgyzstan, projects currently funded via this instrument include torture prevention, youth rights inclusion and political engagement, and monitoring of custody conditions. In Kazakhstan, which has so far hosted the largest number of EIDHR projects in the region, several recent activities have focused on freedom of the press and the existence of independent media (Europa 2012c).

The EU promotes civil rights not only through the provision of technical assistance, but also through instruments under its Common Foreign and Security Policy (CFSP). In addition to the bilateral human rights dialogue, a commonly used CFSP instrument for democracy promotion in Central Asia is CFSP statements. Crawford, for instance, has calculated that between 2005 and 2007, nearly 20 CFSP statements were issued in relations to political events or developments in Central Asian countries, including elections, court cases and legislative acts (2008: 176–7). The majority of CFSP statements in that period were critical in tone and were used to criticize abuses of civil and political rights and to highlight flawed electoral processes. Interestingly, while Kyrgyzstan was often the subject of such declarations, no CFSP statement was released in relation to Kazakhstan (Crawford 2008: 177). For the period 2008–2013, however, a different picture emerges, with Kyrgyzstan and Kazakhstan being the subject of a more or less equal number of CFSP statements. Moreover, while the majority of statements on Kyrgyzstan in this period are positive in tone, most declarations concerning Kazakhstan are critical. The focus of the statements in this six-year period is also on core aspects of democracy, and in particular on the electoral regime, and – to a lesser extent – on political rights of participation and civil rights. For example, the parliamentary (11 October 2010)[2] and presidential (18 December 2010) elections and the constitutional referendum (28 June 2010 and 26 July 2010) in Kyrgyzstan were commended, while the same kind of electoral events in Kazakhstan were rebuked for failing to meet international standards (17 January 2012, 5 April 2011, 21 January 2011, see Europa 2014h). Criticism was also expressed at Kazakhstan's prosecution of political opponents (9 October 2012). It is important to note that core aspects of democracy are promoted in a similar way through the Organization for Security and Cooperation in Europe (OSCE) Permanent Council, where the EU frequently resorts to public condemnation or appraisal of OSCE norm violating or compliant behaviour of Central Asian member countries (Bossuyt 2010: 221–2). These declarations pay attention to the electoral regime, but also to civil and political rights, including Kazakhstan's restrictions on media freedom (1 February 2007 and 3 September 2009) and internet usage (16 July 2009).

In sum, as illustrated in Table A.1 (in the Annex), it is clear that the EU does more to promote 'broad' liberal democracy in Kyrgyzstan than in Kazakhstan. In Kyrgyzstan, the EU concentrates both on the various partial regimes of democracy and on the context conditions

182 Cases: Kazakhstan and Kyrgyzstan

that embed democracy. In Kazakhstan, the EU only promotes some elements of broad liberal democracy. In particular, it puts less emphasis on political rights and horizontal accountability, particularly compared to policy towards Kyrgyzstan. The EU pays attention to the context conditions in both countries, but different conditions are emphasized in each country. In Kazakhstan, the EU places more emphasis on state administrative capacity and less on socio-economic development compared to Kyrgyzstan.

Explaining the substance of EU democracy promotion

This section serves to identify the factors that shape the substance of EU democracy promotion and to explain the variation in substance observed above. To do so, we use the hypotheses presented in the introductory chapter.

Power/interdependence explanation

The power-based hypothesis presented in the opening chapter suggests that if power relationships or issue-specific interdependence favour the EU, it may push a broad democratization agenda. However, the EU may be reluctant to pursue an ambitious democratization agenda if this could harm its own security interests. In these cases, the EU is hypothesized to pursue a shallow democratization agenda, one more focused on stateness or effective governance that will ensure stability.

How do these assumptions apply to the cases of Kazakhstan and Kyrgyzstan? Obviously, both countries are far less powerful than the EU, particularly in terms of economic development. However, it is clear that Kazakhstan is significantly more powerful than Kyrgyzstan, as seen in several indicators displayed in Table 13.1. Kazakhstan is larger and relatively wealthy, particularly by Central Asian standards. While this might make it a more fertile ground for democratization, one should add that much of its wealth derives from oil exports – found to work against democratization (Fish 2005) – and its relative economic strength also makes it less susceptible to foreign pressure compared to countries such as Kyrgyzstan that rely more heavily on foreign assistance. As for issue-specific interdependence, although neither country at present is a major EU trading partner, the presence of significant oil and gas reserves in Kazakhstan (and European interest in gaining access to these resources) puts EU-Kazakh relations on a relatively more equal footing compared to EU-Kyrgyz relations. In sum, based on relative power considerations, it could be argued that one of the reasons why the EU promotes broader democratic substance in Kyrgyzstan than in Kazakhstan is that the EU has more power over Kyrgyzstan compared to Kazakhstan. Security considerations reinforce this outcome as well, as it could be argued that the EU has more strategic interests in Kazakhstan than Kyrgyzstan. This is not to say that Kyrgyzstan has no strategic importance. It has been important to NATO (North Atlantic Treaty Organisation) operations in Afghanistan, and, as with all Central Asian states, there is fear of instability that could spur Islamic radicalism or terrorist networks in the region (see for example Cooley 2008, Crawford 2008, Dave 2008). However, Kazakhstan is a far larger country and aspires to become a regional power. Instability in Kazakhstan would be of far greater significance than in Kyrgyzstan. Moreover, Kazakhstan's oil and gas reserves make it a considerably more attractive economic partner than Kyrgyzstan. Hence, the EU has greater security interests (broadly defined) in not alienating the Kazakh government, which has justified some of its democratic shortcomings by arguing that political liberalization might foster instability. This is further reinforced by the fact that there are other, more powerful players operating in the region, which have no interest in promoting democracy and endorse Kazakhstan's 'stability first' agenda: Russia and China. The EU is thus at a relative disadvantage in this context, which makes it even more difficult for the EU to promote a broad democratization agenda.

Overall then, the expectations from the power hypotheses are broadly in line with what we find, as the EU has pursued a more shallow democratization agenda in Kazakhstan than in Kyrgyzstan.

Institutionalist explanation

As hypothesized in the introductory chapter, the EU's democratic substance might differ depending on the sub-system(s) in charge and/or the policy makers involved in the formulation of EU policies. In the case of Kazakhstan and Kyrgyzstan institutionalist factors offer little explanatory value for the variation in substance, because the EU's policies towards the two countries fall under the same policy framework. Still, institutionalist elements can be drawn upon to gain further insights in the factors that shape the substance. To do so, it is important to distinguish between EU democracy promotion done through the diplomatic/foreign policy channel (embodied by the High Representative and the European External Action Service (EEAS), with a commanding role for the Council – and thus the member states) and democracy promotion done through the assistance channel (embodied by Directorate General for Development and Cooperation (DG DEVCO) in conjunction with the EEAS, with a commanding role for the Commission). Put differently, there is less impact from member states on EU assistance programming (where the Commission is in charge) than at the diplomatic/foreign policy level (where the Council holds the strings). At the latter level, however, it is very difficult to trace the exact impact from the member states on the contents of the EU's democracy promotion, because Council meetings are held behind closed doors and positions taken by individual member states at Council meetings tend to be kept secret. Even so, it is relatively well-known that member states with considerable geostrategic interests in Kazakhstan, in particular Germany and Italy, are reluctant to push for more democratic reforms as they fear this will alienate the democracy-averse regime and thus compromise their national interests.

While this seems to be consistent with the expectations drawn from the power hypothesis explored above, some qualifications are in order. First, as appeared from the CFSP statements, the EU in recent years has been more openly critical of Kazakhstan's poor democratic record. To some extent, this evolution appears to be the result of another institutional factor, notably the fact that the person responsible for the EEAS country desk for Kazakhstan – who, among other things, drafts the CFSP statements concerning Kazakhstan – is an ardent democracy supporter.[3] Overall, however, the EEAS is tied to the strict mandate of the High Representative, giving them little room for manoeuvre vis-à-vis the member states.[4] Second, some member states, while publicly refraining from criticizing democratic flaws in Kazakhstan, so as not to disturb bilateral relations with Kazakhstan, are sometimes rather vocal at Council meetings, pushing the EU to be critical of the regime and do the 'dirty' work.[5]

In the area of development assistance, despite the EEAS having co-programming responsibilities with DG DEVCO for the first three stages of the programming cycle for the financing instruments, that is, country allocation, country/regional strategy papers and national indicative programming, DG DEVCO leads the programming process (Furness 2013). This means that the fact that DG DEVCO, as a development actor, takes a more developmental (as opposed to political) approach to democracy promotion than its counterparts at the EEAS and the Council should be reflected in the democratic substance of the EU's assistance for Kazakhstan and Kyrgyzstan. This indeed appears from the regional assistance strategy for Central Asia, in which good governance and socio-economic development receive much more attention than democratic transition in a narrower sense (see above). At the country level, this applies even more to Kyrgyzstan than Kazakhstan. To explain this variation, the domestic context and the interorganizational field will offer further insights (see below).

As presented in the opening chapter, another hypothesis is that the greater the degree to which EU member states are involved in policy formulation and implementation, the more the substance will resemble the template favoured by the most dominant member state(s). So if we consider that Germany is the most dominant member state in the case of Kazakhstan and Kyrgyzstan, we would expect German national policy characteristics to be reflected at the EU level and to possibly shape the substance of EU democracy promotion. Following the assumption made above that member states have more impact on the diplomatic/foreign policy level than on the level of assistance programming, it is even more useful to distinguish between these two levels in the case of Germany, since there is no unified German approach to democracy promotion, which is instead deeply split along development–foreign policy lines (Youngs 2006: 110–14). However, at the foreign policy level, it is difficult to trace the possible impact of Germany on the substance of EU democracy promotion, both because of the closed nature of policy-making at the Council and because Germany has been reluctant to push openly for democratization.

Domestic context explanation

The domestic context explanation expects the EU to adapt its democratization efforts with some eye to the environment of each country. One possible scenario is that the EU tailors its programmes so that assistance is directed to where it is most needed. Alternatively, EU democracy promotion may be more 'demand-driven' from the target country, meaning the EU tailors its programmes as a reflection of the priorities of the target state. In this scenario, one may find 'democratization producing democracy aid', as 'democratic openings present opportunities for democracy promoters to get involved' (Carothers 1999: 44–5).

With respect to our cases, we find evidence that the EU is sensitive to the domestic context. The EU has gradually backed away from a broader regional approach and towards country-specific policies. At present, 70 per cent of the financial means for Central Asia are now allocated to bilateral programmes. Both EU Strategy Papers point to the importance of taking into account each country's situation; the Commission's assistance strategy explicitly emphasizes 'the need for a differentiated approach depending on the context and the particular needs of individual states' (European Commission 2007i: 6). This is echoed by an EU official, who indicated that EU policies, while based on a template of liberal democratic values promoted around the world, 'is not a copy-paste of these democratic values; it takes into account the region's and countries' specificities and particularities'.[6]

To establish what constitutes the domestic context for our cases, reference is made to data from the Bertelsmann Transformation Index (BTI 2012a), used throughout this volume to assess various components of democracy (see Table A.2 in the Annex). A few items stand out. First, Kyrgyzstan, although far from a consolidated, stable democracy, generally has much higher scores than Kazakhstan on the five core components of democracy.[7] However, on the various context variables, Kazakhstan tends to fare better, particular on issues of stateness (8.5 versus 7), state capacity (6 versus 4) and socio-economic development (5 versus 4).[8] Moreover, in the past decade (2005 and 2010) Kyrgyzstan experienced significant domestic instability, with violence in 2010 making some fear possible civil war. We can therefore consider it a 'post-conflict' country, whereas Kazakhstan has remained relatively stable.[9]

Variation in the substance of EU democracy promotion can be explained by this domestic context. Given that Kyrgyzstan is a weaker and less stable state than Kazakhstan, the EU focuses more on basic elements of political stability in Kyrgyzstan, even more so since the 2010 outburst of violence between ethnic Kyrgyz and Uzbeks, after which the EU called on its Instrument for Stability to help restore order. In Kazakhstan, in contrast, EU capacity-building initiatives focus mostly on assistance for public administration and civil service reform. Moreover, given Kyrgyzstan's relative poverty, one might also expect the EU to prioritize socio-economic development. Indeed, it has done so. Poverty reduction activities are primary in the EU's bilateral assistance to Kyrgyzstan while almost absent in its bilateral assistance to wealthier Kazakhstan.

However, in Kyrgyzstan, as compared to Kazakhstan, one also sees more broad-based democracy assistance, including attention to civil society, development of democratic (as opposed to bureaucratic) institutions, and the electoral regime. By 'objective' assessments, Kazakhstan might have more need for assistance in these areas, but the EU has not made these concerns its primary focus. Why not? The 'demand-driven' hypothesis, which takes into account the political will within the targeted country, provides an answer. Authoritarianism in Kazakhstan is firmly established. There have been some very limited and calculated efforts at political liberalization, exemplified by President Nazarbayev's

'Path to Europe' and modest reforms associated with Kazakhstan's 2010 Chairmanship of the OSCE. However, the priority is maintaining control, and the Kazakh government drew lessons from the 'coloured revolutions' in the post-Soviet space, including the 2005 'Tulip Revolution' in Kyrgyzstan, which work against substantial change (Kubicek 2011). Given the regime's priority on stability, one would expect that it would welcome EU efforts to build state capacity but be hostile to efforts to promote more core elements of democracy. The EU, on its part, may recognize that these are the limits of what it can do. In either event, the expected outcome would be shallow democratization.

In contrast, Kyrgyzstan has experienced more substantial political liberalization. It is the only Central Asian country to have what might be called 'democratic openings', that is, the 'Tulip Revolution' that overthrew President Askar Akaev and the 2010 ouster of his successor, Kurmanbek Bakiev, who failed to deliver on promises of democratization. Moreover, although the current political situation remains fragile, the broad coalition government formed in 2010 after parliamentary elections is leading a process of further democratization and reform. We would therefore expect that domestic resonance with EU calls for broader democratization would be much greater in Kyrgyzstan than in Kazakhstan.[10] This contrast is in line with our finding that the EU focuses more (at least in relative terms) on 'broad' liberal democracy in Kyrgyzstan than in Kazakhstan, and is more assertive in Kyrgyzstan in pressing its democratization agenda. One can note as well that EU assistance is focused, for the most part, on those areas on the BTI on which Kyrgyzstan scores low.

Interorganizational field

The EU, of course, is not the only international actor engaged in democracy promotion in Central Asia. The main external actors involved in democracy promotion in the region can be grouped into three categories: international organizations, most notably the UN, the OSCE and the Council of Europe; individual countries, most notably the US, Japan, Switzerland, Germany, Sweden, the UK and the Netherlands; and international non-governmental organizations (NGOs), including the Soros Foundation.[11]

The OSCE, which has a long and extensive experience with democracy promotion in Central Asia, is the EU's closest partner in the region (OSCE 2014c, 2014d). Coordination activities with the OSCE consist of election monitoring, which the EU leaves almost entirely up to the

OSCE, and programmes on judicial reforms and media freedom. As indicated above, the EU is also active at the OSCE General Assembly, where it has released statements commenting on OSCE norm violating or compliant behaviour of Kazakhstan and Kyrgyzstan. The fact that these declarations pertain to core aspects of democracy, and in particular, the electoral regime, civil rights, and political rights of participation, is of course linked to the OSCE's competence on these issues. In addition, the EU along with several EU member states supports the OSCE Academy in Bishkek, which focuses on training, state capacity and conflict prevention. Efforts for rule of law reforms are coordinated with the Council of Europe's Venice Commission and a number of member states, including France and Germany.

Coordination activities with EU member states comprise mostly civil and political rights-focused programmes and projects, including professional training for journalists (Germany and Sweden), media freedom (Ireland and the UK) and human rights awareness raising (the Netherlands). Both in Kyrgyzstan and Kazakhstan, the EU member state that the EU cooperates with most closely is Germany, which is not surprising given that it has the longest presence in the region.

However, it is difficult to determine to what extent the EU's cooperation on democracy promotion activities has an impact, if at all, on the democratic substance that the EU furthers.

A more visible impact from the interorganizational field can be observed when looking at donor cooperation and coordination as envisaged in the EU's assistance strategy and programming. While the EU engages in donor coordination in both Kazakhstan and Kyrgyzstan, notably in the light of its commitment to the Paris Declaration on Aid Effectiveness, the EU is engaged much more intensively in aid coordination in Kyrgyzstan than in Kazakhstan (see for example European Commission 2007i: 25). This is, of course, not so surprising given that in contrast to middle-income-ranked Kazakhstan, Kyrgyzstan is an aid-dependent developing country, which hosts a large donor community. As with its policy for most developing countries, the EU's assistance programmes for Kyrgyzstan are established through close consultations with relevant stakeholders, which – apart from domestic actors – include EU member states and other donors. Among other things, the EU aligns its priority areas of assistance with Kyrgyzstan's Country Development Strategy, which was set up with a view to implementing the country's Poverty Reduction Strategy Paper (European Commission 2008j: 86). As the latter was prepared in broad consultation with stakeholders and development partners, but in particular the World Bank and the International Monetary Fund, the content and orientation of the EU's assistance for Kyrgyzstan are to a certain extent influenced by the World Bank's agenda, and by implication, the leading international aid paradigm. As such, it is perhaps not a coincidence that the priority areas of the EU assistance to Kyrgyzstan in the field of democratization are socio-economic development (through a poverty-focused approach, which includes the promotion of social spending), effective public administration, capacity-building of the civil service and legal reforms (European Commission 2008j), which are typical ingredients of the dominant aid paradigm. In addition, the EU participates in the Joint Country Support Strategy, which since 2007 has served as a framework for aid coordination between all the main donors (apart from the EU, these are the Asian Development Bank, Switzerland, the UK, the World Bank Group, the International Monetary Fund, the UN Agencies, Germany and Sweden) (European Commission 2011l: 25). With respect to the question of democratic substance, the EU coordinates programmes on administration and public finance management reform with the UK, Switzerland and Sweden (European Commission 2011l: 29). In 2009, for instance, the European Commission established a multi-donor trust fund with these three donors and the World Bank to support public finance management reforms (European Commission 2011l: 29). In sum, the fact that the EU in Kyrgyzstan widely participates in donor coordination with the major donors and as such subscribes to the dominant aid paradigm and principles (cf. Post-Washington Consensus) suggests that these donors, not least the World Bank, have some impact on the democratic substance that the EU promotes in Kyrgyzstan.

Conclusion

This chapter has sought to map the substance of EU democracy promotion in Kazakhstan and Kyrgyzstan, as well as identify factors that help account for the shape of and variation in policy between the two countries. Using the embedded liberal democracy framework, we find that the EU does more to promote 'broad' liberal democracy in Kyrgyzstan than in Kazakhstan. In Kyrgyzstan, the EU concentrates both on the various partial regimes of democracy and on the context conditions that embed democracy. In Kazakhstan, the EU puts less emphasis on the core components of democracy, for example political rights, compared to Kyrgyzstan, but pays a similar amount of attention to the context conditions, although different context conditions are emphasized depending on the country. Indeed, because Kazakhstan is economically (much) more advanced than Kyrgyzstan, the EU places more emphasis on state administrative capacity and less on socio-economic development compared to Kyrgyzstan, which still experiences basic development problems.

Our findings from the two Central Asian cases are broadly in line with the hypotheses suggested in the opening chapter. The outcome – more broad democracy promotion in Kyrgyzstan and shallower promotion in Kazakhstan – is thus over-determined, and we cannot definitely conclude which hypothesis best 'fits' the data. However, utilizing the qualitative nature of our work, we would lend more credence to the domestic context approach. Not only does the EU itself indicate that it tries to tailor its policies to the particular country, but one sees clear evidence of this as the EU has adopted a more bilateral focus over time. Kyrgyzstan, since the collapse of the USSR, has been the most politically liberal – if also unstable – state in the region. One could therefore argue that it is both a 'high-need' state – thus prompting broader democratic substance – and a 'high-demand' state in the sense that it has been more open to international advice and assistance than its neighbours. In the Kazakh case, while the government has been willing to work with the EU on areas of common interest (for example state capacity), it has been less receptive to EU interference on more sensitive issues such as the electoral regime. Here we see an interlinkage with the power/interdependence factor: because the EU is in a less favourable power position, the substance it furthers is dependent on Kazakhstan's political willingness to further democratize.

The most recent developments with respect to the EU's Central Asia policy reinforce the notion that the domestic context is a key factor in shaping the substance. A 15 December 2011 European Parliament Resolution on the implementation of the EU Strategy for Central Asia, for example, asks that the EU 'tailor its strategies to the progress of the states in the region'. The resolution underlines that

> the level and nature of the EU's engagement must be differentiated and conditional, depending on measurable progress in the fields of democratization, human rights, good governance, sustainable socio-economic development, the rule of law and the fight against corruption, offering its assistance where needed to help foster this progress, following lines similar to the principles of the EU's neighbourhood policy (that is, 'more for more').
>
> (European Parliament 2011a)

In terms of substance, both Kazakhstan and Kyrgyzstan have witnessed concrete examples of this approach, albeit at opposing ends. Disappointed with the lack of political liberalization in Kazakhstan, the EU (and in particular, Catherine Ashton and her policy advisors at the EEAS) has been slowing down the pace of the preparatory talks for an enhanced Partnership and Cooperation Agreement with Kazakhstan,[12] which have been tied explicitly to progress on political reforms (Ashton 2012c, see also European Parliament 2012a).

In contrast, reacting to what it considers a democratic opening after the tragic events of 2010, the EU has increased assistance to Kyrgyzstan to support both economic reforms and 'the country's incipient parliamentary democracy' following the ouster of President Bakiev (European Commission 2011m: 1). More specifically, this has included help in designing and implementing constitutional reform and conducting elections in 2010 and 2011.[13] This is clear evidence of 'democratization producing democracy aid', in that the EU has seized recent democratic openings in Kyrgyzstan as an opportunity to get more involved, and in particular to offer more support to broad liberal democracy.

Notes

1. 2007 was the year that the EU launched its political strategy for Central Asia. It is also the year that the European Commission's new multi-annual assistance programme for the region took off, which ended in 2013.
2. Dates refer to the press release of the CFSP statement.
3. Interviews with EEAS officials, 15 February 2012.
4. Interview with EEAS official, 11 October 2012.
5. Interview with EEAS official, 11 October 2012.
6. Interview in Brussels on 14 January 2011.
7. Kyrgyzstan's BTI score in 2012 for electoral regime was 6 (versus 3 for Kazakhstan), for civil rights 6 (versus 4), for political rights 7 (versus 4), for horizontal accountability 4 (versus 3) and for effective power 4 (versus 2).
8. According to the BTI figures from 2012.
9. The BTI score for level of social, ethnic, and religious conflict (Q.13.3) in the 2012 report was 6 (with a maximum of 10) for Kyrgyzstan, and only 2 for Kazakhstan.
10. Elements of this might be captured in the BTI question on domestic leadership support of international parties to implement development plans (Q 17.1). In the 2012 report, Kazakhstan scored a 6 and Kyrgyzstan a 7 (meaning it was more supportive), with the suggestion that its score would likely have been higher had Kyrgyzstan had a more stable, better functioning government.
11. Arguably the most important international actors in the region are Russia and China. Neither, of course, counts as a democracy promoter, and the fact that Central Asian states can play democracy promoters like the EU off

against states like Russia and China may seriously hamper the success of any broad democratization agenda.
12. Interview at the EEAS, Central Asia division, Brussels, 15 February 2012.
13. Interview at the European Commission, DG DEVCO, Brussels, 18 January 2011.

14
Democracy Promotion in Restrictive Environments: Ethiopia and Eritrea

Karen Del Biondo

Introduction

Ethiopia and Eritrea are located in the conflict-ridden Horn of Africa. Ethiopia is currently governed by the Ethiopian People's Revolutionary Democratic Front (EPRDF), which defeated the communist dictatorship of Mengistu Haile Mariam in 1991. Multi-party elections have been held since 1995, but they have been dominated by the ruling party. Eritrea gained independence from Ethiopia in 1993 after a long war against successive Ethiopian governments. President Isaias Afewerki, who led the struggle for independence from Ethiopia as secretary general of the Eritrean People's Liberation Front, took power and promised to hold multi-party elections according to a new constitution adopted in 1997. However, this constitution was never implemented.

Although both countries have remained relatively stable internally, they fought a border war in 1998–2000 and the situation at the border remains tense. In both countries, internal stability has come at the price of democracy: power is strongly centralized in the ruling party, and there is little room for opposing voices. Given the rise of Islamist terrorism and civil wars in Sudan and Somalia, security has become an important consideration of the EU in the region. It has been argued that donors have barely focused on democracy in Ethiopia because they do not want to risk cooperation on counter-terrorism (Brüne 2007, Borchgrevink 2008). At the same time, the EU has few trade interests in Ethiopia, and compared to its actions in other countries such as Angola, it has at least addressed the issue of democracy (Börzel and Hackenesch 2013).

This chapter will reveal two paradoxes as regards power relations and the domestic context. First, the EU has pursued a broader democratic substance where it had – at first sight – less power, namely, in Ethiopia. Second, the EU has not promoted a broader substance where it is most needed, namely, in Eritrea. Rather, the substance of democracy promotion has followed the openness of the government to the support of democracy, which was, though limited in both countries, greater in Ethiopia.

Ethiopia is a 'donor darling' that attracts large amounts of aid funds. In 2010–2011, the EU was Ethiopia's fifth largest donor, after the Global Fund, the UK, the US and the World Bank (OECD 2013). In contrast, Eritrea has been hostile towards foreign aid, and can be considered an aid 'orphan' by its own choice. The European Commission (EC) has been the main EU actor in both cases, although overall the Council has appeared to agree with EC policies. As both states are African, Caribbean and Pacific (ACP) countries, Directorate-General Development (DG DEV) was responsible and the Cotonou Agreement was the general framework of EU policies until the establishment of the European External Action Service (EEAS) in early 2010, when the EEAS became co-responsible with the Commission. This chapter relies on desk research using official documents from EU institutions, indicators and reports from non-governmental organizations (NGOs) and international organizations, academic articles, as well as interviews with EU officials in Brussels (January 2012) and Addis Ababa (January 2011).

EU democracy promotion in sub-Saharan Africa: The rhetoric

The Cotonou Partnership Agreement (2000) between the EU and the ACP group, in its Article 9, underlines the importance of human rights, democratic principles, the rule of law and good governance and defines these norms. On human rights it is emphasized that civil, political, social, economic and cultural rights should be respected. Democratic principles include the legitimacy of the authorities, the legality of their actions and the existence of participatory mechanisms. The rule of law refers to 'accessible means of legal redress, an independent legal system [...] and an executive that is fully subject to the law'. On good governance, the EU approach has shifted from a definition that focused mostly on transparent and accountable management of resources (see Cotonou Agreement) to a 'holistic' definition emphasizing 'the state's ability to serve its citizens' (European Commission 2003a: 3). In a 2006

Communication, democracy and good governance are merged in a broad definition of 'democratic governance', encompassing a wide range of fields, including democracy and respect for human rights, socio-economic governance, security policies, regional integration, respect for the environment and so on (European Commission 2006b). The shift from 'democracy' to 'democratic governance' suggests that the EU is not only concerned about the partial regimes of liberal democracy, but also about the context conditions of embedded democracy, including stateness, state administrative capacity and social and economic requisites (European Commission 2009a: 6). Although civil society was not explicitly mentioned in the definition, the emphasis in the Cotonou Agreement on participatory development and the role of civil society organizations as implementers of the European Development Fund (EDF) shows the importance attached to strengthening civil society (Carbone 2008a).

EU democracy promotion in Eritrea and Ethiopia

In Ethiopia, EU democracy promotion has encompassed most partial regimes of externally embedded liberal democracy. Electoral assistance was provided for the 2005 and 2010 elections, including an observer mission and a project of the European Instrument for Democracy and Human Rights (EIDHR) on voter education in 2005. Apart from the electoral process, the EU has also supported institutions of horizontal accountability. First, the EU provided a contribution of €3 million to the Democratic Institutions Programme (DIP 2007–2012). This was a capacity building programme implemented by the United Nations Development Programme (UNDP) for the National Electoral Board of Ethiopia, the Ethiopian Human Rights Commission, the Ethiopian Institute of the Ombudsman, the Ethics and Anti-Corruption Commission, the House of People's Representatives, Regional State Councils, the House of Federation and the Regional Council of Nationalities (European Community and Ethiopia 2007: 53). In 2003, the EIDHR provided nearly €0.5 million to the parliament via a programme implemented by the UNDP (European Commission n.d.d). Furthermore, the EU is one of the largest donors to the Ethiopian judiciary. Capacity building for the judiciary is provided via the EU's support to the Public Sector Capacity-Building Programme (PSCAP 2005–2012), a multi-donor programme administered by the World Bank, which included a justice system reform sub-programme. More than one-third of the democratic governance envelope under the 10th EDF has been committed to the PSCAP: €18.3 million of a total of €49 million. In addition to this amount, the EU has supported a training centre for judges and prosecutors (€4 million).[1]

In the area of political rights, the EU has addressed press freedom, albeit to a limited extent. In 2002–2004, three EIDHR microprojects, building the capacity of the media to promote human rights, were financed. In December 2009, the Swedish Presidency undertook a démarche on press freedom, followed by a public declaration raising concern about the closure of the independent newspaper *Addis Neger* and the intimidation of journalists (Council of the European Union 2009a). In the area of civil rights, the EU's reaction to the violence and arrests after the 2005 elections should be noted. In December 2005, the EU suspended budget support as a reaction to the violence committed by security forces against demonstrators. Former Commissioner for Development Louis Michel visited those arrested during the demonstrations in February 2006 and raised the issue with then Prime Minister Meles Zenawi. A legal expert was employed to attend the trials (European Parliament 2007a). Similarly, the EU advocated for the release of opposition leader Birtukan Mideksa (Ashton 2010b). On torture, there were two microprojects financed by the EIDHR. Ethiopia was also one of the beneficiaries of a regional EIDHR macroproject in East Africa on the rehabilitation of torture victims. Furthermore, the EIDHR supported projects on human rights education in 2006 and in 2010 (European Commission n.d.d, n.d.e; see also Europa 2013b). The effective power to govern has not been addressed by the EU in Ethiopia.

The EU has also focused on some of the context conditions in Ethiopia, namely, on state administrative capacity, civil society and economic development, but not on stateness. As regards state administrative capacity, the DIP includes support to the Anti-Corruption Commission and the Institute of the Ombudsman (Government of Ethiopia and UNDP 2007). The PSCAP also focuses on administrative capacity, including civil service reform, expenditure management control, tax system reform, information and communication technologies, urban management capacity building and district-level decentralization (World Bank 2004). Furthermore, until 2006, there was substantial support for civil society in Ethiopia. Between 2002 and 2006, the EIDHR financed around 30 microprojects implemented by Ethiopian NGOs in various fields: conflict resolution, women's rights, children's rights, workers' rights, ethnic minorities, disability rights, improving the environment for civil society, support to the development of local civil society organizations and so on (European Commission n.d.b).

Furthermore, €12 million from the EU's Civil Society Fund (CSF) is an important source of funding for local and national civil society organizations in Ethiopia (see Europa 2013c).

Lastly, the EU also focuses extensively on economic development and poverty reduction in Ethiopia. Substantial assistance is provided to two large donor programmes, the Protection of Basic Services and the Productive Safety Net Programme, which cover health, water and sanitation, education, rural roads and agriculture. The EU has equally provided budget support for the road sector. Smaller projects have been funded in water and sanitation, demining, health, agriculture, strengthening the private sector and building resilience to climate change (see OECD 2012).

In Eritrea, there has hardly been any financial support for the partial regimes. Although governance was a 'focal area' of EU cooperation under the 9th EDF (2002-2007), very few projects were eventually implemented. For example, there was no electoral assistance, although this was foreseen in the Country Strategy Paper (CSP) (European Community and Eritrea 2002). Support for horizontal accountability, particularly the justice sector, was equally planned in the CSP but only materialized in a project to support community courts dealing with small disputes (European Commission n.d.c). However, the EU has provided some – albeit limited – support to the effective power to govern. After the border war, Eritrea undertook a demobilization and reintegration process with the aim of reforming the security sector, reducing the size of the armed forces and decreasing military expenditure (European Community and Eritrea 2002: 23-4). The EU supported this process by committing money from the 7th and 8th EDF to a trust fund managed by the World Bank (Pretorius *et al.* 2006: 63).

While financial support has been limited, the EU has used its diplomatic instruments, as well as the threat of aid withdrawal, to encourage the partial regimes. In the area of civil rights, a démarche was undertaken by the Council Presidency in September 2001, in which concern was expressed about the imprisonment of dissidents and the suppression of the independent press (Council of the European Union 2001b). New commitments under the 8th EDF remained frozen until a new CSP was signed in November 2002 (European Community and Eritrea 2002). The question came up again during the negotiations on the CSP for the 10th EDF, but eventually the CSP was signed in 2009 (Vogel 2009). Letters were sent in September 2003, 2004 and 2005 by the Council Presidency to propose a visit of EU ambassadors to the political detainees (European Parliament 2006a). Since 2006, the EU Presidency (and now

High Representative Ashton) has issued a public declaration every year in September asking the Eritrean government to disclose information on the prisoners and to bring them to court. The EU has also raised these issues within the UN framework: it called for the release of political prisoners at the 20th session of the UN Human Rights Council (European Parliament 2012b) and gave its backing to the UN Special Rapporteur on human rights in Eritrea in 2013 (European Parliament 2013, European Union 2013). The issue of political prisoners has further been addressed in political dialogue, which has been held frequently since July 2008, often with President Afewerki himself. In September 2010, a political dialogue session was exclusively devoted to human rights issues (European Parliament 2010).

As far as the context conditions are concerned, the EU has supported state administrative capacity, economic development and stateness, but has not focused much on civil society. The CSP for the 10th EDF foresaw capacity building of public administration (European Community and Eritrea 2009: 31). €3.4 million has been committed to the Eritrean Centre for Organizational Excellence, which provides training to public officials (European Commission n.d.c). Economic development and stateness have been the main focus of the EU in Eritrea, and have been targeted jointly. Under the 9th EDF, the EU's main area of intervention was post-conflict rehabilitation (around 51 per cent), which mainly encompassed economic and social reconstruction and the restoration of economic growth. Furthermore, the EU supported the Eritrean government in defining policies and strategies for food security, transport and education (European Community and Eritrea 2002, 24–5). EC development assistance under the 10th EDF had two main focal sectors: food security (57 per cent) and infrastructure (roads) (28 per cent) (European Community and Eritrea 2009: 27). Capacity building for civil society, however, has been minimal. The EIDHR designated Eritrea as a focal country and, in 2004, a call for proposals was launched for microprojects (European Parliament 2005). However, given the limited freedom for civil society in Eritrea, most of the beneficiaries of the EIDHR have been foreign NGOs (European Commission n.d.b). The only Eritrean 'non-governmental organization' that has received money from the EU (EDF) is the National Confederation of Eritrean Workers, Eritrea's labour union, which is in fact strongly government-controlled (European Commission n.d.c).[2]

In sum, in Ethiopia, the EU has addressed most (but not all) partial regimes of liberal democracy, while it has covered most external conditions (see summary in Table A.1). One could therefore summarize the substance of EU democracy promotion in Ethiopia as relatively broad. In Eritrea, the partial regimes were addressed to a more limited extent, while the EU supported all of the external conditions. Hence, EU democracy promotion in Eritrea has been relatively shallow.

Explanations for the substance of EU democracy promotion

Power-based explanation

The EU has more capabilities than both Ethiopia and Eritrea. However, in the case of Ethiopia, the EU is dependent on cooperation in the field of security. Indeed, Ethiopia's support to counter-terrorism in the Horn of Africa, including its support to the transitional government in Somalia against Islamist rebels, makes it a strategic partner for the West (Clapham 2009: 189–90). Furthermore, the EU has security interests in the sense that it prefers stability in the country. The current government is seen as the best bet for internal stability in Ethiopia, which is deemed crucial to prevent a further rise of Islamist fundamentalism in the region (Borchgrevink 2008: 214). In this sense, democratization could cause a destabilization of the country. In the case of Eritrea, the EU does not depend on the government for security cooperation. Eritrea's alleged support to the Al-Shabaab militia in Somalia and detrimental relations with major US allies Ethiopia and Djibouti make it an unreliable partner for the EU (International Crisis Group 2010: 24–5). As a result, pushing for democratization in Eritrea could advance the EU's security interests as a new leadership may be more receptive to cooperation on security issues. On the other hand, the same argument made for Ethiopia could also be made for Eritrea: given that the country is relatively stable under authoritarian rule, democratization could lead to destabilization. Nonetheless, given that the EU is more dependent on Ethiopia than on Eritrea, one would expect the EU to promote shallow democracy in Ethiopia, and liberal or externally embedded liberal democracy in Eritrea. However, we have found exactly the contrary: the substance of EU democracy promotion has been broader in Ethiopia than in Eritrea.

Development assistance has barely increased the EU's power over either country, although it is a significant donor in both Ethiopia and Eritrea. In Eritrea, EU aid represented 13.8 per cent of Official Development Assistance (ODA) in 2000–2004 and 28.8 per cent in 2005–2009. Although the EU's share of ODA is more limited in Ethiopia, it is still the fifth largest donor with 11.7 per cent of ODA in 2000–2004 and 9.8 per cent in 2005–2009. Nonetheless, in Ethiopia, the suspension of budget support in 2005 did not lead to the desired policy reform (Borchgrevink 2008). Moreover, donors are keen to participate in Ethiopia's development success (see below), and are reluctant to suspend aid (Carothers 2010: 24). Thus, interdependence is equal at best. Similarly, even though the EU is an important donor in Eritrea, this has not increased Eritrea's dependence on the EU. Eritrea is not interested in increasing its legitimacy within the EU, and it does not feel more dependent on cooperation. Since the end of the border war, it has taken a hostile position towards Western powers, protesting against the stance of the international community on the border demarcation, which it finds unjust and favouring Ethiopia. The EU, which was an observer to the Algiers Agreement which demarcated the border between Eritrea and Ethiopia, has never put strong pressure on Ethiopia to abide by the agreement (Bereketeab 2009). The EU has, on the other hand, supported Eritrea's engagement with the international community, which has been valued to some extent by the Eritrean government. Economically, the government of Eritrea has attempted to limit dependence on foreign donors and become self-reliant (International Crisis Group 2010: 24). The result is a paradoxical situation: although the EU might be expected to have less power over Ethiopia than over Eritrea, the opposite seems to be the case. This, in turn, is consistent with the finding that EU democracy promotion in Ethiopia has been broader than in Eritrea.

Institutions

EU policies in Ethiopia and Eritrea fall under the Cotonou Agreement and were – prior to the entry into force of the Lisbon Treaty in late 2009 – implemented by the Commission's DG DEV. This applies of course to development cooperation, but also to political relations where – as we will see below – the Commission often played a role. Given that trade between the EU and both Ethiopia and Eritrea is minor, and does not include energy resources, other DGs do not have a strong interest. The responsibility of DG DEV, rather than (former) DG External Relations (Relex), is likely to have had an influence on the substance of democracy promotion, since DG Development was much more oriented towards poverty reduction, while DG Relex was more geared towards the EU's security interests (Carbone 2007: 48–9, Holden 2009: 41). Hence, the focus on the context conditions in both countries can be assigned to the predominance of the Commission's DG DEV during most of the period under review. Since 2010, however, the EEAS and the EC's DG DEVCO (Development and Cooperation) are jointly in charge of cooperation.

Although this has not resulted in a major shift in approach towards the two countries, one change has been the introduction of local human rights strategies, managed by the Heads of Mission. While no major shift in EU policies towards either country was noted after 2010, in the case of Eritrea we did see the EU taking up the case of political prisoners more strongly in 2012–2013, which could be related to the growing role of the EEAS.

Diplomatic efforts have been mainly undertaken by the Council, although the Commission has also played a role. None of the EU Common Security and Defence Policy missions, such as EUCAP Nestor, EU NAVFOR Somalia or EUTM Somalia, works directly from Eritrea or Ethiopia, nor has the internal situation in these countries been high on the agenda of the Council. Several member states have a special cultural or historical relationship with Eritrea; for example Italy was the former colonizer in Eritrea and Sweden has a large population of Eritrean immigrants. The colonial history did not impede Italy from taking the lead on the démarche on political prisoners in 2001. Sweden has been particularly concerned about the case of the imprisoned Swedish-Eritrean journalist Dawit Isaac. Only a few member states have representation in Asmara: Italy, France, the UK and Germany. The ambassadors from the UK and Germany criticized Louis Michel's negotiations with Eritrean President Afewerki on a new development strategy in 2008 (United States Embassy Eritrea 2008). In Ethiopia, there is wider representation of member states, given the crucial role of Ethiopia in the region, the large donor community there and the fact that Addis Ababa hosts the headquarters of the African Union. On some occasions, member states have been more vocal about the partial regimes in Ethiopia than the EC. In 2009, the Swedish Presidency led a démarche and public statement on the freedom of the press (Council of the European Union 2009a). In 2010, member states prevented the EC from resuming budget support because of the lack of democratic reform.[3] However, despite expressing occasional criticism, the member states largely agree with the EC's stance that dialogue is a better strategy than political conditionality in both cases. The European Parliament (EP) has at times called for the EU to make aid to Ethiopia and Eritrea more conditional on progress on democracy. In 2005, the EP called on the Commission to make aid conditional upon progress in the democratic process in Ethiopia (European Parliament 2006b). In 2009, some Members of the European Parliament (MEPs) protested against the adoption of a new CSP with Eritrea (Vogel 2009). However, neither the EC nor the member states have responded to these calls.

Domestic context: Shortcomings/tailor-made approach

While Eritrea is a fully authoritarian country, Ethiopia could be classified as 'semi-authoritarian' (Carothers 2000) or a 'hybrid regime' (Diamond 2002). Although Eritrea adopted a constitution introducing multi-party democracy in 1997, this constitution has never been implemented. Elections were initially foreseen for 1998, but have been postponed ever since. The ruling People's Front for Democracy and Justice (PFDJ) is the only political party. There is no legal opposition in the country (Reid 2009: 211). Furthermore, in September 2001, political freedom was further restricted. As a reaction to an open letter to the president, 11 dissidents of the PFDJ were jailed, journalists were arrested and a ban on the privately owned press was enacted. Independent civil society organizations do not exist in Eritrea because of the absolute lack of freedom of assembly and legal restrictions on the registration of NGOs (Freedom House 2011).

Compared to Eritrea, Ethiopia's democratization process is more advanced. Whereas the 1995 and 2000 elections were dominated by the ruling party and held in a context of a closed political space, the 2005 parliamentary elections were much more open in terms of campaigning. The opposition increased its presence in parliament from 12 to 161 seats (out of 547) (Abbink 2006). However, surprised by the increased assertiveness of the opposition, press and civil society, which had challenged the results of the vote, the government tightened its grip on these groups with new laws on mass media (2008), civil society (2009) and anti-terrorism (2009) (Aalen and Tronvoll 2009: 200–2). At the same time, the ruling party extended its power base by using microcredit programmes and government jobs as an incentive to attract new members. Together with the weakening and division of the opposition, this strategy succeeded in re-establishing the EPRDF as the sole party in power in the 2008 local and 2010 parliamentary elections (Aalen and Tronvoll 2008, Tronvoll 2010).

The fact that Ethiopia is more democratic than Eritrea is clearly reflected in the Bertelsmann Transformation Index (BTI) indicators on the electoral regime, civil and political rights and horizontal accountability (BTI 2012a). While, for both countries, the scores are rather low, Eritrea's scores are still a few points lower than Ethiopia. Hence, the substance of EU democracy promotion does not reflect the domestic structure: whereas one would expect the EU to have a broader focus where shortcomings are larger (Eritrea), exactly the opposite is the case.

In both countries, the government maintains firm control over the security forces, which can hardly be called 'democratic control of the military' given that the government is not democratically elected (Abbink 2009: 20–1, Reid 2009: 213–14). In Eritrea, military spending is exceptionally high: even after the border war, Eritrea spent around 20 per cent of its GDP on the military. Ethiopia's military expenditure, on the contrary, was only 2.6 per cent on average during 2000–2010 (SIPRI 2012). In this sense, the fact that the EU had a project on the demobilization of the military in Eritrea does reflect the situation on the ground.

Regarding the external conditions, BTI indicators Q 13.3 reflect relatively high conflict intensity in both countries, which decreased in recent years. The substance of democracy promotion does not reflect the conflict intensity, given that the EU only focused on stateness in Eritrea and not in Ethiopia, where conflict intensity was equally high. As mentioned above, the EU has an interest in the internal stability of Ethiopia and Eritrea. Hence, it may not overemphasize the partial regimes in both countries as long as there is no severe conflict. The enormous socio-economic needs of both countries should be noted, which is also reflected in a low score on the BTI indicator for socio-economic development (see Table A.2). While civil society is in both cases underdeveloped, it is especially weak in Eritrea, where BTI scores have been at their lowest levels. As regards state administrative capacity, scores for both countries are higher when compared to those related to the partial regimes. This again contradicts the thesis that the EU would mainly focus on shortcomings: the EU has put more emphasis on state administrative capacity than on the partial regimes in Ethiopia and Eritrea. Moreover, while Ethiopia scored better than Eritrea on state administrative capacity, there has been more focus on this in Ethiopia.

Domestic context: Political will to undertake democratic reform

The degree of political will of the governments of Eritrea and Ethiopia to undertake democratic reform has had a major impact on the substance of EU democracy promotion. To begin with, the broader substance of EU democracy promotion in Ethiopia is related to the fact that the government of Ethiopia is more open to democracy promotion than the government of Eritrea. This is clearly reflected in the BTI indicators on 'international cooperation': over the period 2006–2012, Ethiopia had an average of 5.15, while Eritrea's average score was only 2.25.

However, even in Ethiopia, political will influences the substance of EU democracy promotion. The Ethiopian government has reacted quite harshly to external criticism about democratization. Rather than the Western-inspired liberal democratic model, the EPRDF claims to promote a different kind of democracy, which it terms 'revolutionary democracy' and which focuses on collective rights (as enshrined in the system of ethnic federalism) and direct participatory democracy (via very large local councils of around 300 people) (Human Rights Watch 2010b: 13). The EU has not taken an explicit stance on this revolutionary democratic agenda. The Ethiopian regime has been particularly wary of foreign intervention in the electoral process. Although EU observers were invited to the 2005 and 2010 elections, the reports of both EU Election Observation Missions (EU EOMs) were met with accusations of partiality and violating the memorandum of understanding. The chief observer of the 2010 EU EOM was not allowed to present his report in the capital (Ashton 2010c). Similarly, democracy promotion is affected by the civil society legislation adopted in 2009, which prohibits organizations receiving more than 10 per cent of their funding from foreign sources from working on issues of advocacy, human rights, democratization and good governance. As a result of the legislation, the EU had to refocus on socio-economic issues or women's rights which, despite falling under the scope of prohibited activities, seem to be tolerated by the government-controlled civil society agency.[4]

Even more so than the Ethiopian government, the government of Eritrea has insisted on non-interference on issues of democracy. After an EU troika expressed criticism about the crackdown on political dissent in September 2001, the Eritrean government promptly ousted the Italian ambassador, emphasizing that development cooperation could not be conditional on a 'compromise of Eritrea's sovereignty' (Calchi Novati 2008: 53). There are numerous examples of how political will has limited the substance of EU democracy promotion in Eritrea. Support for the electoral process planned under the 9th EDF did not go ahead, given that elections were never organized. Support for civil society is hampered by the lack of independent civil society organizations. For example, there are no organizations working on political or civil rights (Pretorius *et al.* 2006: 59). The EU has particularly focused on women's, children's and workers' rights, since in these areas, there is some openness from the government.

The closed character of the Eritrean government also applies to the external conditions of embedded democracy. The rather technical focus of most democracy assistance in Eritrea should be seen in this regard:

technical programmes are seen as less threatening to the government. The government has resorted to a policy of self-reliance and has made it very difficult for donors to operate. It does not publish a budget, made the registration of NGOs difficult with a new law in 2004 and prohibits donor officials from travelling outside Asmara (International Crisis Group 2010). This position was taken to the extreme in 2011, when the government refused to sign a new agreement with the UN, instructed all international NGOs to terminate activities and announced the suspension of ongoing projects under the 10th EDF (European Commission n.d.c).

Interorganizational context

The interorganizational context has an influence on the substance of EU democracy promotion in Ethiopia, while in Eritrea this factor is negligible. In Ethiopia, there are various other democracy promoters, the most important of which are the UNDP, the World Bank, the US, the UK, Canada and Norway. Smaller democracy promoters include Austria, Ireland, the Netherlands, Denmark and Sweden. The UNDP and the World Bank are especially important. As noted above, two of the EU-funded programmes in support of the partial regimes and state administrative capacity, namely, the DIP and the PSCAP, were implemented by the UNDP and the World Bank. Both are primarily geared towards development, although there is a difference between the World Bank, which can only support 'good governance', and the UNDP, which explicitly promotes 'democratic governance' (White 2000: 69, Santiso 2002: 584–5). Moreover, some bilateral donors play a particularly important role in some of these multi-donor democracy projects. Canada, the UK and the Netherlands were part of the technical committee of the DIP. In the case of the PSCAP, the EU relied on the expertise of Canada in the justice sector, while the UK took the lead in the sub-programme on civil service reform. The strong focus of the EU on state administrative capacity in Ethiopia has been influenced by the interorganizational context. It seemed easier for the EU to fund multi-donor programmes than to create its own projects for which it would need more expertise and staff. This can explain the relatively large amount of EU funding for the PSCAP. The fact that a much smaller amount was provided to the DIP is also related to the interorganizational context: the DIP was not in need of more funding.[5] Lastly, the EU's absence in the security sector in Ethiopia may be related to the fact that the US and the UK were already involved.

In comparison, the interorganizational context is less important in the case of Eritrea, where the EU is one of the few remaining donors. Most donors have limited their interventions to humanitarian assistance. From this perspective, it is surprising that the EU has not ended its development assistance like other donors. However, for the member states it might be beneficial to have a continuous EU involvement in Eritrea to substitute for their own absence.[6]

Conclusion

This chapter started by mapping the substance of EU democracy promotion in Ethiopia and Eritrea. It was found that, in both cases, the EU has focused on certain partial regimes of liberal democracy and most of the external conditions of embedded liberal democracy. Furthermore, the substance of democracy promotion was relatively broad in Ethiopia, but rather shallow in Eritrea.

Ethiopia and Eritrea are both ACP countries and thus the EC's DG DEV was in charge during most of the period under investigation. The member states have largely concurred with the EC position that development aid should continue despite severe shortcomings in the field of democratization. Whereas in Eritrea the interorganizational context was not that important, in Ethiopia EU democracy assistance should be seen within the wider framework of donor coordination.

The difference between a broader agenda in Ethiopia and a shallower agenda in Eritrea corresponds to a difference in political will. As a fully authoritarian regime, there are hardly any intervention areas for the EU in Eritrea. Particularly in the partial regimes, the lack of cooperation from the Eritrean government has hampered EU assistance. In contrast, Ethiopia is a semi-authoritarian regime and has at least some democratic features that the EU can support, although intervening in sensitive areas such as elections has equally been difficult.

The EU's power position in terms of capabilities has not played an important role. Given the EU's security interests, we expected the EU to be in a more powerful position in Eritrea than in Ethiopia, but found that the contrary was the case. Indeed, Eritrea has been indifferent towards any economic support from the EU, and thus there is no interdependence. EU democracy promotion has not responded well to the shortcomings in both countries: it has had a broader agenda where it was less needed (in Ethiopia). However, the conflict intensity experienced by both countries may have led the EU to place relatively little emphasis on the partial regimes, as it is most important for the EU that Ethiopia and Eritrea are stable.

Notes

1. Anonymous interview, Addis Ababa, January 2011.
2. Anonymous interview, Brussels, February 2012.
3. Anonymous interviews, Addis Ababa, 2011.
4. Anonymous interview, Addis Ababa, January 2011.
5. Anonymous interviews, Addis Ababa, January 2011.
6. Anonymous interview, Brussels, February 2012.

15
Responding to Political Crises in the South Pacific: The Solomon Islands and Fiji

Maurizio Carbone and Karen Del Biondo

Introduction

This chapter investigates the substance of EU democracy promotion in two South Pacific states: the Solomon Islands and Fiji. The Solomon Islands and Fiji are particular in the sense that the domestic context made it necessary for the EU to 'do something' in the field of the partial regimes of liberal democracy. Unconstitutional changes of government are unacceptable to the EU and, as a rule, lead to the opening of the Article 96 procedure of the Cotonou Agreement, which allows the EU to employ sanctions, including the suspension of aid, after consultations with the host government (Portela 2010).

As the EU does not have significant security interests in these countries, we expect the EU to promote a broad democratic substance as it finds itself in a relatively powerful position. However, the EU has expressed support for a regional approach towards democracy promotion, which largely takes place within the Pacific Islands Forum (PIF), which is dominated by regional powers Australia and New Zealand. We will see that the EU finds itself entrapped by its support for a regional approach in the field of democracy and governance.

The political crises in the Solomon Islands and Fiji are strongly related to the ethnic divisions in both countries, and so the EU has been concerned with the issue of stateness. However, we will see that the EU has addressed this issue differently in each case. In the case of the Solomon Islands, the EU has focused on stateness directly, while in Fiji, the EU has promoted stateness indirectly by addressing some of the partial regimes, including the electoral regime, the effective power to govern and horizontal accountability.

The chapter is divided into two main sections. The first section discusses the nature of the political crises, before looking at the substance of EU democracy promotion in the Solomon Islands and Fiji. The second section then reviews the four hypotheses formulated in the introductory chapter of this volume, concluding that the domestic context and interorganizational context are most important in explaining the substance of EU democracy promotion in both cases. To make this argument, the chapter draws on a comprehensive analysis of primary sources, most notably country strategy papers (CSPs), official documents from the EU and the PIF Secretariat, and speeches, as well as 34 interviews with policy-makers.[1]

Mapping the substance of EU democracy promotion in the Solomon Islands and Fiji

Both the Solomon Islands and Fiji have experienced unconstitutional changes of government in the 2000s, yet the EU has responded differently to these crises. In the late 1990s, the Solomon Islands suffered from political turmoil arising from ethnic tensions in Guadalcanal (the main island) between the original inhabitants, represented by the Isatabu Freedom Movement (IFM), and immigrants from Malaita island, represented by the Malaita Eagle Force (MEF). Following two failed peace accords, a 'civil takeover' took place on 5 June 2000. The MEF, assisted by a section of the local police, ousted the IFM government led by Bartholomew Ulufa'alu. Two days later, however, the government and the MEF agreed to seek a 'constitutional' solution and discuss the issue during a special session of parliament. On 30 June 2000, the parliament elected the opposition leader Manasseh Sogavare as the new prime minister, who immediately committed to restoring peace and the rule of law. A ceasefire was signed in August 2000, followed by a peace agreement signed in Townsville, Australia, in October 2000. This agreement, endorsed by the IFM and the MEF, laid the ground for forgiveness, respect and mutual trust among the members of both factions. In December 2001, national elections took place. The electoral process, supported by all major donors, was regarded as free and fair (Carbone 2006).

In Fiji, in May 2000 an armed insurrection led by businessman George Speight and indigenous Fijians took over the parliament and seized the Indo-Fijian Prime Minister, Mahendra Chaudhry, and members of his cabinet. The military then approached President Kamisese Mara and asked him to step aside so that law and order could be restored. The hostages were finally released on 13 July 2000, but Speight's choice for president, Ratu Josefa Iloilo, was selected as the new president. The new president then appointed an interim administration led by Laisenia Qarase, with the former ruling party opposing what they claimed was an illegitimate decision. The Constitutional Review Commission was set up and promised that parliamentary elections would be held in March 2002. Eventually, they were held in 2003, but the formation of the government was questioned by the Fiji Labour Party (FLP), which invoked the constitution that stipulates that any party obtaining at least 10 per cent of the seats in the parliament must be invited to join the government. In July 2003, the supreme court stipulated that the FLP was entitled to be part of a multiparty cabinet. In August 2003, the prime minister thus offered 14 portfolios to the members of the FLP. In May 2006, general elections were held, which led to the formation of a new government. However, Voreqe (Frank) Bainimarama, Fiji's military commander, ousted the ruling government in December 2006 (Carbone 2006).

In the Solomon Islands, the civilian takeover of the government in 2000 led the EU to focus on the electoral regime. After the civilian takeover, the European Commission threatened to cut aid if there was no immediate return to democracy. Although aid was never formally suspended, implementation was negatively affected by the tensions in the country. In the solution to the crisis, the EU mainly focused on the peace process (stateness) and on socio-economic development. While a substantial portion of its activities were halted, projects conducive to the peace process, as well as the various microprojects, continued to be implemented. Moreover, in order for development cooperation to be resumed, the EU demanded an improvement of stateness and socio-economic development. The conditions for a full resumption of cooperation, spelled out in political dialogue, were: (1) a realistic economic restoration programme; and (2) a measurable improvement in the security situation. In November 2003, the European Commission announced that all funds allocated for the Solomon Islands would be unfrozen.

Focal sectors of EU development assistance under the 9th European Development Fund (EDF) (2003–2007) were rural development and support to non-state actors. The latter was mainly focused on supporting civil society organizations in their role as service providers and in their dialogue with the government. After the mid-term review of the Country Strategy Paper in 2005, it was decided to also focus on good governance, leading to a Provincial Governance Support Programme. Under the 10th EDF, EU development assistance focused on one sole focal sector: rural development (European Community and Solomon Islands 2007: 22, 28–9). In 2010, two budget support programmes started, one of which was the Climate Change Assistance Programme and the other the Economic Recovery Assistance Programme (see OECD 2014). Several projects were also set up to support the May 2010 elections. More specifically, the EU financed the coordination of international observation, domestic observation by civil society, civic education and an election expert mission. In addition, some emphasis was put on justice for human rights violations. The EU provided resources to the Truth and Reconciliation Commission established to help redress victims of ethnic unrest between 1998 and 2003. In addition, there was support for two microprojects, one of which supported grassroots democracy and the other human rights training for disadvantaged groups (Europa 2012d).

In Fiji, in the first half of the 2000s there was a clear division of labour in terms of the substance of EU democracy promotion: diplomatic instruments were used to promote liberal democracy, while development assistance focused mainly on the context conditions. Diplomacy and sanctions addressed the partial regimes, particularly the effective power to govern, the electoral regime, horizontal accountability and political rights. In a statement made on 25 July 2000, the EU Presidency deplored the deposing of President Mara and declared its outrage at the repeal of the constitution. It called for the restoration of the rule of law, respect for political rights and a democratically elected government. Interestingly, these conditions were deemed necessary to maintain stability in Fiji, that is, stateness (Council of the European Union 2000). On 6 July 2000, the European Parliament passed a resolution inviting the European Commission to start appropriate procedures to suspend development cooperation if there was no quick return to democracy. On 19 October 2000, the European Commission decided to open consultations with the government of Fiji under Article 96 of the Cotonou Agreement. The consultations ended in April 2001, when the Council adopted a decision, establishing that the allocation of the 9th EDF and the financing and implementation of new programmes and projects under the 7th and 8th EDF would be made once free and fair elections had taken place and a legitimate government had assumed office. Nevertheless, support to regional projects, operations of a humanitarian nature, trade cooperation and trade-related preferences, including the sugar protocol,[2] remained unaffected by the Council decision, in order to avoid causing economic hardship for the population. When elections were held in September 2001, which were considered free and fair by the Commonwealth and by a joint EU–African, Caribbean, and Pacific Group of States (ACP) mission, the EU did not immediately resume development assistance. Instead, the EU chose to await the result of Fiji's supreme court ruling regarding the legitimacy of the new government (see *supra*). In February 2002, the EU decided to release funds under the 7th and 8th EDF, announced the notification of the 9th EDF, but clarified that the National Indicative Programme (NIP) would take effect only after the court ruling on the conformity of the government with the constitution. After the formation of an inclusive government in August 2003, the General Affairs and External Council of the EU decided to resume full cooperation with Fiji in November 2003, almost three years after the coup (Council of the European Union 2003). Hence, in the case of Fiji, respect for the constitution was considered more important than the mere holding of free and fair elections. During the aid suspension, there was hardly any financial support for democratization. For example, despite the focus on holding free and fair elections, the EU did not provide any electoral assistance for the elections in 2003. Instead, EU democracy assistance, which was mostly financed by the European Initiative for Democracy and Human Rights (EIDHR),[3] of which Fiji was a country of focus in 2002–2004, concentrated on inter-ethnic dialogue and conflict prevention, that is, stateness (Carbone 2006).

After 2003, however, development assistance became more focused on the promotion of the partial regimes, particularly the electoral regime, political and civil rights. Apart from a number of projects to promote socio-economic development (education, tourism, measures accompanying the sugar protocol), the EDF supported an EU observer mission for the May 2006 elections (Europa 2014j). EIDHR projects included civic education and support for the human rights commission. However, overall, the focus of EIDHR was on stateness and state capacity: national reconciliation was a cross-cutting issue of most human rights projects and several other projects focused on good governance. In 2007, the EU entered into a new round of Article 96 consultations with the Fiji government after the government was overthrown in a military coup in December 2006. In the consultations, the EU named the following conditions for the resumption of cooperation: respect for human rights and the rule of law, the independence of the judiciary and the constitution and the investigation of human rights violations committed during the coup. The 2008 sugar allocation would become available only once there was evidence of a credible and timely preparation of elections (Council of the European Union 2007c). In September 2009, the EU decided to extend the period of measures, as a response to the abrogation of the constitution by the government, the delay in holding parliamentary elections, and human rights violations (Council of the European Union 2009b). In this period, the EIDHR financed local civil society organizations involved in environmental education, consumer rights and human rights education. To date, the EDF has not been resumed.

Mapping the substance of EU democracy promotion in Fiji and the Solomon Islands reveals the following (see summary in Table A.1 in the Annex). In the case of the Solomon Islands, the EU made a shift from supporting mainly external conditions (2000–2007) to supporting mainly partial regimes (2008–2010). Despite the civilian takeover in 2000, the EU initially remained focused on the external context and hardly paid attention to the partial regimes, although it did condemn the civilian takeover of power. This changed towards 2010, when the EU started providing financial assistance for elections and human rights. Since 2007, the EU has not really further addressed stateness and state capacity, although it does offer support to a small number of civil society organizations and to socio-economic development. In Fiji, a different picture emerges. There, the EU has switched from an approach that concentrates on most partial regimes and some external conditions, to one that touches upon all issues, and in particular on elections. Diplomatic pressure throughout the 2000s addressed the partial regimes, but it took several years before financial assistance followed. For example, despite the fact that elections were considered a condition for the resumption of aid in 2000–2003, the EU did not offer any electoral assistance. Because of the sanctions regime, support for socio-economic development has been relatively small in Fiji. Whereas the sanctions imposed in 2000 were intended to have only a minor impact on development assistance, those imposed in 2006 had a larger impact. Stateness was seen as important by the EU in both cases, but was addressed more intensively in the Solomon Islands than in Fiji. In Fiji, the EU reasoned that the promotion of the partial regimes proved a good way to promote stability. In the Solomon Islands, the EU addressed stability directly, rather than via support for democracy.

Explaining the substance of EU democracy promotion

From the above analysis, it appears that the substance of EU democracy promotion in the Solomon Islands and Fiji has varied between the cases and has changed over time. How can we explain our findings? This question will be addressed in the following section, which discusses the four main explanatory factors of this volume: power, institutions, domestic context and interorganizational context.

Power

From a security point of view, the South Pacific does not present any threat to Europe, not least because of its geographical distance. As for trade relations, these are of marginal significance: the share of the Pacific members of the African, Caribbean and Pacific Group (PACP) in EU–ACP trade in the 2000s was consistently less than 1 per cent, even though Fiji was one of the main trade partners within the PACP group. Fiji signed an interim Economic Partnership Agreement (EPA) in November 2007, mainly to protect its exports of fish and sugar into EU markets (Sheahan *et al.* 2010). With the EU's interest in sugar being in significant decline as a result of various reforms in the Common Agricultural Policy, the fisheries sector is where 'Pacific countries have considerable commodity power as opposed to the EU which is dependent on fish imports from the Pacific' (Serrano 2011). However, it should be noted that the dearth of trade and security interests is matched by relatively high levels of foreign aid, which makes the PACP region the highest per capita recipient of EU foreign aid.[4]

Institutions

Post-colonial links with the two states are rather weak and no EU member state has significant interests in the region. Only the UK (a former colonial power), France (mainly looking after its overseas territories), Portugal (the key partner for Timor-Leste) and more recently Italy and Germany have paid some attention to the PACP region. This situation has been seen positively within the European Commission, as confirmed by a senior official: 'the fact that the member states do not have key interests to protect means that, thanks to the Lisbon Treaty, we are free to experiment in the Pacific and test the EU's wider aspiration to become an influential international actor in the widest sense possible'.[5] However, the EU's member states did play a role in the case of Fiji, as the Article 96 procedure and the suspension of development assistance had to be approved by the Council.

Within the European Commission, Directorate General (DG) Development has been very important for the South Pacific, given the relatively high amount of aid going to the region. For democracy assistance, however, former DG Relex was also an important actor as it controlled the purse for the EIDHR. This led to inter-institutional quarrels with DG Development, which was in charge of the EDF but was hesitant to divert resources away from the objective of poverty reduction. The fact that no electoral assistance was provided to the 2003 elections in Fiji can be explained by such inter-institutional conflict. DG Relex argued that funds for electoral assistance and monitoring had already been allocated and that it could not change the list of beneficiaries; DG Development was against using resources from the EDF for democracy promotion rather than for poverty eradication activities (ECSIEP 2004). However, in 2006 election observation was paid for by the EDF (see *supra*).

The European Parliament has also shown some interest in democracy in the South Pacific. In the case of the Solomon Islands, there was substantial attention from the parliament, particularly during the May 2000 coup, which took place while two Members of the European Parliament (MEPs), Glenys Kinnock and John Corrie, were conducting a mission in the South Pacific. The two MEPs, who were also involved in the Article 96 negotiations, urged the EU and the international community to put pressure on those responsible for the crisis to find a quick solution. Immediately after the coup in Fiji in May 2000, the European Parliament passed a resolution inviting the European Commission to start appropriate procedures to suspend development cooperation if there was no quick return to democracy. In mid-October 2000, a motion was introduced by European members of the EU–ACP Joint Parliamentary Assembly calling for economic sanctions, but it was ultimately rejected due to pressure from the ACP members, who requested a joint fact-finding mission. Although the Parliament has thus played a role in attracting interest in the democratic record, and particularly the electoral regime of the Solomon Islands and Fiji, it was a less important actor than the Commission and the Council, which were the main decision-makers on democracy assistance and sanctions.

Domestic conditions

For a long time, the South Pacific was considered an 'oasis of democracy' and thus the situation of democracy engendered little attention from the EU, which chose instead to focus on socio-economic development. In the words of a Commission official, 'the Pacific is not Africa and we thought there was no need for the EU to focus on democracy and good governance. In our strategies for individual countries we chose to focus on socio-economic development, especially cross-country projects.'[6] However, the two coups that struck Fiji and the Solomon Islands brought the importance of democracy promotion to the fore. Although the crises in Fiji and in the Solomon Islands occurred at the same time, an important difference should be highlighted. In the case of the Solomon Islands, the procedure to appoint the new government was recognized as legitimate by the EU. In the case of Fiji, various pressures, including from the deposed Prime Minister Chaudhry, were directed towards the EU in 2000 not to recognize the legitimacy of the interim administration, accused of promoting an undemocratic and racist agenda. Moreover, another military coup took place in 2006, only a few years after EU aid was resumed. As stated earlier, this triggered a new round of Article 96 consultations and the suspension of EU development assistance in 2007.

The difference between the quickly resolved political crisis in the Solomon Islands and the lingering crisis in Fiji is reflected in indicators regarding the electoral process, civil and political rights, effective power, stateness and civil society. Table 15.1 shows indicators that reflect the different components of embedded democracy. The 2006 military coup in Fiji led to an immediate drop in all these indicators. In comparison, in the Solomon Islands, scores were much higher and remained stable in the last five years. Hence, the EU's strong emphasis on a return to democratic rule in Fiji reflects the challenges on the ground, namely, the grave deterioration of the electoral process, political stability and

Table 15.1 Indicators of embedded democracy

Subsector	Indicator	Range
Electoral regime	Freedom House electoral process	0–12 (higher = better)
Civil rights	CIRI political prisoners, torture, disappearance and killings	0–2 (higher = better)
Political rights	Freedom House political pluralism and freedom of expression and belief (average)	0–16 (higher = better)
Horizontal accountability	Freedom House rule of law	0–16 (higher = better)
Effective power	Freedom House functioning of the government	0–12 (higher = better)
Stateness	WGI political stability	−2.5–+2.5 (higher = better)
State capacity	WGI government effectiveness	−2.5–+2.5 (higher = better)
Civil society	Freedom House freedom of association	0–12 (lower = better)
Socio-economic development	Human Development Index	0–1 (higher = better)

human rights after the military coup. In the Solomon Islands, the situation was less problematic, hence there was less emphasis on democratization. However, the rather average score of the Solomon Islands on the electoral process can explain why the EU deemed it necessary to provide electoral assistance. Moreover, the EU's emphasis on state capacity and development in the Solomon Islands is in line with needs in this sphere. The World Bank Governance Indicators on government effectiveness and the Human Development Index reflect a rather low score for the Solomon Islands, while Fiji scores better on both indicators (Table 15.2).

The initial reluctance to support the partial regimes in the South Pacific, and particularly in the Solomon Islands, corresponds to the particular nature of democracy in the South Pacific, and the unfamiliarity of the EU with this type of democracy. The South Pacific countries differ in terms of political status and institutional performance, yet they share a number of common features that clash with the notion of liberal democracy that the EU seeks to promote. Policy decisions, rather

Table 15.2 Selected indicators Solomon Islands and Fiji

Solomon Islands	2000	2002	2004	2006	2008	2010
Electoral regime	N/A	N/A	N/A	7	6	6
Civil rights	N/A	N/A	1.75	1.75	2	2
Political rights	N/A	N/A	N/A	11.5	11.5	11.5
Horizontal accountability	N/A	N/A	N/A	8	8	8
Effective power	N/A	N/A	N/A	7	5	6
Stateness	−0.83	−0.55	0.06	0.12	0.24	0.41
State capacity	−0.96	−2.04	−1.17	−0.99	−1	−0.94
Civil society	N/A	N/A	N/A	9	9	9
Socio-economic development	0.459	N/A	N/A	N/A	N/A	0.494
Fiji	**2000**	**2002**	**2004**	**2006**	**2008**	**2010**
Electoral regime	N/A	N/A	N/A	6	0	0
Civil rights	1.75	1.75	1.75	1.25	1.25	1.5
Political rights	N/A	N/A	N/A	10	8	7.5
Horizontal accountability	N/A	N/A	N/A	11	7	7
Effective power	N/A	N/A	N/A	6	2	2
Stateness	0.21	0.37	0.37	−0.01	−0.05	−0.16
State capacity	−0.54	0.06	−0.43	−0.13	−0.76	−0.73
Civil society	N/A	N/A	N/A	9	4	4
Socio-economic development	0.651	N/A	N/A	N/A	N/A	0.699

than being the result of confrontation between government and opposition, are often taken by consensus. A pluralistic multiparty system is seen as exacerbating ethnic tensions; an excessive emphasis upon individual human rights clashes with highly regarded collective interests, such as the community, the village or the chief system; an effective system of checks and balances is difficult to implement because educated elites who form the judiciary, the military and the bureaucracy are often closely connected through family ties. For these reasons, some analysts even conclude that democracy itself is a 'foreign flower' rooted in particular social conditions and perhaps unable to flourish without them – something that was introduced by the outside but that has still not translated well in Pacific societies (Larmour 2005, Crocombe 2008). The political crises in the Solomon Islands and Fiji are linked to ethnic clashes and to the perception of group inequalities, combined with the struggle to control natural resources and tensions over land ownership (Reilly 2004, Crocombe 2008). Although the EU seemed concerned about ethnic cleavages in both the Solomon Islands and Fiji, the solutions it has offered differed between the countries. In the Solomon Islands, the EU focused on stateness directly, while in Fiji, it promoted stateness indirectly by addressing some of the partial regimes, including the electoral regime, the effective power to govern and horizontal accountability.

From a socio-economic point of view, most indicators have not improved or have even deteriorated. Indicators on government effectiveness and the Human Development Index have improved only slightly or have even worsened, as was the case with corruption in the Solomon Islands. For these reasons, Reilly (2000) has spoken, provocatively, of the 'Africanisation of the South Pacific'. Fraenkel (2004) has contested this thesis, arguing that the socio-economic situation in the South Pacific is still much better than in most African countries. Nonetheless, the rather undeveloped status of the economy in the Solomon Islands can explain why the EU put so much emphasis on development and, to a lesser extent, on state capacity. In the case of Fiji, however, the military coup and the subsequent sanctions put severe limits on development assistance.

Interorganizational context

The interorganizational context has had a significant influence on EU democracy promotion policies towards both countries. One element to consider is the regional integration process in the South Pacific, and the efforts made by the PIF in particular. The PIF represents heads of government of all the independent and self-governing Pacific Island countries, as well as Australia and New Zealand. Some differences exist between Pacific and metropolitan values and methods. Pacific Islanders adhere to principles of face-saving, consensus, and non-interference, whereas Australia and New Zealand, with some differences, have increasingly overridden these principles and emphasized more effective intervention (Von Strokirch 2005).

Nonetheless, the Forum has issued several documents on the topic of democratization. In 2000, the Forum signed the Biketawa Declaration, which included a commitment to good governance, liberty of the individual, democratic processes that reflect national and local circumstances, equitable economic, social, and cultural development, indigenous rights, values and traditions, and an inclusive democracy that involves civil society organizations (Von Strokirch 2005). In 2005, the Pacific Plan for Strengthening Regional Cooperation and Integration was adopted. The aim was to foster economic growth and promote regional security, but one of its central components was the idea that good governance is a prerequisite for sustainable development and economic growth. Moreover, the Plan emphasized the need to move towards harmonization at the regional level, which would also help to overcome the variety of traditions of democracy and governance on the basis of indicators developed outside the region – and this rather technocratic view of governance was criticized by most PACP countries as being in contrast with local traditions emphasizing broader participation and consensual decision-making processes.

The EU strongly endorsed the Pacific Plan, which is reflected in its *Strategy for the Pacific Islands* published in 2006, just after the former's adoption. Its three main components – political dialogue through the enhancement of the relationship with the PIF; focused development action with greater emphasis on governance, regionalism and sustainable management of natural resources; and aid efficiency through better coordination with Australia and New Zealand – seemed to suggest that regional integration is the solution to all problems (European Commission 2006j).[7] In the case of democracy promotion, significant emphasis was placed on political dialogue with the PIF, which was identified as 'the main regional institution for political issues [...] which has a mandate and coherent regional policies set out in the *Pacific Plan*' (European Commission 2006j: 5, emphasis added).

The unintended consequence of this focus on regional integration was that the EU (unwillingly) delegated the substance of democracy promotion in the South Pacific to Australia and New Zealand (Carbone

2011). Indeed, these regional powers had increasingly managed to impose their views within the PIF.[8] Following the terrorist attacks in the US (September 2001) and in Bali (October 2002), Australia and New Zealand started seeing the PACP region as a potential source of threats to their national security and therefore adopted a more interventionist stance. The PIF's principle of non-interference was softened, which allowed Australia to launch a 'cooperative intervention' operation in the Solomon Islands in 2003 to restore law and order and reinvigorate the local economy. Furthermore, an Australian official, Greg Urwin, was imposed as the Secretary-General of the PIF, in the face of opposition from various PACP countries (Firth 2008: 119–34).[9] More generally, because of their larger economies, more assertive foreign policies and major contribution to the PIF's budget, the two regional powers have been 'able to be simultaneously members *of* the region (and regional groupings as the Pacific Islands Forum) and powerful actors executing pressure *on* the poorer countries in the region' (Roberts *et al.* 2007: 972). The EU's approach to the crises in the Solomon Islands and Fiji was largely in line with that of the regional powers. In the 2000 political crisis in the Solomon Islands, the EU condemned the civilian takeover but then focused on stateness and socio-economic development. This resembles the Australian intervention, which focused on restoring law and order and reinvigorating the local economy. In the context of the December 2006 coup in Fiji, Australia and New Zealand pressured the EU into taking a tough stance by using sanctions to push for elections. While sanctions were initially limited to 'smart sanctions', by 2009 both countries advocated stronger sanctions as the commitment to hold general elections by March 2009 was not honoured, the constitution was abrogated and various measures curtailing individual freedoms were adopted. This led to the suspension of Fiji from the PIF in May 2009 (P. Smith 2008).

Although the EU initially favoured a more conciliatory approach, it eventually succumbed to pressure from Australia and New Zealand to take a harder line (Carbone 2011). As a result, several rounds of consultations with the Fijian authorities on the restoration of democracy could not prevent the suspension of aid in October 2007. In addition, while the EU was reluctant to suspend the sugar protocol, it eventually did so in response to bilateral pressure from Australia and New Zealand. Moreover, when in late 2009 the EU started thinking of the resumption of development assistance, which would be targeted directly to the vulnerable population and focus on democracy support, this was strongly resisted by Australia and New Zealand. In a self-critical evaluation, a senior Commission official admitted that 'we trusted Australia and New

Zealand way too much. They convinced us that they knew how to proceed. They asked us to stop aid on the sugar protocol because they were sure that order would be in place within a few weeks, but clearly they were wrong.'[10]

Conclusion

This chapter has mapped and explained the substance of EU democracy promotion in two South Pacific countries: the Solomon Islands and Fiji. In the Solomon Islands, the EU made a shift from promoting mainly external context conditions (2000–2007) to focusing more on the partial regimes (2008–2010). In Fiji, the EU's approach also shifted over time, from focusing on some partial regimes and some external conditions (2000–2003) to a more comprehensive approach that touched upon all issues, and particularly on the electoral regime (2003–2010). However, compared to the Solomon Islands, the EU focused less on the external context in the case of Fiji.

This difference is related to two factors. First, the domestic context of the two countries was different. In the Solomon Islands, the 2000 civilian takeover and the resulting political crisis were resolved rather quickly and in a manner that was satisfactory to the EU. In Fiji, the political crisis lingered and a second military takeover followed in 2006. That the EU focused more on development and state capacity in the Solomon Islands could also be related to the fact that problems in both areas were seen as more pressing in the Solomon Islands than in Fiji. Second, in the case of Fiji, the EU was influenced by the position of the PIF, where the two regional powers Australia and New Zealand strongly advocated for tough sanctions until free and fair elections were held. The EU succumbed to diplomatic pressure and has kept sanctions in place to this day, which limited its possibilities for development assistance.

The analysis also shows that, while the context condition 'stateness' is important to the EU in societies that are ethnically divided, the EU addresses this problem in different ways. In Fiji, the holding of free and fair elections was seen as the best way to achieve internal stability. In the Solomon Islands, the EU was satisfied with the local solution and addressed stateness directly by focusing on national reconciliation.

Notes

1. These semi-structured interviews were conducted in the South Pacific in May–June 2005 and in Brussels in January–February 2011 with policy-makers from the European Commission, the EU Council, the PIF Secretariat and some Pacific countries (including Fiji).

2. The sugar protocol was a preferential trade agreement with certain ACP countries, whereby the EU undertook to purchase a certain amount of sugar annually at guaranteed prices.
3. In 2006 the EIDHR was renamed European Instrument for Democracy and Human Rights.
4. This outcome can be justified as a substitution for the declining bilateral assistance of the member states, as a consequence of the high costs of aid delivery caused by the distance between and within ACP countries, or as a result of the region's extreme vulnerability to natural hazards and climate change.
5. Interview with EU official, February 2011. If, 'in the Pacific, the EU has become a green donor', to use the words of the same official, it is due not only to its vast experience in environmental policy, but also to the attempt to form a bloc with the Pacific Islands in international negotiations. For this, democracy promotion may be affected not only by material interests, by also by other, more normative goals.
6. Interview with EU official, June 2005.
7. Interview with EU official, February 2011.
8. By contrast, the Post-Forum Dialogue, which was the interface between the EU and the Pacific taking place in the margins of PIF annual meetings, was criticized because of 'a number of shortcomings, such as limited visibility, interaction and impact and too little time for preparation and discussion at a point when the EU-Pacific agenda is growing' (European Commission 2006j: 5).
9. Interviews with PIF officials, May–June 2005.
10. Interview with EU official, January 2011.

16
Much Ado About Nothing? Brazil and Venezuela

Andrea Ribeiro Hoffmann

Introduction

Latin America does not hold a prominent place in the literature on European Union (EU) democracy promotion (Youngs 2008, Magen et al. 2009), and experts on EU–Latin America relations do not tend to focus on democracy promotion either (Freres 2000, Grugel 2004, Gratius 2011). The scarce literature on EU democracy promotion in Latin America suggests that these policies and activities are not seen as relevant, or do not inspire a demand for more bilateral engagement in this area. Possible justifications are that Latin America has been on the right track in its democratization process, or that local actors or other donors already do enough. Is the concern with EU democracy promotion in Latin America, then, simply 'much ado about nothing'?

This chapter challenges the underlying assumption that EU democracy promotion in Latin America is of little relevance. To start with, this argument implicitly assumes a narrow definition of democracy, according to the categories defined in this volume, that is, elections, political rights, civil rights, horizontal accountability and effective power (see the introductory chapter). If one expands the definition of democracy to incorporate context conditions such as socio-economic development, civil society, stateness and state administrative capacity, then EU democracy promotion in Latin America becomes a very important topic. This chapter explores these arguments and presents an explanation of the substance of EU democracy promotion in Latin America based on the analytical framework presented in this volume. It focuses on two case studies: Brazil and Venezuela. The analysis is based on primary sources, that is, bilateral treaties, databases and documents from the EU, such as the Country Strategy Papers and Council Statements, and the existing secondary literature.

Brazil and Venezuela are important cases given their increasing presence in international politics. In addition, they present a considerable variation in possible explanatory factors taken into consideration in this volume. First, while they are both weaker partners in asymmetric relations with the EU, the difference in their regional and global power position accounts for variance with regard to this factor. In 2010, Brazil's GDP was the largest in the Latin America and Caribbean region, accounting for approximately 44 per cent of the regional total, and Venezuela was the fifth largest, accounting for around 5 per cent (CEPAL 2012: 68). Brazil is, in addition, a global emerging market and one of the BRICS (Brazil, Russia, India, China and South Africa) group of countries. Second, the domestic shortcomings in the two countries are of very different nature. Venezuela is an example of what Susanne Gratius has called 'the new political challenges of democratic backlash' (2011: 689). Despite its better record in most of the indicators related to the narrow definition of democracy, Brazil has a serious problem of state administrative capacity and one of the highest levels of income inequality in the region, important indicators for the context conditions. Finally, the fact that in absolute terms Brazil and Venezuela have been the main recipients of EU funding from the European Instrument for Democracy and Human Rights (EIDHR) in Central and Latin America makes them important cases to be studied in depth in order to understand the substance of EU democracy promotion in the world. According to the multiannual indicative planning, Venezuela was supposed to be the main recipient of EIDHR funding in Central and Latin America in 2011, with €1.2 million, 1.9 per cent of the total; and Brazil is the second, together with Guatemala, Honduras and Peru, with €0.9 million, 1.4 per cent of the total (European Commission 2011n).

The chapter proceeds by mapping the substance of EU democracy promotion in the next section, and then explaining the peculiarities of each country, based on the analytical framework discussed in the introductory chapter of this volume.

The substance of EU democracy promotion in Brazil and Venezuela

In order to assess the substance of EU democracy promotion in Brazil and Venezuela, a number of documents and policy instruments are analysed, such as bilateral agreements, EU Country Strategy Papers (CSPs) and National Indicative Programmes (NIPs), Common Foreign and Security Policy (CFSP) statements, documents and actions from the European Parliament (EP), cooperation projects and election observation missions. Bilateral agreements are compromises between both partners and in this sense the expectation is that when references to promotion of democracy are made, the substance reflects a consensus. The other sources indicate EU preferences, even the EU CSPs, which in principle take partner countries' ownership into account (Carbone 2008b).

Bilateral agreements

Bilateral relations between the EU and Brazil are regulated by the EC–Brazil Framework Cooperation Agreement (1992), the EU–Mercosur Framework Cooperation Agreement (1995) and the Agreement for Scientific and Technological Cooperation (2004). In addition, a Strategic Partnership was concluded in 2007. In the context of the Partnership, two EU–Brazil Joint Action Plans (JAPs) have been concluded so far, for 2009–2011 and for 2012–2014.

A general pattern that can be found in these documents is that democracy, human rights and the rule of law are considered essential values and principles of bilateral relations, and are always referred to in preambles and general statements, but are vague, and do not contain any allocation of funding for specific cooperation projects. The preamble of the 1992 agreement, for instance, reaffirms the importance that the EU and Mercosur member states attach to the principles of the United Nations Charter, to democratic values and to respecting human rights, and recognizes the need to promote social rights and in particular the rights of the most disadvantaged segments of society. Article 1 of the 1995 agreement states that the basis for cooperation is the respect for the democratic principles and fundamental human rights established by the Universal Declaration of Human Rights.

The references to democracy in the JAPs are much more specific. Both JAPs include the promotion of human rights and democracy at the international level as part of the promotion of peace and security, establishing regular human rights consultations on multilateral and bilateral issues. JAP 2009–2011 treats cooperation in social cohesion and inclusion in detail in the context of the achievement of the Millennium Development Goals, and refers to social and employment issues, institutional strengthening and state modernization, consolidation of democratic instruments for consulting civil society, and promotion of inter-parliamentary exchange. With regard to the last of these, it states that both partners will work towards the establishment of a regular structured dialogue between the members of the Brazilian national congress and of the EP. Regarding civil society, the document encourages the establishment of an EU–Brazil civil society forum on human rights protection and respect for democratic principles, and requests the European Economic and Social Committee (EESC) and the Brazilian Council for Economic and Social Development (CDES) to set up an EU–Brazil civil society round table. These documents refer to both the partial regimes and external conditions of democracy, but civil society and socio-economic development prevail.

In the case of Venezuela, bilateral relations are less institutionalized; the EU has no formal bilateral agreements with the country. Venezuela was a member of the Andean Community (CAN) from 1973 until 2006. EU–CAN relations are based on the Political Dialogue and Cooperation Agreement signed in 2003, but it is not yet in force. Venezuela's accession treaty to Mercosur entered in force in 2012, but only in December 2013 did the Paraguayan Congress approve its ratification and conclude the legal dispute about the legality of the accession during the suspension of the country from Mercosur. Relevant bi-regional cooperation initiatives were included in the documents analysed below.

EU CSPs

The EU sets the main objectives for its relations with third countries in the so-called Country Strategy Papers. Some CSPs include an estimate of the allocation of funds in the format of NIPs. For Brazil, two CSPs have been published, for the periods of 2002–2006 and 2007–2013. For Venezuela, there are CSPs for the periods of 2002–2006, 2007–2013, and a mid-term review for 2011–2013.

The two strategy papers for Brazil are quite similar. The document for 2002–2006 states that it has become clear that a stable democracy and the rule of law, well-functioning institutions and policies based on good governance are key factors for sustainable development. The NIP for 2002–2006 focused, however, on the areas of economic reform (47 per cent of the total budget), social development (23 per cent) and environment (9 per cent); in other words, the main priorities regarding the substance of democracy promotion have not been topics from the partial regimes but rather external conditions. Most initiatives are related to socio-economic development and civil society. Some proposals were related to state administrative capacity, such as tax and public administration reform. The CSP for 2007–2013 called for support to the existing sectoral dialogues (such as in social issues, trade, transport, nuclear cooperation, science and technology, information society and the environment), and small-scale initiatives or soft measures that could have a multiplier effect, such as the encouragement of the mutual understanding and promotion of Europe's image and culture in Brazil, and academic exchanges. These initiatives also refer more to external conditions than partial regimes.

According to the CSP 2002–2006, EU development cooperation with Venezuela became significant only in the 2000s. The initiatives for this period focused mainly on prevention of environmental catastrophes, trade diversification and the transfer of knowledge, that is, not on democracy promotion. A number of non-governmental organizations (NGOs) in Venezuela received funding from the EIDHR, but under the regional programme with the Andean Community (see below). In 2005, the country became eligible for national projects.[1] The only additional reference to democracy in the CSP 2002–2006 was support for Organization of American States (OAS) activities, such as its electoral mission and investigation of the events of the failed coup of April 2002. Interestingly, the CSP for 2007–2013 emphasizes that the aims of EU cooperation are neither to supplant nor displace the activities of the Venezuelan government, but rather to provide added value through intervention in carefully targeted areas, which have been agreed and consulted upon with the Venezuelan authorities. The aims advanced for the cooperation are to reinforce political, economic, social and cultural relations, accompany the government in its efforts to reduce poverty and foster greater social cohesion, and advance Venezuela's participation in the process of regional integration. The CSP emphasizes that these objectives will be carried out following a participative approach in all identified sectors of intervention by including non-state actors in the dialogue, and that among the guiding principles that underlie all EC cooperation activities are the promotion of equal opportunities for men and women, and respect for human rights, highlighting the importance of indigenous rights. The specific sectors identified for EC support were the modernization and decentralization of the Venezuelan state and its institutions, including through increased participation in policy-making by civil society and local government, and diversification of the economy. The mid-term review for the period of 2011–2013 referred to the 'Bolivarian Revolution',[2] stating that Venezuelan society is polarized, and many of the ongoing economic and political reforms (nationalization, the creation of new forms of property) accentuate this trend. The focal sectors defined in the NIP remained unchanged, with a minor adjustment. While the amount of funds available to the modernization of the state increased, the amount for diversification of economy decreased. This was justified by the analysis that the frequent, often drastic, changes in economic policy make it more difficult to identify feasible and useful projects in this domain, while capacity building to strengthen the institutional fabric remains a firm priority.

To sum up, Venezuela CSPs for the periods of 2002–2006 and 2007–2013 (including the mid-term review) indicate that the substance of democracy promotion is mostly related to external conditions such as socio-economic development, social cohesion and poverty alleviation. Modernization of the state (administrative capacity) has been increasingly prioritized. References to support to civil society were also recurrent. Regarding the partial regimes, civil rights, indigenous rights and elections have been included.

Cooperation projects

A closer look at the cooperation projects implemented confirms the arguments advanced so far. The main instruments by which the EU promotes democracy in Latin America are the EIDHR, the Thematic Programmes 'non-state actors and local authorities in development' (NSA-LA), and 'investing in people'. Also important is the co-financing of NGOs through the 'European Development NGOs – Actions in developing countries' programme (NGOs-PVD).

For the case of Brazil, it was possible to access a comprehensive list including all cooperation projects for the period analysed (Europa 2014k). The data shows that most projects went to civil society (co-financing of NGOs and development projects by non-state actors and local authorities), with 58 projects; the environment (PPG7, FLORELOS, and so on), with 50 projects; academic cooperation (Erasmus Mundus, Institute of European Studies), with 40 projects; and human rights (EIDHR, Investing in People), with 38 projects. Other topics addressed were: urbanization and infrastructure, with ten projects; energy security, with six projects; poverty alleviation/social cohesion, with four projects; economic competition (small- and medium-sized enterprises), with three projects; modernization of state administration, with two projects; and sectoral dialogues, with one project.[3] If seen in terms of the classification of the substance of democracy outlined in this volume, civil society would be the most targeted item, followed by human rights, including both civil and socio-economic rights.

In the case of Venezuela, only the cooperation projects funded under the EIDHR were accessed given their availability. Most of the projects under this programme refer to human rights (28 out of the 34 projects), and among these, most refer to civil and socio-economic rights such as rehabilitation of torture victims, rights of indigenous peoples, children rights, non-discrimination rights, rights of persons with disabilities, gender equality rights and freedom of speech. The others refer to governance (one project), peaceful conciliation (one), rule of law (two) and civil society (two). In terms of the classification of the substance of democracy, civil and socio-economic rights (social and economic context) were the most frequently targeted.

Political initiatives

Three types of political initiatives can be distinguished: Council statements, EP actions, and electoral observation missions. The Council of the EU has addressed both Brazil and Venezuela in its CFSP statements. For Brazil, most statements refer to the results of bilateral meetings and do not emphasize democracy matters, except for some which congratulate on electoral results (according to the database of Council Press Releases, see Europa 2014h). As for Venezuela, most statements refer to concerns with the democratic situation in the country at different moments, such as during the political crisis in 2002/2003, or congratulations on successful referenda or elections. In 2007, a statement expressed concerns with the freedom of speech and of the press in the country following the suspension of the broadcasting licence of Radio Caracas (Council of the European Union 2007d). To the extent that the CFSP statements are relevant, they refer mostly to electoral matters and political rights.

The EP is often cited as an important promoter of democracy in Latin America; one of its main activities is the establishment of inter-parliamentary dialogues with Latin American regional parliaments such as the Latin American Parliament (PARLATINO), the Mercosur Parliament (PARLASUR) and the Central American Parliament (PARLACEN) (Herranz 2005, Corbett *et al.* 2007). In addition to inter-parliamentary dialogues with regional parliaments, the EU also established an inter-parliamentary dialogue with the Brazilian Congress, whose first meeting took place in 2011 (European Parliament 2011b).[4] The inter-parliamentary dialogues increase the mutual knowledge of partners and provide a more complex matrix of interests and values, since they include members from all parties, and not only those in power. These dialogues also strengthen the parliaments themselves as political actors, and their awareness of mechanisms of demanding accountability from the executive power.

A good example of the EP demanding accountability from the European Commission in the case of EU–Brazilian relations is the EP

Resolution on the draft Commission decisions establishing Country Strategic Papers and Indicative Programmes for Malaysia, Brazil and Pakistan, in which the EP 'takes the view that in its draft Strategic Paper and draft National Indicative Programme 2007–2010 for Brazil the Commission exceeds its implementing powers laid down in the basic act by earmarking 70 per cent of the NIP for priority I "Enhancing bilateral relations"' (European Parliament 2007b: 2), whose specific objectives, according to the EP, do not fulfil the criteria for official development assistance (ODA) established by the Development Assistance Committee from the Organization for Economic Cooperation and Development (OECD-DAC).

Another important mechanism of the EP to promote democracy is the Office for Promotion of Parliamentary Democracy (OPPD 2014) created in 2008. The OPPD assists the EP in the establishment and the reform of new parliaments, particularly regional parliaments, and aims at strengthening their capacity to implement essential functions including law-making, over sight and representation. The OPPD also supports the EP in its efforts to move democracy promotion further up the EU agenda, and to develop a comprehensive EU democracy policy (OPPD n.d.: 14–18, OPPD 2009, OPPD 2010). These actions are related to political rights and horizontal accountability.

As for the election observation missions, these have not been an important instrument of EU democracy promotion in Brazil and Venezuela. No mission has been sent to Brazil, and only two to Venezuela, for the December 2005 legislative elections and the presidential election in 2006 (Europa 2014d). It should, however, be kept in mind that other regional organizations such as the OAS and the Union of South American Nations (UNASUR) are active in election observation.

Summary of the mapping

The analysis of the EU–Brazil and EU–Venezuela bilateral agreements, the EU CSPs and NIPs, CFSP statements, EP documents and actions, EU cooperation projects and electoral missions to both countries indicate some patterns regarding the substance of EU democracy promotion. Firstly, bilateral agreements are vague but always make reference to democracy and human rights as common values and principles. Secondly, socio-economic development and socio-economic rights are priorities in both Brazil and Venezuela. Civil society has also been a main target. For Venezuela, state modernization and decentralization have been emphasized in the documents, but not addressed as much in the cooperation projects, which refer mostly to human rights, mainly civil, indigenous and socio-economic. Political rights have been addressed in both countries by the Council and the Parliament, but are more marginal comparatively. Electoral missions are not relevant. The assessment of the substance of democracy promotion in Brazil and Venezuela according to the categories outlined in the introductory chapter of this volume is summarized in Table A.1 (in the Annex).

Explaining the substance of EU democracy promotion to Brazil and Venezuela

Brazil

Among the power-related explanatory factors pointed out in the analytical framework presented in the introductory chapter of this volume, power position plays an important role in the determination of the substance of EU democracy promotion in Brazil, while security threat and issue-specific interdependence are not relevant. On the one hand, the EU is more powerful than Brazil in terms of material capacities, which, according to hypothesis 1, would lead to the expectation that the EU will promote liberal democracy. However, on the other hand, when the power configuration in Latin America is taken into consideration, that is, US hegemony and the contestation of this hegemony by Brazil (instead of the (a)symmetries between the EU and Brazil), the assessment of power position becomes more complex. This leads to a situation in which the EU foreign policy is formulated in order to balance US hegemony, and therefore, to be more open to the demands of substance by the third country in exchange for more influence.

Regarding the institutionalist variables, the sectoral policy-makers more involved in the formulation of EU foreign policy in general were from the former Commission's Directorate-General for External Relations, DG RELEX, especially in the context of the EU–Brazil Strategic Partnership. In the area of democracy promotion, however, the EP has been the most engaged, above all via the inter-parliamentary dialogues. It is possible to distinguish a focus on context conditions by the Commission, while the Council and EP emphasized more partial regimes. Regarding the interorganizational field, the existence of other institutions beyond the EU, such as the OAS and UNASUR, assuming a strong role in the area of electoral observation missions undermined the possibility for the EU to assume a relevant role (Carothers and Youngs 2011).

Regarding the EU member states, Spain's role is less strong in Brazil than the rest of Latin America, but it is still the most important member state in the EU foreign policy system towards Latin America. Its role has contributed to the focus on socio-economic development. Gratius, for instance, argues that Spain is still the most engaged member state in Latin America, but that its non-political approach in development assistance (due to the prioritization of other objectives such as trade and investment) has contributed to reducing the EU's democracy profile in the Americas (2011: 690, Gratius and Legler 2013). The prominent role of Spain, and its focus on good governance, which is framed in terms of social cohesion, rather than democracy promotion, is also confirmed by Youngs (2008: 166–67). Other member states such as Germany and Italy do promote democracy in Brazil, but they act primarily at the national or sub-national level, via political party foundations.[5]

The variables from the domestic context also play an important role in the determination of the substance of EU democracy promotion in Brazil. This is due mainly to a high level of consensus between both partners regarding the urgent necessities. In that sense, both government agenda and shortcomings are assessed as variables of major relevance. The data from the Bertelsmann Transformation Index (BTI 2012a) shows an improvement of some indicators. Otherwise, they have been quite stable in the last decade, as indicated in Table A.2 (see Annex). The weaker indicators are socio-economic development, followed by state capacity and civil rights. These have been addressed by the local government and by the EU bilateral cooperation. The post-conflict scenario is assessed as not directly relevant (see BTI Q13.3 – 3 for all years), but if the policies of 'pacification' in the shantytowns (favelas) are included in this variable, then a few examples of cooperation are found, under the label of infrastructure/urbanization.

To sum up, power constellation and domestic context are both relevant, and, moreover, they are interconnected: power position and desire to counter US influence makes the EU follow the local agenda, which is in turn based on deficiencies that are consensual.

Venezuela

The power variables are less relevant for Venezuela than Brazil as they are all only partially confirmed. The EU is in a stronger power position than Venezuela, even if a degree of interdependence against it can be found in the sector of oil, and Venezuela is not considered a security threat either, despite its confrontational diplomacy discourse against the 'west' at the global level. However, the EU's strategy to balance the US's more confrontational approach in democracy promotion plays an important role in the substance of EU democracy promotion (Gratius and Legler 2013). Despite an overall similar approach to democracy promotion in the world, the EU and the US have often adopted different approaches in Latin America (Risse 2009: 245). This divergence was very clear in the case of Central America in the 1980s, but is also the case for contemporary approaches to democracy promotion, at least in Cuba and Venezuela, countries which, together with Ecuador and Bolivia, are members of the Bolivarian Alliance for the Peoples of Our America (ALBA), and promote a (social) model of democracy that is often presented as in opposition to liberal democracy (Gratius and Legler 2013; see note 2 as well). The US's approach has actually led to ALBA countries issuing a resolution in 2012 requesting its member states to expel United States Agency for International Development (USAID) (Venezuelanalysis 2012).

In terms of institutionalist variables, former Directorate-General RELEX seems to have agreed for the agenda to be determined by former Directorate-General Development, which suggests, as in the case of Brazil, an interconnection between the power and institutionalist variables. With regard to EU member states, Spain is clearly the most influential, but democracy promotion has not been a priority in its approach towards Latin America. Rather, trade and investments have been. As Youngs argues, Spain has taken a hard line on Venezuela under the conservative government of Jose Maria Aznar (1996–2004), criticizing the democratic credentials of the governments of Venezuelan President Chavez, but not engaging in democracy promotion per se. After 2004, Spain took a more pragmatic approach, but when dealing with democracy promotion the focus has been on good governance and social cohesion aspects (Youngs *et al.* 2006: 19, 170–71).

To sum up, power considerations and the institutional context allow Spain to play a decisive role in shaping the substance. Finally, regarding the domestic context, the most urgent shortcomings according to BTI data (see Table A.2), such as horizontal accountability and effective power, are not the priorities addressed by the EU. Instead, the substance of democracy promotion has followed the government's agenda to a high degree. The match with the government agenda has actually been a target of criticism (Youngs 2008, Gratius 2011). In other words, the attempt to balance the US and taking a differentiated approach to the regime in Venezuela is linked to the EU's acceptance of the government's agenda. The slightly modified approach away from diversification of the economy and towards modernization of the state in the mid-term review of the 2007–2013 CSP could indicate the possibility of change in the future.

Concluding remarks

This chapter has analysed the substance of EU democracy promotion in Brazil and Venezuela. It was seen that the priority in both countries has been socio-economic development and civil society, that is, contextual conditions rather than partial regimes. This explains why the traditional literature tends to neglect EU activities of democracy promotion in Latin America: a narrow definition of democracy in the literature underplays the role of the EU. EU democracy promotion in Latin America is not, therefore, 'much ado about nothing'! There is a need to explore further the EU's role in the region. This chapter has focused on only two countries; it is hard to generalize from them despite their relevance for this study.

The chapter also explored the driving forces behind the existing activities of EU democracy promotion in Brazil and Venezuela. Despite the peculiarities and differences of the two countries, it was seen that power position matters for both, in the sense of the triangular relations between Latin America, Europe and the US. The US is not only the global hegemonic power in the region, but it has also adopted a different approach in its policy of democracy promotion, which is less tolerant than the EU's of the social model of democracy advanced by Latin American governments, especially in the case of Venezuela since the Bolivarian Revolution. Finally, in both cases, the countries' governmental agendas have played an important role in the determination of the substance of democracy promotion. The EU has tried to impose some of its unilateral priorities, such as modernization and decentralization of the state in Venezuela, but has been in general very sensitive or flexible, with local demands given power considerations. In the case of Brazil, the governmental agenda focused on deficiencies that are consensual with the EU's and, therefore, even in the light of power considerations, unilateral priorities could be pursued.

Notes

1. The focus of this chapter is on the bilateral and not bi-regional level. Although some overlap exits, the main objective of the bi-regional cooperation has been the promotion of regional integration per se, and not on democracy promotion.
2. The Bolivarian Revolution and '21st-century socialism' are concepts elaborated by former Venezuelan President Hugo Chavez, who was elected in 1998 and re-elected in 2000, 2006 and 2012 (Chavez died in 2013). They refer to a new model of democracy and economic development which mixes elements of the liberal models of democracy with a focus on direct participation, and

socialist models of democracy and economic development. They also draw on local indigenous culture and practices, and criticism of North American and European imperialism and hegemony over Latin America, glorifying the independence movement's hero Simon Bolivar. Former President Chavez created, together with Cuba, a regional organization in 2004: the Bolivarian Alliance for the Peoples of Our America (ALBA). ALBA advances these models of democracy and development in Latin America. Other members joined later, including Bolivia and Ecuador.
3. The data does not allow for a reliable assessment of distribution of allocation per topic as there are overlaps in the indicated contributions between several projects.
4. In this meeting, the main focus was on the exchange of ideas about the negotiations of the EU–Mercosur Agreement.
5. The analysis presented in this volume does not focus on the bilateral relations between EU member states, but rather on the EU level. More detailed analysis of the EU member states' bilateral patterns of development cooperation would be necessary in order to understand its relation with EU development cooperation. However, assuming that the information on the bilateral patterns indicates the preferred substance of different EU member states (which might be uploading their preferences to the EU level), the position of Spain indicated in the literature is confirmed. As indicated on the Brazilian Agency of International Cooperation homepage (www.abc.gov.br), its main donor partners are Spain, Germany and Japan. France and Italy are also highlighted in the bilateral cooperation. According to this source, the priorities of Germany are environment and energy; of Spain, environment, professional development, tourism, agriculture and public administration; of France, agriculture and environment; and of Italy, democratic governance and territorial development. Italian projects are the most directly related to democracy promotion (democratic governance), followed by Spain (public administration). The activities of democracy promotion by the German party foundations are also not included in this analysis despite their importance in Latin America in general and Brazil in particular, as they cannot be defined as part of the EU policy of democracy promotion either. For their projects, see the homepages of the Konrad Adenauer Foundation and the Friedrich Ebert Foundation especially, and for their historical role in democracy promotion abroad, see for instance European Parliament (2010).

17
Comparing Country Cases: Output-Oriented EU Democracy Promotion?

Anne Wetzel and Jan Orbie

Introduction

The purpose of this book has been to map and explain the substance of European Union (EU) democracy promotion. The adapted framework of embedded liberal democracy provided the analytical framework for the mapping exercise, whereas the four hypotheses guided the authors' search for explanations (see the introductory chapter). Based on our systematic and comparative analysis involving the EU's policy towards 22 countries, this concluding chapter will formulate a number of general conclusions. We find that the 'default substance' of the EU's democracy promotion is output-oriented, specifically targeting 'socio-economic development' and 'state administrative capacity'. Partial regimes, and in particular 'horizontal accountability' and 'effective power to govern', tend to be under-addressed.

However, we also find some interesting deviations from this general pattern, not least in relation to countries that are located close to the EU. The different hypotheses, and in particular the power and domestic context hypotheses, shed light on this diversity. Based on the results, the rough distinction between 'partial regimes' and 'external conditions', and the concomitant distinction between 'narrow' and 'shallow' democracy promotion (Wetzel and Orbie 2011; the introductory chapter), can also be refined.

Before elaborating on these conclusions, some methodological notes should be made on how we have come to our findings. Most importantly, we differentiate between 'absolute' and 'relative' substance. The absolute substance concerns the extent to which a specific component of the framework has been addressed. This is in line with the scores provided by the contributors to Table A.1 (see Annex). The shading provides an initial indication of which components and which countries have been more or less important for the EU. However, while this table provides a good overview of what has been the focus of the EU's attention, it is a purely descriptive device that tells us little about possible explanations. For example, some countries and components may receive more attention than others because domestic deficiencies are stronger (cf. the domestic context hypothesis).

Therefore, in a second step, we compared the scores of the substance table with the democratic 'deficiencies' in the third countries, which gives us an idea of the 'relative' substance, denoting the difference between the 'absolute' values in the above-mentioned substance table and the domestic situation in the third country. The differences allow us to gauge the extent to which the EU 'overperforms' or 'underperforms' in relation to domestic 'deficits', in line with the domestic context hypothesis. Specifically, we compared the available Bertelsmann Transformation Index (BTI) values for all components for the year 2006, represented in a condensed form in Table A.2, with the values of the substance table (for the original values, see BTI 2012). The original BTI values that range between 1 ('worst') and 10 ('best') were subsumed into four categories that conversely correspond to the four values in the substance tables. The BTI table thus shows where there are the biggest deficits in those countries for which values are available.[1] This approach reveals that there is a clear and underlying output-oriented tendency, even if the EU does not recommend the same 'size' of this model to the different target states. The 'basso continuo' of EU democracy promotion consists of socio-economic development and state capacity.

Output democracy as the default substance

Previous research has led to the conclusion that the EU emphasizes the external context conditions more than the partial regimes (Wetzel and Orbie 2011). The cases presented in this edited volume generally confirm this pattern. In absolute terms, but also after the comparison with the 'deficiencies' in the countries, 'socio-economic development' and 'state administrative capacity' are the major focal points of the EU's international democracy promotion policy. Not only did the EU put most emphasis on these two components, but overall the EU's substance also matches most closely with the domestic deficiencies in these fields and sometimes the EU even overperforms. This close match relates to almost all cases (with the exception of state administrative capacity in the Solomon Islands) – that is to say, we do not see any major deviances to the positive or negative, which suggests that it is an underlying default option.

This careful attention to socio-economic development and state capacity stands out in comparison with the other components of the adapted framework of embedded liberal democracy, which the EU tends to under-address, although to widely varying degrees both with regard to differences between components and differences between countries. The two most under-addressed components are 'effective power to govern' and 'horizontal accountability', which belong to the partial regimes. While 'effective power to govern' receives the least attention also in absolute terms, the EU's attention to horizontal accountability does not actually deviate from the remaining three partial regimes in absolute terms but displays a large gap between the existing deficiencies and the degree to which the deficiencies were addressed. With the extremes on both sides – that is, best match and worst match of substance with domestic conditions – relating to the context conditions and partial regimes, respectively, the earlier finding (Wetzel and Orbie 2011) that the EU addresses the external context conditions of democracy more, and thus that the substance of EU democracy promotion tends towards the shallow side, is confirmed.

At the same time, the contributions to this volume show that this finding can be further specified. As becomes clear from the above, not all components related to the external context are central to the EU's democracy promotion. Large differences in attention can also be detected among the partial regimes. These more fine-grained conclusions result not only from the larger number of country cases and the more systematic approach, but also from the new distinction made between 'stateness' and 'state administrative capacity'. In view of the above finding that the most addressed and also most adequately addressed components are 'socio-economic development' and 'state administrative capacity' and the least addressed and also least adequately addressed component is 'effective power to govern', we conclude that the 'default substance' of EU democracy promotion can be described as 'output democracy', with a particular emphasis on effective problem solving.

With this term, we refer to the established distinction between 'input' and 'output' as the basis of democratic legitimacy (see Scharpf 1999). Given the need to legitimize policies, Scharpf presents two ways to ensure legitimacy. While input legitimacy relates to the general responsiveness of governing processes 'to the manifest preferences of the governed', output legitimacy ensures 'that the policies adopted will generally represent effective solutions to common problems of the governed' (Scharpf 2003). Reduced to a short formula, input legitimacy refers to 'government by the people', whereas output legitimacy resonates with 'government for the people' (Scharpf 2003). This distinction has also been taken up in work on EU democracy promotion by Tanja Börzel and her collaborators (Börzel *et al.* 2008, Börzel and Hackenesch 2013).

With their emphasis on performance, both 'socio-economic development' and 'state administrative capacity' clearly correspond to the notion of 'output democracy'.[2] 'Effective power to govern', on the other hand, addresses the translation of the will of the electorate into policies by ensuring that it is those who are democratically elected that govern. This largely neglected component thus clearly relates to input legitimacy. Horizontal accountability, which was also neglected in relative terms, in Scharpf's account corresponds to 'output democracy', too, but to the sub-category of preventing wrongdoing (Scharpf 2003). In the case of democracy promotion this component arguably sits in between input and output legitimacy, because a strengthening of checks and balances can be assumed to contribute to enhancing responsiveness to the electorate's preferences, for instance by making the parliament a body that is able to effectively control the government. Scharpf himself admits that there may emerge a certain trade-off between checks and balances and effective problem solving. So, the sub-categories in fact address different issues. When we speak of output democracy, we refer to effective problem solving. Furthermore, speaking of an output-democracy agenda does not imply that the EU completely neglects input-related components and focuses exclusively on output-related components. In fact, as emphasized by Kurki (Chapter 3), no systematic conceptual model or clear ideological vision emerges from the EU's documents and practice on what democracy means. By output-democracy agenda we rather summarize a tendency in EU democracy promotion that favours performance and spans across the narrow–shallow distinction.

The findings on civil society also support our general finding about the EU's output-oriented agenda. In absolute terms, the EU devotes considerable attention to civil society across our range of cases, and only slightly less than state administrative capacity (Table A.1). However, when looking at the relative substance, the EU tends to slightly underperform, with the two exceptions of Tunisia (before the Arab

Spring) and Eritrea, where the discrepancies are quite large. It seems fair to conclude that, despite the EU's own discourse, there is room for improvement with regard to civil society support. For instance, it was pointed out that despite the official aim of empowering civil society in the Euro-Mediterranean Partnership the concrete realization of this aim was hollowed out by intergovernmental tendencies and the exclusion of a large share of civil society actors from EU support (Simon and Jünemann 2013: 82–3). More importantly, a judgment regarding 'civil society' should take into account the qualitative assessments in the chapters (see also the introductory chapter), which support the EU's output-democracy agenda. As Börzel shows, the support of civil society can go together very well with an output-oriented agenda (for evidence from the EU eastern enlargement, see Börzel 2010: 5–6). Such an approach 'places emphasis on *output-oriented* reform goals as well but either includes non-state actors in the implementation process to produce better policies by pooling resources and increasing acceptance or facilitates the building and strengthening of non-state organizations that will help to implement policies better' (Börzel and Hackenesch 2013: 539). As the chapters on Russia/Ukraine (Chapter 9), Bosnia and Herzegovina/Kosovo (Chapter 8), Georgia/Armenia (Chapter 10), Croatia/Turkey (Chapter 7) and Ethiopia/Eritrea (Chapter 14) show, EU civil society promotion at least partly displays an instrumental tone. In many cases, civil society organizations have been supported in order to help implement the EU's *acquis*, the European Development Fund or reforms more generally in the third countries. Also, in terms of topics that civil society organizations have addressed with the help of EU support, an effective problem-solving logic can be detected at least in some cases (see for example projects on environmental protection or conflict resolution). Again, this does not mean that the EU did not foster civil society's involvement with a view to the input dimension (cf. Chapter 5 on the governance approach), but it shows that the strong focus on civil society does not, as such, contradict the overall description of the EU's democracy promotion agenda as output-oriented, and that it often tends to reinforce it.

With regard to the other components, the results are not so pronounced but, overall, support the characterization of the substance of EU democracy promotion as output-oriented. Political and civil rights generally receive attention at a medium level and on average less than they should, given the local circumstances in third countries. Elections have received more attention than one might have expected based on criticisms of the EU's technocratic democracy promotion (see the introductory chapter), but far less than would justify speaking of an 'electoralist fallacy'.[3] The largest gap emerges in the component of 'political rights'. As is the case with 'horizontal accountability', the three components also display strong deviations from an imagined 'appropriate' substance. Cases of overperformance are in sharp contrast to cases of underperformance, which suggests a higher 'volatility' for these mainly input-related components as part of democratic substance.

How can this output-democracy bias be explained? The hypotheses advanced in the introductory chapter do not fully answer this question since they serve to explain differentiation of EU policies across the countries covered in this book – as will be illustrated below. We can rely on existing literature and on evidence provided by the authors in this book to explain the output-oriented character of EU democracy promotion. First, there is the 'nature of the beast' explanation. Scharpf (1999: 12) has already asserted that 'the European polity is fundamentally different from national democracies' given its tendency towards output-oriented legitimacy. Several other scholars have depicted the EU as a regulatory, technocratic or output-oriented political system (Majone 1994, Moravcsik 2002). It has been argued that this internal configuration predisposes the EU to act accordingly in its external relations (cf. Orbie 2011, Damro 2012). In our previous study, we emphasized that '[t]he EU project itself has been geared towards deepening economic integration and building multi-level governance structures', which sheds light on the substance of its democracy promotion policy (Wetzel and Orbie 2011: 724). In his 'skeptical' contribution to this volume, Kochenov also emphasizes that the intra-EU and extra-EU dimensions are 'intimately interconnected'. From a law perspective, he states that democracy may be a political 'value' for the EU and its member states, but it is 'not a real principle of law' in the EU *acquis*. Furthermore, he argues that 'the EU, given its nature, is a very poor candidate for a standard setter not only in the field of democracy as such, but also in all the related fields, which are necessarily connected with democracy, whether we want it or not' (see Chapter 2). The 'whether we want it or not' qualification also resonates with the argument made by Kurki (Chapter 3), who emphasizes that the pragmatic approach of the EU has the effect of being market-oriented, although there is no clear and deliberate template behind it. However, the lack of such an explicit and agreed template that would possibly include more input-related elements (cf. the demand by the European Parliament to adopt a United Nations (UN) definition of democracy mentioned in the introductory chapter) forms a perfect ground for democracy promotion in 'known terrain' and in a kind of 'autopilot mode' that may be adjusted under certain circumstances.

Specifically, the 'nature of the beast' explanation connects with the institutional hypothesis of the introductory chapter, although on a more fundamental explanatory level. Rather than being tied to a particular EU institution or sub-system, it refers to a general disposition of the EU, closely connected to the institutional structure of the European polity.

Second, and complementary, the EU's emphasis on output-oriented substance also stems from feasibility concerns. When the EU faces (strong) resistance from third countries, it seems to be particularly quick to revert to output-related democracy promotion through fostering socio-economic development and state administrative capacity. In this context the EU has also used the less sensitive term 'democratic governance', which includes exactly these output-related components. Eritrea would be an example: as shown by Del Biondo (Chapter 14), the EU saw no other option than engaging in technical programmes and initiatives in areas such as women's, children's and workers' rights that are seen as less threatening to the government. The EU's policies towards China, which have not been covered in this volume, may also illustrate the feasibility argument. In the late 1990s, the EU abandoned its direct focus on the political system that characterized its response to the Tiananmen Square massacre, focusing on a less confrontational approach involving cooperation in less sensitive areas such as the rule of law (e.g. training of lawyers and judges), culture and youth (Shen 2013).

This example makes it clear that it is indeed difficult to discern whether we can still speak of democracy promotion. As stated in the introductory chapter to this volume, activities labelled as democracy promotion are counted as such when they are designed to support democracy in the sense of the framework regardless of their actual effectiveness. However, it has already been pointed out elsewhere that a sole focus on the context conditions may not necessarily further democratization (Wetzel and Orbie 2012).

In our view, feasibility concerns are subordinated to the 'nature of the beast' explanation. They can be seen as complementary in the sense that they may even enhance the EU's output-related substance of democracy promotion. We conclude this from several observations. Firstly, a low willingness and ability of third countries to cooperate with external actors (as indicated by the respective BTI score; see the introductory chapter) does not translate to the same degree to a negative discrepancy between deficiencies and substance promoted, especially with regard to the partial regimes. While, for instance, Russia, Egypt, Eritrea, Ethiopia and Venezuela had a score of 4 (with 10 indicating highest willingness to co-operate) in 2006, discrepancies were negative but still modest in the latter two, and larger in Russia, Egypt and Eritrea (in order of deterioration). Thus it can be concluded that even in cases of reluctant third countries, the EU has some room for manoeuvre that it can choose to use or not, and that in most cases it chooses not to use it.

Secondly, while it is true that the size of negative discrepancies increases with increasing levels of authoritarianism in the five countries as measured by Freedom House's Freedom Rating for 2006,[4] it cannot automatically be concluded that this necessitates a focus on output-related substance. This becomes particularly evident with regard to the differences with US democracy promotion, which is often seen as more political, even in the face of authoritarian resistance. It has long been argued that the EU, in contrast to the US, is less a political and more a 'developmental' actor (Carothers 2009). From a different perspective, Schmidt (Chapter 4) also argues that the EU is less focused on political issues of 'how authority is exercised and who is in power' (in favour of a more sociological view). As Youngs and Pishchikova conclude (2013: 14),

> ensuring real democratic reform requires [...] a willingness to delve into the messy and conflicting politics of change, and address the concerns over power that divert reform momentum. The EU lags behind the United States in this area. [...] In Europe, democracy debates lack a high-politics tenor and are couched more in terms of generic identity and standards.

While we do not make the case here for more political democracy promotion, this evidence shows that unfavourable domestic conditions do not have to be answered by a purely output-oriented strategy. After all, it is at least partly the choice of the democracy supporter to opt for such a strategy among alternatives.

The third observation relates to the fact that we did not detect much reflection and discussion among EU actors involved in democracy promotion on the potential consequences of almost entirely 'output-related' approaches.[5] We see this as evidence for routine behaviour: although they might even be contrary to the intended aim of advancing democracy in a third country, the EU conducts them as the default option, rather than completely withdrawing assistance from the country.

The rare instances of sanctions in cases of democratic shortcomings are an exception. The sanctions against Fiji illustrate this (see Chapter 15). However, since the mid-2000s, the EU has become less active in applying sanctions. This is not only because their impact has been questioned and because the power of traditional donors (including the EU) has declined. It also relates to the principle of ownership that is central to international engagements on aid effectiveness, including the Paris Declaration (2005) and the Accra Agenda for Action (2008), which the EU has fully supported. Developing country governments often prefer output-oriented assistance and are hesitant regarding politically intrusive policies (Del Biondo 2011: 666–7). This, in turn, resonates particularly well with the EU's default substance.

With the conclusions to this volume, we aim to arrive at a more precise understanding of what the EU promotes. Our main finding is that the EU's default policy is not just about promoting external conditions (Wetzel and Orbie 2011) and/or about neoliberal market reform (cf. Reynaert 2011), but it is specifically about promoting socio-economic development in tandem with state administrative capacity. We have called this the output-oriented substance of EU democracy promotion. There is also a lack of reflection by the EU on the potentially positive *and* negative impact of supporting socio-economic development and state administrative capacity for democracies. Both the institutional nature of the EU and, related to this, feasibility considerations can explain these general tendencies. However, notwithstanding this general picture, there is considerable variation across the countries and over the components, which require more specific explanations.

Accounting for diversity

Despite this underlying output-oriented approach, the EU does not promote the same 'size' of this model in the different target states. Both the absolute and relative substance of EU democracy promotion policies differ across countries and regions. There are instances where socio-economic development and state administrative capacity are promoted less (e.g. in Russia), and others where horizontal accountability and even effective power to govern are promoted more (e.g. in Turkey and Bosnia and Herzegovina) than one might expect based on the above analysis. There is also a high volatility of certain (mostly input-related) components where the EU sometimes overperforms and sometimes underperforms. This general picture corresponds with Kurki's argument that despite the general (neo)liberal, market-oriented 'undercurrent' of EU democracy promotion, there is a considerable degree of 'fuzziness' with regard to the meaning of 'democracy'. She argues that this fuzziness is compatible with a range of different socio-economic models that can be promoted, and points to the 'possibility of a broad range of "substances" that arises from this broad conceptual basis'. Despite its downsides, the lack of a clear model also has the advantage that it allows the EU to adopt a flexible approach according to different contexts (Chapter 3).

Based on the hypotheses presented in the introductory chapter, which also informed the country chapters throughout the book, we aim to make a more systematic assessment of different explanations for the diversity in the EU's substance. The power and domestic context factors emerge as the most salient explanations, even if the institutional and inter-organizational hypotheses also explain some parts of the puzzle. As anticipated in the introductory chapter, the different factors are also interrelated.

The power hypothesis has been confirmed in two ways. On the one hand, the EU's agenda becomes shallower when the EU expects that a broader substance would damage its (perceived) security. The same is true when the difference in capabilities and/or when the (favourable) asymmetric interdependence with the third country is relatively small. This sheds light on the few cases where *even* socio-economic reform and state administrative capacity are not strongly pursued by the EU, even though there would have been room for improvements. Russia is the most obvious example, where the EU underperforms in terms of relative substance, even in relation to the external context conditions. Here, (perceived) energy dependence and, to a lesser extent, general security concerns have influenced the EU's agenda (in combination with the reluctance of the Russian government to accept democracy promotion measures from the outside; see Chapter 9). The situation is similar in Kazakhstan, in contrast to Kyrgyzstan, which relies more on external assistance and is less relevant with regard to EU security concerns (see Chapter 13). In the cases of Egypt and Tunisia, there is evidence that security considerations have led the EU to take a more shallow approach, although to a different degree (see Chapter 11). This resonates with the existing literature on the democracy–stability dilemma (Andrés Viñas 2009, Jünemann 2009, Powel 2009, Börzel and van Hüllen 2014). In Israel and Palestine, the security issue was found to dominate any democracy promotion efforts. This has not only led to shallow democracy promotion but also implies that all democracy promotion measures have to be seen in the light of security concerns (see Chapter 12).

The opposite is true in a different set of countries. Here, on the other hand, the EU has over-addressed some components towards countries that are less powerful. This includes the component of horizontal accountability, which was on average found to be under-addressed (see above). Less powerful countries most obviously include those that are located close to the EU, and that aspire to and have a (distant) perspective of the EU membership, such as Croatia (pre-2013) and Turkey, and, to a lesser extent, Bosnia and Herzegovina and Kosovo. In these cases, the EU tends to be over-attentive. This example shows how the institutional and power hypotheses interact. When relations between the EU and the third country take place within an enlargement (institutional) framework, the EU gains considerable leverage and the power to define the agenda. Apart from the asymmetric power relationship that is inherent to the accession process and that increases the feasibility of democracy promotion policies, other factors, including constructivist dynamics, may contribute to the EU's broad agenda towards these countries. Higher expectations may be held towards countries that are considered as 'European' and want to become members of the 'European family'. It also seems plausible that the EU aims to lock in democratic commitments within the domestic system of candidate countries before admitting them. Whatever the exact dynamics, it is clear that these countries are of a higher importance to the EU than further-away countries. This resonates with Börzel's finding that '[t]he closer a candidate country moves towards accession, the more the EU shifts from the effective government to the democratic government approach' (2009: 36). It should, however, be noted that in these cases the substance is also inspired by the standards of other organizations such as the Council of Europe, the UN and the Organisation for Economic Co-operation and Development (in the cases of the Czech Republic and Slovakia, see Chapter 6), the International Criminal Tribunal for the Former Yugoslavia (ICTY), the Organization for Security and Co-operation in Europe (OSCE) (in the case of Croatia, see Chapter 7) and even the International Monetary Fund (see Chapter 7). Thus, while the EU provided the power in terms of leverage, these organizations often shaped the substance by providing expertise and legitimacy (Skovgaard 2011). In this sense, inter-organizational context was relevant in these cases.

However, the EU becomes much less ambitious towards countries that are further away, even if it is clearly in a dominant position. In this regard, the power hypothesis has to be qualified. In general, the

EU has under-addressed partial regimes in countries outside the EU neighbourhood. In Fiji and the Solomon Islands, for instance, the EU is clearly more powerful and at the same time there are no (perceptions of) security threats. Still, the EU generally underperforms in these cases, even in the external context conditions, including state capacity, albeit with the exception of elections in the case of Fiji. A similar picture emerges for Venezuela. This indicates that a powerful position and the absence of security concerns do not automatically translate to the promotion of a broad substance.

The case of Fiji also illustrates how the power hypothesis and the inter-organizational hypothesis interrelate. The atypical substance promoted towards Fiji – that is to say, significant attention given to elections, combined with neglect of other components – can be explained because the EU has been following the regional hegemony of Australia and New Zealand (and by extension the Pacific Island Forum; see Chapter 15). The relatively broad substance towards Kyrgyzstan can be explained not only by the high asymmetrical interdependence and the comparatively low security interests (power hypothesis), but also by the relative openness of the country's government (see Chapter 13).

This leads us to elaborate on the two forms of the domestic context hypothesis, namely, the assumptions that the substance corresponds to the existing democratic deficiencies within the third country or is adjusted to governments' agendas, respectively. At first sight its explanatory value with regard to the former reading seems limited: there are significant divergences between the 'absolute' and 'relative' substance promoted by the EU (see Tables A.1 and A.2). The EU's underlying or 'default' output orientation and other factors seem more important than domestic deficiencies in terms of explaining the EU's substance. However, this should also be nuanced. All of the chapters provide evidence that the EU takes the domestic context into consideration at least to some extent, even if this does not always radically change the big picture. Moreover, the EU's tendency to emphasize socio-economic development and state administrative capacity is often in line with the domestic situation and with preferences of the ruling government (see above). Finally, there are instances where the EU has overall adequately addressed domestic deficiencies, such as in Kyrgyzstan, Ukraine and Brazil, or has responded to specific problems, such as in Kosovo and Bosnia and Herzegovina. Explanations for the EU's policy towards Kyrgyzstan have already been touched upon. In the case of Ukraine, Stewart shows how the EU has responded to the deterioration of democracy under former President Yanukovych (see Chapter 9). In Kosovo and Bosnia and Herzegovina, the EU paid attention to minority rights and constitutional issues, respectively. In the latter case, the EU also responded to the hardships of the 2008/09 financial and economic crisis by increasing funds from its Instrument for Pre-Accession Assistance (IPA). Overall, the EU was found to take into account that both countries are post-conflict societies (see Chapter 8).

The case of Brazil is particular, because the two readings of the domestic hypothesis are congruent and are at the same time interconnected with the power hypothesis. As Ribeiro-Hoffmann argues, the EU's responsiveness to the Brazilian domestic context, understood as the *preferences* of the government, relates to the EU's desire to counterbalance US hegemony. This has led the EU to be more lenient towards the domestic government's preferences (see Chapter 16). In turn, accommodating the Brazilian government's preferences is congruent with addressing 'objective' deficiencies that mainly relate to the socio-economic situation (Table A.2). There was a high level of consensus between both partners on the necessary areas for reform, which with a view to socio-economic development resonates well with the EU's default substance (see above). However, as other cases show, accommodating the preferences of the third country government does not necessarily mean that domestic *deficiencies* will be taken into account. For instance, the EU has also followed Venezuela's preferences, which have been less geared towards democratic reforms (especially in the partial regimes). Together with the limited interest and agenda of Spain as the dominant EU actor in democracy promotion towards Latin America (i.e. the institutional hypothesis), this explains why domestic deficiencies in Venezuela have generally been under-addressed. Eritrea is another case where the EU has largely followed the government's preferences, even if this means that domestic deficiencies are severely under-addressed. What determines the EU's substance in this case (also in comparison to Ethiopia) is not so much the 'objective' democratic situation, but rather the reluctance of the government to accept external intervention to support democracy and the EU's readiness to adjust its agenda accordingly (Chapter 14).

Thus, while our contributors found some evidence for the adaption of the substance of democracy promotion to the domestic context in terms of governments' preferences, in no case did the EU leave the definition of substance exclusively to the third country. Still, there are differences in the degree to which the EU accepts ownership in democracy promotion. At one end of the spectrum, there are the candidate countries that do not have much leeway in defining which substance of democracy is being promoted. As the case of Turkey shows, their governments can only influence the substance on the implementation side, that is, by refusing to transpose certain parts of the agenda. At the other end, in its development policy the EU adheres to agreements such as the 2005 Paris Declaration on Aid Effectiveness that remind donors to take ownership seriously. This is clearly reflected in the regulation on the European Development Fund (EDF) and, eventually, in the profile of EDF-funded assistance (see also Del Biondo 2015). As mentioned above, the application of ownership principles often reinforces the EU's output-oriented tendency. In theoretical terms, this variation shows how the domestic context interrelates with institutional factors.

Another finding from a range of case studies is that despite its acknowledgement of domestic particularities, the EU does not engage with democratic concepts that emerge in third countries' domestic contexts. Be it 'revolutionary democracy' in Ethiopia (Chapter 14), or the model of democracy related to the Bolivarian revolution in Venezuela (Chapter 16), the EU does not take up and get involved in such discourses. Only in Russia has the EU tried to connect the promotion of functioning administration and of corruption to the discourse on 'modernization', without, however, discussing it further or even elaborating on the prevailing notion of 'sovereign democracy' (Chapter 9).

Institutional factors have not emerged as of major explanatory value. It is clear that different member states and sub-systems within the EU hold different templates of what democracy promotion should entail (see e.g. Ribeiro-Hoffmann in Chapter 16 on Spain, but also the difference between the Commission, the Council and the European Parliament, and Stewart in Chapter 9 on Poland). Some chapters have also confirmed that EU actors and institutions with a developmental background rather favour a shallow democracy promotion agenda (see e.g. Chapter 15 on the inter-institutional quarrels between Directorate General (DG) Development and DG Relex on whether the EDF should be used for poverty reduction or electoral assistance). Here, the interrelatedness between institutional factors and attention to the third country government's agenda also comes into play (see above). Furthermore, the case of the European Parliament's complaint about the limited attention paid to socio-economic development in the Commission's draft Country Strategy Paper on Brazil shows that the legal basis of the financial source is important for the content of the policy. Since in this case the funding was based on rules that relate to development co-operation, the Parliament argued that the Commission had to follow the respective (development) priorities instead of others (see Chapter 16). As Kochenov underlines in his contribution, the absence of certain legal rules related to democracy from the EU's *acquis* is a characteristic of EU democracy promotion (Chapter 2). This becomes evident with regard to the component of 'stateness', which has generally not been overly important in EU democracy promotion. One of the reasons that has been identified in the literature is the lack of respective rules in this sphere (Bieber 2011: 1793). This shows that institutional factors also reflect and further reinforce the more fundamental 'nature of the beast' explanation. Related to this is the characteristic role of the European Commission in the EU system of governance that can be said to contribute to the EU as a rather output-oriented political construction, as argued above. That EU external relations have, to a large extent, been driven by the Commission partly explains its output-oriented character, as argued by Reynaert in relation to Tunisia and Egypt (Chapter 11). Interestingly, this reasoning implies that the EU may take a broader approach to democracy promotion when the European External Action Service (EEAS) becomes more closely involved, as found by Del Biondo in relation to Ethiopia and Eritrea (Chapter 14). In a similar vein, one might also hypothesize that the growing role of the European Parliament would broaden the EU's democracy promotion agenda, as has been suggested in several chapters (e.g. Chapter 9 on Russia and Ukraine, Chapter 16 on Brazil and Venezuela, and Chapter 15 on Fiji and Solomon Islands).

However, these generalizations remain speculative. While the diversity of substances within the EU has been recognized throughout this volume, overall the chapters have not provided much evidence that the institutional factor is a decisive one. Furthermore, many chapters show that the same institutional configuration towards two countries (e.g. Kazakhstan and Kyrgyzstan; Ethiopia and Eritrea; Brazil and Venezuela) can still lead to diverse findings on the substance.

Three closely related reasons for the limited specific explanatory value of the institutional hypothesis come to mind. First, within the EU there are few cases where one member state and/or one sub-system is dominant. European foreign policy usually involves a compromise and/or coexistence of various policies. Arguably, this is even more true in a 'horizontal' domain such as democracy promotion, which is (in contrast to trade, aid, climate change, etc.) not confined to a (mainly) single institutional sub-system. This diversity of models is precisely why some authors, such as Kurki and De Ridder, talk about the 'fuzziness' or 'vagueness' (Chapters 3 and 6, respectively) of the EU's substance. Second, in the few cases where dominant member states or sub-systems can be identified, these tend to be the ones that are less interested in democracy promotion. This has been shown in the cases of Brazil/Venezuela (Chapter 16), Israel/Palestine (Chapter 12) and Russia

(Chapter 9). In each of these cases, the limited attention to democracy issues by key actors has gone hand in hand with a shallow or a superficial agenda. Third, other factors such as the EU's power relationship with third countries, the domestic context on the recipient side, and of course the EU's 'default' output-oriented tendencies, are generally more important than the intra-EU institutional configuration. All this does not imply that the institutional dimension is irrelevant, but rather that it is closely connected with, and often subordinate to, other factors.

Apart from the above explanations, there may be a methodological reason for why the institutional hypothesis seems to be less important. Opening the black box of EU institutions proves difficult and demands intense fieldwork. For instance, it was pointed out that it is difficult to trace individual member states' influence in the Council because its meetings take place behind closed doors (Chapter 13). Thus, while we do not think that intensified studies would change the general picture, they could still provide important further insights with regard to different understandings of democracy (promotion) in different DGs, the translation of paradigms into action, scope conditions under which institutional factors matter and the interaction of institutional factors with others.

Similar to the situation regarding institutions, inter-organizational context does not emerge as a decisive factor. This resonates with the observation that 'there is a lack of global coordination among developed countries supporting democracy promotion throughout the world' (Epstein *et al.* 2007: 22). Usually, each democracy promoter pursues its own democratization agenda (Burnell 2008: 416, Merkel 2010: 154–59). Still, there are instances where the EU's substance of democracy promotion is shaped in coordination with other actors, or at least with a view to other actor's activities. Some cases have already been mentioned above. With regard to elections, more generally, the OSCE is mentioned in several chapters as an important actor that has limited the role of the EU. The same is true for specific EU member states and other states. As Del Biondo argues, the involvement of the UK and the US in security sector reform in Ethiopia has reduced the need for EU involvement in this field (Chapter 14). On the other hand, the same chapter shows that initiatives conducted by other actors may attract EU financial support. Given that staff and expertise are valuable resources that the EU does not always have, supporting joint projects such as the World Bank-administered Public Sector Capacity-Building Programme in Ethiopia seems to be an alternative. Similar to the case of Fiji mentioned above, in the case of Israel and Palestine the EU's activities take place in an environment that is dominated by another external actor (here the US), which has an impact on the EU's policy.

This makes it clear that further research should explore not only the relative explanatory value of different factors, but also how they interrelate and correspond to different strata or layers of explanation. As argued within critical realist scholarship, research constitutes a never-ending search for ever more accurate explanations beyond observable events. This implies that diverse theories and explanations can be integrated into a multi-causal analysis, whereby some work at deeper levels than others (Kurki 2008, Bailey 2009). In our case, the 'nature of the beast' seems the most fundamental explanation (see also Wetzel *et al.* 2015), whereas the other factors play a role in a number of ways that deserve further study.

Conclusions

The main objective of this book was to map and explain the substance of EU democracy promotion. Briefly summarized, this concluding chapter has found that the 'default substance' or 'basso continuo' of the EU's democracy promotion is output-oriented, specifically targeting 'socio-economic development' and 'state administrative capacity'. At the same time, the EU has, in most cases, and in particular in recent candidate countries, addressed at least some of the partial regimes that lie at the core of the definition of embedded liberal democracy. This finding helps to shed light on the puzzle outlined in the introductory chapter. While EU democracy promotion generally includes key elements of liberal democracy, we detect a focus and the closest match with existing 'deficiencies' in third countries with regard to 'output-oriented' components that belong to the context conditions instead of the definitional core of embedded liberal democracy.

Looking for explanations, the 'nature of the beast' seems the most fundamental factor (see also Wetzel *et al.* 2015), while feasibility concerns, power relations and domestic context conditions are also important. The institutional and inter-organizational hypotheses appear to have less immediate explanatory value, although it should be mentioned that all explanations are interrelated in complex ways.

Further research could elaborate these findings by extending the mapping as well as specifying the explanations. In order to do so, both carefully designed case studies and quantitative, statistical analyses should be considered. Although this volume addresses a large number of third countries spanning around the globe, there is room for further comparative analysis. In the process of the editing of this book, it has proven particularly difficult to find researchers working on EU democracy promotion in Asia and Latin America. Whereas the EU's broader normative agenda, including human rights, has been studied extensively, the literature on EU democracy promotion largely focuses on Africa and on the European neighbourhood. The reason for this may be that academics and policy-makers consider other concerns to be more pressing and more relevant, whereas democracy promotion is either unnecessary because countries are already democratized to a large extent (e.g. in Latin America) or unfeasible because it faces strong opposition from the government (e.g. in China). However, these assumptions can be seriously questioned. As Ribeiro-Hoffmann rightly argues in Chapter 16, a wider view on democracy allows identifying different, previously unexplored dimension in the EU's relations with Latin America. It would also be a shame if China continues to be neglected in further research, not only because it is 'the de facto leader of those countries that are resisting the global advance of democracy' but especially because its authoritarian rule may not endure alongside economic openness (Nathan *et al.* 2013: 6). A broader, 'embedded liberalism' perspective could be particularly fruitful in this regard, since it allows for not only capturing the potential richness of democracy, but also the various ways through which it could be promoted. Carefully selected additional case studies could help advance our knowledge about the substance of (EU) democracy promotion by controlling for particular variables or by detailed process tracing.

Beyond case studies, there is also room for advancement with regard to quantitative methods. With the BTI there exists a dataset that includes a large number of countries, that is updated every two years and that breaks down the notion of democracy into single components which are measured individually. It would therefore be conceivable to extend the mapping exercise to more countries (see above) and use statistical methods to learn about the match or mismatch between the promoted substance and the existing deficiencies on a larger scale.

When it comes to explanations, further theorizing on the different hypotheses would be desirable, for example by conceiving of different 'layers' of explanations and how they interrelate. Our findings indicate that the 'nature of the beast' plays at a more fundamental level, which may also be the case for institutions and inter-organizational context. While the latter two did not display strong explanatory power at a specific level across our cases, their relevance could be studied further with a view to underlying attitudes. With regard to institutions, in particular, such a perspective could be applied in a detailed study of attitudes towards democracy promotion held by the EU policymakers, which may relate back to the 'nature of the beast' explanation. It should also be kept in mind that the importance of a factor such as inter-organizational field may vary over time and in view of changing paradigms and patterns of donor coordination. Such changes may be subject to further study themselves. Feasibility concerns, power relations and domestic context conditions seem to operate at an intermediate level, and further research could aim to identify scope conditions under which these hypotheses apply or build chains of explanations that include these factors as independent and intervening variables. Thus, future research should engage in more intricate analysis of the different explanations for the substance of EU democracy promotion, thereby also identifying the conditions under which the substance might change.

Notes

1. Values for Fiji and the Solomon Islands were constructed from the scores given in the respective country chapter. We opted for the 2006 BTI values as a reference because many Country Strategy Papers (CSPs) and the respective Indicative Programmes that the authors refer to relate to the time frame of 2007–2013. These documents were drawn up at the beginning of the 2007–2013 programming period. Thus, if the domestic context has played a role in drafting the CSPs and related documents and eventually in designing the substance of democracy promotion, the situation shortly before the start of this funding period, which is reflected in the 2006 BTI values, should have been relevant for the policy-makers.
2. With regard to socio-economic development, it can be argued that the scores are a modest judgment given the fact that we did not include the EU measures aimed at the development of a functioning market economy, which the EU deems to contribute to the (output-related) improvement of the socio-economic situation in third countries. Thus, including market-building activities (cf. the Chapter by Kurki) would justify the characterization as output-related even more.
3. 'Electoralist fallacy' refers to an exclusive focus on and over-evaluation of elections for successful democratization (see for instance Schneider and Schmitter 2004: 88, Endnote 14).
4. With Ethiopia and Venezuela rated as partly free and Russia, Egypt and Eritrea rated as not free: http://www.freedomhouse.org/report/freedom-world/freedom-world-2006#tabs-0-bottom-2.
5. Apart from the lack of such discussion in the EU documents, the issue was not raised in various discussions we had with the EU officials (Brussels, 2 July 2012; see www.eu-ipods.eu).

Annex: Summary of Substance and BTI Values

Table A.1 Summary of substance of EU democracy promotion based on country case studies

Country	Elections	Political rights	Civil rights	Horizontal account-ability	Effective power	Stateness	State admin. capacity	Civil society	Socio-economic develop-ment
Czech Rep.	–	+	++	++	–	–	++	++	++
Slovakia	+	+	++	++	–	–	++	++	++
Bosnia-Herzegovina	+++	+	+	+++	+	++	+++	++	++
Kosovo	++	+	+	+++	+	++	+++	++	+++
Croatia	+	++	+++	+++	–	++	++	++	++
Turkey	+	+++	+++	+++	++	++	++	++	+++
Ukraine 2005–2009	+	++	+	+	–	–	++	++	++
Ukraine 2010–2013	++	++	++	++	–	–	++	++	++
Russia	+	+	+	+	–	–	+	+	+
Armenia	+++	+	+	+	–	+	+++	++	++
Georgia	++	+	++	+	–	++	++	++	+++
Egypt	+	+	+	–	–	–	++	+	++
Tunisia 2003–2010	–	–	–	–	–	–	++	–	+

Table A.1 (Continued)

Country	Elections	Political rights	Civil rights	Horizontal accountability	Effective power	Stateness	State admin. capacity	Civil society	Socio-economic development
Tunisia 2011–2012	+	+	+	–	–	–	++	+	+
Israel	–	+	+	+	–	–	++	+++	+
Palestine	+	+	+	+	+	+++	+++	+++	+++
Kazakhstan	+	+	++	++	–	–	+++	++	+
Kyrgyzstan	++	++	+++	+++	–	+	++	++	+++
Ethiopia	+++	+	++	+++	–	–	+++	++	+++
Eritrea	–	–	++	–	+	++	+	–	+++
Solomon Islands 2000–2007	+	–	–	–	–	++	++	++	+++
Solomon Islands 2008–2010	++	+	+	–	–	–	–	+	+++
Fiji 2000–2002	++	+	–	+	+	+	–	–	++
Fiji 2003–2010	+++	+	+	+	+	+	+	+++	+
Brazil	–	+	+	–	–	–	+	–	+++
Venezuela	–	+	+	–	–	–	++	++	+++

– no or very minor attention, + some attention, ++ focused attention, + + + major attention.
Source: See country chapters in this volume.

Table A.2 BTI values

Country	Elections	Political rights	Civil rights	Horizontal account-ability	Effective power	Stateness	State admin. capacity	Civil society	Socio-economic development
	1-3 = ---	1-3,5 = ---	1-3 = ---	1-3,5 = ---	1-3 = ---	1-3,5 = ---	1-3,5 = ---	1-3,5 = ---	1-3 = ---
	4-6 = --	4-6,5 = --	4-6 = --	4-6,5 = --	4-6 = --	4-6,5 = --	4-6,5 = --	4-6,5 = --	4-6 = --
	7-9 = -	7-9,5 = -	7-9 = -	7-9,5 = -	7-9 = -	7-9,5 = -	7-9,5 = -	7-9,5 = -	7-9 = -
	10 = +	10 = +	10 = +	10 = +	10 = +10 = +	10 = +	10 = +	10 = +	10 = +
Bosnia-Herzegovina	-	-	-	-	-	-	-	-	-
Kosovo (BTI 2010)	-	-	-	-	-	-	-	-	-
Croatia	+	+	-	-	+	-	-	-	-
Turkey	-	-	-	-	-	-	-	-	-
Ukraine 2005–2009	-	-	-	-	-	-	-	-	-
Ukraine 2010–2013 (BTI 2012)	-	-	-	-	-	-	-	-	-
Russia	--	--	--	--	--	--	--	--	--
Armenia	--	--	--	--	--	--	--	--	--

Table A.2 (Continued)

Country	Elections	Political rights	Civil rights	Horizontal accountability	Effective power	Stateness	State admin. capacity	Civil society	Socio-economic development
	1-3 = --- 4-6 = -- 7-9 = - 10 = +	1-3,5 = --- 4-6,5 = -- 7-9,5 = - 10 = +	1-3 = --- 4-6 = -- 7-9 = - 10 = +	1-3,5 = --- 4-6,5 = -- 7-9,5 = - 10 = +	1-3 = --- 4-6 = -- 7-9 = - 10 = +10 = +	1-3,5 = --- 4-6,5 = -- 7-9,5 = - 10 = +	1-3,5 = --- 4-6,5 = -- 7-9,5 = - 10 = +	1-3,5 = --- 4-6,5 = -- 7-9,5 = - 10 = +	1-3 = --- 4-6 = -- 7-9 = - 10 = +
Georgia	-	-	-	-	-	-	-	-	-
Egypt 2003–	---	---	--	---	--	--	--	--	--
Tunisia 2003–2010	---	---	--	--	-	+	--	--	--
Tunisia 2011–2012 (BTI 2014)	-	--	-	-	-	-	--	-	--
Kazakhstan	---	--	--	---	--	-	--	--	--
Kyrgyzstan	-	--	--	--	--	--	---	--	--
Ethiopia	---	--	--	---	--	-	--	--	--
Eritrea	---	---	---	---	--	-	--	---	--
Brazil	+	-	-	-	+	-	-	-	-
Venezuela	-	--	--	--	-	-	--	-	--

Source: See BTI (2012a). BTI values for 2006 unless otherwise indicated. On the construction of the values for the components, see Chapter 1.

References

Aalen, L. and K. Tronvoll (2008) 'The 2008 Ethiopian Local Elections: The Return of Electoral Authoritarianism', *African Affairs* 108(430): 111–20.

Aalen, L. and K. Tronvoll (2009) 'The End of Democracy? Curtailing Political and Civil Rights in Ethiopia', *Review of African Political Economy* 36(120): 193–207.

Abbink, J. (2006) 'Discomfiture of Democracy? The 2005 Election Crisis in Ethiopia and Its Aftermath', *African Affairs* 105(419): 173–99.

Abbink, J. (2009) 'The Ethiopian Second Republic and the Fragile "Social Contract"', *Africa Spectrum* 44(2): 3–28.

Agné, H. (2014) 'Is Successful Democracy Promotion Possible? The Conceptual Problem', *Democratization* 21(1): 49–71.

Alexander, E.R. (1993) 'Interorganizational Coordination: Theory and Practice', *Journal of Planning Literature* 7(4): 328–43.

Andrés Viñas, D. (2009) *EU's Democracy Promotion Policy in the Mediterranean: Squaring the Stability-Democracy Circle?*, Bellaterra (Barcelona), Institut Universitari d'Estudis Europeus: Observatorio Politico Working Papers 80.

Ashton, C. (2010a) *Statement by EU High Representative Catherine Ashton on the Elections to the People's Assembly of Egypt*, A 249/10, Brussels, 6 December, http://www.consilium.europa.eu/uedocs/cms_data/docs/pressdata/EN/foraff/118243.pdf, date accessed 7 June 2014.

Ashton, C. (2010b) *Statement by EU High Representative Catherine Ashton on the Pardon of Ethiopian Opposition Leader Birtukan Midekssa*, A 199/10, Brussels, 7 October.

Ashton, C. (2010c) *Declaration by the High Representative Catherine Ashton on Behalf of the European Union on the Publication of the Final Report of the EU Election Observation Mission to Ethiopia 2010*, 15964/10 (PRESSE 295), Brussels, 8 November.

Ashton, C. (2011a) *Statement by High Representative Catherine Ashton on the Adoption of a General Amnesty in Armenia*, A 214/11, Brussels, 27 May, http://www.consilium.europa.eu/uedocs/cms_data/docs/pressdata/EN/foraff/122297.pdf, date accessed 2 January 2013.

Ashton, C. (2011b) *Statement by High Representative Catherine Ashton on the Elections in Tunisia*, A 429/11, Brussels, 24 October, http://www.consilium.europa.eu/uedocs/cms_data/docs/pressdata/EN/foraff/125531.pdf, date accessed 7 June 2014.

Ashton, C. (2011c) *Speech by EU High Representative Catherine Ashton at the Women's Rights Forum in Tripoli*, A 450/11, Brussels, 12 November, http://www.consilium.europa.eu/uedocs/cms_data/docs/pressdata/EN/foraff/126034.pdf, date accessed 7 June 2014.

Ashton, C. (2012a) *Statement by High Representative of the European Union Catherine Ashton on the Presidential Elections in Russia on 4 March 2012*, A 100/12, Brussels, 5 March, http://www.consilium.europa.eu/uedocs/cms_Data/docs/pressdata/EN/foraff/128733.pdf, date accessed 22 May 2014.

Ashton, C. (2012b) *Statement by EU High Representative Catherine Ashton on the Sentencing of "Pussy Riot" Punk Band Members in Russia*, A 370/12, Brussels, 17 August, http://www.consilium.europa.eu/uedocs/cms_data/docs/pressdata/EN/foraff/132192.pdf, date accessed 22 May 2014.

Ashton, C. (2012c) *Statement by High Representative Catherine Ashton Following Her Meeting with the Minister of Foreign Affairs of Kazakhstan, Mr. Yerzhan Kazykhanov*, A 40/12, Brussels, 2 February.

Ashton, C. (2013) *Remarks by EU High Representative Catherine Ashton on the Current Situation in Egypt*, A 132/13, Strasbourg, 13 March, http://www.consilium.europa.eu/uedocs/cms_data/docs/pressdata/EN/foraff/136078.pdf, date accessed 7 June 2014.

Ashton, C. and Š. Füle (2011) *Joint Statement by Catherine Ashton, High Representative of the Union for Foreign Affairs and Security Policy, and Commissioner Štefan Füle, on the Constituent Assembly Elections in the Republic of Tunisia*, MEMO/11/747, Brussels, 28 October, http://www.consilium.europa.eu/uedocs/cms_data/docs/pressdata/EN/foraff/125725.pdf, date accessed 7 June 2014.

Ashton, C. and Š. Füle (2012a) *Joint Statement by EU High Representative Catherine Ashton and Commissioner Štefan Füle on the Upcoming Parliamentary Elections in Ukraine*, A 453/12, 12 October 2012, http://www.consilium.europa.eu/uedocs/cms_data/docs/pressdata/EN/foraff/132805.pdf, date accessed 22 May 2014.

Ashton, C. and Š. Füle (2012b) *Statement by High Representative Catherine Ashton and Commissioner Štefan Füle on the Parliamentary Elections in Armenia on 6 May 2012*, A 212/12, Brussels, 8 May, http://www.consilium.europa.eu/uedocs/cms_data/docs/pressdata/EN/foraff/130097.pdf, date accessed 2 January 2012.

Ashton, C. and Š. Füle (2012c) *Joint Statement by EU High Representative Catherine Ashton and Commissioner Štefan Füle on the Results of Georgia's Parliamentary Elections*, A 433/12, Brussels, 2 October, http://www.consilium.europa.eu/uedocs/cms_Data/docs/pressdata/EN/foraff/132699.pdf, date accessed 4 January 2013.

Ashton, C. and Š. Füle (2013a) *Joint Statement by EU High Representative Catherine Ashton and Commissioner Štefan Füle on Elections in Armenia*, MEMO/13/125, Brussels, 20 February, http://europa.eu/rapid/press-release_MEMO-13-125_en.htm?locale=en, date accessed 13 April 2014.

Ashton, C. and Š. Füle (2013b) *Joint Statement by EU High Representative Catherine Ashton and Commissioner Štefan Füle on the Results of Georgia's Presidential Election*, MEMO/13/940, Brussels, 28 October, http://europa.eu/rapid/press-release_MEMO-13-940_en.htm, date accessed 13 April 2014.

Ayers, A. J. (2008) ' "We All Know a Democracy when We See One": (Neo)liberal Orthodoxy in the "Democratisation" and "Good Governance" Project', *Policy and Society* 27(1): 1–13.

Bach, D. and A. L. Newman (2010) 'Transgovernmental Networks and Domestic Policy Convergence: Evidence from Insider Trading Regulation', *International Organization* 64(3): 505–28.

Bäck, H. and A. Hadenius (2008) 'Democracy and State Capacity: Exploring a J-Shaped Relationship', *Governance* 21(1): 1–24.

Bailey, D. J. (2009) *The Political Economy of European Social Democracy: A Critical Realist Approach*, London: Routledge.

Balkır, C. (2010) 'Turkey's Road to EU Membership: Economic Outlook', *Köz-Gazdaság* 5(3): 25–40.

Balkır, C. and D. Soyaltın (2010) 'The Limits to Europeanization: Analyzing Domestic Change in Turkey', in C. Nas and R. Izci (eds), *Re-conceptualizing EU-Turkey Relations: Conceptual and Theoretical Approaches*, Istanbul: Marmara University, 29–58.

Bánkuti, M., G. Halmai and K. L. Scheppele (2012) 'Hungary's Illiberal Turn: Dismantling the Constitution', *Journal of Democracy* 23(3): 138–46.

Bartolini, S. (2005) *Restructuring Europe: Centre Formation, System Building and Political Structuring between the Nation-State and the European Union*, Oxford: Oxford University Press.

Baumann, R., V. Rittberger and W. Wagner (2000) 'Power and Power Politics: Neorealist Foreign Policy Theory and Expectations About German Foreign Policy since Unification', University of Tübingen: Tübinger Arbeitspapiere zur Internationalen Politik und Friedensforschung 30a.

Beetham, D. (1997) 'Market Economy and Democratic Polity', *Democratization* 4(1): 76–93.

Beetham, D. (1999) *Democracy and Human Rights*, Cambridge: Polity Press.

Bereketeab, R. (2009) 'The Eritrea-Ethiopia Conflict and the Algiers Agreement: Eritrea's Road to Isolation', in R. Reid (ed.), *Eritrea's External Relations*, London: Chatham House, 98–124.

Berman, S. (2006) *The Primacy of Politics: Social Democracy and the Making of Europe's Twentieth Century*, Cambridge: Cambridge University Press.

Beurdeley, L. (2003) *L'élargissement de l'Union Européenne aux pays d'Europe Central et Orientale et aux îles du Bassin Méditerranéen*, Paris/Montréal: L'Harmattan.

Bez, K. (2010) *Persecution of Asylum Seekers by Ukrainian Authorities Constitutes a Violation of Law and Ukraine's Obligations*, Press Release, www.noborders.org.ua, 22 July 2010, date accessed 22 May 2014.

Bicchi, F. (2009) 'Democracy Assistance in the Mediterranean: An Overview', *Mediterranean Politics* 14(1): 61–78.

Bicchi, F. (2010) 'Dilemmas of Implementation: EU Democracy Assistance in the Mediterranean', *Democratization* 17(5): 976–96.

Bieber, F. (2011) 'Building Impossible States? State-Building Strategies and EU Membership in the Western Balkans', *Europe-Asia Studies* 63(10): 1783–802.

Boas, V. (2012) *Energy and Human Rights: Two Irreconcilable Foreign Policy Goals? The Case of the Trans-Caspian Pipeline in EU-Turkmen Relations*, Rome: Istituto Affari Internazionali: IAI Working Papers No. 12–07.

Boonstra, J. (2010) 'Assessing Democracy Assistance: Georgia', *Project Report: Assessing Democracy Assistance*, Madrid: FRIDE.

Borchgrevink, A. (2008) 'Limits to Donor Influence: Ethiopia, Aid and Conditionality', *Forum for Development Studies* 35(2): 195–220.

Börzel, T. A. (2009) *Transformative Power Europe? The EU Promotion of Good Governance in Areas of Limited Statehood*, European Report on Development Workshop "Transforming Political Structures: Security, Institutions, and Regional Integration Mechanisms", Florence: Robert Schumann Centre for Advanced Studies, 16–17 April.

Börzel, T. A. (2010) Why You Don't Always Get What You Want: EU Enlargement and Civil Society in Central and Eastern Europe', *Acta Politica* 45(1–2): 1–10.

Börzel, T. A. and T. Risse (2009) 'Venus Approaching Mars? The European Union's Approaches to Democracy Promotion in Comparative Perspective', in

A. Magen, T. Risse and M. McFaul (eds), *Promoting Democracy and the Rule of Law: American and European Strategies*, Basingstoke: Palgrave Macmillan, 34–60.

Börzel, T. A. and C. Hackenesch (2013) 'Small Carrots, Few Sticks: EU Good Governance Promotion in Sub-Saharan Africa', *Cambridge Review of International Affairs* 26(3): 536–55.

Börzel, T. A. and V. van Hüllen (2014) 'One Voice, One Message, But Conflicting Goals: Cohesiveness and Consistency in the European Neighbourhood Policy', *Journal of European Public Policy* 21(7): 1033–49.

Börzel, T. A., Y. Pamuk and A. Stahn (2008) *The European Union and the Promotion of Good Governance in Its Near Abroad: One Size Fits All?* Berlin: Free University Berlin: SFB-Governance Working Paper Series, 18.

Bossuyt, F. (2010) *The EU's Transnational Power over Central Asia: Developing and Applying a Structurally Integrative Framework to the Study of the EU's Power over Central Asia*, PhD Dissertation, Birmingham: Aston University.

Bossuyt, F. and P. Kubicek (2011) 'Advancing Democracy on Difficult Terrain: EU Democracy Promotion in Central Asia', *European Foreign Affairs Review* 16(5): 639–58.

Brinkerhoff, D. W. (2000) 'Democratic Governance and Sectoral Policy Reform: Tracing Linkages and Exploring Synergies', *World Development* 28(4): 601–15.

Brüne, S. (2007) 'Testfall Äthiopien: Die neue Afrikastrategie der Europäische Union', in M. Knodt and A. Jünemann (eds), *European External Democracy Promotion*, Baden Baden: Nomos, 35–70.

BTI – Bertelsmann Transformation Index (2012a) http://www.bti-project.de, date accessed 3 May 2014.

BTI – Bertelsmann Transformation Index (2012b) *Codebook for Country Assessments*, Gütersloh: Bertelsmann Stiftung.

BTI – Bertelsmann Transformation Index (2012c) Armenia Country Report, Gütersloh: Bertelsmann Stiftung, http://www.bti-project.de/fileadmin/Inhalte/reports/2012/pdf/BTI%202012%20Armenia.pdf, date accessed 9 January 2013.

Bulmer, S. and C. Radaelli (2005) 'The Europeanization of National Policy', in S. Bulmer and C. Lequesne (eds), *The Member States of the European Union*, Oxford: Oxford University Press, 338–59.

Burnell, P. (2008) 'From Evaluating Democracy Assistance to Appraising Democracy Promotion', *Political Studies* 56(2): 414–34.

Cain, B. E., R. J. Dalton and S. E. Scarrow (eds) (2003) *Democracy Transformed? Expanding Political Opportunities in Advanced Industrial Democracies*, Oxford: Oxford University Press.

Calchi Novati, G. (2008) 'Italy and Africa: How to Forget Colonialism', *Journal of Modern Italian Studies* 13(1): 41–57.

Carbone, M. (2006) 'Normative Power and Political Dialogue: The European Union in the South Pacific', *Asia-Pacific Journal of EU Studies* 4(1): 27–42.

Carbone, M. (2007) *The European Union and International Development*, New York: Routledge.

Carbone, M. (2008a) 'Theory and Practice of Participation: Civil Society and EU Development Policy', *Perspectives on European Politics and Society* 9(2): 241–55.

Carbone, M. (2008b) 'Mission Impossible: The EU and Policy Coherence for Development', *Journal of European Integration* 30(3): 323–42.

Carbone, M. (2011) 'Trapped in Regionalism: The EU and Democracy Promotion in the South Pacific', *European Foreign Affairs Review* 16(5): 673–87.

Carothers, T. (1997) 'Democracy Assistance: The Question of Strategy', *Democratization* 4(3): 109–32.
Carothers, T. (1999) *Aiding Democracy Abroad*, Washington, DC: Carnegie Endowment for International Peace.
Carothers, T. (2000) 'Struggling with Semi-Authoritarians', in P. Burnell (ed.), *Democracy Assistance*, London: Frank Cass Publishers, 210–25.
Carothers, T. (2009) 'Democracy Assistance: Political vs. Developmental?' *Journal of Democracy* 20(1): 5–19.
Carothers, T. (2010) 'The Elusive Synthesis', *Journal of Democracy* 21(4): 12–26.
Carothers, T. and R. Youngs (2011) *Looking for Help: Will Rising Democracies Become International Democracy Supporters? Democracy and Rule of Law*, Washington, DC: Carnegie Endowment for International Peace: Carnegie Papers, July 2011.
Chandler, D. (2009) *Hollow Hegemony*, London: Pluto Press.
Chandler, D. (2010) 'The EU and Southeastern Europe: The Rise of Post-Liberal Governance', *Third World Quarterly* 31(1): 69–85.
Cheneval, F. and F. Schimmelfennig (2013) 'The Case for Democracy in the European Union', *Journal of Common Market Studies* 51(2): 334–50.
Clapham, C. (2009) 'Post-War Ethiopia: The Trajectories of Crisis', *Review of African Political Economy* 36(120): 181–92.
Closa, C., D. Kochenov and J. H. H. Weiler (2014) *Reinforcing Rule of Law Oversight in the European Union*, Badia Fiesolana, European University Institute: Robert Schuman Centre for Advanced Studies Paper 2014/25.
Comisión Económica para América Latina (CEPAL) (2012) *Estudio Economico de America Latina y el Caribe*, Documento Informativo, http://www.eclac.cl/cgi-bin/getProd.asp?xml=/publicaciones/xml/2/48062/P48062.xml&xsl=/tpl/p9f.xsl&base=/tpl/top-bottom.xslt, date accessed 15 February 2014.
Cooley, A. (2008) 'Principles in the Pipeline: Managing Transatlantic Values and Interests in Central Asia', *International Affairs* 84(6): 1173–1188.
Corbett, R., F. Jacobs and M. Shackleton (2007) *The European Parliament*, 3rd edition, London: John Harper Publishing.
Cotonou Partnership Agreement (2000) http://www.acp.int/sites/acpsec.waw.be/files/cotonou_2006_en.pdf
Council of Europe (2009) *Support to Good Governance: Project Against Corruption in Ukraine (UPAC)*, http://www.coe.int/t/DGHL/cooperation/economiccrime/corruption/Projects/upac/upac_en.asp, date accessed 22 May 2014.
Council of the European Union (2000) *Declaration by the Presidency on Behalf of the European Union on the Development of the Situation in Fiji*, 10578/00, Brussels, 25 July.
Council of the European Union (2001a) *General Affairs Council Conclusions on Human Rights and Democratisation in Third Countries*, 10228/01 (Presse 250 – G). 25 June.
Council of the European Union (2001b) *Declaration by the Presidency on Behalf of the European Union on Eritrea*, 12381/2/01 REV 2 (Presse 339), Brussels, 5 October.
Council of the European Union (2003) *Resumption of Full Cooperation After the Partial Suspension of Cooperation Under Article 96 of the Cotonou Agreement*, ACP Working Party I/A note, Brussels, 3 November.
Council of the European Union (2004) *Declaration by the Presidency on Behalf of the European Union on the Presidential and Parliamentary Elections in Tunisia*,

13932/1/04 REV 1 (Presse 304), P 122/04, Brussels, 26 October, http://www.consilium.europa.eu/uedocs/cms_data/docs/pressdata/en/cfsp/82390.pdf, date accessed 7 June 2014.

Council of the European Union (2005a) *Declaration by the Presidency on Behalf of the European Union on the Presidential Elections in Egypt*, 12084/05 (Presse 229), P 99/05, Brussels, 8 September, http://www.consilium.europa.eu/uedocs/cms_data/docs/pressdata/en/cfsp/86162.pdf, date accessed 7 June 2014.

Council of the European Union (2005b) *Declaration by the Presidency on Behalf of the European Union on the Obstruction of the Activities of the "Ligue Tunisienne pour la Défense des Droits de l'Homme"*, 12240/05 (Presse 232), P 100/05, Brussels, 13 September, http://www.consilium.europa.eu/uedocs/cms_data/docs/pressdata/en/cfsp/86235.pdf, date accessed 7 June 2014.

Council of the European Union (2006) *Declaration by the Presidency on Behalf of the EU on Measures by the Egyptian Authorities Against Civil Society Activists*, 9364/06 (Presse 143), P 070, Brussels, 15 May, http://www.consilium.europa.eu/uedocs/cms_data/docs/pressdata/en/cfsp/89608.pdf, date accessed 7 June 2014.

Council of the European Union (2007a) *Declaration by the Presidency on Behalf of the European Union on the Current Situation in Georgia*, 14818/07, P 099, Brussels, 8 November, www.consilium.europa.eu/uedocs/NewsWord/en/cfsp/97018.doc, date accessed 2 January 2013.

Council of the European Union (2007b) *European Union and Central Asia: Strategy for a New Partnership*, Brussels: General Secretariat of the Council.

Council of the European Union (2007c) *Council Decision on the Conclusion of Consultations with the Republic of the Fiji Islands Under Article 96 of the ACP-EC Partnership Agreement and Article 37 of the Development Cooperation Instrument*, 12708/07, Brussels, 26 September.

Council of the European Union (2007d) *Declaration of the Presidency on Behalf of the EU on the Nonrenewal of the Broadcasting Licence of the Venezuelan Channel RCTV*, P/07/46, 10135/07 (Presse 121), Brussels, 29 May.

Council of the European Union (2008a) 'Council Decision of 12 February 2008 on the Principles, Priorities and Conditions Contained in the Accession Partnership with Croatia and Repealing Decision 2006/145/EC', 2008/119/EC, *Official Journal of the European Union*, L 42, 16 February, 51–62.

Council of the European Union (2008b) 'Council Decision of 18 February 2008 on the Principles, Priorities and Conditions Contained in the Accession Partnership with the Republic of Turkey and repealing Decision 2006/35/EC', 2008/157/EC, *Official Journal of the European Union*, L 51, 26 February, 4–18.

Council of the European Union (2008c) 'Council Decision of 18 February 2008 on the Principles, Priorities and Conditions Contained in the European Partnership with Serbia Including Kosovo as Defined by United Nations Security Council Resolution 1244 of 10 June 1999 and Repealing Decision 2006/56/EC', (2008/213/EC), *Official Journal of the European Union*, L 80, 19 March, 46–70.

Council of the European Union (2008d) *Declaration by the Presidency on Behalf of the European Union on the Presidential Elections in Georgia on 5 January 2008*, 5057/1/08 REV 1, P 004, Brussels, 8 January, http://www.consilium.europa.eu/uedocs/cms_Data/docs/pressdata/en/cfsp/97906.pdf, date accessed 2 January 2013.

Council of the European Union (2008e) *Conclusions on Georgia*, EU External Relations 2870th Council Meeting, 9868/08, Brussels, 26–27 May.

Council of the European Union (2009a) *Declaration by the Presidency on Behalf of the European Union on the Freedom of Expression in Ethiopia*, 17684/1/09 REV 1 (Presse 384), P 141/09, Brussels, 21 December.

Council of the European Union (2009b) *Council Decision Extending the Period of Applications of the Measures in Decision 2007/64/ EC Concluding Consultations with the Republic of the Fiji Islands Under Article 96 of the ACP-EC Partnership Agreement and Article 37 of the Development Cooperation Instrument*, 13087/09, Brussels, 22 September.

Council of the European Union (2010), *14th EU-Ukraine Summit (Brussels, 22 November 2010): Joint Press Statement*, http://www.consilium.europa.eu/uedocs/cms_data/docs/pressdata/en/er/117912.pdf, 22 November 2010, date accessed 22 May 2014.

Council of the European Union (2011) *Accession Treaty: Treaty Concerning the Accession of the Republic of Croatia*, 14409/11, Brussels, 7 November, http://register.consilium.europa.eu/pdf/en/11/st14/st14409.en11.pdf, date accessed 12 June 2014.

Council of the European Union (2013) *EU Annual Report on Human Rights and Democracy in the World in 2012*, 9431/13, COHOM 82, 13 May, http://register.consilium.europa.eu/doc/srv?l=EN&f=ST%209431%202013%20INIT, date accessed 15 May 2014.

Council of the European Union and European Parliament (2006) 'Regulation (EC) No. 1638/2006 Laying Down General Provisions Establishing a European Neighbourhood and Partnership Instrument', *Official Journal of the European Union*, L310, 9 November, 1–14.

Crawford, G. (2008) 'EU Human Rights and Democracy Promotion in Central Asia: From Lofty Principles to Lowly Self-interests', *Perspectives on European Politics and Society* 9(2): 172–91.

Cremona, M. (2011) 'Values in EU Foreign Policy', in M. Evans and P. Koutrakos (eds), *Beyond the Established Legal Orders: Policy Interconnections Between the EU and the Rest of the World*, Oxford: Hart, 275–315.

Crocombe, R. (2008) *The South Pacific*, 7th edition, Suva: University of the South Pacific.

Dahl, R. A. (1994). 'A Democratic Dilemma: System Effectiveness Versus Citizen Participation', *Political Science Quarterly* 109(1): 23–34.

Dalton, R. J., S. E. Scarrow and B. E. Cain (2003a) 'New Forms of Democracy? Reform and Transformation of Democratic Institutions', in B. E. Cain, R. J. Dalton and S. E. Scarrow (eds), *Democracy Transformed? Expanding Political Opportunities in Advanced Industrial Democracies*, Oxford: Oxford University Press, 1–20.

Dalton, R. J., B. E. Cain and S. E. Scarrow (2003b) 'Democratic Publics and Democratic Institutions', in B. E. Cain, R. J. Dalton and S. E. Scarrow (eds), *Democracy Transformed? Expanding Political Opportunities in Advanced Industrial Democracies*, Oxford: Oxford University Press, 250–75.

Damro, C. (2012) 'Market Power Europe', *Journal of European Public Policy* 19(5): 682–99.

Dave, B. (2008) 'The EU and Kazakhstan: Is the Pursuit of Energy and Security Cooperation Compatible with the Promotion of Human Rights and Democratic Reforms?' in N. J. Melvin (ed.), *Engaging Central Asia: The European Union's New Strategy in the Heart of Eurasia*, Brussels: CEPS Paperbacks, 43–67.

de Búrca, G. (1997) 'The Role of Equality in European Community Law', in A. Dashwood and S. O'Leary (eds), *The Principle of Equal Treatment in EC Law*, London: Sweet and Maxwell, 13–34.
de Búrca, G. (2013) 'Europe's Raison D'être', in D. Kochenov and F. Amtenbrink (eds), *European Union's Shaping of the International Legal Order*, Cambridge: Cambridge University Press, 21–37.
Del Biondo, K. (2011) 'Democracy Promotion Meets Development Cooperation: The EU as a Promoter of Democratic Governance in Sub-Saharan Africa', *European Foreign Affairs Review* 16(5): 659–72.
Del Biondo, K. (2015) 'Promoting Democracy or the External Context? Comparing the Substance of EU and US Democracy Assistance in Ethiopia', *Cambridge Review of International Affairs* 28(1).
Delegation of the European Union to Georgia (2012) *Local EU Statement on Prisoner Abuse*, Tbilisi, 19 September, http://eeas.europa.eu/delegations/georgia/documents/news/20120919-eu_statement_on_prison_abuse_en.pdf, date accessed 26 May 2014.
Delegation of the European Commission to Turkey (2008) *European Instrument for Democracy and Human Rights (EIDHR) Turkey Programme*, January, http://ec.europa.eu/europeaid/what/human-rights/documents/turkey_eidhr_projects_en.pdf, date accessed 12 June 2014.
Delegation of the European Union to Ukraine (2012) *Annual Work Programme for Grants. Non-State Actors and Local Authorities in Development – Ukraine, 2012 Annual Action Programme (NSA&LA 2012 AAP Ukraine) and Neighbourhood Civil Society Facility 2011*, http://ec.europa.eu/europeaid/documents/awp/2012/awp_2012_ukr_p2_en.pdf, date accessed 22 May 2014.
De Ridder, E. (2009) 'EU Aid for Fighting Corruption in the Czech Republic and Slovakia: Where Did It Go Wrong?' *Journal of Contemporary European Research* 5(1): 61–81.
De Ridder, E., A. Schrijvers and H. Vos (2008) 'Civil Power Europe and the Eastern Enlargement: The More the Merrier?' in J. Orbie (ed.), *Europe's Global Role: External Policies of the European Union*, Aldershot: Ashgate, 239–57.
De Soto, A. (2007) *End of Mission Report*, United Nations, http://image.guardian.co.uk/sys-files/Guardian/documents/2007/06/12/DeSotoReport.pdf, date accessed 13 August 2008.
De Witte, B. (2011) 'The EU and the International Legal Order: The Case of Human Rights', in M. Evans and P. Koutrakos (eds), *Beyond the Established Legal Orders: Policy Interconnections Between the EU and the Rest of the World*, Oxford: Hart Publishing, 127–47.
Diamond, L. (2002) 'Thinking About Hybrid Regimes', *Journal of Democracy* 13(2): 21–35.
Diamond, L., M. Plattner and A. Schedler (1999) 'Introduction', in A. Schedler, L. Diamond and M. Plattner (eds), *The Self-Restraining State: Power and Accountability in New Democracies*, Boulder: Lynne Rienner, 1–10.
Dillon, M. and J. Reid (2000) 'Global Governance, Liberal Peace, and Complex Emergency', *Alternatives: Global, Local, Political* 25(1): 117–40.
Dimitrova, A. (2002) 'Enlargement, Institution-Building and the EU's Administrative Capacity Building', *West-European Politics* 25(4): 171–90.
Dimitrova, A. (2005) 'Europeanization and Civil Service Reform in Central and Eastern Europe', in F. Schimmelfennig and U. Sedelmeier (eds), *The*

Europeanization of Central and Eastern Europe, Ithaca, NY: Cornell University Press, 71–90.
Dimitrova, A. and G. Pridham (2004) 'International Actors and Democracy Promotion in Central and Eastern Europe: The Integration Model and Its Limits', *Democratization* 11(5): 91–112.
Di Palma, G. (1990) *To Craft Democracies: An Essay on Democratic Transitions*, Los Angeles: University of California Press.
Donais, T. (2005) 'A Tale of Two Towns: Human Security and the Limits of Post-War Normalization in Bosnia-Herzegovina', *Journal of Southern Europe and the Balkans*, 7(1): 19–32.
Dryzek, J. S. (2009) 'Democratization as Deliberative Capacity Building', *Comparative Political Studies* 42(11): 1379–1402.
Duffield, M. (2001) *Global Governance and the New Wars: The Merging of Development and Security*, London: Zed Books.
Duleba, A. (1997) 'Democratic Consolidation and the Conflict over Slovakian International Alignment', in S. Szomolányi and J. Gould (eds), *Slovakia: Problems of Democratic Consolidation and the Struggle for the Rules of the Game*, Bratislava: Slovak Political Science Association, Friedrich Ebert Foundation, 209–30.
Dunne, T. and T. Flockhart (eds) (2013) *Liberal World Orders*, Oxford: Oxford University Press.
Džihić, V. and A. Wieser (2011) 'Incentives for Democratisation? Effects of EU Conditionality on Democracy in Bosnia & Hercegovina', *Europe-Asia Studies* 63(10): 1803–25.
EAR (European Agency for Reconstruction) (2002) *Annual Report 2001 for the European Parliament and the European Council*, Final, Thessaloniki, 19 April, http://ec.europa.eu/enlargement/archives/ear/publications/main/documents/EARAnnualReport2001.pdf, date accessed 3 May 2014.
EAR (European Agency for Reconstruction) (2004) *Annual Report to the European Parliament and the Council: January to December 2003*, Thessaloniki, 7 June, http://ec.europa.eu/enlargement/archives/ear/publications/main/documents/EARAnnualReport2003.pdf, date accessed 3 May 2014.
EAR (European Agency for Reconstruction) (2007) *Annual Report 2006 to the European Parliament and the Council*, Thessaloniki, 30 May, http://ec.europa.eu/enlargement/archives/ear/publications/main/documents/AnnualReportJan-Dec2006.pdf, date accessed 3 May 2014.
EAR (European Agency for Reconstruction) (2008) *Annual Report 2007*, Thessaloniki, 30 May, http://ec.europa.eu/enlargement/archives/ear/publications/main/documents/AnnualReportJan-Dec2007.pdf, date accessed 3 May 2014.
Eastern Partnership (2012). 'Platform 1 "Democracy, Good Governance and Stability". Core Objectives and Work Programme for 2012–2013', http://eeas.europa.eu/eastern/platforms/docs/work_programme_2012_13_platform1_en.pdf, date accessed 3 July 2014.
ECLO (European Commission Liaison Office to Kosovo) (2008) *European Commission Newsletter*, 7, April, http://eeas.europa.eu/delegations/kosovo/documents/newsletter/eu_newsletter_07_en.pdf, date accessed 3 May 2014.
Economides, S. (2003) 'Balkan Security: What Security? Whose Security?' *Journal of Southeast European and Black Sea Studies* 3(3): 105–29.

ECSIEP (2004) *Seminar on the Cotonou Agreement and the Conflicts in the Pacific*, Brussels, 30 November.
EEC-Turkey (1963) 'Agreement Establishing an Association Between the European Economic Community and Turkey', *Official Journal of the European Communities* 16, C113, 24 December 1973: 2–80.
Egeberg, M. (2005) 'EU Institutions and the Transformation of European-Level Politics: How to Understand Profound Change (If It Occurs)', *Comparative European Politics* 3(1): 102–17.
EMHRN – Euro-Mediterranean Human Rights Network (2011) *The EU and the Palestinian Arab Minority in Israel*, Copenhagen: Euro-Mediterranean Human Rights Network.
Epstein, S. B., N. M. Serafino and F. T. Miko (2007) *Democracy Promotion: Cornerstone of U.S. Foreign Policy?* Washington, DC: Congressional Research Service, CRS Report for Congress.
EUobserver (2009) *Turkey Angered by Franco-German Enlargement Remarks*, 18 May, http://euobserver.com/enlargement/28138, date accessed 13 June 2014.
EurActiv (2011) *EU Concerned About Russian Election*, http://www.euractiv.com/global-europe/eu-concerned-russia-election-news-509490, 7 December 2011, date accessed 22 May 2014.
Europa (2009) European External Action Service, *European Union Launches Twinning Project 'Support to the Academy of Judges of Ukraine'*, http://eeas.europa.eu/delegations/ukraine/press_corner/all_news/news/2009/20090916_1_en.htm, accessed 23 May 2014.
Europa (2010) Council of the European Union, *EU-Russia: Partnership for Modernisation*, http://eeas.europa.eu/delegations/russia/eu_russia/tech_financial_cooperation/partnership_modernisation_facility/index_en.htm, accessed 23 May 2014.
Europa (2011) Delegation of the EU to Ukraine, *The European Union and the Council of Europe Continue Promoting European Standards in the Ukrainian Media*, http://ec.europa.eu/delegations/ukraine/press_corner/all_news/news/2011/2011_01_24_01_en.htm, 24 January 2011, date accessed 22 May 2014.
Europa (2012a) Delegation of the European Union to Armenia, *EU and OSCE to Support Democratic Elections in Armenia*, 17 January, http://eeas.europa.eu/delegations/armenia/press_corner/all_news/news/2012/2012_01_17_en.htm, date accessed 2 January 2013.
Europa (2012b) Delegation of the European Union to Armenia, *Project Fiche: Support to Justice Reform in Armenia*, http://eeas.europa.eu/delegations/armenia/projects/list_of_projects/226208_en.htm, date accessed 2 January 2013.
Europa (2012c) European Commission – EuropeAid, *European Instrument for Democracy & Human Rights (EIDHR)*, http://ec.europa.eu/europeaid/how/finance/eidhr_en.htm, date accessed 9 June 2014.
Europa (2012d) Delegation of the European Union to Solomon Islands, *List of Projects*, http://www.eeas.europa.eu/delegations/solomon/projects/list_of_projects/projects_en.htm#governance-human-rights, date accessed 19 November 2012.
Europa (2013a) European Commission-EuropeAid, *Election Observation Missions*, http://ec.europa.eu/europeaid/what/human-rights/election_observation_missions/index_en.htm, date accessed 3 February 2013.

References 269

Europa (2013b) European Commission – EuropeAid, *Beneficiaries of Grants and Contracts*, http://ec.europa.eu/europeaid/work/funding/beneficiaries/index.cfm?lang=en&mode=SM&type=, date accessed 9 August 2013.
Europa (2013c) Delegation of the European Union to Ethiopia, *EC Civil Society Fund II*, http://eeas.europa.eu/delegations/ethiopia/eu_ethiopia/eu_civil_society_fund/index_en htm, date accessed 7 October 2014.
Europa (2014a), European Commission, *Instrument for Pre-accession Assistance (IPA). Bosnia and Herzegovina Financial Assistance*, http://ec.europa.eu/enlargement/instruments/funding-by-country/bosnia-herzegovina/index_en.htm, date accessed 6 June 2014.
Europa (2014b) Delegation of the European Union to Bosnia and Herzegovina and EU Special Representative, *Structured Dialogue*, http://europa.ba/Default.aspx?id=87&lang=EN, date accessed 8 July 2014.
Europa (2014c) Delegation of the European Union to Bosnia and Herzegovina and EU Special Representative, *EIDHR*, http://europa.ba/Default.aspx?id=16&lang=EN
Europa (2014d) European External Action Service, *Ongoing Missions*, http://eeas.europa.eu/eueom/missions/index_en.htm, date accessed 6 June 2014.
Europa (2014e) European Commission, *Instrument for Pre-accession Assistance (IPA). Kosovo Financial Assistance*, http://ec.europa.eu/enlargement/instruments/funding-by-country/kosovo/index_en.htm, date accessed 6 June 2014.
Europa (2014f) European External Action Service, *EU-Russia Common Spaces*, http://eeas.europa.eu/russia/common_spaces/index_en.htm, accessed 23 May 2014.
Europa (2014g) Delegation of the EU to the Russian Federation, *Partnership for Modernisation*, http://eeas.europa.eu/delegations/russia/eu_russia/tech_financial_cooperation/partnership_modernisation_facility/index_en.htm, accessed 23 May 2014.
Europa (2014h) Council of the European Union, *Common Foreign and Security Policy (CFSP) Statements*, http://www.consilium.europa.eu/press/press-releases/common-foreign-and-security-policy-%28cfsp%29-statements?lang=en&BID=73, accessed 5 June 2014.
Europa (2014i) Delegation of the European Union to the Kyrgyz Republic, *List of Projects*, http://ec.europa.eu/delegations/kyrgyzstan/projects/list_of_projects/projects_en.htm, date accessed 9 June 2014.
Europa (2014j) European External Action Service, *EU Election Observation Mission to Fiji in 2006*, http://eeas.europa.eu/eueom/missions/2006/fiji/index_en.htm, date accessed 11 June 2014.
Europa (2014k) Delegation of the European Union to Brazil, *Technical Cooperation Activities*, http://eeas.europa.eu/delegations/brazil/projects/overview/index_en.htm, date accessed 15 February 2014.
EuropeAid (2005) *Institutional Assessment and Capacity Development: Why, What and How?* Tools and Methods Series, Reference Document 1, European Commission, http://ec.europa.eu/europeaid/multimedia/publications/documents/tools/europeaid_institutional_assessment_capacity_devlpmt_2006_en.pdf, date accessed 15 May 2014.
EuropeAid (2008) *Analysing and Addressing Governance in Sector Operations*, Tools and Methods Series, Reference Document 4, European Commission, http://ec.

europa.eu/europeaid/infopoint/publications/europeaid/documents/149a_en. pdf, date accessed 15 May 2014.

European Commission (1995) *The European Union and the External Dimension of Human Rights Policy: From Rome to Maastricht and Beyond*, COM (95) 567 final, 22 November, http://eur-lex.europa.eu/LexUriServ/LexUriServ.do?uri=COM:1995:0567:FIN:EN:PDF, date accessed 15 May 2014.

European Commission (1998a) *Democratisation, the Rule of Law, Respect for Human Rights and Good Governance: The Challenges of the Partnership Between the European Union and the ACP States*, COM(98) 146, 24 February, http://archive.idea.int/lome/bgr_docs/eucom.pdf, date accessed 15 May 2014.

European Commission (1998b) *1998 Regular Report from the Commission on Turkey's Progress Towards Accession*, http://ec.europa.eu/enlargement/archives/pdf/key_documents/1998/turkey_en.pdf, date accessed 12 June 2014.

European Commission (1999) *1999 Regular Report from the Commission on Turkey's Progress Towards Accession*, 13 October, http://ec.europa.eu/enlargement/archives/pdf/key_documents/1999/turkey_en.pdf, date accessed 12 June 2014.

European Commission (2000) *Regular Report from the Commission on Turkey's Progress Towards Accession*, http://ec.europa.eu/enlargement/archives/pdf/key_documents/2000/strat_en.pdf, date accessed 12 June 2014.

European Commission (2001a) *The European Union's Role in Promoting Human Rights and Democratisation in Third Countries*, COM (2001)252, Brussels, 8 May, http://eur-lex.europa.eu/legal-content/EN/TXT/PDF/?uri=CELEX:52001DC0252&from=EN, date accessed 15 May 2014.

European Commission (2001b) *Regular Report from the Commission on Turkey's Progress Towards Accession*, SEC (2001) 1756, Brussels, 13 November, http://ec.europa.eu/enlargement/archives/pdf/key_documents/2001/tu_en.pdf, date accessed 12 June 2014.

European Commission (2001c) *Country Strategy Paper 2002–2006 & National Indicative Programme 2002–2004 Egypt*, http://eeas.europa.eu/egypt/csp/02_06_en.pdf, date accessed 7 June 2014.

European Commission (2001d) *Country Strategy Paper 2002–2006 & National Indicative Programme 2002–2004 Tunisia*, http://eeas.europa.eu/tunisia/csp/02_06_fr.pdf, date accessed 7 June 2014.

European Commission (2002) *Regular Report from the Commission on Turkey's Progress Towards Accession*, SEC (2002) 1412, Brussels, 9 October, http://ec.europa.eu/enlargement/archives/pdf/key_documents/2002/tu_en.pdf, date accessed 12 June 2014.

European Commission (2003a) *Governance and Development*, COM (2003) 615 final, Brussels, 20 October.

European Commission (2003b) *Regular Report from the Commission on Turkey's Progress Towards Accession*, http://ec.europa.eu/enlargement/archives/pdf/key_documents/2003/rr_tk_final_en.pdf, date accessed 12 June 2014.

European Commission (2003c) *Report from the Commission to the Council on the Preparedness of Bosnia and Herzegovina to Negotiate a Stabilisation and Association Agreement with the European Union*, COM(2003) 692 final, Brussels, 18 November, http://eur-lex.europa.eu/legal-content/EN/TXT/PDF/?uri=CELEX:52003DC0692, date accessed 6 June 2014.

European Commission (2003d) *Wider Europe – Neighbourhood: A New Framework for Relations with our Eastern and Southern Neighbours*, COM (2003) 104 final, Brussels, 11 March.

European Commission (2004a) *Opinion on Croatia's Application for Membership of the European Union*, COM (2004) 257 final, Brussels, 20 April, http://eur-lex.europa.eu/legal-content/EN/TXT/PDF/?uri=CELEX:52004DC0257&from=en, date accessed 14 June 2014.

European Commission (2004b) *Regular Report from the Commission on Turkey's Progress Towards Accession*, SEC(2004) 1201, Brussels, 6 October, http://ec.europa.eu/enlargement/archives/pdf/key_documents/2004/rr_tr_2004_en.pdf, date accessed 12 June 2014.

European Commission (2004c) *European Neighbourhood Policy Strategy Paper*, COM(2004) 373 final, Brussels, 12 May.

European Commission (2004d) *National Indicative Programme 2005–2006 Egypt*.

European Commission (2004e) *National Indicative Programme 2005–2006 Tunisia*, http://eeas.europa.eu/tunisia/csp/nip_05_06_en.pdf, date accessed 7 June 2014.

European Commission (2005a) *Enlargement Strategy Paper*, COM(2005) 561 final, Brussels, 9 November, http://eur-lex.europa.eu/LexUriServ/LexUriServ.do?uri=COM:2005:0561:FIN:EN:PDF, date accessed 12 June 2014.

European Commission (2005b) *Progress Report Croatia*, SEC(2005) 1424, Brussels, 9 November, http://ec.europa.eu/transparency/regdoc/rep/2/2005/EN/2-2005-1424-EN-1-0.Pdf, date accessed 14 June 2014.

European Commission (2005c) *Progress Report Turkey*, SEC(2005) 1426, Brussels, 9 November, http://ec.europa.eu/enlargement/archives/pdf/key_documents/2005/package/sec_1426_final_progress_report_tr_en.pdf, date accessed 12 June 2014.

European Commission (2005d) *Progress Report Bosnia and Herzegovina*, SEC(2005) 1422, Brussels, 9 November, http://ec.europa.eu/enlargement/archives/pdf/key_documents/2005/package/sec_1422_final_progress_report_ba_en.pdf, date accessed 3 May 2014.

European Commission (2005e) *Progress Report Kosovo (Under UNSCR 1244)*, Brussels, 9 November 2005, SEC(2005) 1423, Brussels, 9 November, http://ec.europa.eu/transparency/regdoc/rep/2/2005/EN/2-2005-1423-EN-1-0.Pdf, date accessed 6 June 2014.

European Commission (2006a) *Increasing the Impact of Aid: A Common Framework for Drafting Country Strategy Papers and Joint Multiannual Programming*, COM(2006) 88 final, Brussels, 2 March.

European Commission (2006b) *Governance in the European Consensus on Development: Towards a Harmonised Approach Within the European Union*, COM (2006) 421 final, 30 August, http://eur-lex.europa.eu/legal-content/EN/TXT/PDF/?uri=CELEX:52006DC0421&from=EN, date accessed 15 May 2014.

European Commission (2006c) *Enlargement Strategy and Main Challenges 2006–2007*, COM(2006) 649, Brussels, 8 November, http://eur-lex.europa.eu/legal-content/EN/TXT/PDF/?uri=CELEX:52006DC0649&from=en, date accessed 14 June 2014.

European Commission (2006d) *Progress Report Croatia*, SEC (2006) 1385, Brussels, 8 November, http://ec.europa.eu/enlargement/pdf/key_documents/2006/nov/hr_sec_1385_en.pdf, date accessed 12 June 2014.

European Commission (2006e) *Progress Report Turkey*, SEC (2006) 1390, Brussels, 8 November, http://ec.europa.eu/enlargement/pdf/key_documents/2006/Nov/ tr_sec_1390_en.pdf, date accessed 12 June 2014.

European Commission (2006f) *Progress Report Bosnia and Herzegovina*, SEC (2006) 1384, Brussels, 8 November, http://ec.europa.eu/enlargement/pdf/key_documents/2006/nov/bih_sec_1384_en.pdf, date accessed 3 May 2014.

European Commission (2006g) *Country Strategy Paper 2007–2013 & National Indicative Programme 2007–2010 Egypt*, http://eeas.europa.eu/enp/pdf/pdf/country/enpi_csp_egypt_en.pdf, date accessed 7 June 2014.

European Commission (2006h) *Country Strategy Paper 2007–2013 & National Indicative Programme 2007–2010 Tunisia*, http://eeas.europa.eu/enp/pdf/pdf/country/enpi_csp_nip_tunisia_summary_en.pdf, date accessed 7 June 2014

European Commission (2006i) *ENP Progress Report: Israel*, SEC (2006) 1507/2, Brussels, 29 November.

European Commission (2006j) *EU Relations with Pacific Islands: A Strategy for a Strengthened Partnership*, COM (2006) 248, Brussels, 29 May.

European Commission (2007a) *Enlargement Strategy and Main Challenges 2007–2008*, COM (2007) 663 final, Brussels, 6 November, http://eur-lex.europa.eu/legal-content/EN/TXT/PDF/?uri=CELEX:52007DC0663&from=en, date accessed 12 June 2014.

European Commission (2007b) *Croatia 2007 Progress Report*, SEC (2007) 1431, Brussels, 6 November, http://ec.europa.eu/enlargement/pdf/key_documents/2007/nov/croatia_progress_reports_en.pdf, date accessed 12 June 2014.

European Commission (2007c) *Turkey 2007 Progress Report*, SEC (2007) 1436, Brussels, 6 November, http://ec.europa.eu/transparency/regdoc/rep/2/2007/EN/2-2007-1436-EN-1-0.Pdf, date accessed 12 June 2014.

European Commission (2007d) *Progress Report Bosnia and Herzegovina*, SEC (2007) 1430, Brussels, 6 November, http://ec.europa.eu/enlargement/pdf/key_documents/2007/nov/bosnia_herzegovina_progress_reports_en.pdf, date accessed 3 May 2014.

European Commission (2007e) *Instrument for Pre-Accession Assistance (IPA) Bosnia and Herzegovina. Multi-Annual Indicative Planning Document 2007–2009, Annex to Commission Decision C(2007) 2255 of 01/06/2007 on a Multi-annual Indicative Planning Document (MIPD) 2007–2009 for Bosnia and Herzegovina*, http://ec.europa.eu/enlargement/pdf/mipd_bosnia_herzegovina_2007_2009_en.pdf, date accessed 5 June 2014.

European Commission (2007f) *Multi-Annual Indicative Planning Document for Kosovo (Under UNSCR 1244), 2007–2009. Annex to Commission Decision C(2007)2271 of 01/06/2007 on a Multi-Annual Indicative Planning Document (MIPD) 2007–2009 for Kosovo Under UNSCR 1244*.

European Commission (2007g) *Black Sea Synergy – A New Regional Cooperation Initiative*, COM (2007) 160 final, Brussels, 11 April.

European Commission (2007h) *European Neighbourhood and Partnership Instrument. Israel. Strategy Paper 2007–2013 and Indicative Programme 2007–2010*, http://eeas.europa.eu/enp/pdf/pdf/country/enpi_csp_nip_israel_en.pdf, date accessed 20 May 2014.

European Commission (2007i) *European Community Regional Strategy Paper for Assistance to Central Asia for the Period 2007–13*, Brussels.

References 273

European Commission (2007j) *Annual Action Programme 2007. Action Fiche for Kazakhstan*, Brussels.
European Commission (2008a) *Progress Report Croatia*, SEC (2008) 2694, Brussels, 5 November, http://ec.europa.eu/enlargement/pdf/press_corner/key-documents/reports_nov_2008/croatia_progress_report_en.pdf, date accessed 12 June 2014.
European Commission (2008b) *Enlargement Strategy and Main Challenges 2008–2009*, COM (2008) 674 final, Brussels, 5 November, http://eur-lex.europa.eu/legal-content/EN/TXT/PDF/?uri=CELEX:52008DC0674&from=en, date accessed 14 June 2014.
European Commission (2008c) *Progress Report Turkey*, SEC (2008) 2699, Brussels, 5 November, http://ec.europa.eu/enlargement/pdf/press_corner/key-documents/reports _nov_2008 /turkey _progress_report_en.pdf, date accessed 12 June 2014.
European Commission (2008d) *European Instrument for Democracy and Human Rights (EIDHR) Turkey Programme*, http://ec.europa.eu/europeaid/what/human-rights/documents/eidhr_2008_projects_in_turkey_en.pdf, date accessed 12 June 2014.
European Commission (2008e) *Progress Report Bosnia and Herzegovina*, SEC (2008) 2693, Brussels, 5 November, http://ec.europa.eu/enlargement/pdf/press_corner/key-documents/reports_nov_2008/bosnia_herzegovina_progress_report_en.pdf, date accessed 3 May 2014.
European Commission (2008f) *Instrument for Pre-Accession Assistance (IPA) Bosnia and Herzegovina. Multi-Annual Indicative Planning Document (MIPD) 2008–2010. Annex to Commission Decision of on a Multi-Annual Indicative Planning Document (MIPD) 2008–2010 for Bosnia and Herzegovina*, http://ec.europa.eu/enlargement/pdf/mipd_bosnia_herzegovina_2008_2010_en.pdf, date accessed 5 June 2014.
European Commission (2008g) *Multi-Annual Indicative Planning Document (MIPD) for Kosovo 2008–2010 (Under UNSCR 1244/99). Annex to Commission Decision on a Multi-Annual Indicative Planning Document (MIPD) 2008–2010 for Kosovo Under UNSCR 1244/99*, http://ec.europa.eu/enlargement/pdf/mipd_kosovo_2008_2010_en.pdf, date accessed 5 June 2014.
European Commission (2008h) *Eastern Partnership*, COM (2008) 823 final, Brussels, 3 December.
European Commission (2008i) *Progress Report Israel*, SEC (2008) 394, Brussels, 3 April.
European Commission (2008j) *Joint Country Support Strategy for the Kyrgyz Republic 2007–2010*, Document prepared by the EC funded project "Support to JCSS in the Kyrgyz Republic" (implemented by Atos Origin), Bishkek, April.
European Commission (2009a) *Supporting Democratic Governance Through the Governance Initiative: A Review and the Way Forward*, SEC (2009) 58 final, 19 January, http://ec.europa.eu/development/icenter/repository/CSWP_SEC_2009_0058_governance_en.pdf, date accessed 15 May 2014.
European Commission (2009b) *Enlargement Strategy and Main Challenges 2009–2010*, COM (2009) 533 final, Brussels, 14 October, http://eur-lex.europa.eu/LexUriServ/LexUriServ.do?uri=COM:2009:0533:FIN:EN:PDF, date accessed 12 June 2014.

European Commission (2009c) *Progress Report Croatia*, SEC (2009) 1333, Brussels, 14 October, http://ec.europa.eu/enlargement/pdf/key_documents/2009/hr_rapport_2009_en.pdf, date accessed 12 June 2014.

European Commission (2009d) *Progress Report Turkey*, SEC (2009) 1334, Brussels, 14 October, http://ec.europa.eu/enlargement/pdf/key_documents/2009/tr_rapport_2009_en.pdf, date accessed 12 June 2014.

European Commission (2009e) *Progress Report Bosnia and Herzegovina*, SEC (2009) 1338, Brussels, 14 October, http://ec.europa.eu/enlargement/pdf/key_documents/2009/ba_rapport_2009_en.pdf, date accessed 3 May 2014.

European Commission (2009f) *Multi-Annual Indicative Planning Document (MIPD) for Kosovo (Under UNSCR 1244/99), 2009–2011*. Annex to Commission Decision of 2009 on a Multi-Annual Indicative Planning Document (MIPD) 2009–2011 for Kosovo (Under UNSCR 1244/99).

European Commission (2009g) *Progress Report Israel*, SEC (2009) 516/2, Brussels, 23 April.

European Commission (2010a) *Enlargement Strategy and Main Challenges 2010–2011*, COM (2010) 660, Brussels, 9 November, http://ec.europa.eu/enlargement/pdf/key_documents/2010/package/strategy_paper_2010_en.pdf, date accessed 12 June 2014.

European Commission (2010b) *Progress Report Croatia*, SEC (2010) 1326, Brussels, 9 November, http://ec.europa.eu/enlargement/pdf/key_documents/2010/package/hr_rapport_2010_en.pdf, date accessed 12 June 2014.

European Commission (2010c) *Progress Report Turkey*, SEC (2010) 1327, Brussels, 9 November, http://eur-lex.europa.eu/legal-content/EN/TXT/PDF/?uri=CELEX:52010SC1327&from=en, date accessed 12 June 2014.

European Commission (2010d) *European Instrument for Democracy and Human Rights (EIDHR) Compendium 2007–2009. Promoting Democracy and Human Rights in Asia*, http://ec.europa.eu/europeaid/what/human-rights/documents/compendium_asia_2007-2009_en.pdf, date accessed 12 June 2014.

European Commission (2010e) Instrument for Pre-Accession Assistance (IPA) Project. Component 1 – Decentralized Management, http://ec.europa.eu/enlargement/pdf/turkey/ipa/2010/129_tr2010013609_justice_academy.pdf, date accessed 12 June 2014.

European Commission (2010f) *Progress Report Bosnia and Herzegovina*, SEC (2010) 1331, Brussels, 9 November, http://ec.europa.eu/enlargement/pdf/key_documents/2010/package/ba_rapport_2010_en.pdf, date accessed 3 May 2014.

European Commission (2010g) *Progress Report Kosovo*, SEC (2010) 1329, Brussels, 9 November, http://ec.europa.eu/enlargement/pdf/key_documents/2010/package/ks_rapport_2010_en.pdf, date accessed 3 May 2014.

European Commission (2010h) *EU-Russia Common Spaces Progress Report 2009*, http://www.eeas.europa.eu/russia/docs/commonspaces_prog_report_2009_en.pdf, date accessed 22 May 2014.

European Commission (2010i) *National Indicative Programme 2011–2013 Egypt*, http://www.enpi-info.eu/library/content/egypt-national-indicative-programme-2011-2013, date accessed 7 June 2014.

European Commission (2010j) *National Indicative Programme 2011–2013 Tunisia*, http://www.enpi-info.eu/library/content/tunisia-national-indicative-programme-2011-2013, date accessed 7 June 2014.

European Commission (2010k) *Progress Report Israel*, SEC (2010) 520, Brussels, 12 May.
European Commission (2010l) *Central Asia DCI Indicative Programme 2011–2013*, Brussels.
European Commission (2010m) *Annual Action Plan for Central Asia 2010*, http://ec.europa.eu/europeaid/documents/aap/2010/af_aap_2010_central-asia_p3.pdf, date accessed 9 June 2014.
European Commission (2011a) *Progress Report Croatia*, SEC (2011) 1200 final, Brussels, 12 October, http://ec.europa.eu/enlargement/pdf/key_documents/2011/package/hr_rapport_2011_en.pdf, date accessed 12 June 2014.
European Commission (2011b) *Enlargement Strategy and Main Challenges 2011–2012*, COM (2011) 666 final, Brussels, 12 November, http://ec.europa.eu/enlargement/pdf/key_documents/2011/package/strategy_paper_2011_en.pdf, date accessed 12 June 2014.
European Commission (2011c) *Progress Report Turkey*, SEC (2011) 1201 final, Brussels, 12 October, http://eur-lex.europa.eu/legal-content/EN/TXT/PDF/?uri=CELEX:52011SC1201&from=en, date accessed 12 June 2014.
European Commission (2011d) *Strengthening Institutional Capacity of Centre for Labour and Social Security Training and Research (ÇASGEM)*, http://ec.europa.eu/enlargement/pdf/turkey/ipa/2011/part2/tr2011.0319.22_institutional_capacity_of_centre_for_labor_and_socialsecurity%28casgem%29.pdf, date accessed 14 June 2014.
European Commission (2011e) *Bosnia and Herzegovina 2011 Progress Report*, SEC (2011) 1206 final, Brussels, 12 October.
European Commission (2011f) *Instrument for Pre-Accession Assistance (IPA). Multi-Annual Indicative Planning Document (MIPD). 2011–2013 Bosnia and Herzegovina*, http://ec.europa.eu/enlargement/pdf/mipd_bih_2011_2013_en.pdf, date accessed 3 May 2014.
European Commission (2011g) *Progress Report Kosovo*, SEC (2011) 1207 final, Brussels, 12 October, http://ec.europa.eu/enlargement/pdf/key_documents/2011/package/ks_rapport_2011_en.pdf, date accessed 3 May 2014.
European Commission (2011h) *Instrument for Pre-Accession Assistance (IPA). Multi-Annual Indicative Planning Document (MIPD) 2011–2013 Kosovo. Annex to Commission Implementing Decision of 27.6.2011 Adopting a Multi-Annual Indicative Planning Document (MIPD) 2011–2013 for Kosovo*, C (2011) 4381 final, Brussels, 27 June.
European Commission (2011i) *2011 Annual Programme – Judiciary: 03-2011/1*, http://ec.europa.eu/enlargement/pdf/kosovo/ipa/2011/3._rol_-_judiciary.pdf, date accessed 3 May 2014.
European Commission (2011j) *Annex 3 – Action Fiche Ukraine AAP 2011*, http://ec.europa.eu/europeaid/documents/aap/2011/af_aap_2011_ukr_p2.pdf, date accessed 22 May 2014.
European Commission (2011k) *EU Response to the Arab Spring: The Civil Society Facility*, MEMO/11/638, Brussels, 27 September, http://europa.eu/rapid/pressReleasesAction.do?reference=MEMO/11/638, date accessed 2 January 2013.
European Commission (2011l) *European Union – Central Asia Development Cooperation*, Luxembourg: Publications Office of the European Union, http://ec.europa.

eu/europeaid/infopoint/publications/europeaid/documents/263a_en.pdf, date accessed 9 June 2014.

European Commission (2011m) *Proposal for a Decision of the European Parliament and of the Council Providing Macro-Financial Assistance to the Kyrgyz Republic*, COM (2011) 0925 final – 2011/0458 (COD), http://eur-lex.europa.eu/LexUriServ/LexUriServ.do?uri=COM:2011:0925:FIN:EN:HTML, date accessed 9 June 2014.

European Commission (2011n) *EIDHR 2011–2013 Multiannual Indicative Planning. Global Calls for Proposals + CBSS*, http://ec.europa.eu/europeaid/what/human-rights/documents/20110321_mip_eidhr_2011-2013_for_publication3_en.pdf, date accessed 4 June 2014.

European Commission (2012a) *Comprehensive Monitoring Report on Croatia*, SWD (2012) 338 final, Brussels, 10 October, http://eur-lex.europa.eu/legal-content/EN/TXT/PDF/?uri=CELEX:52012SC0338, date accessed 12 June 2014.

European Commission (2012b) *Enlargement Strategy and Main Challenges 2012–2013*, COM (2012) 600 final, Brussels, 12 October, http://eur-lex.europa.eu/legal-content/EN/TXT/PDF/?uri=CELEX:52012DC0600&from=en, date accessed 12 June 2014.

European Commission (2012c) *Turkey 2012 Progress Report*, SWD (2012) 336 final, Brussels 10 October, http://eur-lex.europa.eu/legal-content/EN/TXT/PDF/?uri=CELEX:52012SC0336&from=en, date accessed 14 June 2014.

European Commission (2012d) *Progress Report Bosnia and Herzegovina*, SWD (2012) 335 final, Brussels, 10 October.

European Commission (2012e) *Commission Implementing Decision Amending Commission Implementing Decision C(2011) 9081 final of 5 December 2011*, C(2012) 5705 final, Brussels, 9 August, http://ec.europa.eu/enlargement/pdf/financial_assistance/ipa/2013/multi-beneficiary/ipa_amend_1_csf_2011-2012-_allocation_2013_-_c2012-5705-090812.pdf, date accessed 6 June 2014.

European Commission (2012f) *Feasibility Study for a Stabilisation and Association Agreement Between the European Union and Kosovo*, COM (2012) 602 final, Brussels, 10 October.

European Commission (2013a) *Progress Report Bosnia and Herzegovina*, SWD (2013) 415 final, Brussels, 16 October, http://ec.europa.eu/enlargement/pdf/key_documents/2013/package/brochures/bosnia_and_herzegovina_2013.pdf, date accessed 3 May 2014.

European Commission (2013b) *Progress Report Kosovo*, SWD (2013) 416 final, Brussels, 16 October, http://ec.europa.eu/enlargement/pdf/key_documents/2013/package/brochures/kosovo_2013.pdf, date accessed 3 May 2014.

European Commission (2013c) *EU's Response to the Arab Spring: The State-of-Play after Two Years*, MEMO/13/81, Brussels, 8 February, http://europa.eu/rapid/press-release_MEMO-13-81_en.htm, date accessed 7 June 2014.

European Commission (2013d) *European Endowment for Democracy – Additional Support for Democratic Change*, IP/13/17, Brussels, 9 January, http://europa.eu/rapid/press-release_IP-13-17_en.htm, date accessed 7 June 2014.

European Commission (n.d.a) *Fostering Ethics in the Turkish Public Administration, Turkey, Reform of Public Administration*, http://ec.europa.eu/enlargement/pdf/case-studies/20111011_turkey2.pdf, date accessed 12 June 2014.

European Commission (n.d.b) *Principles for the Implementation of a Governance Facility under ENPI*, http://www.enpi-info.eu/library/content/principles-implementation-governance-facility-under-enpi, date accessed 7 June 2014.
European Commission (n.d.c) *Country Fiche: Eritrea*, Internal Document.
European Commission (n.d.d) *EIDHR Compendium 2000–2006*, http://ec.europa.eu/europeaid/what/human-rights/documents/updated_report_by_location_en.pdf, date accessed 19 October 2012.
European Commission (n.d.e) *EIDHR Compendium 2007–2009*, http://ec.europa.eu/europeaid/what/human-rights/documents/eidhr_compendium_en.pdf, date accessed 19 October 2012.
European Commission and High Representative of the European Union for Foreign Affairs and Security Policy (2011a) *Human Rights and Democracy at the Heart of EU External Action – Towards a More Effective Approach*, COM (2011) 886 final, Brussels, 12 December.
European Commission and High Representative of the Union for Foreign Affairs and Security Policy (2011b) *A New Response to a Changing Neighbourhood*, COM(2011) 303 final, Brussels, 25 May.
European Commission and High Representative of the Union for Foreign Affairs and Security Policy (2011c) *Implementation of the European Neighbourhood Policy in 2010. Country Report: Georgia*, SEC (2011) 649 final, Brussels, 25 May.
European Commission and High Representative of the European Union for Foreign Affairs and Security Policy (2011d) *A Partnership for Democracy and Shared Prosperity with the Southern Mediterranean*, COM (2011) 200 final, Brussels, 8 March.
European Commission and High Representative of the European Union for Foreign Affairs and Security Policy (2012a) *EU Support for Sustainable Change in Transition Societies*, JOIN(2012) 27 final, Brussels, 3 October.
European Commission and High Representative of the Union for Foreign Affairs and Security Policy (2012b) *Delivering on a new European Neighbourhood Policy*, COM (2012) 14 final. 15 May 2012.
European Commission and High Representative of the Union for Foreign Affairs and Security Policy (2012c) *Implementation of the European Neighbourhood Policy in Armenia. Progress in 2011 and Recommendations for Action*, SWD (2012) 110 final, Brussels, 15 May.
European Commission and High Representative of the Union for Foreign Affairs and Security Policy (2013) *Joint Staff Working Document. Implementation of the European Neighbourhood Policy in 2012: Statistical Annex*, SWD (2013) 87 final, Brussels, 20 March.
European Community and Eritrea (2002) *Country Strategy Paper and National Indicative Programme for the Period 2002–2007*.
European Community and Eritrea (2009) *Country Strategy Paper and National Indicative Programme for the Period 2009–2013*.
European Community and Ethiopia (2007) *Country Strategy Paper and National Indicative Programme for the Period 2007–2013*.
European Community and Solomon Islands (2007) *Country Strategy Papers and National Indicative Programme for the period 2008–2013*, http://ec.europa.eu/development/icenter/repository/summary_sb_csp10_en.pdf, date accessed 28 May 2014.

European Council (1991) *Resolution on Human Rights, Democracy and Development*, 28 November, http://archive.idea.int/lome/bgr_docs/resolution.html, date accessed 15 May 2014.

European Court of Auditors (2012) *European Union Assistance to Kosovo Related to the Rule of Law*, Special Report 18, Luxembourg.

European Forum (2010) *Dutch Social Democrat MEP Assaulted by Russian Police in Protests*, http://www.europeanforum.net/news/945/dutch_social_democrat_mep_assaulted_by_russian_police_in_protests, 1 September 2010, date accessed 22 May 2014.

European Parliament (2005) *Answer to Parliamentary Question E-1962/2005 by Cristiana Muscardini*, 29 June.

European Parliament (2006a) *Answer to Parliamentary Question E-3542/2005 by Jonas Sjöstedt*, 10 March.

European Parliament (2006b) *European Parliament Resolution on Ethiopia*, 13 October.

European Parliament (2007a) *Answer to Parliamentary Question E-5353/2006 by Baroness Sarah Ludford*, 10 January.

European Parliament (2007b) *European Parliament Resolution on the Draft Commission Decisions Establishing Country Strategy Papers and Indicative Programmes for Malaysia, Brazil and Pakistan*, P6_TA (2007)0045, Strasbourg, 15 February.

European Parliament (2009) *European Parliament Resolution of 22 October 2009 on Democracy Building in the EU's External Relations*, P7_TA (2009)0056, Strasbourg, 22 October.

European Parliament (2010) *Answer to Parliamentary Question P-5393/2010 by Marita Ulvskog*, 5 August.

European Parliament (2011a) *Resolution of 15 December 2011 on the State of Implementation of the EU Strategy for Central Asia*, P7_TA-PROV (2011) 0588, 2011/2008(INI), Brussels, 15 December.

European Parliament (2011b) 'Minutes of the 1st EU – Brazil Interparliamentary Meeting', Delegation for Relations with the Mercosur Countries, DMER_PV (2011) 0607, Strasbourg, 6 July, http://www.europarl.europa.eu/meetdocs/2009_2014/documents/dmer/pv/872/872995/872995en.pdf, date accessed 15 April 2014.

European Parliament (2012a) *Resolution of 15 March 2012 on Kazakhstan*, P7_TA (2012)0089, RSP(2012) 2553, Strasbourg, 15 March, http://www.europarl.europa.eu/sides/getDoc.do?type=TA&reference=P7-TA-2012-0089&language=EN&ring=B7-2012-0142, date accessed 9 June 2014.

European Parliament (2012b) *Answer Given by High Representative/Vice President Ashton on Behalf of the Commission*, 30 October.

European Parliament (2013) *Answer to Parliamentary Question E-005863/2013 by High Representative/Vice President Ashton on Behalf of the Commission*, 18 July.

European Union (2008a) *Declaration by the Presidency on Behalf of the European Union on the Presidential Elections in Russian Federation on 2 March 2008*, http://www.eu2008.si/en/News_and_Documents/CFSP_Statements/March/0304MZZ_Ruska_federacija_volitve.html, date accessed 22 May 2014.

European Union (2008b) *Declaration by the Presidency on Behalf of the EU on the Situation After the Presidential Elections in Armenia on 1st March 2008*,

5 March, http://www.eu2008.si/en/News_and_Documents/CFSP_Statements/March/0403MZZ_Armenia.html, date accessed 2 January 2013.

European Union (2008c) *EU Presidency Statement on the Situation in Armenia*, 12 March, http://www.eu2008.si/en/News_and_Documents/CFSP_Statements/March/0312MZZarmenia.html, date accessed 2 January 2013.

European Union (2010) *Fifteen Years of Partnership and Cooperation*, Astana.

European Union (2011a) *EU Statement on Recent Developments in Armenia*, OSCE Permanent Council Nr 861, Vienna, 12 May, http://eeas.europa.eu/delegations/vienna/documents/eu_osce/permanent_council/2011/20110512_861recent_development_in_armenia_en.pdf, date accessed 2 January 2013.

European Union (2011b) *EU Statement on the Demonstrations in Georgia*, OSCE Permanent Council Nr 864, Vienna, 2 June, http://eeas.europa.eu/delegations/vienna/documents/eu_osce/permanent_council/2011/20110602_864_demonstrations_in_georgia_en.pdf, date accessed 2 January 2013.

European Union (2012a) *Statement by the Spokesperson of EU High Representative Catherine Ashton on the Abuse of Prisoners in Georgian Penitentiary System*, A411/12, Brussels, 20 September, http://www.consilium.europa.eu/uedocs/cms_Data/docs/pressdata/EN/foraff/132510.pdf, date accessed 2 January 2013.

European Union (2012b) *Statement by the Spokesperson of the HR Ashton on the Presidential Elections in Egypt*, Brussels, 25 May, http://www.consilium.europa.eu/uedocs/cms_data/docs/pressdata/EN/foraff/130446.pdf, date accessed 7 June 2014.

European Union (2012c) *Statement by the Spokesperson of High Representative Catherine Ashton on the Election of Mohammed Morsi as the President of Egypt*, A 286/12, Brussels, 24 June, http://www.consilium.europa.eu/uedocs/cms_data/docs/pressdata/EN/foraff/131145.pdf, date accessed 7 June 2014.

European Union (2013) *United Nations Human Rights Council 23rd Session. Interactive Dialogue with Special Rapporteur on Eritrea*, http://eeas.europa.eu/delegations/un_geneva/documents/eu_statments/human_right/20130605_id_sr_eritrea.pdf, date accessed 7 January 2013.

EU/Israel (2005) *EU-Israel Action Plan*, http://eeas.europa.eu/enp/pdf/pdf/action_plans/israel_enp_ap_final_en.pdf, date accessed 13 May 2014.

EU/Ukraine (2009) *EU-Ukraine Association Agenda to Prepare and Facilitate the Implementation of the Association Agreement*, http://www.eeas.europa.eu/ukraine/docs/2010_eu_ukraine_association_agenda_en.pdf, date accessed 22 May 2014.

Fagan, A. (2015) 'Democracy Promotion in Kosovo: Mapping the Substance of Donor Assistance and a Comparative Analysis of Strategies', *Cambridge Review of International Affairs* 28(1).

Firth, S. (2008) 'The New Regionalism and Its Contradictions', in G. Fry and T.T. Kabutaulaka (eds), *Intervention and State-Building in the Pacific*, Manchester: Manchester University Press, 119–34.

Fish, M. S. (2005) *Democracy Derailed*, Cambridge: Cambridge University Press.

Føllesdal, A. and S. Hix (2005) *Why There Is a Democratic Deficit in the EU*, European Governance Papers (EUROGOV), No. C-05-02.

Foucault, M. (1991 [1975]) *Discipline and Punish: The Birth of the Prison*, London: Penguin Books.

Foucault, M. (2009) *Security, Territory, Population: Lectures at the Collège de France 1977–1978*, Basingstoke: Palgrave Macmillan.

Fraenkel, J. (2004) 'The Coming Anarchy in Oceania? A Critique of the "Africanisation" of the South Pacific Thesis', *Commonwealth & Comparative Politics* 42(1): 1–34.
Freeden, M. (1996) *Ideologies and Political Theory: A Conceptual Approach*, Oxford: Oxford University Press.
Freedom House (2011) *Freedom in the World*, http://www.freedomhouse.org/reports, date accessed 18 October 2012.
Freedom House (2013) *Freedom in the World 2013*, www.freedomhouse.org, date accessed 30 September 2013.
Freire, M. R. and L. Simão (2007) *The Armenian Road to Democracy. Dimensions of a Tortuous Process*, Brussels: CEPS Working Document 267.
Freres, C. (2000) 'The European Union as a Global "Civilian Power": Development Cooperation in EU-Latin American Relations', *Journal of Interamerican Studies and World Affairs* 42(2): 63–85.
Freyburg, T., S. Lavenex, F. Schimmelfennig, T. Skripka and A. Wetzel (2015) *Democracy Promotion by Functional Cooperation: The European Union and Its Neighbourhood*, Basingstoke: Palgrave Macmillan.
Freyburg, T., T. Skripka and A. Wetzel (2007) *Democracy Between the Lines? EU Promotion of Democratic Governance via Sector-Specific Co-Operation*, Zurich: NCCR Democracy Working Paper, No. 5.
Fukuyama, F. (1992) *The End of History and the Last Man*, New York: The Free Press.
Fukuyama, F. (2005) ' "Stateness" First', *Journal of Democracy* 16(1): 84–8.
Furness, M. (2013) 'Who Controls the European External Action Service? Agent Autonomy in EU External Policy', *European Foreign Affairs Review* 18(1): 103–25.
Gilpin, R. (1981) *War and Change in World Politics*, Cambridge: Cambridge University Press.
Government of Ethiopia and United Nations Development Programme (UNDP) (2007) *Multi-Donor Support for the Democratic Institutions Programme*, http://www.undp.org/content/dam/undp/documents/projects/ETH/00047799_Democratic%20Instituions%20Programme%20%2800057667%29.pdf, date accessed 7 June 2014.
Grabbe, H. (1999) *A Partnership for Accession? The Implications of EU Conditionality for the Central and East European Applicants*, Badia Fiesolana: EUI Working Papers, RSC No. 1999/12.
Grabbe, H. (2001) 'How Does Europeanization Affect CEE Governance? Conditionality, Diffusion and Diversity', *Journal of European Public Policy* 8(6): 1013–31.
Grabbe, H. (2003) 'Europeanization Goes East: Power and Uncertainty in the EU Accession Process', in K. Featherstone and C. Radaelli (eds), *The Politics of Europeanization*, Oxford: Oxford University Press, 303–27.
Grabbe, H. (2006) *The EU's Transformative Power: Europeanization Through Conditionality in Central and Eastern Europe*, Basingstoke: Palgrave Macmillan.
Grant, R. W. and R. O. Keohane (2005) 'Accountability and Abuses of Power in World Politics', *American Political Science Review* 99(1): 29–43.
Gratius, S. (2011) 'EU Democracy Promotion in Latin America: More a Tradition than a Policy', *European Foreign Affairs Review* 16(5): 689–703.
Gratius, S. and T. Legler (2013) 'Latin America Is Different: Transatlantic Discord on How to Promote Democracy in "Problematic" Countries', in A. Magen,

T. Risse and M. A. McFaul, (eds), *Promoting Democracy and the Rule of Law: American and European Strategies*, New York: Palgrave Macmillan, 185–216.
Grugel, J. B. (2004) 'New Regionalism and Modes of Governance – Comparing US and EU Strategies in Latin America', *European Journal of International Relations* 10(4): 603–26.
Gunning, J. (2010) 'The Conflict and the Question of Engaging with Hamas', in E. B. Aymat (ed.), *European Involvement in the Arab-Israeli Conflict*, Paris: EU ISS, Chaillot Paper 124, 97–108.
Hall, P. A. (1993) 'Policy Paradigms, Social Learning, and the State: The Case of Economic Policymaking in Britain', *Comparative Politics* 25(3): 275–96.
Hall, P. A. and R. C. R. Taylor (1996) 'Political Science and the Three New Institutionalisms', *Political Studies* 44: 936–57.
Halmai, G. (2012) 'From the "Rule of Law Revolution" to the Constitutional Counter-Revolution in Hungary', in W. Benedek, F. Benoît-Rohmer, W. Karl and M. Nowak (eds), *European Yearbook of Human Rights*, Wien: Duncker and Humblot, 365–82.
Haran, O. (2011) 'From Viktor to Viktor: Democracy and Authoritarianism in Ukraine', *Demokratizatsiya: The Journal of Post-Soviet Democratization* 19(2): 93–110.
Hautala, H. (2010) *Human Rights in Russia – The European Parliament's Point of View*, http://www.khodorkovskycenter.com/news-resources/stories/human-rights-russia-%E2%80%93-european-parliament%E2%80%99s-point-view, 13 April 2010, date accessed 23 August 2013.
Head of EU Office in Kosovo/EU Special Representative and the Heads of Mission of the EU Member States Present in Kosovo (2014) *We Expect European Standards for Democratic Elections to Be Fully Respected*, Joint Statement, 06 June, http://eeas.europa.eu/delegations/kosovo/press_corner/all_news/news/2014/20140606_en.htm, date accessed 20 June 2014.
Held, D. (2006) *Models of Democracy*, Cambridge: Polity.
Héritier, A. (1999) 'Elements of Democratic Legitimation in Europe: An Alternative Perspective', *Journal of European Public Policy* 6(2): 269–82.
Herlin-Karnell, E. (2013) 'EU Values and the Shaping of the International Context', in D. Kochenov and F. Amtenbrink (eds), *European Union's Shaping of the International Legal Order*, Cambridge: Cambridge University Press, 89–107.
Herranz, A. (2005) 'The Inter-Parliamentary Delegations of the European Parliament. National and European Priorities at Work', in E. Barbe and A. Herranz (eds), *The Role of Parliament in European Foreign Policy*, Barcelona: Universitat Autonoma de Barcelona, http://www.iuee.eu/pdf-publicacio/20/djAuHe5Xblihu1BuXf5Y.PDF, date accessed 15 February 2014.
Hillion, C. (2002) 'Enlargement of the European Union: A Legal Analysis', in A. Arnull and D. Wincott (eds), *Accountability and Legitimacy in the European Union*, Oxford: Oxford University Press, 401–18.
Hirst, P. (1993) 'Associational Democracy', in D. Held (ed.), *Prospects for Democracy: North, South, East, West*, Cambridge: Polity, 112–35.
Holden, P. (2009) *In Search of Structural Power. EU Aid Policy as a Global Political Instrument*, Farnham: Ashgate.
Holden, P. (2010) 'Developing Polyarchy? The European Union and Its Structural Policies for Middle Eastern Neighbours', *European Foreign Affairs Review* 15(5): 589–609.

Hood, C. (2010) 'Accountability and Transparency: Siamese Twins, Matching Parts, Awkward Couple?' *West European Politics* 33(5): 989–1009.
Hout, W. (2010) 'Governance and Development: Changing EU Policies', *Third World Quarterly* 31(1): 1–12.
Huber, D. (2008) 'Democracy Assistance in the Middle East and North Africa: A Comparison of US and EU Policies', *Mediterranean Politics* 13(1): 43–62.
Hughes, J. and G. Sasse (2003) 'Monitoring the Monitors: EU Enlargement Conditionality and Minority Protection in the CEECs', *Journal on Ethnopolitics and Minority Issues in Europe* 1/2003: 1–35.
Hughes, J., G. Sasse and C. Gordon (2004) 'Conditionality and Compliance in the EU's Eastward Enlargement: Regional Policy and the Reform of Sub-national Government', *Journal of Common Market Studies* 42(3): 523–51.
Human Rights Watch (2010a) *Ukraine: Migrants and Asylum Seekers Tortured, Mistreated*, http://www.hrw.org/en/news/2010/12/16/ukraine-migrants-and-asylum-seekers-tortured-mistreated, 16 December 2010, date accessed 22 May 2014.
Human Rights Watch (2010b) *Development Without Freedom: How Aid Underwrites Repression in Ethiopia*, New York: Human Rights Watch.
Hyden, G., J. Court and K. Mease (2004) *Making Sense of Governance: Empirical Evidence from Sixteen Developing Countries*, Boulder, CO: Lynne Rienner.
Ingelhart, R. and C. Welzel (2009) 'How Development Leads to Democracy', *Foreign Affairs* 88(2): 33–48.
Inglis, K. (2000) 'The Europe Agreements Compared in the Light of Their Pre-Accession Reorientation', *Common Market Law Review* 37(5): 1173–210.
International Crisis Group (2010) *Eritrea: The Siege State*, Africa Report No. 163, Nairobi/Brussels, 21 September.
Interprovincial Security Associates Consulting Group (ISA Consult) (1997) *Final Report: Evaluation of the PHARE and TACIS Democracy Programme. 1992–1997*, European Commission, Ref. 951432.
Jann, W. and K. Wegrich (2003) 'Phasenmodelle und Politikprozesse: Der Policy Cycle', in K. Schubert and N. C. Bandelow (eds), *Lehrbuch Politikfeldanalyse*, München: Oldenbourg, 71–103.
Jünemann, A. (2009) 'Externe Demokratieförderung im Südlichen Mittelmeerraum: Ein Rollentheoretischer Erklärungsansatz für die Kluft zwischen Anspruch und Wirklichkeit in den EU-Außenbeziehungen', in M. Beck, C. Harders, A. Jünemann and S. Stetter (eds), *Der Nahe Osten im Umbruch: Zwischen Transformation und Autoritarismus*, Wiesbaden: VS Verlag für Sozialwissenschaften, 151–74.
Jünemann, A. and M. Knodt (eds) (2007) Externe Demokratieförderung durch die Europäische Union, Baden-Baden: Nomos.
Karktuli, N. and D. Bützler (1999) *Final Report: Evaluation of the MEDA Democracy Programme 1996–1998*, Brussels, http://ec.europa.eu/europeaid/how/evaluation/evaluation_reports/reports/med/951460_en.pdf, date accessed 23 October 2014.
Keohane, R. O. and J. S. Nye (1974) 'Transgovernmental Relations and International Organizations', *World Politics* 27(1): 39–62.
Keohane, R. O. and J. S. Nye (1989 [1977]) *Power and Interdependence*, New York: Harper Collins.

Ketola, M. (2010) *Europeanization and Civil Society: The Early Impact of EU Pre-Accession Policies on Turkish NGOs*, PhD Dissertation, London: School of Economics.
Khodorkovsky Center (2010) *EU High Representative Catherine Ashton Comments on Khodorkovsky Trial*, http://www.khodorkovskycenter.com/news-resources/stories/high-representative-catherine-ashton-khodorkovskylebedev-case, 31 December 2010, date accessed 23 August 2013.
Knodt, M. and A. Jünemann (2008) 'EU External Democracy Promotion: Approaching Governments and Civil Societies', in B. Kohler-Koch, D. De Bièvre and W. Maloney (eds), *Opening EU Governance to Civil Society. Gains and Challenges*, Mannheim: Connex, 259–93.
Knook, A. (2005) 'The Court, the Charter, and the Vertical Division of Powers in the European Union', *Common Market Law Review* 42(2): 367–98.
Kochenov, D. (2004) 'Behind the Copenhagen Façade: The Meaning and Structure of the Copenhagen Political Criterion of Democracy and the Rule of Law', *European Integration online Papers* 8(10), http://eiop.or.at/eiop/texte/2004-010a.htm, date accessed 20 May 2014.
Kochenov, D. (2007) *EU Enlargement and the Failure of Conditionality: Pre-Accession Conditionality in the Fields of Democracy and Rule of Law*, Netherlands: Wolters Kluwer.
Kochenov, D. (2008a) *EU Enlargement and the Failure of Conditionality: Pre-Accession Conditionality in the Fields of Democracy and the Rule of Law*, The Hague: Kluwer Law International.
Kochenov, D. (2008b) 'The Summary of Contradictions: Outline of the EU's Numerous Approaches to Minority Protection', *Boston College International and Comparative Law Review* 31(1): 1–51.
Kochenov, D. (2009) *The Eastern Partnership, the Union for the Mediterranean and the Remaining Need to Do Something with the ENP*, Glasgow, University of Glasgow: CRCEES Working Paper 1.
Kochenov, D. (2010) *Citizenship Without Respect: The EU's Troubled Equality Ideal*, New York, New York Law School: Jean Monnet Working Paper 08/10, 8 October.
Kochenov, D. (2011) 'New Developments in the European Neighbourhood Policy: Imitating Change, Ignoring the Problems', *Comparative European Politics*, 9(4–5): 581–95.
Kochenov, D. (2013a) 'The Citizenship Paradigm', *Cambridge Yearbook of European Legal Studies* 15: 197–225.
Kochenov, D. (2013b) 'The Essence of EU Citizenship Emerging from the Last Ten Years of Academic Debate: Beyond the Cherry Blossoms and the Moon', *International and Comparative Law Quarterly* 62(1): 97–136.
Kochenov, D. (2014a) 'On Policing Article 2 TEU Compliance', *Polish Yearbook of International Law* 33, Warsaw: Institute of Legal Studies PAN, 145–70.
Kochenov, D. (2014b) 'The Issue of Values', in R. Petrov and P. Van Elsuwege (eds), *Legislative Approximation and Application of EU Law in the Eastern Neighbourhood of the European Union*, London: Routledge, 46–62.
Kochenov, D. and R. Plender (2012) 'EU Citizenship: From an Incipient Form to an Incipient Substance', *European Law Review* 37: 369–96.
Kochenov, D., G. de Búrca and A. Williams (eds) (2014a), *Europe's Justice Deficit?* Oxford: Hart Publishing.

Kochenov, D., G. de Búrca and A. Williams (2014b) 'Justice Deficit Introduced', in D. Kochenov, G. de Búrca and A. Williams (eds), *Europe's Justice Deficit?* Oxford: Hart Publishing.

Kohler-Koch, B. and B. Rittberger (2006) 'Review Article: The "Governance" Turn in EU Studies', *Journal of Common Market Studies* 44(1): 27–49.

Koivisto, M. and T. Dunne (2010) 'Crisis, What Crisis? Liberal Order Building and World Order Conventions', *Millennium* 38(3): 615–40.

Kostanyan, H. (2012) *The EEAS and the Eastern Partnership: Let the Blame Game Stop*. Brussels: CEPS Commentary, 4 September.

Kostanyan, H. and B. Vandecasteele (2013) *The EuroNest Parliamentary Assembly: The European Parliament as a Socializer of Its Counterparts in the EU's Eastern Neighbourhood?* Bruges: College of Europe, EU Diplomacy Papers, 5/2013.

Kramer, H. (2009) *Turkey's Accession Process to EU: The Agenda Behind the Agenda*, Berlin: German Institute for International and Security Affairs, SWP Comments 25.

Krasner, S. D. (1993) 'Sovereignty, Regimes, and Human Rights', in V. Rittberger and P. Mayer (eds), *Regime Theory and International Relations*, Oxford: Clarendon Press, 139–67.

Kubicek, P. (2011) 'Are Central Asian Leaders Learning from Upheavals in Kyrgyzstan?' *Journal of Eurasian Studies* 2(2): 115–24.

Kurki, M.(2008) *Causation in International Relations: Reclaiming Causal Analysis*, Cambridge: Cambridge University Press.

Kurki, M. (2010) 'Democracy and Conceptual Contestability: Reconsidering Conceptions of Democracy in Democracy Promotion', *International Studies Review* 12(3): 362–86.

Kurki, M. (2011a) 'Democracy Through Technocracy', *Journal of Intervention and State-Building* 5(2): 211–34.

Kurki, M. (2011b) 'Human Rights and Democracy Promotion: Reflections on the Contestation in, and the Politico-Economic Dynamics of, Rights Promotion', *Third World Quarterly* 32(9): 1573–587.

Kurki, M. (2011c) 'Governmentality and EU Democracy Promotion: The European Instrument for Democracy and Human Rights and the Construction of Democratic Civil Societies', *International Political Sociology* 5(4): 349–66.

Kurki, M. (2012) *How the EU Can Adopt a New Type of Democracy Promotion*, Working Paper, Madrid: FRIDE, http://www.fride.org/publication/998/how-the-eu-can-adopt-a-new-type-of-democracy-support, date accessed 21 June 2014.

Kurki, M. (2013) *Democratic Futures: Revisioning Democracy Promotion*, London: Routledge.

Kyiv Post (2010) *Ukraine's Visa-Free Travel Action Plan with European Union (Full Text of Document)*, http://www.kyivpost.com/content/ukraine/ukraines-visa-free-travel-action-plan-with-europea-91142.html, 24 November 2010, date accessed 23 May 2014.

Kyiv Post (2011) 'Tymoshenko, Fule Discuss Oppression of Opposition in Ukraine', http://www.kyivpost.com/news/politics/detail/94538/, 11 January 2011, date accessed 24 May 2014.

Laffan, B. (1998) 'The European Union: A Distinctive Model of Internationalization', *Journal of European Public Policy* 5(2): 235–53.

Large, J. and T. Sisk (2006) *Democracy, Conflict and Human Security*, http://www.idea.int/publications/dchs/upload/Inlaga.pdf, date accessed 15 May 2014.

Larmour, P. (2005) *Foreign Flowers: Institutional Transfer and Good Governance in the Pacific Islands*, Honolulu: University of Hawaii Press.

Larner, W. and W. Walters (eds) (2004) *Global Governmentality: Governing International Spaces*, London: Routledge.

Lavenex, S. and F. Schimmelfennig (2009) 'EU Rules Beyond EU Borders: Theorizing External Governance in European Politics', *Journal of European Public Policy* 16(6): 791–812.

Lavenex, S. and F. Schimmelfennig (2011) 'EU Democracy Promotion in the Neighbourhood: From Leverage to Governance?' *Democratization* 18(4): 885–909.

Legrand, T. (2012) 'The Merry Mandarins of Windsor: Policy Transfer and Transgovernmental Networks in the Anglosphere', *Policy Studies* 33(6): 523–40.

Lenaerts, K. and K. Gutman (2006) ' "Federal Common Law" in the European Union: A Comparative Perspective from the United States', *American Journal of Comparative Law* 54(1): 1–121.

Levy, C. J. (2011) 'Ukraine Raises the Pressure on Opposition Leaders', *New York Times*, http://www.nytimes.com/2011/02/10/world/europe/10ukraine.html, 9 February 2011, date accessed 22 May 2014.

Light, M. (2001) 'Exporting Democracy', in K. E. Smith and M. Light (eds), *Ethics and Foreign Policy*, Cambridge: Cambridge University Press, 75–92.

Linz, J. J. and A. Stepan (1996a) *Problems of Democratic Transition and Consolidation: Southern Europe, South America, and Post-Communist Europe*, Baltimore: The Johns Hopkins University Press.

Linz, J. J. and A. Stepan (1996b) 'Toward Consolidated Democracies', *Journal of Democracy* 7(2): 14–33.

Magen, A., T. Risse and M. A. McFaul (eds) (2009) *Promoting Democracy and the Rule of Law: American and European Strategies*, Basingstoke: Palgrave Macmillan.

Majone, G. (1998) 'Europe's "democratic deficit": The Question of Standards', *European Law Journal* 4(1): 5–28.

Maniokas, K. (2004) 'The Method of the European Union's Enlargement to the East: A Critical Appraisal', in A. Dimitrova (ed.), *Driven to Change: The European Union's Enlargement Viewed from the East*, Manchester: Manchester University Press, 17–37.

Manners, I. (2002) 'Normative Power Europe: A Contradiction in Terms?' *Journal of Common Market Studies* 40(2): 235–58.

Manners, I. (2006) 'The Constitutive Nature of Values, Images and Principles in the European Union', in S. Lucarelli and I. Manners (eds), *Values and Principles in European Union Foreign Policy*, London: Routledge, 19–41.

Mansfield, E. D. and J. Snyder (2002) 'Democratic Transitions, Institutional Strength, and War', *International Organization* 56(2): 297–337.

Maresceau, M. (2001) 'The EU Pre-Accession Strategy: A Political and Legal Analysis', in M. Maresceau and E. Lanon (eds), *The EU's Enlargement and Mediterranean Strategies: A Comparative Analysis*, Basingstoke: Palgrave, 3–28.

Maresceau, M. (2006) 'Quelques Réflexions sur l'Application des Principes Fondamentaux dans la Stratégie d'Adhésion de l'UE', in J. Raux (ed.), *Le droit de l'Union Européenne en Principes: Liber Amicorum en l'Honneur*, Paris: LGDJ, 69–97.

McCann, D. (2010) *The Political Economy of the European Union*, Cambridge: Polity Press.

Merkel, W. (2004) 'Embedded and Defective Democracies', *Democratization* 11(5): 33–58.
Merkel, W. (2010) 'Strategien der Demokratieförderung: Konzept und Kritik', in J. Raschke and R. Tils (eds), *Strategie in der Politikwissenschaft. Konturen eines neuen Forschungsfelds*, Wiesbaden: VS Verlag für Sozialwissenschaften, 151–79.
Merkel, W., H.-J. Puhle, A. Croissant, C. Eicher and P. Thiery (2003) *Defekte Demokratien. Theorien und Probleme*, Opladen: Leske+Budrich.
Meyer-Resende, M. and D. Toornstra (2009) 'Defining Democracy – An EU Imperative', *EUobserver*, 5 October, http://euobserver.com/opinion/28775, date accessed 27 June 2014.
Middle East Quartet (2006) *Statement by the Middle East Quartet*, http://unispal.un.org/unispal.nsf/fdc5376a7a0587a4852570d000708f4b/ 354568cce5e38e5585257106007a0834?OpenDocument, date accessed 30 September 2013.
Moravcsik, A. (2000) 'The Origins of Human Rights Regimes: Democratic Delegation in Postwar Europe', *International Organization* 54(2): 217–52.
Moravcsik, A. (2002) 'In Defence of the Democratic Deficit: Reassessing Legitimacy in the European Union', *Journal of Common Market Studies* 40(4): 603–24.
Morlino, L. (2004) 'What Is a "Good" Democracy?', *Democratization* 11(5): 10–32.
Müller, J. W. (2013) *Safeguarding Democracy Inside the EU: Brussels and the Future of Liberal Order*, Washington, DC: Transatlantic Academy.
Muskhelishvili, M. and G. Jorjoliani (2009) 'Georgia's Ongoing Struggle for a Better Future Continued: Democracy Promotion through Civil Society Development', *Democratization* 16(4): 682–708.
Musu, C. (2010) *European Union Policy Towards the Arab-Israeli Peace Process: The Quicksands of Politics*, Basingstoke: Palgrave Macmillan.
Nathan, A. J., L. Diamond and M. F. Plattner (2013) 'Introduction', in Nathan, A. J., L. Diamond and M. F. Plattner (eds) *Will China Democratize?* Baltimore, MD: Johns Hopkins University Press, xi–xx.
Neumann, I. and O. J. Sending (2010) *Governing the Global Polity: Practice, Mentality, Rationality*, Ann Arbor: The University of Michigan Press.
O'Donnell, G. A. (2001) 'Democracy, Law, and Comparative Politics', *Studies in Comparative International Development* 36(1): 7–36.
O'Donnell, G. and P. C. Schmitter (1989): *Transitions from Authoritarian Rule: Tentative Conclusions About Uncertain Democracies*, 2nd edition, Baltimore: The Johns Hopkins University Press.
OECD – Organisation for Economic Co-Operation and Development (2012) *OECD Creditor Reporting System*, http://stats.oecd.org/index.aspx, date accessed 19 October 2012.
OECD – Organisation for Economic Co-Operation and Development (2013) *OECD Aid at a Glance*, http://www.oecd.org/dac/stats/ETH.gif, date accessed 12 August 2013.
OECD – Organisation for Economic Co-Operation and Development (2014) *Creditor Reporting System*, http://stats.oecd.org/Index.aspx?datasetcode=CRS1, date accessed 11 June 2014.
Ogerschnig, L. (2012) *EU Democracy Assistance: An Analysis of Theory and Practice 1991–2011*, Ph.D. thesis defended at EUI, Florence, on 25 January 2012.

Olsen, G. R. (2000) 'Promotion of Democracy as a Foreign Policy Instrument of "Europe": Limits to International Idealism', *Democratization* 7(2): 142–67.
Olsen, J. (2002) 'The Many Faces of Europeanization', *Journal of Common Market Studies* 40(5): 921–52.
OPPD (2009) *Democracy Revisited: Which Notion of Democracy for the EU's External Relations?* Brussels: Office for Promotion of Parliamentary Democracy, http://www.europarl.europa.eu/pdf/oppd/Page_1/OPPD-Democracy_revisited.pdf, date accessed 15 February 2014.
OPPD (2010) *Getting Acquainted: Setting the Stage for Democracy Assistance*, Brussels: Office for Promotion of Parliamentary Democracy, http://www.europarl.europa.eu/pdf/oppd/Page_8/getting_acquainted_web.pdf, date accessed 15 February 2014.
OPPD (2014) Office for Promotion of Parliamentary Democracy, http://www.europarl.europa.eu/aboutparliament/en/008407cea1/Office-for-Promotion-of-Parliamentary-Democracy.html, date accessed 15 February 2014.
OPPD (n.d.) *Strengthening Parliaments Worldwide*, Brussels: Office for Promotion of Parliamentary Democracy, http://www.europarl.europa.eu/pdf/oppd/Page_1/OPPD-Strengthening_Parliaments_Worldwide.pdf, date accessed 15 February 2014.
Orbie, J. (2011) 'Promoting Labour Standards Through Trade: Normative Power or Regulatory State Europe?', in R. G. Whitman (ed.), *Normative Power Europe: Empirical and Theoretical Perspectives*, Basingstoke: Palgrave, 161–87.
OSCE (2007) *ODIHR Unable to Observe Russian Duma Elections*, Press release, http://www.osce.org/odihr/elections/49175, 16 November 2007, date accessed 22 May 2014.
OSCE (2011) *Organization for Security and Co-Operation in Europe Mission in Kosovo. Fact Sheet*, http://www.osce.org/files/documents/5/3/76507.pdf, date accessed 3 May 2014.
OSCE (2014a) Organization for Security and Co-Operation in Europe, *Croatia*, http://www.osce.org/odihr/elections/croatia, date accessed 12 June 2014.
OSCE (2014b) Organization for Security and Co-Operation in Europe, *Turkey*, http://www.osce.org/odihr/elections/turkey, date accessed 12 June 2014.
OSCE (2014c) Organization for Security and Co-Operation in Europe, *Kazakhstan*, www.osce.org/odihr/elections/kazakhstan, date accessed 9 June 2014.
OSCE (2014d) Organization for Security and Co-Operation in Europe, *Kyrgyzstan*, www.osce.org/odihr/elections/kyrgyzstan, date accessed 9 June 2014.
Ott, A. and K. Inglis (2002) *Handbook on EU Enlargement: A Commentary on the Enlargement Process*, The Hague: T.M.C. Asser Press.
Ottaway, M. (1997) 'African Democratisation and the Leninist Option', *The Journal of Modern African Studies* 35(1): 1–15.
Ottaway, M. (2003) 'Promoting Democracy after Conflict: The Difficult Choices', *International Studies Perspectives* 4(3): 314–22.
Ottaway, M. (2005) 'The Limits of Women's Rights', in T. Carothers and M. Ottaway (eds), *Uncharted Journey: Promoting Democracy in the Middle East*, Washington: Carnegie Endowment for International Peace, 115–30.
Owens, P. (2012) 'Human Security and the Rise of the Social', *Review of International Studies*, 38(3): 547–67.
Pace, M. (2010) 'Paradoxes and Contradictions in EU Democracy Promotion in the Mediterranean: The Limits of EU Normative Power', in M. Pace

and P. Seeberg (eds), *The European Union's Democratization Agenda in the Mediterranean*, Oxon: Routledge, 39–58.
Parekh, B. (1993) 'Cultural Particularity of Liberal Democracy', in D. Held (ed.), *Prospects for Democracy: North, South, East, West*, Cambridge: Polity, 156–75.
Pech, L. (2013) 'Promoting the Rule of Law Abroad', in D. Kochenov and F. Amtenbrink (eds), *European Union's Shaping of the International Legal Order*, Cambridge: Cambridge University Press, 108–14.
Permanent Mission of the Russian Federation to the European Union (2011) *Russia and EU Hold an Expert Meeting on Anti-corruption*, http://www.russianmission.eu/en/news/russia-and-eu-hold-expert-meeting-anti-corruption, 26 December 2011, date accessed 22 May 2014.
Pescatore, P. (2003) 'La Cooperation Entre la Cour Communautaire, les Juridictions Nationales et la Cour Européenne des Droits de l'Homme Dans la Protection des Droits Fondamentaux: Enquête sur un Problème Virtuel', *Revue du Marché Commun et de l'Union Européenne* 466: 151–59.
Petrovic, B. and E. Solingen (2005) 'Europeanisation and Internationalisation: The Case of the Czech Republic', *New Political Economy* 10(3): 281–303.
Pickering, P. M. (2011) 'The Constraints on European Institutions' Conditionality in the Western Balkans', *Europe-Asia Studies*, 63(10): 1939–44.
Pogodda, S. (2012) 'Inconsistent Interventionism in Palestine: Objectives, Narratives, and Domestic Policy-making', *Democratization* 19(3): 535–52.
Poiares Maduro, M. (2012) *A New Governance for the European Union and the Euro: Democracy and Justice*, Badia Fiesolana: Robert Schuman Centre for Advanced Studies Working Paper, RSCAS PP 2012/11.
Poleshchuk, V. (2009) *Shans vyzhit': Prava men'shinstv v Èstonii i Latvii*, Tallinn: Foundation for Historical Outlook.
Pollack, M. A. (2005) 'The New Transatlantic Agenda at Ten: Reflections on an Experiment in International Governance', *Journal of Common Market Studies* 43(5): 899–919.
Portela, C. (2010) *European Union Sanctions and Foreign Policy: When and Why Do They Work?* Abingdon Oxon: Routledge.
Pouligny, B. (2000) 'Promoting Democratic Institutions in Post-Conflict Societies: Giving Diversity a Chance', *International Peacekeeping* 7(3): 17–35.
Powel, B. T. (2009) 'A Clash of Norms: Normative Power and EU Democracy Promotion in Tunisia', *Democratization* 16(1): 193–214.
Pretorius, C., R. Ooijen, K. Boersma and M. Visser (2006) *Evaluation of the European Commission's Support to the State of Eritrea*, Rotterdam: ECORYS-NEI.
Pridham, G. (2005) *Designing Democracy: EU Enlargement and Regime Change in Post-Communist Europe*, Basingstoke: Palgrave Macmillan.
Pridham, G. (2006) 'European Union Accession Dynamics and Democratization in Central and Eastern Europe: Past and Future Perspectives', *Government and Opposition* 41(3): 373–400.
Pridham, G. (2007) 'The Scope and Limitations of Political Conditionality: Romania's Accession to the European Union', *Comparative European Politics* 5(4): 347–76.
Pridham, G., E. Herring and G. Sanford (1997 [1994]) 'Introduction', in G. Pridham, E. Herring and G. Sanford (eds), *Building Democracy: The International Dimension of Democratization in Eastern Europe*, Revised Edition, London: Leicester University Press, 1–6.

Raik, K. (2004) 'EU Accession of Central and Eastern European Countries: Democracy and Integration as Conflicting Logics', *East European Politics and Societies* 18(4): 567–94.
Reding, V. (2013) *The EU and the Rule of Law – What Next?* Speech at the College of Europe, 4 September, SPEECH/13/677.
Reid, R. (2009) 'The Politics of Silence: Interpreting Stasis in Contemporary Eritrea', *Review of African Political Economy* 36(120): 209–21.
Reilly, B. (2000) 'The Africanisation of the South Pacific', *Australian Journal of International Affairs* 54(3): 115–38.
Reilly, B. (2004) 'State Functioning and State Failure in the South Pacific', *Australian Journal of International Affairs* 58(4): 479–93.
Republic of Croatia (2007) *Operational Programme for Human Resources Development 2007–2009. Instrument for Pre-Accession Assistance 2007*, HR05IPO001, http://ec.europa.eu/enlargement/pdf/croatia/ipa/4_croatia_human_resources_development_operational_programme_2007-2009_en.pdf, date accessed 14 June 2014.
Republic of Turkey, Ministry of EU Affairs (2011) TR-EU Financial Co-Operation, http://www.abgs.gov.tr/index.php?p=5&l=2, date accessed 12 June 2014.
Reynaert, V. (2011a) 'Preoccupied with the Market: The EU as a Promoter of "Shallow" Democracy in the Mediterranean', *European Foreign Affairs Review* 16(5): 623–37.
Reynaert, V. (2011b) 'Explaining EU Aid Allocation in the Mediterranean: A Fuzzy-Set Qualitative Comparative Analysis', *Mediterranean Politics* 16(3): 405–26.
Reynaert, V. (2012) *Talking Democracy and Creating Identity: A Poststructuralist Analysis of the EU's Discourse Towards the Mediterranean Region (1989–2011)*, PhD Thesis, Ghent: Ghent University.
Risse, T. (2009) 'Conclusions: Towards Transatlantic Democracy Promotion?' in A. Magen, T. Risse and M. A. McFaul (eds), *Promoting Democracy and the Rule of Law: American and European Strategies*, Basingstoke: Palgrave Macmillan, 244–71.
Roberts, D. (2010) *Global Governance and Biopolitics: Regulating Human Security*, London: Zed Books.
Roberts, S., S. Wright and Ph. O'Neill (2007) 'Good Governance in the Pacific? Ambivalence and Possibility', *Geoforum* 38(5): 967–84.
Rupnik, J. (2000) 'Eastern Europe: The International Context', in M. Plattner and A. Smolar (eds), *Globalization, Power and Democracy*, London: The John Hopkins University Press, 57–79.
Sadurski, W. (2010) 'Adding Bite to a Bark: The Story of Article 7, EU Enlargement, and Jörg Haider', *Columbia Journal of European Law* 16(3): 385–426.
Sadurski, W. (2013) *Constitutionalism and Enlargement*, Oxford: Oxford University Press.
Santiso, C. (2002) 'Promoting Democratic Governance and Preventing the Recurrence of Conflict: The Role of the United Nations Development Programme in Post-Conflict Peace-Building', *Journal of Latin American Studies* 34(3): 555–86.
Sasse, G. (2005) *EU Conditionality and Minority Rights: Translating the Copenhagen Criterion into Policy*, Badia Fiesolana: EUI Working Papers, RSC No. 2005/16.
Scharpf, F. W. (1999) *Governing in Europe. Effective and Democratic?* Oxford: Oxford University Press.

Scharpf, F. W. (2003) *Problem-Solving Effectiveness and Democratic Accountability in the EU*, Cologne: Max Planck Institute for the Study of Societies, MPIfG Working Paper, No. 03/1.
Schedler, A. (1999) 'Conceptualizing Accountability', in A. Schedler, L. Diamond and M. F. Plattner (eds), *The Self-restraining State: Power and Accountability in New Democracies*, Boulder, CO: Lynne Rienner, 13–28.
Scheppele, K. L. (2013) *What Can the European Commission Do When Member States Violate Basic Principles of the European Union? The Case for Systemic Infringement Actions*, Paper presented at 'The Assises de la Justice', Brussels, 21 and 22 November, http://ec.europa.eu/justice/events/assises-justice-2013/files/contributions/45.princetonuniversityscheppelesystemicinfringementaction brusselsversion_en.pdf, date accessed 5 July 2014.
Scherpereel, J. (2009) *Governing the Czech Republic and Slovakia: Between State Socialism and the European Union*, London: First Forum Press.
Schimmelfennig, F. (2011) 'How Substantial Is Substance? Concluding Reflections on the Study of Substance in EU Democracy Promotion', *European Foreign Affairs Review* 16(5): 727–34.
Schimmelfennig, F. (2012) 'Europeanization beyond Europe', *Living Reviews in European Governance* 7(1): 1–31.
Schimmelfennig, F. and H. Scholtz (2010) 'Legacies and Leverage: EU Political Conditionality and Democracy Promotion in Historical Perspective', *Europe-Asia Studies* 62(3): 443–60.
Schimmelfennig, F. and U. Sedelmeier (2004) 'Governance by Conditionality: EU Rule Transfer to the Candidate Countries of Central and Eastern Europe', *Journal of European Public Policy* 11(4): 661–79.
Schimmelfennig, F. and U. Sedelmeier (2005) 'Conclusions: The Impact of the EU on the Accession Countries', in F. Schimmelfennig and U. Sedelmeier (eds), *The Europeanization of Central and Eastern Europe*, Ithaca, NY: Cornell University Press, 210–28.
Schimmelfennig, F., S. Engert and H. Knobel (2005) 'The Impact of EU Political Conditionality', in F. Schimmelfennig and U. Sedelmeier (eds), *The Europeanization of Central and Eastern Europe*, Ithaca, NY: Cornell University Press, 29–50.
Schimmelfennig, F., S. Engert and H. Knobel (2006) *International Socialization in Europe: European Organizations, Political Conditionality and Democratic Change*, Basingstoke: Palgrave Macmillan.
Schmidt, M. G. (2008) *Demokratietheorien: Eine Einführung*, 4th edition, Wiesbaden: VS Verlag für Sozialwissenschaften.
Schmitter, P. C. (1992) 'The Consolidation of Democracy and Representation of Social Groups', *American Behavioral Scientist* 35(4/5): 422–49.
Schmitter, P. C. (2001) 'The Influence of the International Context upon the Choice of National Institutions and Policies in Neo-Democracies', in L. Whitehead (ed.), *The International Dimension of Democratization: Europe and the Americas*, Oxford: Oxford University Press, 26–54.
Schmitter, P. C. and T. L. Karl (1991) 'What Democracy Is...and Is Not', *Journal of Democracy* 2(3): 75–88.
Schmitter, P. C. and I. Brouwer (1999) *Conceptualizing, Researching and Evaluating Democracy Promotion and Protection*, Badia Fiesolana, San Domenico: EUI Working Paper SPS, No. 99/9.

Schneider, C. Q. and P. C. Schmitter (2004) 'Liberalization, Transition and Consolidation: Measuring the Components of Democratization', *Democratization* 11(5): 59–90.
Schraeder, P. J. (2003) 'The State of the Art in International Democracy Promotion: Results of a Joint European-North American Research Network', *Democratization* 10(2): 21–44.
Schütze, R. (2009) *From Dual to Cooperative Federalism*, Oxford: Oxford University Press.
Scott, W. R. (2001) *Institutions and Organizations*, Thousand Oaks: Sage.
Sebastian, S. (2010) *Assessing Democracy Assistance: Bosnia*, Project Report, Madrid: FRIDE, http://www.fride.org/publication/775/bosnia, date accessed 3 May 2014.
Sedelmeier, U. (2005) *Constructing the Path to Eastern Enlargement: The Uneven Policy Impact of EU Identity*, Manchester, New York: Manchester University Press.
Sedelmeier, U. (2006a) 'The EU's Role as a Promoter of Human Rights and Democracy. Enlargement Policy Practice and Role Formation', in O. Elgström and M. Smith (eds), *The European Union's Roles in International Politics: Concepts and Analysis*, Abingdon: Oxon; New York: Routledge, 118–35.
Sedelmeier, U. (2006b) 'Europeanisation in New Member and Candidate States', *Living Reviews in European Governance* 1(3). Online Article, http://europeangovernance.livingreviews.org/Articles/lreg-2006-3/download/lreg-2006-3Color.pdf, date accessed 20 May 2014.
Sen, A. (1999) *Development as Freedom*, Oxford: Oxford University Press.
Serrano, K. (2011) 'The Trade-Development Nexus in EU-Pacific Relations: Realism, Dependence or Interdependence?' *Global Change, Peace & Security* 23(1): 89–112.
Sheahan, L., N. Chaban, O. Elgström and M. Holland (2010) 'Benign Partner or Benign Master? Economic Partnership Agreement Negotiations Between the EU and the Pacific Islands', *European Foreign Affairs Review* 15(3): 347–66.
Shen, W. (2013) 'EU-China Relations on Human Rights in Competing Paradigms: Continuity and Change', in T. Christiansen, E. Kirchner, and P. B. Murray (eds), *The Palgrave Handbook of EU-Asia Relations*, 165–80.
Simon, J. and A. Jünemann (2013) 'Europa und die Arabellions: Zur Wiederentdeckung der Zivilgesellschaft in der EU-Mittelmeerpolitik', in E. D. Stratenschulte (ed.), *Grenzen der Integration. Europas strategische Ansätze für die Nachbarregionen*, Baden-Baden: Nomos, 79–120.
SIPRI (2012) The SIPRI Military Expenditure Database, http://milexdata.sipri.org/, date accessed 7 June 2014.
Skovgaard, J. (2011) 'Power Beyond Conditionality: European Organisations and the Hungarian Minorities in Romania and Slovakia', *Journal of International Relations and Development* 14(4): 440–68.
Slaughter, A.-M. (1997) 'The Real New World Order', *Foreign Affairs* 76(5): 183–97.
Slaughter, A.-M. (2000) 'Government Networks: The Heart of the Liberal Democratic Order', in G. H. Fox and B. R. Roth (eds), *Democratic Governance and International Law*, Cambridge: Cambridge University Press, 199–235.
Slaughter, A.-M. (2004) *A New World Order*, Princeton: Princeton University Press.

Slivkova, E. (1999) *Slovakia's Response on the Regular Report from the European Commission on Progress Towards Accession*, Bonn: University of Bonn, Center for European Integration Studies Discussion Paper C57.
Slye, R. C. (1996) 'The Dayton Peace Agreement: Constitutionalism and Ethnicity', *Yale Journal of International Law* 21: 459–74.
Smith, H. (2000) 'Why Is There No International Democratic Theory?' in H. Smith (ed.) *Democracy and International Relations: Critical Theories/Problematic Practices*, Basingstoke: Macmillan.
Smith, K. E. (2004) *The Making of EU Foreign Policy: The Case of Eastern Europe*, 2nd edition, Basingstoke: Palgrave Macmillan.
Smith, K. E. (2008) *European Union Foreign Policy in a Changing World*, Cambridge: Polity.
Smith, P. (2008) 'Fiji's Military Leader Boycotts Pacific Talks', *Financial Times*, 18 August 2008.
Smith, T. (2004) *America's Mission: The United States and the Worldwide Struggle for Democracy in the Twentieth Century*, Princeton: Princeton University Press.
Smith, T. (2011) 'From "Fortunate Vagueness" to "Democratic Globalism": American Democracy Promotion as Imperialism' in C. Hobson and M. Kurki (eds), *Conceptual Politics of Democracy Promotion*, London: Routledge, 201–14.
Sørensen, E. and J. Torfing (2005) 'The Democratic Anchorage of Governance Networks', *Scandinavian Political Studies* 28(3): 195–218.
Stewart, S. (2009) 'NGO Development in Ukraine Since the Orange Revolution', in J. Besters-Dilger (ed.), *Ukraine on Its Way to Europe: Interim Results of the Orange Revolution*, Frankfurt: Peter Lang Verlag, 179–94.
Sushko O. and O. Prystayko (2011) 'Ukraine', *Nations in Transit 2011*, http://www.freedomhouse.org/report/nations-transit/2011/ukraine#.U38Q8iiYJ8E, date accessed 22 May 2014.
Tansey, O. (2009) *Regime-Building: Democratization and International Administration*, Oxford: Oxford University Press.
Tocci, N. (2007) *The EU and Conflict Resolution: Promoting Peace in the Backyard*, Abingdon: Routledge.
Tocci, N. (2010) 'The Conflict and EU-Israel Relations', in E. B. Aymat (ed.), *European Involvement in the Arab-Israeli Conflict*, Paris: EU ISS, Chaillot Paper 124, 55–64.
Tocci, N. (2011) *The EU, the Middle East Quartet and (In)effective Multilateralism*, Mercury Reports 9.
Tocci, N. and B. Voltolini (2011) 'Eyes Wide Shut: The European Union and the Arab Minority in Israel', *European Foreign Affairs Review* 16(4): 521–38.
Transparency International Georgia (2011) *Corruption Perceptions Index 2011*, http://transparency.ge/en/node/1460, 1 December 2011, date accessed 2 January 2013.
Tronvoll, K. (2010) 'The Ethiopian 2010 Federal and Regional Elections: Re-Establishing the One-Party State', *African Affairs* 110(438): 121–36.
UNDP – United Nations Development Programme (2002) *Arab Human Development Report*, http://www.arab-hdr.org/publications/other/ahdr/ahdr2002e.pdf, date accessed 7 June 2014.
United States Embassy Eritrea (2008) 'Eritrea Garners More Money from the EC', *US Embassy Cable 08ASMARA328*, 19 June.

US/EU (2009) *Joint US-EU Statement on Georgia*, Council Doc. 10284/09 (Presse 154), Brussels, 25 May, http://europa.eu/rapid/pressReleasesAction. do?reference=PRES/09/154&format=HTML&aged=0&language=EN& guiLanguage=en, date accessed 2 January 2013.
Vachudová, M. A. (2005) *Europe Undivided: Democracy, Leverage and Integration After Communism*, Oxford: Oxford University Press.
Valenzuela, J. S. (1992) 'Democratic Consolidation in Post-Transitional Settings: Notion, Process, and Facilitating Conditions', in S. Mainwaring, G. O'Donnell and J. S. Valenzuela (eds), *Issues in Democratic Consolidation: The New South American Democracies in Comparative Perspective*, Notre Dame (Indiana): University of Notre Dame Press, 57–104.
Van den Brink, M. (2012) 'EU Citizenship and EU Fundamental Rights: Taking EU Citizenship Seriously?' *Legal Issues of Economic Integration* 39(2): 273–89.
van Hüllen, V. and A. Stahn (2009) 'Comparing EU and US Democracy Promotion in the Mediterranean and the Newly Independent States', in A. Magen, T. Risse and M. A. McFaul (eds), *Promoting Democracy and the Rule of Law: American and European Strategies*, Basingstoke: Palgrave Macmillan, 118–49.
Van Parijs, P. (2012) *The Machiavelli Programme*, London: ECPR Press.
Venezuelanalysis (2012) *ALBA Expels USAID from Member Countries*, http:// venezuelanalysis.com/news/7069, date accessed 15 April 2014.
Verba, S. (1967) 'Democratic Participation', *The Annals of the American Academy of Political and Social Science* 373(1): 53–78.
Vogel, T. (2009) 'Aid Plan for War-Torn Eritrea Causes Concern', *European Voice*, 19 February, http://www.europeanvoice.com/article/aid-plan-for-war-torn-eritrea-causes-concern, date accessed 23 October 2014.
von Bogdandy, A., M. Kottmann, C. Antpöhler, J. Dickschen, S. Hentrei and M. Smrkolj (2012) 'Reverse *Solange* – Protecting the Essence of Fundamental Rights against EU Member States', *Common Market Law Review* 49: 489–520.
Von Strokirch, K. (2005) 'The Region in Review: International Issues and Events, 2004', *The Contemporary Pacific* 17(2): 416–33.
Weiler, J. H. H. (1999) *The Constitution for Europe*, Cambridge: Cambridge University Press.
Weiler, J. H. H. (2003) 'In Defence of the Status Quo: Europe's Constitutional *Sonderweg*', in J. H. H. Weiler and M. Wind (eds), *European Constitutionalism beyond the State*, Cambridge: Cambridge University Press, 7–26.
Weiler, J. H. H. (2009) 'Europa "Nous Coalisons des Etats, Nous n'Unissons pas des Hommes"', in M. Cartabia and A. Simoncini (eds), *La Sostenibilità della Democrazia nel XXI Secolo*, Bologna: il Mulino.
Wetzel, A. (2011) 'The Promotion of Participatory Governance in the EU's External Policies: Compromised by Sectoral Economic Interests?' *Democratization* 18(4): 978–1000.
Wetzel, A. and J. Orbie (eds) (2011a) 'The Substance of EU Democracy Promotion', *European Foreign Affairs Review*, Special Issue, 16(5): 565–734.
Wetzel, A. and J. Orbie (2011b) 'With Map and Compass on Narrow Paths and Through Shallow Waters: Discovering the Substance of EU Democracy Promotion', *European Foreign Affairs Review* 16(5): 705–25.

Wetzel, A. and J. Orbie (2012) *The EU's Promotion of External Democracy: In Search of the Plot*, Brussels: CEPS Policy Brief 281, 13 September.
Wetzel, A., F. Bossuyt and J. Orbie (2015) (eds) One-of-What-Kind? Comparative Perspectives on the Substance of EU Democracy Promotion, *Cambridge Review of International Affairs* 28(1).
White, N. (2000) 'The United Nations and Democracy Assistance' in P. Burnell (ed.), *Democracy Assistance*, London: Frank Cass Publishers, 67–89.
Whitehead, L. (ed.) (2001) *The International Dimensions of Democratization: Europe and the Americas*, Oxford: Oxford University Press, expanded edition.
Williams, A. (2009) 'Taking Values Seriously: Towards a Philosophy of EU Law', *Oxford Journal of Legal Studies* 29(3): 549–77.
Williams, A. (2010) *The Ethos of Europe*, Cambridge: Cambridge University Press.
Williams, A. (2013) 'European Union, Interim Global Justice, and the International Legal Order', in D. Kochenov and F. Amtenbrink (eds), *European Union's Shaping of the International Legal Order*, Cambridge: Cambridge University Press, 38–61.
Wolff, J. and I. Wurm (2011) 'Towards a Theory of External Democracy Promotion: A Proposal for Theoretical Classification', *Security Dialogue* 42(1): 77–96.
World Bank (2004) *Public Sector Capacity-Building Programme Project Appraisal Document*, Washington, DC: World Bank.
World Bank (2010), www.worldbank.org, accessed 2010.
World Movement of Democracy (2010) *Let the People Breathe the Air of Freedom! Statement on the International Day of Democracy*, 15 September, http://www.wmd.org/about/statements/day-democracy-2010, date accessed 15 May 2014.
Yannis, A. (2002) 'The Creation and Politics of International Protectorates in the Balkans: Bridges over Troubled Waters', *Journal of International Relations and Development* 5(3): 258–74.
Youngs, R. (2001a) *The European Union and the Promotion of Democracy: Europe's Mediterranean and Asian Policies*, Oxford: Oxford University Press.
Youngs, R. (2001b): 'European Union Democracy Promotion Policies: Ten Years On', *European Foreign Affairs Review* 6(3): 355–73.
Youngs, R. (2003) 'European Approaches to Democracy Assistance: Learning the Right Lessons?' *Third World Quarterly* 24(1): 127–38.
Youngs, R. (ed.) (2006) *Survey of European Democracy Promotion Policies 2000–2006*, Madrid: FRIDE.
Youngs, R. (2008) 'Trends in Democracy Assistance: What Has Europe Been Doing?' *Journal of Democracy* 19(2): 160–69.
Youngs, R. (2009) 'Democracy Promotion as External Governance?' *Journal of European Public Policy* 16(6): 895–915.
Youngs, R. (ed.) (2010a) *The European Union and Democracy Promotion: A Critical Global Assessment*, Baltimore: The Johns Hopkins University Press.
Youngs, R. (2010b) *Europe's Role in Global Politics: A Retreat from Liberal Internationalism*, London: Routledge.
Youngs, R. and K. Pishchikova (2013) *A More Pluralist Approach to European Democracy Support*, Washington, DC: Carnegie Endowment for International Peace.
Youngs, R., K. Kausch, D. Mathieson, I. Menéndez and J. de Zeeuw (2006) *Survey of European Democracy Promotion Politics 2000–2006*, Madrid:

FRIDE, http://www.fride.org/publication/132/survey-of-european-democracy-promotion-policies-2000-2006, date accessed 15 February 2014.
Zielonka, J. (2006) *Europe as an Empire*, Oxford: Oxford University Press.
Zulueta-Fülscher, K. (2008) *Elections and the European Neighbourhood Policy in Armenia*, Madrid: FRIDE.

Index

Abkhazia, *see* Georgia
absorption capacity, *see* enlargement
academic, *see* research
Accession Partnership, *see* enlargement
accession, *see* enlargement
accountability, 4, 5, 6, 23, 60, 61, 63, 64, 65, 75, 76, 77, 78, 79, 83, 87, 89, 92, 94, 95, 97, 98, 100, 106, 110, 112, 114, 115, 122, 137, 141, 143, 144, 146, 148, 157–8, 171, 172, 178, 180, 182, 191, 194, 195, 197, 202, 208, 211, 216, 217, 218, 223, 229–30, 233, 236, 238, 239, 241, 244, 246, 255–8
acquis communautaire, 27, 29, 31, 32, 33, 72, 73, 76–7, 78, 79, 80, 85, 91, 95, 96, 99, 101, 240, 241, 249
administration, *see* public administration
Afewerki, Isaias, *see* Eritrea
Afghanistan, 183
African, Caribbean and Pacific countries (ACP), 194, 206, 212, 214, 215, 222
    Cotonou Agreement, 194, 195, 200, 208, 211
    Economic Partnership Agreement (EPA), 214
    EU-ACP Joint Parliamentary Assembly, 215
    see also Article 96; European Development Fund
agenda, *see* democracy promotion agendas
agriculture, 166, 197, 214, 235
aid, 12, 16, 43, 72, 73, 78, 79, 81, 83, 84, 145, 151, 152, 167, 169, 170, 185, 188, 189, 191, 194, 197, 199, 200, 201, 206, 208, 210, 212, 213, 214, 216, 219, 220, 221, 222, 244, 249, 250

budget support, 141, 179, 196, 197, 200, 201, 211
Coordination, 20–1, 100, 160, 187–9, 206, 211, 219, 251, 254
Development Cooperation Instrument (DCI), 178
Donor, 105, 114, 140, 174, 188, 189, 193, 194, 195, 197, 199–200, 201, 205–6, 209, 222, 223, 235, 244, 249
humanitarian assistance, 167, 170, 206, 211
microcredits, 202
microprojects, 154, 156, 196, 198, 210, 211
Official Development Assistance (ODA), 179, 199, 230
re-distribution, 130
technical assistance, 22, 43, 62, 90, 102, 113, 141, 142, 166, 179, 204
see also Democratic Institutions Programme (DIP); European Development Fund; European Neighbourhood and Partnership Instrument (ENPI); Investing in People; European Instrument for Democracy and Human Rights (EIDHR); capacity building; civil society
Akaev, Askar, *see* Kyrgyzstan
Al-Shabaab, *see* Somalia
Andean Community (CAN), *see* Latin America
Angola, 193
Arab Spring, 117, 138, 149–60, 239–40
Arafat, Yasser, *see* Palestine
Argentina, 102
armed forces, *see* military
Armenia, 17, 102, 134–48, 240, 255, 257
Armenian National Congress (HAK), 139–40

Index 297

Sargsyan, Serzh, 140
  see also Nagorno-Karabakh
Article, 7, see Treaty on European Union
Article 96 (Cotonou Agreement), see sanctions
Ashton, Catherine, see High Representative of the Union for Foreign Affairs and Security Policy
Asian Development Bank, 189
Association Agreement, 73, 85, 101, 106, 108, 119, 121–6, 136, 139, 142, 165–6
asylum, see migration
Australia, 208–9, 219–21, 247
Austria, 32–3, 85, 98–100, 205
authoritarian, 87, 89, 126, 133, 154–6, 171, 186, 199, 202, 206, 243, 253
  semi-authoritarian, 202, 206
  see also hybrid regime
Azerbaijan, 32, 133, 136
  Nagorno-Karabakh, 141

Bainimarama, Voreqe (Frank), see Fiji
Bakiev, Kurmanbek, see Kyrgyzstan
Bali, 220
Baltic, see Estonia; Latvia
Beetham, David, 7, 64
Belarus, 28, 118, 120, 134, 136, 140
Bertelsmann Transformation Index (BTI), 4, 18, 20, 23, 87, 89–96, 99–100, 112, 115, 122, 128–30, 137–8, 146, 148, 151, 186–7, 191, 202–3, 232–3, 237, 242, 253–8
Black Sea Synergy, 134, 136
Bloc Yulia Tymoshenko (BYuT), see Ukraine
Bolivarian Alliance for the Peoples of Our America (ALBA), see Venezuela
Bolivarian Revolution, see revolution
Bolivia, 233, 235
Börzel, Tanja, 3, 7–8, 12, 18–19, 134, 153, 193, 239–40, 245–6
Bosnia and Herzegovina (BiH), 14, 17, 21, 90, 104–16, 240, 244, 246–7, 255, 257
  EUFOR-ALTHEA, 107–8
  EU Police Mission (EUPM), 107–8

Brazil, 10, 20, 45, 102, 223–35, 247–50, 256–8
  Brazilian Council for Economic and Social Development (CDES), 226
BRICs(Brazil, Russia, India and China), 45, 224
broad agenda, see democracy agendas
budget support, see aid
bureaucracy, see public administration
Bush, George W., see United States
business, 64, 91, 128, 144, 157, 209

campaigning, 122, 138, 202
Canada, 205
candidate country, see enlargement
capacity building, 3, 48, 51–2, 54, 62, 95, 152–3, 165, 167, 172–3, 179, 186, 189, 195–6, 198, 228, 251
  see also Comprehensive Institution Building Programme (CIB); Public Sector Capacity-Building Programme (PSCAP)
capitalism, 45
Caribbean, 224
  see also African, Caribbean and Pacific countries (ACP)
Carothers, Thomas, 3, 16, 56, 185, 200, 202, 231, 243
censorship, see freedom, of press
Central American Parliament (PARLACEN), see parliament
Central Asia, 22, 177–92
Central and Eastern Europe (CEE)/Central and Eastern European countries (CEECs), 33, 59, 71–84, 117, 150
Charter of Fundamental Rights, 30
Chaudhry, Mahendra, see Fiji
Chavez, Hugo, see Venezuela
Chechnya, see Russia
checks and balances, see horizontal accountability
children
  children's rights, 156, 170–1, 196, 204, 229, 242
  see also juvenile justice

China, 45, 59, 183, 191–2, 224, 242, 253
  see also BRICS
citizenship, citoyens, 5, 7–8, 33, 90, 95, 107
CIVETs (Colombia, Indonesia, Vietnam, Egypt, Turkey and South Africa), 45
civilian oversight, 75, 94, 106, 112
  see also military
civil rights, 4–6, 23, 75, 77–8, 83, 87–8, 92–4, 97–8, 100, 106, 111, 113, 115, 122, 128, 137, 140–1, 144, 146, 156–9, 161, 168, 172, 175, 178, 180–1, 188, 191, 194, 196–7, 202, 204, 212, 216, 228, 230, 232, 240, 255–8
Civil Service Bureau (CSB), 142
civil service, see public administration
civil society, 3–5, 7–8, 23, 41, 43, 57, 60, 64–5, 74, 77–9, 82–3, 90–1, 96–7, 101, 103, 109, 113–15, 123–4, 130–1, 137, 141–4, 146, 150, 153–4, 156, 158–61, 164–5, 168, 170–5, 179–80, 186, 195–8, 202–4, 210–11, 213, 216–17, 219, 223, 225–30, 234, 239–40, 255–8
Civil Society Forum of the Eastern Partnership, 130, 143
Civil Society Fund (CSF), 197
civil society organization (CSO), 101, 150, 153–4, 156, 159
IPA Civil Society Facility, 101, 109, 114, 143, 154
Neighbourhood Civil Society Facility, 124, 142–4, 154, 164–5
non-state actors, 8, 19, 65, 136, 143, 180, 210, 227–8, 240
Non-State Actors and Local Authorities in Development Programme (NSA-LA), 180, 228
  see also Non-Governmental Organization (NGO)
civil war, 12, 109, 186, 193
climate change, see environment
Cold War, 36, 48–50
collective rights, 204
colonial, 201, 214

Commission, see European Commission
Common Foreign and Security Policy (CFSP), 107, 110–12, 150, 154, 156, 181, 184, 191, 225, 229–30
competition, anti-trust, 131, 151, 228
compliance, 16, 32, 72–4, 78, 80, 106, 119
  see also implementation
Comprehensive Institution Building Programme (CIB), see Eastern Partnership
conditionality, 72–3, 76, 78, 80–3, 86, 98, 100–1, 104–6, 111, 119, 137, 139, 155, 164–6, 168–9, 173, 201
conflict, 18, 23, 74, 85, 92, 104, 115, 136–7, 141, 162–4, 166–70, 173–5, 191, 193, 196, 203, 206, 240
conflict prevention, 60, 86, 188, 212
post-conflict, 19, 99, 104, 115, 186, 198, 232, 248
constitutionalism, 28
context conditions, 4, 6–9, 77–9, 81, 83, 96, 110, 112–15, 120, 136–7, 147, 150–1, 158, 161–2, 170, 172–5, 178, 181–2, 189, 195–6, 198, 200, 203, 206, 211, 213, 221, 223–4, 231, 234, 236–8, 242, 245, 247, 252, 254–8
coordination, see aid
Copenhagen criteria, see enlargement
corruption, see crime
Cotonou Agreement, see ACP; Article, 96
Council of the EU, 11, 16, 22, 35, 40, 57, 59, 73, 76, 89–90, 92, 94–7, 101, 106, 113–14, 123, 135–6, 139–40, 150, 155–6, 178, 183–5, 196–7, 201, 211–15, 221, 224, 229, 231, 249, 251
Council Presidency, 111, 196–7, 201, 211
  see also European Council
Council of Europe, 76, 82, 93, 119, 123, 147, 187, 246
Parliamentary Assembly of the Council of Europe, 147
Venice Commission, 188

Country-Based Support Scheme
  (CBSS), 171–2, 175
Country Development Strategy,
  188, 201
Country Strategy Papers (CSP), 21–2,
  150, 152–3, 155, 158–9, 197–8,
  201, 209, 224–8, 230, 233,
  249, 254
coup, 212, 215–18, 220, 227
  see also revolution
court, *see* judicial
crime, 79, 105
  corruption, 5, 65, 75–9, 82, 89–90,
    95, 99, 101, 108–9, 113,
    119–20, 123, 125, 129–30, 137,
    142, 151–2, 195–6, 218, 249
  cybercrime, 9
  fraud, 76, 152
  (money) laundering, 76, 119, 157
  organized crime, 89–90, 99, 108,
    113, 157
Crimea, *see* Ukraine
crisis, 85, 142
  economic/financial, 45, 110, 124
  political, 210, 215–16, 220–1,
    229
Croatia, 85–103, 104, 143, 240, 246,
  255, 257
Cuba, 233, 235
customs, customs union, 85, 134, 153
Cyprus, 85, 99
Czech Republic, 14, 17, 20, 23, 71–84,
  246, 255

Dahl, Robert, 6, 49, 63
Dayton Peace Agreement, 105, 116
death penalty, 171
Deep and Comprehensive Free Trade
  Area (DCFTA), *see* trade
deep democracy, *see* democracy
democracy
  deep, 154
  embedded liberal, 2–5, 8, 13, 36, 58,
    65–6, 80, 83, 92, 97, 109,
    118–19, 134, 137, 150, 159,
    168, 170–1, 173, 189, 195, 199,
    204, 206, 216, 236, 238,
    252–3
  fuzzy liberalism, 1, 35–46

global, 36, 39
market-oriented, 31, 119, 241,
  245
output-oriented, 3, 7, 8, 19, 55, 66,
  113, 153–4, 236–54
participatory, 36, 38–9, 41, 48, 194,
  195, 204
reform liberal, 45
revolutionary, 204, 249
social, 42, 109, 233
democracy agendas
  broad agenda, 9, 79, 83, 92, 97, 99,
    110, 114, 145, 147, 150, 182–3,
    192, 206, 246
  full agenda, 9, 83
  narrow agenda, 9–10, 80, 83, 184,
    223–4, 234, 236, 239
  shallow agenda, 9–10, 13, 16, 19,
    80, 83, 105, 110, 114, 137, 147,
    158, 161–2, 164, 172–3, 182–3,
    187, 190, 199, 206, 236, 238–9,
    245, 249, 251
democratic governance, 33, 36, 55,
  58–67, 149, 195, 205, 235, 242
Democratic Institutions Programme
  (DIP), 195–6, 205
democratic peace, 14
demonstration, *see* freedom of
  demonstration
demos, 5, 90, 95
depoliticization, *see* politicization
development
  DG Development/DEVCO, *see*
    European Commission
  Human Development Index, 149,
    216–18
  Millennium Development Goals,
    225
  see also aid
developmental approach to
  democracy promotion, 3, 184,
  243, 249
Development Cooperation Instrument
  (DCI), *see* aid
DG DEVCO (DG Development and
  Cooperation), *see* European
  Commission
DG Relex (DG for External Relations),
  see European Commission

differentiation, 135–7, 147, 159, 241
diplomatic pressure, 50, 62, 89, 94, 138, 169–70, 182, 200, 213, 215–16, 220–1
disability rights, 143, 196, 229
disadvantaged groups, *see* vulnerable groups
discrimination, anti-discrimination, 88, 93, 95, 100, 102, 124, 157, 171–2, 175–6, 229
Djibouti, 199
domestic context, domestic resonance, domestic shortcomings, *see* explanations domestic context
donor, *see* aid
double standards, inconsistency, 12, 114, 135, 146
Dzurinda, Mikuláš, *see* Slovakia

Eastern Partnership (EaP), 9, 32, 117–33, 134–48
  Comprehensive Institution Building Programme (CIB), 123, 136, 153
  see also civil society
economic crisis, *see* crisis
Economic Partnership Agreement (EPA), *see* ACP
Ecuador, 233, 235
education, 5, 88, 91, 93, 97, 100, 103, 109, 114, 142, 144, 151, 168, 172, 195–8, 211–13
  see also socio-economic development
effective power to govern, 5–7, 23, 75, 81, 87, 90, 92, 94, 97, 99, 106, 112, 123, 129, 137, 144, 146, 158–9, 191, 196–7, 208, 211, 216–18, 223, 236, 238–9, 244
e-government, 142
Egypt, 14, 45, 149–61, 166, 242–3, 245, 250, 254, 255, 258
  Mubarak, Hosni, 155
  Supreme Council of Armed Forces (SCAF), 156
  see also CIVETs
election observer missions, *see* elections

elections, 5–6, 19, 40–1, 50, 53–4, 73–5, 77, 81, 87, 92, 99, 105–6, 110–11, 114, 116, 120–1, 125, 127–8, 136, 138–9, 141, 144–6, 151, 154–6, 158, 164–5, 167, 169–71, 175, 180–1, 187, 191, 193, 195–6, 202, 204, 206, 209–13, 215, 220–1, 223, 228–30, 247, 251, 255–8
  observation, 22, 100–1, 127, 132, 147–8, 155, 169, 204, 215, 225, 229–31
  electoral regime, 4–6, 8, 41, 74, 77–8, 87, 92, 97, 105, 127, 137–8, 146–7, 154–5, 158, 161, 178, 181, 186, 188, 190–1, 202, 208, 210–12, 216–18, 221
  (universal) suffrage, (right to) vote, 5–6, 87, 92
embedded democracy, embedded liberal democracy, *see* democracy
employment, unemployment, *see* labour
  see also social policy
empowerment, 8, 12, 19, 57, 99, 168, 171, 173, 240
civil society, non-state actors, *see* civil society
women, *see* gender
energy, 60, 117, 125–6, 128, 130–1, 136, 143–5, 200, 228, 235, 245
  Nord Stream/South Stream, 126
  nuclear, 126, 226
  oil, 130, 160, 179, 182–3, 232
  (shale) gas, 126, 130, 182–3
enlargement, 9, 14, 16–17, 33, 71–84, 100, 103, 114–15, 117, 127, 134, 145, 240, 246
  absorption capacity, 86
  accession, pre-accession/pre-accession strategy, 28, 36, 71–84, 85–103
  candidate country, 28, 31, 71–84, 85–103, 246, 248, 252
  Copenhagen criteria, 16, 72–3, 75, 77, 82–3, 86
  enlargement fatigue, 114

Instrument for Pre-Accession
  Assistance (IPA), 90, 91, 94, 95,
  97, 98, 101–2, 106–14, 248; see
  also civil society
Phare, 74, 78–9, 82–4, 110
Regular Reports, 73, 76, 83, 92–4,
  98, 103, 106–7, 109, 111,
  114, 121
see also conditionality; Bosnia and
  Herzegovina; Croatia; Czech
  Republic; Kosovo; Slovakia;
  Turkey
enlargement fatigue, see enlargement
entrapment, 208
environment, 59, 109, 136, 143–4,
  153–4, 195, 213, 222, 226–8,
  235, 240
climate change, 143, 197, 211,
  222, 250
equality, 6, 8, 29–31, 36, 40, 46, 91,
  96, 157, 175, 224, 229
see also gender equality
Ergenekon, see Turkey
Eritrea, 10, 17, 20, 193–207, 239–40,
  242–3, 248, 250, 254, 256, 258
Afewerki, Isaias, 193, 198, 201
Isaac, Dawit, 201
People's Front for Democracy and
  Justice (PFDJ), 202
see also conflict; post-conflict
Estonia, 34
see also Baltics
ethics, see norms
Ethiopia, 17, 20, 193–207, 240, 243,
  248–51, 254, 256, 258
Ethiopian People's Revolutionary
  Democratic Front (EPRDF), 193,
  202, 204
Haile Mariam, Mengistu, 193
Mideksa, Birtukan, 196
Zenawi, Meles, 196
see also conflict; post-conflict
ethnic, 11, 95, 105, 107, 115, 186,
  191, 196, 204, 208–9, 211–12,
  218, 221
EU-ACP Joint Parliamentary Assembly,
  see ACP
EUFOR-ALTHEA, see Bosnia and
  Herzegovina

EU Monitoring Mission (EUMM),
  110, 142
EU Police Mission (EUPM), see Bosnia
  and Herzegovina
eurocrisis, see crisis, economic; crisis,
  financial
Euro-Mediterranean, 3, 149–61, 162,
  164, 168, 176, 240
  Euro-Mediterranean Parliamentary
    Assembly (EMPA), 157
  Euro-Mediterranean Partnership
    (EMP), 149, 158, 164, 165, 172,
    174
  MEDA (Measures D'Adjustment),
    151, 153, 155, 160
  North Africa, 3, 133
  Union for the Mediterranean (UfM),
    149, 158
EuroNest Parliamentary Assembly, see
  parliament
EuropeAid, 49, 54–5
see also aid
European Agency for Reconstruction
  (EAR), see Kosovo
European Commission, 16, 18, 21–2,
  28, 31, 33, 35, 47, 53–6, 59, 61,
  73, 75–7, 79–80, 82–4, 86–98,
  105, 110, 112, 118–19, 124,
  135–9, 142, 148, 149, 153–4,
  158–9, 168, 175–6, 177, 185, 192,
  194, 201, 210–11, 214–15, 221,
  229–30, 249–50
  DG DEVCO (DG Development and
    Cooperation), 17, 43, 127, 145,
    148, 183–4, 192, 200
  DG Relex (DG for External
    Relations), 17, 127, 131, 145,
    148, 176, 200, 214–15, 231, 233
  DG Trade, 127, 131, 145, 148, 200
European Commission Liaison
  Office (ECLO), 110, 112–13
  Michel, Louis, 196, 201
European Council summit, 72–3,
  85–6, 100, 116
see also Council
European Court of Justice (ECJ), 31–2
European Development Fund (EDF),
  195, 197–8, 204–5, 210–15, 249
see also aid; ACP

European Economic and Social
  Committee (EESC), 226
European Endowment for Democracy
  (EED), 137
European External Action Service
  (EEAS), see High Representative of
  the Union for Foreign Affairs and
  Security Policy (HR/VP)
European Instrument for Democracy
  and Human Rights (EIDHR), 92–3,
  95, 98, 102, 106, 109, 113, 118,
  124, 130, 140, 143, 150, 153–4,
  156–7, 164–5, 168, 170–5,
  178–80, 195–6, 198, 212–14, 222,
  224, 227–8
European Neighbourhood Policy
  (ENP), 22, 43, 60, 117–18, 120–1,
  133, 134–48, 149–60, 164–74
European Neighbourhood and
  Partnership Instrument (ENPI),
  135, 138, 143–4, 151, 153,
  155, 166
Neighbourhood Investment Facility
  (NIF), 144
see also Eastern Partnership;
  Euro-Mediterranean; EuroNest
  Parliamentary Assembly; civil
  sociey
European Parliament (EP), 42, 87, 121,
  128, 140–1, 147–8, 157, 190, 201,
  211, 215, 225, 226, 229–30, 231,
  241, 249–50
Member of European Parliament
  (MEP), 111, 128, 140, 201, 215
see also parliament
European Security and Defence Policy
  (ESDP), 107
European Union Rule of Law Mission
  in Kosovo (EULEX), see Kosovo
EU Special Representative (EUSR), 105,
  107–8, 111, 142
executive, 5–6, 60, 75, 112, 123, 129,
  141, 143, 157–8, 194, 229
explanations
  domestic context/domestic
    resonance/domestic
    shortcomings/tailor, 81–2,
    99–100, 115, 120–32, 146, 148,

159, 161, 185–7, 190, 202–6,
  215–18, 221, 232–4, 236–54
institutions/sub-systems, 80–1,
  98–9, 115, 127, 145–6, 148,
  158–9, 174, 183–5, 200–1,
  214–15, 231–3, 236–54
inter-organizational context, 82,
  100–1, 115–16, 127, 147–8, 160,
  174, 187–9, 205–6, 218–21,
  236–54
power/interdependence/hegemony,
  2, 10–14, 80, 98, 114–15,
  127–32, 144–5, 147, 159–61,
  173–4, 182–3, 190, 199–200,
  206, 214, 231–2, 234, 236–54

feasibility, 50, 59, 242, 244, 246, 254
Fiji, 14, 21, 208–22, 244, 246–7,
  250–1, 254, 256
  Bainimarama, Voreqe (Frank), 210
  Chaudhry, Mahendra, 209, 216
  Fiji Labour Party (FLP), 210
  Iloilo, Ratu Josefa, 210
  Mara, Kamisese, 209
  Qarase, Laisenia, 210
  Speight, George, 209–10
see also Pacific
financial aid, see aid
fisheries, 166, 214
food security, 178, 198
former Yugoslav Republic of
  Macedonia (FYROM), 104
see also ICTY
Foucault, Michel, 48–52, 54, 56
foundation, 35, 41, 232, 235
  Friedrich Ebert Foundation, 41, 235
  Konrad Adenauer Foundation, 235
  Olof Palme Centre, 41
  Soros Foundation, 187
Four Common Spaces, 129–30
France, 98–9, 141, 146, 188, 201, 214,
  235
  Sarkozy, Nicolas, 99
fraud, see crime
freedom, 5, 135, 152, 166, 202
  of association, 5, 6, 75–6, 100, 121,
    126, 128, 136, 139, 156, 171,
    198, 202
  of demonstration, 5

of petition, 5
of press, 5, 6, 77, 106, 128, 136, 139, 156–7, 181, 188, 196, 201
of religion, 5, 88, 157
of speech, 5, 75, 89, 93, 100, 172, 229
Freedom House (FH), 18, 163, 216, 243
free and fair elections, *see* elections
Friedrich Ebert Foundation, *see* foundation
Fukuyama, Francis, 7, 49
full agenda, *see* democracy agendas
functional cooperation, 58–66
fuzzy liberalism, *see* democracy

gas, *see* energy
Gaza, *see* Palestine
Gazprom, 131
gender, gender equality, 143, 156–7, 229
 women, women's rights, 57, 92, 97, 154, 156–7, 170–1, 196, 204, 227, 242
Generalised Scheme of Preferences (GSP)/GSP+, *see* trade
Georgia, 14, 17, 134–48, 240, 255, 258
 Abkhazia, 141, 145
 Rose Revolution, 138, 140, 145–6
 Saakashvili, Mikheil, 138
 South Ossetia, 141, 145
Germany, 98–100, 146, 184–5, 187–9, 201, 214, 232, 235
global democracy, *see* democracy
Global Fund, 194
good governance, 3, 7, 8, 9, 19, 43, 54, 59, 105, 108, 119, 129, 136, 143, 152, 157, 158, 161, 178, 179, 184, 190, 194–195, 204, 205, 210, 212, 215, 219, 226, 232, 233
governance, *see* democratic governance; good governance
government, *see* executive
grassroots, *see* local
Greece, 102
Guatemala, 224

Haider, Jörg, 32
Haile Mariam, Mengistu, *see* Ethiopia
Hamas, *see* Palestine
Hayek, Friedrich, 41
health, 96, 143, 152, 197
hegemon/hegemonic, *see* explanations, power
High Representative of the Union for Foreign Affairs and Security Policy (HR/VP), Ashton, 121, 128–9, 138–40, 153–5, 157, 164, 166, 183–4, 191, 196, 198, 204
 European External Action Service, 16, 127, 135, 148, 156, 176, 183, 194, 250
Honduras, 224
horizontal accountability, 4–6, 23, 64, 75–9, 83, 89, 92, 94, 97–8, 100, 106, 110, 112, 114, 122, 141, 144, 146, 148, 157–8, 172, 178, 182, 191, 197, 208, 211, 216–18, 223, 230, 233, 236, 238–9, 241, 244, 246
Horn of Africa, 193, 199
 see also Ethiopia; Eritrea
Human Development Index, *see* development
human rights, 11, 18, 30, 43, 54, 57, 59, 72–3, 75–6, 82, 88, 92, 94, 97, 102, 106, 111, 113, 118–20, 128, 135–40, 143, 147, 149–50, 152, 156–7, 159–60, 162, 164–6, 168, 170–2, 176, 178–81, 188, 190, 194–6, 198, 201, 204, 211–13, 216, 218, 222, 224–8, 230, 253
Human Rights Defender's Office (HRDO), 138, 140
Hungary, 28, 32–4
hybrid regime, 202
 see also authoritarian
hypothesis, *see* explanations

ICTY, 88, 100, 246
identity, *see* role
ideology, 36–46, 239
Iloilo, Ratu Josefa, *see* Fiji
immigration, *see* migration

implementation, 8, 16–17, 19, 21–3, 43, 62, 65, 73, 76, 90, 93, 101, 108, 123, 130, 135, 137, 142–3, 145–8, 150, 170–1, 174, 177, 180, 185, 190, 210–11, 240, 248
  see also compliance
inclusion, 7, 8, 48, 53–5, 91, 97, 101, 180, 225
inconsistency, *see* double standards
indigenous rights, 219, 227–9, 231
individual rights, *see* civil rights
infrastructure, 91, 144, 167, 198, 228, 232
instability, *see* stability
institutions, *see* explanations institutions
Instrument for Pre-Accession Assistance (IPA), *see* enlargement
interdependence, *see* explanations power
internal market, 73, 85, 151–2, 158, 160, 241
International Election Observation Mission (IEOM), *see* elections
international financial institutions (IFIs)/World Bank/International Monetary Fund, 18, 35, 44, 82, 101, 107, 110, 160, 188–9, 194–7, 205, 217, 251
  see also Post-Washington Consensus
International Labour Organization (ILO), 141
International Monetary Fund (IMF), *see* international financial institutions
internet, *see* freedom, of press
inter-organizational context, *see* explanations inter-organizational context
Investing in People, 228
investment/public procurement, 91, 97, 122, 129, 137, 144, 180, 232–3
Ireland, 188, 205
Isaac, Dawit, *see* Eritrea
Isatabu Freedom Movement (IFM), *see* Solomon Islands
Israel, 10, 20, 154, 162–76, 245, 250–1, 256
Italy, 184, 201, 214, 232, 235

Japan, 187, 235
jews, 102, 163
Joint Action Plan (JAP), 137, 141, 225
Joint Country Support Strategy, 189
journalism, *see* freedom, of press
judge, *see* judicial
judicial/court/judge, 5–6, 19, 60, 65–6, 75, 88–9, 94–5, 99, 101–2, 107, 112, 120, 122–3, 126, 129, 140–1, 157, 165, 172, 179–81, 188, 196–8, 210, 212, 242
justice, 27, 29–31, 40–1, 54, 76, 93, 95, 100, 102, 107, 126, 140–1, 143, 153–4, 157, 167–8, 171–2, 195, 197, 202, 211
juvenile, 140
Justice and Development Party (AKP), *see* Turkey
justice and home affairs (JHA), 76–7, 79, 95
juvenile justice, *see* justice; children

Kazakhstan, 134, 177–92, 245, 250, 256, 258
Keohane, Robert, 13, 60, 62, 64, 66
Khodorkovsky, Mikhail, *see* Russia
Konrad Adenauer Foundation, *see* foundation
Kosovo, 21, 28, 66, 104–16, 240, 246–7, 255, 257
  European Agency for Reconstruction (EAR), 110, 112, 113
  European Union Rule of Law Mission in Kosovo (EULEX), 110, 112–13
Krasner, Stephen, 11
Kuchma, Leonid, *see* Ukraine
Kurds, 85, 92, 102
Kurdistan Workers' Party (PKK), 92, 94
Kurki, Milja, 1, 3, 5, 35–46, 239, 241, 244, 250, 252, 254
Kyrgyzstan, 177–92, 245, 247, 250, 256, 258
  Akaev, Askar, 187
  Bakiev, Kurmanbek, 180, 187, 191
  Tulip Revolution, 187

Index 305

labour, 96, 210
  employment/unemployment, 76, 91, 96, 97, 101, 114, 124, 143, 166, 173, 225
  market, 61, 91, 96, 97, 101, 124, 151
  rights, 41, 96, 102, 109, 118, 159
  trade union/unionist, 76, 93, 96, 102, 143, 157, 198
  see also social policy; freedom of association
labour market, *see* labour
land ownership, *see* property
language, 43, 76, 93
Latin America, 223–35, 248, 253
  Andean Community (CAN), 226
  Mercosur, 225–6, 229, 235
  Union of South American Nations (UNASUR), 230–1
  Latin American Parliament (PARLANTINO), *see* parliament
Latvia, 134
  see also Baltics
laundering, *see* crime
Lavenex, Sandra, 10, 18, 47, 60, 62, 66
law, 2, 5–6, 22, 27–34, 48, 51–2, 65, 77–8, 88–9, 93, 95, 102, 106, 110, 123, 130, 138–9, 157, 169, 172, 202, 220, 230, 241
learning, 61–2
Lebanon, 155, 162
legislative, *see* parliament
legitimacy, 3, 18, 61, 98, 100, 153, 194, 200, 212, 216, 238–9, 241, 246
Leninist option, 50, 53–5
liberalism, *see* democracy; neoliberalism
liberalization, 73, 122, 131, 134, 136, 151–2, 158–61, 186, 191
libertarian, 40
Linz, Juan J., 4, 6–7, 163
Lisbon Treaty, *see* Treaty
local
  administration, 77, 90, 109, 111, 121, 124, 179–80, 202, 204, 208, 223, 227–8, 232
  context/grassroots, 18, 44, 48–50, 53–7, 162, 164, 168, 170–1, 175, 178–9, 196–7, 201, 211, 213, 219–21, 223, 232, 234–5, 240
  region/regional government/regional development, 76, 82–3, 86, 90–1, 93, 97, 104, 121, 123, 143–4, 149, 164, 174, 177–80, 183–8, 195–6, 208, 211, 218–20, 224, 226–7, 229–30, 234–5
  village/town/municipality, 65, 77, 87, 90, 102, 105, 124, 172, 218, 232

Madagascar, 102
Magnitsky, Sergei, *see* Russia
Maidan movement, *see* Ukraine
Majone, Giandomenico, 64, 241
majoritarianism, 40
Malaita Eagle Force (MEF), *see* Solomon Islands
Manners, Ian, 14, 44
Mara, Kamisese, *see* Fiji
market
  economy, 3, 5, 91, 136, 153, 158–60, 254
  paradigm, *see* neoliberal
  see also labour market; internal market; democracy, market-oriented democracy
Mečiar, Vladimír, *see* Slovakia
MEDA (Measures D'Adjustment), *see* Euro-Mediterranean
media, *see* freedom, of press
Mediterranean, *see* Euro-Mediterranean
Member of European Parliament (MEP), *see* European Parliament
member state (EU), 14, 17, 20–1, 27–32, 42, 54, 59, 71, 80–1, 85–6, 98–100, 103, 111, 113, 115, 117, 124, 126–7, 135, 142, 145–8, 158, 166, 169, 173–4, 178, 183–5, 188, 201, 206, 214, 222, 225, 231–3, 235, 241, 249–51
Mercosur Parliament (PARLASUR), *see* parliament
Mercosur, *see* Latin America

Merkel, Wolfgang, 4–8, 39, 46, 251
Michel, Louis, *see* European Commission
microcredits, *see* aid
microprojects, *see* aid
Middle East, 3, 133, 162–76
  Quartet, 170, 174
  see also Palestine; Israel
Mideksa, Birtukan, *see* Ethiopia
migration, 9, 59, 152, 157
  asylum/refugee, 87–8, 109, 122, 152, 157
  immigration, 59
  see also visa
military/armed forces, 5, 7, 12–13, 75, 86, 94, 100, 102, 106–8, 136–7, 145, 156, 172, 197, 203, 209–10, 212, 216–18, 221
Millennium Development Goals, *see* development
minority, 91, 93, 102, 163, 167–9, 172–6
  rights, 75–9, 82, 87–8, 93, 99–100, 102, 111, 113, 164, 168–9, 175, 248
  Roma, 77–8, 88, 91, 102, 113
mission civilisatrice, 56
model, *see* role
money laundering, *see* crime
monopoly of force, *see also* stateness, 5, 7, 90, 94, 107–8, 163
Montenegro, 90, 104
Moravcsik, Andrew, 11, 30, 241
Morocco, 59, 102, 154, 163
Mubarak, Hosni, *see* Egypt
multilateral, 21, 42, 120, 136, 225
municipality, *see* local
Muslim, 86, 102

Nagorno-Karabakh, *see* Azerbaijan
narrow agenda, *see* democracy agendas
National Indicative Programme (NIP), 135, 143–4, 150, 153, 158–9, 184, 212, 225–7, 230
Neighbourhood Investment Facility (NIF), *see* European Neighbourhood Policy (ENP)

neoliberal institutionalism/neo-institutionalism, 11, 13–14, 145
neoliberal/neoliberalism/market paradigm, 27, 40, 43–4, 158–61, 244, 254
neorealism/realism, 11–13, 145
Netherlands (the), 31, 105, 187–8, 205
network, 6, 21, 52, 58, 60–3, 66–7, 101, 109, 183
newspaper, *see* freedom, of press
New Zealand, 208, 219–21, 247
non-governmental organization (NGO), 35, 43, 65, 77, 93, 109, 123–4, 127, 130, 143, 157, 166, 171–2, 194, 196, 198, 202, 205, 227–8
  see also civil society
non-state actors, *see* civil society
norms, 5, 11, 14–16, 39–40, 42, 48–9, 51–5, 59, 61, 124, 140, 160, 181, 188, 194, 222, 253
  normative power/norm promotion, 35, 46, 49, 52
  values/ethics, 2, 7, 12, 16, 27–33, 36–7, 40–1, 44–6, 59, 117–20, 149, 162, 164–6, 179, 186, 219, 225, 229–30, 241
North Africa, *see* Euro-Mediterranean
North Atlantic Treaty Organization (NATO), 82, 107, 125, 183
Norway, 105, 205
nuclear, *see* energy
Nye, Joseph, 13, 60, 62, 66

Occupied Palestinian Territory (OPT), *see* Palestine
Office for Democracy and Human Rights (ODIHR), 119, 127, 132, 147–8
Office for Promotion of Parliamentary Democracy (OPPD), *see* parliament
Official Development Assistance (ODA), *see* aid
oil, *see* energy
Olof Palme Centre, *see* foundation

ombudsperson, 65, 88, 95, 106, 180, 195–6
one-size-fits-all approach, 38, 55, 135
openness, 37, 194, 204, 247, 253
opposition, 62, 74, 126, 128, 138–40, 202, 209, 233, 253
Orange Revolution, *see* revolution
Organisation for Economic Co-operation and Development (OECD), 23, 40, 57, 65, 76, 82, 147–8, 194
Organization of American States (OAS), 227, 230–1
Organization for Security and Co-operation in Europe (OSCE), 76, 82, 100–1, 105–6, 111, 115, 119, 127, 132, 141, 147–8, 181, 187–8, 246, 251
organized crime, *see* crime
output-oriented democracy, *see* democracy
ownership, 21, 53–4, 76, 159, 218, 225, 244, 248–9
see also property; Paris Declaration on Aid Effectiveness

Pacific, 194, 208–22, 232, 247
Pacific Islands Forum (PIF), 208–22
South Pacific, 208–22
Urwin, Greg, 220
see also ACP; Fiji; Solomon Islands
Palestine/Occupied Palestinian Territory (OPT), 14, 162–76, 245, 250–1, 255–6
Arafat, Yasser, 167
Gaza, 154, 162–3, 167, 170–1, 175
Hamas, 163–4, 167–70, 173–4
Palestinian Authority (PA), 32, 163, 167–70, 173, 175
West Bank, 154, 162–3, 167, 170–1, 173, 175
paradigm, *see* role
Paris Declaration on Aid Effectiveness, 188, 244, 249
ownership, 21, 53–4, 76, 159, 218, 225, 244, 248–9
see also aid

parliament/legislative, 5, 75, 86–7, 92, 107, 111–12, 121, 128–9, 138–9, 146, 155, 157–8, 169, 180–1, 187, 195, 202, 209–11, 213, 215, 229–31, 239
Central American Parliament (PARLACEN), 229
EU-ACP Joint Parliamentary Assembly, 215
EuroNest Parliamentary Assembly, 140
Latin American Parliament (PARLATINO), 229
Mercosur Parliament (PARLASUR), 229
Office for Promotion of Parliamentary Democracy, 1, 42, 230
Parliamentary Assembly of the Council of Europe (PACE), *see* Council of Europe
see also European Parliament
partial regime, 4–9, 63, 65, 67, 77, 87, 89–90, 92–4, 97, 99, 105, 110, 114–15, 120, 135–8, 147, 150, 154, 159–61, 167–8, 171–3, 180–1, 189, 195, 197–9, 201, 203, 205–6, 208, 211, 213, 217–18, 221, 226–8, 231, 234, 236–8, 243, 247, 248, 252
see also elections; civil rights; political rights; horizontal accountability; effective power to govern
participatory democracy, *see* democracy
Partnership and Cooperation Agreement (PCA), 117, 119, 134
party, *see* political party
peace, 12, 14, 19, 29, 95, 104–5, 118, 138, 168, 174–5, 209–10, 225, 229
People's Front for Democracy and Justice (PFDJ), *see* Eritrea
Peru, 224
petition, *see* freedom of petition
Phare, *see* enlargement
pluralism, 36, 38, 41–2, 44, 74, 89, 118, 121, 216, 218

Poland, 31, 127, 146, 249
police, 5, 9, 75, 88, 100, 106–7, 112, 136–8, 165, 167, 209
Policy Dialogue and Advice Programme (PDAP), 179
political dialogue, 22, 121, 157, 198, 201, 210, 219, 226, 229
political economy, 2, 11–12, 35–46
political party, 73, 87, 92, 100, 121, 140–1, 193, 202, 210, 218, 232, 235
see also foundation
political prisoner, *see* prison
political rights, 4–5, 49, 54, 57, 65, 73, 75–8, 87, 89, 92–4, 97–9, 106, 111–12, 115, 121, 128, 137, 139–40, 144, 146, 148, 156–61, 163, 167–8, 172, 178, 180–2, 188–91, 194, 196–8, 202, 204, 211–12, 216–17, 223, 229–32, 240–1, 255–8
political society, 40
politicization/depoliticization, 37, 43
post-conflict, *see* conflict
Post-Washington Consensus, 189
poverty, 5, 91, 96, 186, 189
  poverty reduction, 124, 144, 178–9, 186, 197, 200, 215, 227–8, 249
  Poverty Reduction Strategy Paper, 188
power, *see* explanations power
pragmatic, 45, 81, 233, 241
press, *see* freedom, of press
prison, political prisoner, 126, 128, 140, 197–8, 201, 216
privacy, 76, 89
privatization, 43, 91, 151
property/(land) ownership, 5, 15, 76, 89, 106, 111, 151, 172, 218, 227
protectorate, 104
Przeworski, Adam, 49
public administration/public service/public sector/civil service/bureaucracy, 5–7, 19, 36, 44, 60, 64, 90, 95–6, 123, 142, 179, 186, 189, 196, 205, 218

public finance/tax, 128, 142, 189, 196, 226
public procurement, *see* investment
Public Sector Capacity-Building Programme (PSCAP), 195–6, 205
public sector, *see* public administration
public service, *see* public administration
public sphere, 6, 19, 49, 57, 64–5, 88–91, 95–6, 102, 107–8, 113, 138, 142, 152–3, 167, 179, 186, 189, 195, 198, 226, 235, 251
Pussy Riot, *see* Russia
Putin, Vladimir, *see* Russia

Qarase, Laisenia, *see* Fiji
Quartet, *see* Middle East

racism, 76, 171, 216
  see also ethnic
realism, *see* neorealism
reconciliation, 102, 211–12, 221
reconstruction, relief and rehabilitation, 139
referendum, 99, 181, 229
reform liberal democracy, *see* democracy
refugee, *see* migration
regional integration, 143, 160, 195, 218–19, 227, 234
  see also Mercosur; Andean Community; Union of South American Nations; Organization of American States (OAS)
region, *see* local
Regular Reports, *see* enlargement
regulatory state, 60, 241
religion, *see* freedom of religion
research/academic, 2, 12, 15, 17, 22, 39, 46, 58, 60–1, 63, 66, 71, 96, 114, 151
revolution, 102, 121, 125, 138, 140, 145–6, 149, 155, 187, 193, 204, 227, 234, 249
  Bolivarian Revolution, 227, 234, 249
  Orange Revolution, 121, 125

Rose Revolution, 138, 140, 145–6
Tulip Revolution, 187
see also coup
revolutionary democracy, *see* democracy
rhetoric, 30–1, 33, 37, 41, 120, 122, 125–6, 129, 132, 135, 139, 147, 166, 194
rights, *see* human rights; collective rights; disability rights; social policy, social rights; indigenous rights; individual rights; political rights; gender, women's rights; Charter of Fundamental Rights
role, 14–15, 35, 42, 44, 87, 92, 104, 174, 201, 234, 235
identity, 14–15, 76, 86, 94–5, 99, 243
model, template, 2–6, 10, 14–17, 20, 23, 30–1, 36–9, 41–6, 49, 55–7, 58–9, 66, 76, 81–3, 100, 115, 132, 134, 137, 146, 148, 150, 160–1, 171, 173, 185–6, 204, 233–5, 237, 239, 241, 244–5, 249–50
paradigm, 16, 27, 50, 52, 158–61, 175, 189, 251, 254
see also explanations institutions
Romania, 28, 32, 34, 146
Roma, *see* minority
Rose Revolution, *see* revolution
rule of law, 4–6, 19, 27–34, 54, 59, 61, 63, 72–5, 86, 94, 99, 110, 112, 117–19, 125–6, 128–9, 131–2, 135–8, 140, 151–2, 167, 171, 178–9, 188, 190, 194, 209, 212, 216, 225–6, 229, 242
Russia/Russian Federation, 14, 45, 117–33, 134, 136, 141, 143, 145, 147, 183, 191–2, 224, 240, 242–5, 249–50, 254, 255, 257
Chechnya, 117
Khodorkovsky, Mikhail, 128–9, 133
Magnitsky, Sergei, 128
Pussy Riot, 129
Putin, Vladimir, 129, 132
see also BRICS; Crimea; USSR

Saakashvili, Mikheil, *see* Georgia
sanctions, 13, 22, 62, 64, 128, 131, 208, 211, 213, 215, 218, 220–1, 243–4
stick, 104, 166, 173
see also conditionality; Article, 96
Sargsyan, Serzh, *see* Armenia
Sarkozy, Nicolas, *see* France
Saudi Arabia, 33
Scharpf, Fritz W., 238–9, 241
Schimmelfennig, Frank, 2, 10, 12, 18, 47, 58, 60, 62, 64–6, 71–2, 86
Schmitter, Philippe, 58, 63, 67, 81, 254
school, *see* education
Schumpeter, Joseph, 49
Šečić case, *see* Croatia
security, 10–16, 76, 80, 86, 94, 96, 100, 105, 107, 112, 122, 130–1, 135–6, 138, 141–3, 145, 150, 152–3, 157, 160–1, 162–76, 178, 181–3, 193, 195–202, 204, 206, 208, 210, 214, 219–20, 228, 231–2, 245–7
Şemdinli bombing, *see* Turkey
semi-authoritarian, *see* authoritarian
Sen, Amartya, 56
Serbia, 87, 90, 104, 113
shallow agenda, *see* democracy agendas
skepticism, 241
Slaughter, Anne-Marie, 60–3, 66
Slovakia, 14, 23, 71–84, 246, 254
Dzurinda, Mikuláš, 74
Mečiar, Vladimír, 74
Slovenia, 34, 90
social democracy, *see* democracy
social dialogue, *see* social policy
socialization, 61–2, 140, 173
social policy, 9, 14–15, 36, 38–46, 48–9, 61, 77, 79, 88, 93, 96–7, 110, 114, 117, 124, 144, 153–4, 172, 194–5, 219, 225–9, 232–5
social dialogue, 154
social inclusion, 91, 97, 101, 225
social protection, 97, 124
social rights, 75–6
social security, 96, 114
see also labour

socio-economic development (context condition), 3, 8–9, 16, 23, 40–1, 60, 79, 82–3, 91, 96–8, 101, 110, 124, 141, 143–4, 146, 148, 151–2, 161, 163, 173, 178–9, 182, 184, 186, 189–90, 203–4, 210, 212–13, 215–18, 220, 223, 226, 228, 230, 232, 234, 236–8, 242, 244, 247–9, 252, 254–8
sociological, 50, 53, 243
Sogavare, Manasseh, *see* Solomon Islands
solidarity, 36, 46
Solomon Islands (the), 14, 21, 208–22, 238, 247, 250, 254, 256
   Isatabu Freedom Movement (IFM), 209
   Malaita Eagle Force (MEF), 209
   Sogavare, Manasseh, 209
   Ulufa'alu, Bartholomew, 209
   see also Pacific
Somalia, 193, 199, 201
   Al-Shabaab, 199
South Caucasus, *see also* Armenia; Azerbaijan, 134–48
South Ossetia, *see* Georgia
South Pacific, *see* Pacific
sovereignty, 48, 51, 54, 204, 249
Soviet, *see* USSR
Spain, 17, 231–3, 235, 248–9
Speight, George, *see* Fiji
Stabilisation and Association Agreement (SAA), 85, 106, 108
Stabilisation and Association Process (SAP), 108, 116
stability/instability, 9, 11–13, 72, 104, 118–20, 135, 138–9, 143, 154, 159, 160–1, 182–3, 186–7, 193, 199, 203, 213, 216, 245
Stabilization and Association Process Dialogue (SAPD), 114
state
   administrative capacity, 5, 7, 75–9, 83, 90, 95, 97, 108, 113, 123, 141–2, 144, 146–7, 152–3, 158, 161, 163, 167–8, 172–3, 179, 190, 195–6, 198, 203, 205, 223, 226, 228, 236–9, 242, 244–5, 247, 252

state-building, 19, 60, 108, 112, 115, 165, 167, 172–3, 175, 198
stateness, 5–7, 13, 23, 81, 90, 94, 97, 107, 112, 115, 129, 141, 144, 146, 152, 158, 163, 167–8, 173, 182, 186, 195–6, 198, 203, 208, 210–13, 216–18, 220–1, 223, 238, 250, 255–8
   see also public administration; monopoly of force
Stepan, Alfred, 4, 6–7, 163
stick, *see* sanctions
structural adjustment programme (SAP), 160
sub-system/sub-state institutions, *see* explanation institutions
Sudan, 193
suffrage, *see* elections
sugar protocol, 211–12, 220–2
Support for Improvement in Governance and Management programme (SIGMA), 142, 147–8
supranational, 145
Supreme Council of Armed Forces (SCAF), *see* Egypt
sustainable development, 59, 136, 144, 169, 178, 190, 219, 226
   see also development
Sweden, 105, 187–9, 201, 205
Switzerland, 187, 189

Tacis, 74, 84
tailor/tailor-made approach, *see* explanations domestic
tax, *see* public finance
Technical Assistance Information Exchange (TAIEX), 22, 90, 101, 142, 147–8, 166
technical assistance, *see* aid
technocratic, 3, 43, 45–6, 240–1
   see also output-oriented democracy, *under* democracy
template, *see* role
terrorism, 94, 157, 193, 199, 202
Thailand, 102

torture, 5, 88, 92–3, 102, 106, 156, 170, 180, 196, 216, 229
tourism, 212, 235
trade, 15–16, 42–3, 59, 73, 85, 124–5, 127, 131, 134, 137, 143–6, 148, 151–2, 157, 193, 200, 211, 214, 222, 226–7, 232–3, 239, 250
   Deep and Comprehensive Free Trade Area (DCFTA), 134, 136, 142, 145
   DG Trade, see European Commission
   Generalised Scheme of Preferences (GSP)/GSP+, 22, 144
   see also ACP, Economic Partnership Agreement
trade union, see labour
transgovernmental relations, 58, 60–3, 66–7
transition/democratic transition, 19, 57, 81–4, 95, 106, 178–9, 184, 199
Transition Facility, 83–4
transparency, 1, 60, 63–5, 95, 122–3, 142, 152, 169, 178, 180, 194
Transparency International, 142
transport, 60, 144, 166, 198
Treaty
   Treaty on the European Union (TEU), 21, 28, 30, 32
   Treaty on the Functioning of the European Union (TFEU)/Lisbon Treaty, 21, 145, 148, 158, 176, 200, 214
Troika (EU), 204
Tudjman, Franjo, 87, 99
Tulip Revolution, see revolution
Tunisia, 14, 149–61, 166, 239, 245, 250, 255–8
   Ben Ali, Zine El Abidine, 155
Turkey, 14, 17, 45, 85–103, 136, 143, 240, 244, 246, 248, 255–8
   Ergenekon, 94, 102
   Justice and Development Party (AKP), 100
   Şemdinli bombing, 94, 102
   see also CIVETs; Kurds
Turkmenistan, 33

twinning, 22, 122, 142, 147–8, 166
Tymoshenko, Yulia, see Ukraine

Ukraine, 20, 28, 32, 117–33, 136, 143, 240, 247, 250, 255–8
   Bloc Yulia Tymoshenko (BYuT), 121
   Crimea, 130
   Kuchma, Leonid, 121
   Maidan movement, 124–5
   Orange Revolution, 121, 125
   Tymoshenko, Yulia, 121–2, 126
   Yanukovych, Viktor, 120–3, 124, 126, 132–3, 247
   Yushchenko, Viktor, 121, 125–6, 132
Ulufa'alu, Bartholomew, see Solomon Islands
unemployment, see employment
unionist, see labour
Union of South American Nations (UNASUR), see Latin America
United Kingdom (UK), 31, 187–9, 194, 201, 205, 214, 251
United Nations (UN), 76, 107, 110, 141, 149, 160, 163, 170, 195, 225, 241
   United Nations Development Programme (UNDP), 149, 195–6, 205
   United Nations General Assembly, 1, 163
   United Nations Interim Administration Mission in Kosovo (UNMIK), 110; see also Kosovo
   United Nations Relief and Works Agency (UNRWA), 170
United States (US), 35, 36, 40, 41, 43, 44–5, 105, 127, 131, 140, 141, 147, 163, 170, 173, 174, 187, 194, 199, 205, 220, 231, 232–3, 234, 243, 248, 251, 252
   Bush, George W., 41, 44–5
Urwin, Greg, see Pacific
USSR/Soviet Union/post-Soviet, 117, 132, 134, 177, 187, 190
   see also Russia
Uzbekistan, 186

values, *see* norms
Venezuela, 17, 223–35, 243, 247–50, 254, 255–8
   Bolivarian Alliance for the Peoples of Our America (ALBA), 233, 235
   Chavez, Hugo, 233–5
Venice Commission, *see* Council of Europe
visa
   visa facilitation/readmission/visa liberalization, 114, 122, 131, 134, 136
   see also migration
vulnerable groups/disadvantaged groups, 57, 97, 101, 140, 168, 211, 225
   see also indigenous rights

Weiler, Joseph, 27, 30
West Bank, *see* Palestine
Western, 45, 50, 61, 86, 105, 125, 167, 171, 200, 204
Women/women's rights, *see* gender
World Bank, *see* international financial institutions
World Movement of Democracy, 56
Worldwide Governance Indicators (World Bank), 18, 216

Yanukovych, Viktor, *see* Ukraine
Youngs, Richard, 3, 17, 44, 47, 49, 56, 59, 170, 185, 223, 231–3, 243
Yushchenko, Viktor, *see* Ukraine

Zenawi, Meles, *see* Ethiopia

CPI Antony Rowe
Chippenham, UK
2017-03-06 09:46